The Making of Haiti

The Making of Haiti

The Saint Domingue Revolution from Below

Carolyn E. Fick

The University of Tennessee Press

KNOXVILLE

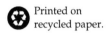
Library of Congress Cataloging in Publication Data

Fick, Carolyn E., 1947–
        The making of Haiti: the Saint Domingue revolution from below/
        Carolyn E. Fick. —1st ed.
            p.   cm.
        Includes bibliographical references.
        ISBN 0-87049-658-1 (cloth: alk. paper)
        ISBN 0-87049-667-0 (pbk.: alk. paper)
        1. Haiti—History—Revolution, 1791–1804. 2. Slavery—Haiti—
        Insurrections, etc. 3. Government, Resistance to—Haiti—
        History—18th Century. I. Title.
        F1923.F5   1990
        972.94'03—dc20   90-30956   CIP

To Haiti,
her people, her obscure leaders,
and her future

Contents

Maps

Preface

The present work is an attempt to illustrate the nature and the impact of the popular mentality and popular movements on the course of revolutionary (and, in part, postrevolutionary) events in eighteenth-century Saint Domingue. Today, Haiti is undergoing radical change, and it is to the popular movements that emerged in 1985–86, at Gonaïves, Saint Marc, Léogane, Jacmel, les Cayes, Jérémie, in the rural areas, and only subsequently in Port-au-Prince, that we must direct our attention for an explanation of what has happened. That the churches and other community organizations in Haiti (without mentioning the U.S. State Department) all played a role in the unfolding of those events is certain. But, ultimately, it was the creative energies and popular organizational capacities of the Haitian masses, with no single leader and without arms, that proved to be the decisive factor in bringing down one of the world's most ghastly and seemingly most enduring dictatorships. It is this popular movement—in its diverse dimensions, social, demographic, and cultural, as well as political—that deserves not only to be recognized but to be understood in the present context of developing political change and upheaval. While liberal-minded politicians and intellectuals have their role to play, it is my firm belief that the fundamental changes that are absolutely vital in the process of national reconstruction will ultimately come from the wisdom and common sense of the masses— from their own popular modes of social organization, their local skills and implicit understanding of rural needs, and above all, their unquestioned acceptance of sacrifice as the price to pay to live—or those changes will never come at all.

Finally, it is to these individuals, to "the people and their obscure leaders" who have collectively pushed Haiti one step forward, that this book is dedicated.

Acknowledgments

There are two individuals who have left an indelible mark on the original conception and eventual evolution of the present study. The book is a product of what each, under particular circumstances, has taught me about history and the world we live in. But in the face of the sheer magnitude of their life's work, the present book stands as only a minor contribution to the field of history and world politics that each, in his own way, pioneered. One is the late C. L. R. James, and the other, George Rudé. Many years ago Dr. James proposed to Professor Rudé a study of this nature for my doctoral dissertation, and it is from that dissertation, supervised and directed by Professor Rudé, that the book has developed. My debts to each are great. Whatever weaknesses or flaws the reader may find in the book are a result of my own limitations.

Many others have also contributed, in diverse capacities and at various stages, to the development and realization of this study. In particular, the works of Jean Fouchard and of Gabriel Debien on marronage and on colonial Saint Domingue have, almost contradistinctively, contributed to the elaboration of my own interpretations. M. Debien, in spite of my sheer obstinacy in believing that there was something more to slave desertion, or marronage, than what the Saint Domingue colonists saw in it, as he would argue, has always faithfully encouraged my work, and I am particularly grateful for his friendship and scholarly support. M. Fouchard, in addition to making his personal library available to me at all times, in Paris and in Pétionville, Haiti, enthusiastically directed me to an important body of correspondence located at the Public Record Office in London, covering popular slave movements in Saint Domingue's South province, and suggested that a major section of the work might be devoted to the South—a region, until recently, generally neglected in studies of the Saint Domingue revolution. This correspondence was first uncovered and then archivally classified by M. Bernard Foubert, who also forwarded to me quoted passages from his research that have helped to fill certain gaps in my own work.

Among my North American colleagues, I owe a large personal debt to Roger N. Buckley, who, at a very early stage, took a keen interest in the dissertation, and who also read the entire manuscript. His unflinching belief in the validity and importance of the study of Caribbean slave resistance and of the Saint Domingue revolution from a popular perspective has greatly contributed to the eventual realization of this study as a book. Thomas O. Ott also read and criticized the manuscript at various stages and offered several pertinent suggestions that have helped to improve the manuscript. At the former Centre de Recherche Caraïbes (Université de Montréal), Liliane Dévieux, Monique Desroches, and Serge Larose each offered helpful observations on a few of the more particular aspects of slave culture and oral traditions, while Francine M. Mayer and Yolande Lavoie, in a few of my more wretched moments, both provided insistent encouragement and useful advice. John M. Janzen, at the University of Kansas, very generously offered a translation from the original Kikongo language of one of the most ambiguous and perplexing of the colonial voodoo chants. I also wish to thank Lucien Goupil at the Université de Montréal for drawing the schematic map in Chapter 4 of the August 1791 slave revolt in the North province. Equally as important in the final realization of the manuscript are Christiane St-Pierre, who, with unfailing conscientious professionalism and efficiency, typed the entire manuscript throughout the many stages of revising, rewriting, and correcting to the very end; and Sandra Kwavnick, who not only lent a much-needed hand in proofreading the final draft, but also offered useful grammatical advice.

Permission to reproduce in Chapters 6 and 7 selected material from an article published in *History from Below: Studies in Popular Protest and Popular Ideology* (1988), has been kindly extended by both Basil Blackwell in London and Frederick Krantz at Concordia University in Montreal. The National Army Museum in London, the John Carter Brown Library at Brown University, and the Bibliothèque Nationale in Paris have also granted permission to reproduce the photographic maps and table. For their services and accommodation of my research needs, thanks and recognition are also extended to the directors and staff at the Archives Nationales in Paris; the Public Record Office in London; the University of Florida Libraries, in particular to Carmen Williams at the Rare Books and Manuscripts section; to the late Frère Lucien and to Frère Constant at the Institut Saint-Louis de Gonzague in Port-au-Prince; and to the Interlibrary Loans personnel at Concordia University. Here, Gail Flicker was more than helpful over the many years, especially in retrieving several extremely obscure documents. The research and writing have also been made possible through diverse fellowships and grants from the Social Sciences and Humanities Research Council of Canada, including the current Canada Research Fellowship, and from the Fonds pour la formation de chercheurs et l'aide à la recherche (FCAR) of the Quebec government.

Finally, I wish to extend a personal note of appreciation to Carol Wallace

Orr, director, to the editorial board, the staff: Lee Campbell Sioles, Dariel Mayer, Jennifer Siler, and June Hussey—as well as to Cynthia Maude-Gembler, former acquisitions editor—all at The University of Tennessee Press, and to my copyeditor, Alexa Selph, who have each worked with the manuscript at various stages. Their encouragement from the very beginning and enthusiasm throughout have, in the end, made the seemingly endless process of publishing a book a pleasurable one.

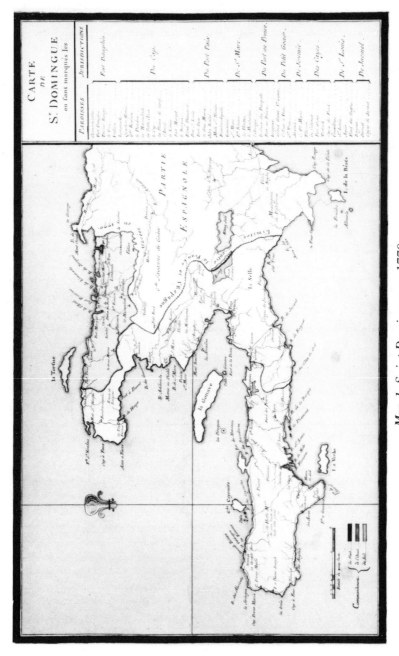

Itineraire for the Island of St. Domingo in Leagues.

Explanation

Example

Table: Itineraire for the Island of St. Domingo in Leagues. Courtesy of the Director, National Army Museum, London.

The Making of Haiti

Introduction

Every form of enslavement generates in one way or another an opposing struggle for liberation. The slaves in the former French colony of Saint Domingue (present-day Haiti), as everywhere in New World plantation societies, were not only denied their freedom as human beings, but as slaves were denied their essential humanity. For the masters, they were property, units of production, things to be bought and sold and used for profit. The all-too-human struggle against such a denial took many forms, and in Saint Domingue it culminated in revolution.

The Saint Domingue, or Haitian, revolution of 1791–1804 was not merely a West Indian slave revolt that succeeded in abolishing slavery, though that in itself was a unique and monumental feat. The black slave revolt that began in 1791 and ended in Haitian independence in 1804 constituted one of the great revolutions of the modern world. The new economic forces at play during the eighteenth century, the dynamic growth of capitalism, the concomitant emergence of the bourgeoisie and gradual breakup of feudalism, the unfolding of the French Revolution—such were the world and the times in which the slaves of Saint Domingue took charge of their own destiny, and in so doing "were to make history which would alter the fate of millions of men and shift the economic currents of three continents."[1] The Haitian revolution was, on the one hand, specifically and uniquely Caribbean and, on the other, an integral part of the history of Western civilization. In this struggle, a twofold one, first for the abolition of slavery, then for national independence, the uneducated black masses often played an instrumental, if not a leading, and sometimes even a determining, role.

To date, very little research, at least from the standpoint of primary archival sources, has been devoted specifically to the mass of black slave laborers who participated in this revolution on their own terms and with interests and goals embodying their own needs and aspirations, often at variance with, if not in direct opposition to, the path being staked out by those in positions of leadership or control. Historians of the Haitian revolution have traditionally treated the masses in a vague, summary fashion, almost as a mere footnote to the roles played by the more distinguished and prominent leaders of the revolution, such as Toussaint Louverture, Henri Christophe, or Dessalines, the latter generally acclaimed as the "founder" of Haitian independence. Yet this is perhaps not so surprising. The writing of history has traditionally focused either on great men and great leaders or on the prevailing economic and political forces shaping the world at a given time. Only in recent times has study been devoted to the individuals who participated, willingly or not, in the profound transformations of history and whose lives were thereby necessarily altered, for better or for worse.

The existing body of literature on the Haitian revolution provides an abundance of straightforward narrative political histories, most of these appearing during the decades following Haitian independence. Sir James Barskett's *History of the Island of St. Domingo* (1818) or Dr. Johnathan Brown's *History and Present Condition of St. Domingo* (1837), for example, treat the case for independent Haiti and her rulers from an optimistic and generally sympathetic stance; on the other hand, James Franklin's *The Present State of Hayti* (1828) was written as both a critical assessment of Haitian independence and as a warning to the British government against the dangers of abolition in the British colonies. From the French writers of the same period, some of them participants in the upheavals, the works are richly detailed and provide immensely valuable sources of information on revolutionary events. They appear, nevertheless, as an overall critique ultimately deploring the loss to France of her most valuable colony and view Haitian independence more as a tragedy than as the supreme accomplishment of a people scarcely ten years out of servile bondage. [2]

The most exhaustive treatments of the revolution by nineteenth-century postrevolutionary writers, however, are those of two foremost Haitian national historians, Thomas Madiou, in *Histoire d'Haïti* (1817), and Beaubrun Ardouin, in *Etudes sur l'histoire d'Haïti* (1853). Though biased to a degree in favor of the mulattoes and their leaders, both of these works present a mass of material on the events of the revolution, including material on the popular insurrections and movements, some of which was passed on to the writers through the oral tradition and would therefore otherwise be unavailable.

One of the most prominent works on the revolution during the second half of the nineteenth century was Victor Schoelcher's *Vie de Toussaint Louverture* (1899). Writing from the French radical tradition of the nineteenth century, Schoelcher was an arch opponent of slavery, of colonialism, and of Napoleon, but as one well-known writer has put it, "though his heart is in the right place, he is too uncritical to be trustworthy." [3] His work does, however, present numerous original documents until then largely ignored and represents a clear departure from the earlier colonialist works on the revolution.

Another work, that of R. P. Adolphe Cabon, presents an excellent exhaustive study of slavery and the revolution in Saint Domingue, which appeared as the major part of a four-volume history of Haiti, *Histoire d'Haïti* (1895–1919). What was new and noteworthy here was Cabon's treatment of the socio-political economy of slavery and the problematics of the various post-emancipation systems of land and labor, with the divergent aspirations of the black laborers brought into view.

Among the American writers, the turn of the century and the advent of worldwide conflict gave rise to sharply contrasting views on the colonial question and the accompanying race question. T. G. Steward's *The Haitian Revolution, 1791–1804*, written in 1914 on the eve of World War I, puts forward the claim that "the Haitian revolution is indeed the heritage of all the races, as it exhibits the unfitness of any man for slavery and the capability of all for freedom. [It] is the special heritage of the Negro Race."[4] With a fundamentally optimistic view regarding the possibilities of the human race, the author tends, however, to be uncritically sympathetic of Toussaint Louverture. It does merit attention, though, as one of the first serious histories of the revolution to see the slaves as the principal architects of their own freedom and independence. Almost diametrically opposed to this interpretation of the Haitian revolution is the ideologically racist thesis of T. Lothrop Stoddard, *The French Revolution in San Domingo*, also written in 1914, which sees the history of the French Revolution in the colony as a great tragedy —the tragedy not of slavery, the slave trade, and the tremendous fortunes built thereon (as French socialist Jean Jaurès so aptly stated it), but "the tragedy of the annihilation of the white population."[5] The fundamental problem of the twentieth century is thus seen in terms of a worldwide struggle between the primary races, and the color question as the gravest problem facing the great [white] communities like the United States, the South African Confederation, and Australasia.

During the 1920s a new scholarly history of the revolution, written largely from untapped French archival, contemporary newspaper and manuscript sources, as well as family archival sources in Haiti, was produced by a Haitian historian, Pauléus Sannon. Written during the occupation of Haiti by the U.S. Marines, the three-volume *Histoire de Toussaint Louverture* (1920–33) was at once a tribute to Haitian independence and national pride, the heritage of the Saint Domingue revolution and its leaders, and a major contribution to the historical scholarship of the revolution. As an in-depth political history of the revolution through the biography of its foremost leader, this study brings the popular movements and popular leaders into the sphere of events and highlights their importance, though they do not assume a predominant role.

In 1938, on the eve of World War II, an entirely new approach to the colonial question was put forward by the West Indian Marxist scholar and writer C. L. R. James in *The Black Jacobins*, written in part as a forecast for African independence movements. James saw the economic forces and concomitant social and political relations of the colonial era, redefined through the outbreak of revolution in France, as central to the unfolding and development of the Saint Domingue revolution. And as to the perpetual race question: "[It] is subsidiary to the class question in politics and to think of imperialism in terms of race is disastrous. But to neglect the racial factor as merely incidental is an error only less grave than to make it fundamental."[6] This was, and has always remained, James's essential outlook on the interrelated questions of class and race.

Although he was chiefly concerned in 1938 with the role of the leadership of the revolution, i.e., the black Jacobins and particularly Toussaint Louverture, the inarticulate masses are never lost from view, and though their activities are not always explicitly documented in the book, it is they, nonetheless, who provide the initiative and impetus, if not the driving force of any insurrectionary movement.[7] So for the first time, the revolutionary potential of the masses is treated as an integral part of the revolutionary process, but again these masses, though vitally important, are not in themselves the direct subject of the book, chiefly concerned as it was with the problem of leadership and colonial struggle. And like Sannon's book, it is a study of the revolution through the historical biography of its greatest leader, Toussaint Louverture.

Subsequent histories of the revolution, written either as biographies or analytical studies of one or another of its chief leaders, include Ralph Korngold's *Citizen Toussaint* (1944), Aimé Césaire's *Toussaint Louverture* (1961), Hubert Cole's *Christophe, King of Haiti* (1967), *Toussaint Louverture* (1973), edited by George Tyson, Wenda Parkinson's *'This Gilded African'*, *Toussaint Louverture* (1978), and Pierre Pluchon's *Toussaint Louverture, de l'esclavage au pouvoir* (1979). While a few of these (especially Korngold's *Citizen Toussaint*) do provide some useful and interesting material on the activities of the maroon bands and popular leaders throughout the revolution, the major theme of these works is, of course, developed around the individual in their respective titles. The most recent treatment of the revolution through the historical biography of one of its leading figures is Robert L. Stein's *Léger Félicité Sonthonax: The Lost Sentinel of the Republic* (1985). Here it is Sonthonax, the French radical commissioner whose abolitionist beliefs reached far beyond his own time, who is seen as the founder of slave emancipation in Saint Domingue.

Among other recent studies of the revolution is Thomas O. Ott's *The Haitian Revolution*, written in 1973. But here the predominant features of the revolution are seen fundamentally in terms of social and racial conflict, to which "the important influences of the French Revolution, key personalities and foreign intervention" are subsidiary. Another major theme is the quest for power. Thus the entire revolution and its lessons appear to be little more than the recurrent struggles of its leaders to gain and to retain power. As for the masses, they are often characterized as "tigers on the prowl," "swarming hordes of rebels," and other such epithets reminiscent of Taine's depiction of the French revolutionary crowds.

Quite a different approach to the problem of slavery and revolution has been adopted by the British historian David P. Geggus in his recent *Slavery, War and Revolution: The British Occupation of Saint Domingue, 1793–1798* (1982). A well-documented and comprehensive sociopolitical study concerned chiefly with the period, the problems, and the areas in Saint Domingue of British occupation, it touches on the relationships of the slaves in these areas to the ongoing events and forces in the colony before and during this period. But on the whole, slave insurrections and popular movements during the revolution are treated either as isolated eruptions of little consequence to slavery and the plantation system or as unwilling embroilments of the slaves in the conflicts of one or another political-interest group. Rarely, if ever, are the insurrectionary movements of the slaves inspired by genuinely autonomous motives or on their own initiative. In fact, what Geggus finds paradoxical "is the fact that the world's sole successful slave revolt took place in a colony where slave resistance had been comparatively slight. Hence any explanation of the slave revolution must also explain its lack of significant precedents."[8]

But was there *really* a lack of significant precedents? And how does one define "significant"? If one considers chiefly the overt slave revolts as indications of resistance in Saint Domingue, compared with a greater number of such revolts in other slave colonies during the period of slavery, then perhaps one may pose the problem in those terms. However, alternative forms of resistance did exist in Saint Domingue that were possibly more effective there than elsewhere. One study that deals with slave resistance in a comparative context is Gwendolyn Midlo Hall's *Social Control in Slave Plantation Societies: A Comparison of Saint Domingue and Cuba* (1971). The findings here are that, although overt uprisings and conspiracies aimed at seizing power were indeed rare in Saint Domingue as compared with Cuba, "more systematic, insidious and, in the long run, more effective forms of resistance" placing "a considerable amount of real power in the hands of the slaves" were practiced in Saint Domingue. Among those alternative forms of resistance was marronage, wherein "open confrontation gave way to guerrilla warfare."[9]

It was mainly during the decade of the 1970s that special attention was given over directly to the question of the maroons and marronage (the act or state of being a fugitive slave) in relation to slave society and revolution.[10] As a form of slave resistance, marronage became the subject of particular inquiry by both French and Haitian scholars, and the cause of several serious points of contention between them. The French sociologist Yvan Debbasch,[11] the eminent historian Gabriel Debien, in his many works on colonial French Caribbean plantation systems, and historian François Girod[12] all adopted the position in one form or another, and to varying degrees, that statistically speaking the desire for freedom counted for very little among the real causes of marronage, that those causes motivating slaves to escape were almost invariably related to the conditions of slavery and rarely, if ever, had anything to do with the lofty "European" ideal of liberty. Haitian scholar Jean Fouchard retaliated that although factors relating to the brutal conditions of slavery did, indeed, play a role, the most basic motive for marronage was the desire of the slave to escape the bondage of slavery itself and thereby to obtain his own freedom, and that freedom is itself intrinsically unquantifiable.

Another point of contention between the two interpretations concerns the nature of marronage as practiced at various times by the slaves. On the one hand, Debien makes a somewhat arbitrary distinction between "small" marronage, i.e., flights lasting only a day or two, or a week, and which involve only one individual or very small groups, and "big" marronage—the real thing, the more spectacular and more alarming sort which involves large numbers of slaves grouped in bands.[13] In his *Marrons de la liberté*, Fouchard, on the other hand, questions the validity of making such distinctions.[14] In other words, whether marronage was the result of a sudden change of temper in the slave or an actual rebellion against the colonial regime, in each case it came down to nothing less than continual resistance to slavery, under one form or another.

Finally, there is a third source of contention: Debien seriously doubts a fundamental tenet of the Haitian national writers regarding the role and significance of marronage, i.e., that this phenomenon contained both the antecedents and general form of the great slave uprising of 1791 in the North Province—the real beginning of the black revolution.[15] In so doing, however, he relies entirely upon a distinction sometimes made by contemporaries between "maroons" and the armed slaves that they called "brigands," "rebels," or "insurgents," as if the latter were not maroons themselves. The whole point here is that categories relevant to the comparatively stable conditions of the colonial regime tend, for that very reason, to break down and change during times of revolutionary upheaval.

A long-overdue contribution to this whole debate was made by Leslie Manigat during a 1976 symposium on comparative slavery studies.[16] Manigat actually draws together these two opposing perspectives, each of which deals with marronage on an ideologically preferential "level of analysis," the one empirical, "atomistic," descriptive, and dismissing the overall impact of marronage on the plantation system as trivial; the other sociopolitical, cultural, "collectivist," viewing marronage as a total phenomenon within the objective structural framework of slave society, a constant threat in whatever its manifestation to the very foundations of slavery. Manigat argues that the two perspectives need not be mutually exclusive. Each of the individualistic motives for running away described by the French school—hunger, punishments, harsh working conditions, maltreatment, inadaptation, inadequate living conditions—may in fact be but particular expressions of, or may "trigger off," the desire for freedom.[17] Finally, insofar as marronage is a reaction against the property relations of slavery, it is therefore inscribed within the dynamics of class and race struggle in Saint Domingue and, facing the historical conjuncture of the prerevolutionary decade of the 1780s, evolved from a preconscious form of colonial protest to a political revolutionary force.[18]

In an earlier study of the Jamaican maroons, sociologist Orlando Patterson has argued in a somewhat similar vein, and this can equally be applied to the case of Saint Domingue, that the maroons were merely one feature of the revolt of the slaves. He goes even further to suggest that "all sustained slave revolts must acquire a Maroon dimension, since the only way in which a slave population can compensate for the inevitably superior military might of their masters is to resort to guerilla warfare."[19] There is no need nor is there any justification to treat the maroons as a separate entity; they were themselves ex-slaves that the colonists sought to defeat and to return to slavery; the slaves on the plantations saw them as fellow slaves lucky enough to have gotten away; and the maroons saw their plantation counterparts as potential allies on whom they depended for provisions and shelter. In light of these observations, then, the dynamics of marronage can be understood from a fresh perspective that carries the discussion beyond the limitations of the French/Haitian paradigm.

Yet another approach to the problem of marronage in slave societies has been delineated by historian Eugene Genovese. His provocative book, *From Rebellion to Revolution* (1979), treats the evolution of marronage and slave revolt throughout the New World from the early seventeenth-century "restorationist" movements that sought personal freedom from slavery and attempted to reconstruct, by withdrawing from slave society, a form of social organization roughly reminiscent of African modes of life, toward slave movements in the latter part of the eighteenth and early nineteenth centuries. These movements ultimately involved the overthrow of slavery itself, occurring as they did within the context of the "bourgeois-democratic revolutionary wave" of the Age of Revolution. They necessarily took on a new and broader dimension as they became part of the mainstream of world history as it was then unfolding. Their aim was not escape from slave society, but the destruction of slavery and hence the transformation of that society. The turning point in this historical evolution of slave resistance was the great Saint Domingue revolution. And so, whether they knew it or not, the maroons of the modern period were challenging part of the foundations of the emerging world and the capitalist system to which slavery itself was so integrally bound.

This separation of marronage into distinct historical categories such as "restorationist"/"revolutionary" or "backward-looking"/"modern" may perhaps be somewhat too reductionist, at least in regard to Saint Domingue, where many of the early slave revolts aimed as much at the massacre and elimination of the white masters as at escape from slavery.[20] Indeed, in the one really significant slave conspiracy prior to the revolution, the Makandal affair of 1757,[21] the intent was not only the total destruction of the white masters but independence as well; the new masters were to be the blacks. It revealed an incipient, prerevolutionary consciousness, certainly, but was hardly "escapist" or "backward-looking." And then we have during the revolutionary years of 1792–93 the maroon settlement at Platons in the South that might, according to the Genovese thesis, be called "restorationist" (as the slaves organized themselves in the hills outside of plantation society, elected themselves a ruler/king, and called the territory they occupied the Kingdom of Platons), but which actually played an active, armed, and integral role in the revolutionary process whereby slavery was finally abolished. [22]

What the Genovese thesis points out, however, is that whether marronage was "restorationist," as the great peasant revolts of Europe, or "revolutionary"—and these terms may be debated—its mere presence in slave society was a continual blow to the plantation system and the foundations of slavery in the New World. The argument also underscores the qualitative change in marronage as it had adapted to a new world context in 1789–91 and onward and had become a popular revolutionary form of collective resistance, which it could not have been in Makandal's time, just thirty years earlier, given the historical limitations of that period.

From whatever standpoint one may choose to consider marronage (and this will to one degree or another be influenced by the ideological biases of the researcher), qualifications such as "restorationist," "backward-looking," "revolutionary," "contradictory," "modern," or "paradoxical" all have meaning only for the historian who, from an academic standpoint, is looking back at history. For the slaves, it was a matter of life and death. The choices they made depended upon the circumstances they faced. Marronage, then, is not a category but is something that occurs in the human dynamics of the master-slave relationship; for some slaves it was part of what being a slave was all about, just as acquiescence could be another.

In words that may equally apply to the slaves (and then, the postabolition peasantry) of Saint Domingue as to the "lost causes" of the pre-industrial artisans in England, E. P. Thompson reminds us that

> they lived through these times of acute social disturbance, and we did not. Their aspirations were valid in terms of their own experience; and, if they were casualties of history, they remain, condemned in their own lives, as casualties. Our only criterion of judgement should not be whether or not a man's actions are justified in the light of subsequent evolution. After all, we are not at the end of social evolution ourselves. In some of the lost causes . . . we may discover insight into social evils which we have yet to cure. . . . Causes which were lost in England might, in Asia of Africa, yet be won. [23]

Surely the case of the Haitian peasantry is no exception. So whether the slaves, or the maroons, or the "insurgents," or "brigands," or the ordinary black plantation laborers were acting paradoxically or not in their prolonged fight for freedom and then for land, they were acting according to self-defined needs and aspirations. And these are the chief concern of the present study.

To examine the autonomous activities, the organizational capacities, and the particular character of these masses in the midst of a revolution is a difficult enough task in itself, only compounded by the fact that the slaves, the principal actors in the revolution, left no written records of their own. For the vast majority of them, the ability to read or write was an unknown luxury. So they left no memoirs, tracts, pamphlets, nor accounts of events. Their participation in the revolution was written rather in fire and blood and by the sacrifice of their own lives, by whatever means they could find within their power to destroy slavery and the tyranny of the masters. The difficulty and even impossibility, in some cases, of securing precise, conclusive, "statistically valid" data on the activities of the black masses has naturally influenced historians, up to now, more in the direction of political, leadership, military, or economic studies on the revolution, than toward an area of study they might, at best, consider interesting but scientifically precarious. However it is an aspect of the Haitian revolution that need, indeed ought, not be ignored, and enough evidence does exist to justify such a study.

Wherever it has been possible and the documents permitting, I have tried to show who these slaves and their chosen leaders were, what their aspirations were, and how they were able to organize themselves in active rebellion; in a sense, from 1791 on, I have tried to present the development of the Saint Domingue revolution from below. Finally, I should like to make two points concerning slave resistance in regard to the present study. The first is that, although marronage is given particular importance as a form of resistance, and is at times treated at some length, it is hoped that this work will not be taken simply as a case study of New World marronage. Marronage, at least in Saint Domingue, is not a separate phenomenon or entity to be studied in and of itself or to be viewed from the outside in relation *to* the slave system, but rather an integral and active part of the dynamics of slavery and slave resistance and a form of resistance that facilitated others, including insurrectionary activities within the revolution

The second point, on the other end of the spectrum, is addressed to those readers who may find that not enough attention has been paid to the more passive side of the slave personality, to accommodation as a response to slavery and indeed as a means of survival,[24] or to those slaves who did not rebel or who may even have fought at various times in defense of the masters. Accommodation as a strategy of survival within the slave system no doubt enabled slaves, on the one hand, to acquire much useful experience and knowledge, as well as concrete skills that would later prove vital. However, resistance, at least in its extreme revolutionary form in Saint Domingue, was a strategy of liberation and of the eventual destruction of slavery itself. In its more restricted forms under the colonial regime, it was a means of striking back and provided the possibility of individual release, if only temporary, from the weight of slavery. It is thus from the vantage point of history and of the operative historical forces in Saint Domingue society, as concerns the slaves, that greater emphasis will be placed in this study upon resistance and the diverse traditions of resistance that contributed so much to the success of the black revolution.[25] The present work, then, is not in itself a slavery study of a New World plantation society; it is a study of popular participation in a revolution, a type of activity that, by definition, cannot be seen in terms of status quo. This is not to say, however, that the "passive" slave did not exist, nor for that matter that apparent passivity necessarily meant acquiescence, but only that, among those who chose for various reasons not to resist at the outset of the revolution, there were also those who may later have been prompted to do so depending upon the alternatives they faced at any given moment. And in times of revolution, those moments can become decisive.

While this study will principally focus on the independent activities of the black masses and the various forms of rebellion used to resist and finally to overthrow the rule of the white masters, to destroy slavery itself, and to achieve independence, I have felt it important, nonetheless, to begin with a brief background summary of the social and economic structure of Saint Domingue. The first chapter of Part One will include a brief discussion of the class and caste relationships that existed prior to the revolution, as well as a general discussion of the plantation system, followed by a fairly lengthy section depicting the black slave culture at the outset of the revolution (1789–91). Chapter 2 will deal almost entirely with the continuity of slave resistance throughout the eighteenth century. Finally, Part One will end with a short chapter discussing the impact of the French Revolution on

the political context within which the revolt of the colonists, the ensuing revolt of the *affranchis*, or free blacks and free mulattoes, and the continuing
struggle of the slaves successively erupted.

From then on, the study will be concerned chiefly with the activities, both
individual and collective, of those slaves who participated in and contributed to the revolution. Thus, Part Two will deal with the revolts of 1791,
beginning with the August 1791 revolt in the North and continuing with an
account of events in the West and the South up to early 1792. Part Three
will give a more detailed analysis of the popular movements in a single province and will deal almost exclusively with the South. Although in much less
detail, the politically significant activities of the masses in the North and the
West will be chronologically integrated into the discussion of the popular
movement in the South from 1792 onward.

However, I have made no special attempt to deal with autonomous slave
activities as they may have occurred in the zones of British occupation
(1793–98) where slavery had not yet effectively been abolished. Such a
study would indeed raise additional questions and problems that might well
constitute fertile ground for further intensive research and perhaps even the
basis of another monograph. Thus, in a more modest vein, I have limited my
analysis to those areas of Saint Domingue that remained under the French
republican regime during these years.

The sources used for the general background of Part One consist mainly
of manuscript materials, contemporary printed sources, and secondary literature, which are found in abundance, not only at the Bibliothèque Nationale in Paris, but at the A. Schomburg Collection of the New York Public
Library, the Institut Saint-Louis de Gonzague in Port-au-Prince, as well as
at university libraries throughout North America. In addition, the general
correspondence in Series C9 A and C9 B and the F 3 series of the Bibliothèque
Moreau de Saint-Méry at the Archives Nationales in Paris provide numerous
accounts of slave conspiracies, poisonings, infanticides, and other forms of
resistance to the slave system. In addition to the manuscript sources mentioned above for the period from 1789 to 1791, one can find an overwhelming
mass of primary materials, including the correspondence of the civil commissioners, colonists, and *affranchis*, as well as records of the Colonial
Assembly and contemporary pamphlets in Series DXXV (Colonies) of the
Archives Nationales in Paris. Also, contemporary newspapers from a few
of the Atlantic port cities such as Philadelphia, Boston, or New York contain accounts by American merchants and ship captains resident in le Cap
during the August 1791 revolt, and have proved helpful.

I have chosen, however, to devote an entire section of this work to a particular study of the South, and for two main reasons. First, one of the major
sources of primary materials relating to the masses (Series DXXV at the

Archives Nationales) contains an abundance of documents providing vital information on the individual activities of slaves in the South, be they correspondence, prison records, court interrogations, or contemporary eyewitness accounts of specific events. While similar documentation can be found for the North and West, it does not always include the type of information that I used in Chapter 7, for example, where I was able to analyze the reactions of the black workers to emancipation in the South. Additionally, the Public Record Office in London holds a wealth of correspondence in the High Court of Admiralty (HCA) Series that gives detailed day-to-day accounts of the massive revolt at Platons in 1792 and in the early months of 1793, an insurrection by which some seven hundred slaves achieved their own freedom prior to the abolition of slavery. In addition to descriptive accounts of their activities, the correspondence provides us with valuable insights into the general mentality and political attitudes of the slave participants and indicates in many cases the plantations to which they belonged. This correspondence was found aboard a French ship, *La Fédératif*, captured by the British in 1793, and therefore complements and completes the material at the Archives Nationales for the same period.[26] The second reason for devoting special attention to the South lies in the fact that, while events in the North and West have been focally treated by almost all historians of the Haitian revolution, no adequate or systematic analysis has yet been made of the popular revolutionary movements in the South.

The period from roughly 1795 to 1801 was, from the available evidence, or lack of it, a relatively stable one in the South, where either popular resistance had actually subsided for reasons I have tried to explain in Chapter 8 or else the data revealing forms of protest among the black laborers have yet to be uncovered. Whatever the case may be, popular resistance did resurface once the French expeditionary army landed to restore slavery. For this period, the war for independence (1802–03), I have used as primary sources military correspondence and, wherever available, official reports and interrogations of the black plantation workers. Most of this material is found in the Rochambeau Papers located at the University of Florida Libraries.

It is my hope, then, that a study of this nature may in some way help not only to fill what has until very recently been a regrettable gap in the overall history of the Saint Domingue revolution, but that it may also make a contribution, if only a modest one, to the ever-increasing body of literature on slave resistance in the New World.

PART ONE
Background to Revolution

1
Slavery and Slave Society

At its height in 1789, the French colony of Saint Domingue, the Pearl of the Antilles and the pride of France, was by far the wealthiest and most flourishing of the slave colonies in the Caribbean. The tremendous fortunes amassed by the white planters, as well as the merchant bourgeoisie of that era, had been generated by the forced labor of over half a million black slaves, raided from their homelands in Africa and forcibly brought to the New World to fill the preeminent and ever-expanding demand for labor and profits.

Yet there was very little in its early seventeenth-century beginnings to indicate that Saint Domingue would become the colonial Hercules that she was by the eve of the revolution. The first French settlers were, in fact, of a dubious nature, composed of former *flibustiers*, or pirates and freebooters operating in the coastal waters, along with the inland *boucaniers* involved in hunting and the trafficking of hides.[1] What little subsistence farming the *boucaniers* did engage in eventually gave way, by the 1670s, to the more lucrative exploitation of tobacco and, by 1685, of indigo, thus initiating the transition to a plantation-oriented economy and the introduction of forced labor.

The first imported laborers to Saint Domingue, however, were the *engagés,* or white indentured servants of peasant and laboring class origins, initially from the western maritime regions of France, who came to serve under three-year contracts and eventually worked and lived side by side in near-equal numbers with black slaves.[2] It was the conversion to indigo, though, financed in part through capital derived from spurious *flibuste* operations, that accelerated the utilization of Africans as plantation laborers. The larger-scale, labor-intensive production of sugar and the exclusive induction of black slaves into the colonial work force were by then hardly two decades away, with the *engagés* eventually occupying the lower ranks of *économe*, or overseer, specialized tradesmen, and, occasionally, steward on the plantations. [3]

It was from these disparate elements that a dominant white colonial planter class emerged in the eighteenth century,[4] and by the eve of the revolution constituted the most significant segment of the white population, for it was upon the plantation system and slave labor that the entire economy and wealth of Saint Domingue depended. During the latter decades of the colonial regime, however, most planters no longer claimed permanent residence in the colony. Indeed, one rarely came to Saint Domingue with the desire to stay any longer than it would take to make a quick fortune. Simply stated, the first and foremost aim of the planters was to make money, to make more money, and to make it all as quickly as possible in order to return to France to enjoy the luxuries and comforts that their overseas investments ensured them. In general, most colonists considered themselves as mere travelers in the colony and spoke continually of revisiting or of returning to France within the following year. In fact, a significant portion of the planter class seldom, if ever, even set foot on the island. [5]

These absentee planters were represented in the colony either by their agents or plantation managers, who kept them more or less informed of production levels, profits, expenses, and the general operations of the plantation. The agent, or *procureur*, usually a permanent resident in the colony, thus took over full administration of the plantation and assumed all the rights and prerogatives of the owner;[6] in his turn, the *procureur* could become a plantation owner himself. But the delegation of powers to an agent almost invariably meant harsher treatment for the slave than if the master were present to check the excesses of an overzealous or often sadistic overseer. [7]

For the colonial planter, life was generally one of monotony and isolation, compensated by sheer dissipation and indulgence.[8] The arrogance and conceit of the white planters was sustained by surrounding themselves with a swarm of domestic slaves to satisfy every need, want, or caprice. Indeed, the most visible sign of wealth and the most flagrant indication of superiority consisted in the number of domestic slaves at one's disposal, for "the dignity of a rich man consisted in having four times as many domestics as he needed."[9] To further ensure their prestige and enhance their status, some planters would usurp nobility by merely inventing a fictitious past, laying false claims to their ancestry, and thereby hiding their lowly origins. [10]

Yet all this extravagance merely contributed to the boredom and social alienation of the typical planter, separated as he was by long distances over deplorable roads from the nearest neighbor. Whatever social life existed in Saint Domingue was to be found in the two principal cities of le Cap and Port-au-Prince, where the cultural and intellectual activities of the colony were centered. Although attempting to imitate French culture, the cities were nonetheless vulnerable to local habit, debauchery, and decadent lifestyles; so for the rural planter, social life centered invariably around his business: his slaves, his sugar, his cotton, his coffee, his profits.

These planters, as well as their white counterparts in the cities—the representatives of the French maritime bourgeoisie and the French-born bureaucrats—were collectively known in the island as the *grands blancs*. At the head of the bureaucracy were the governor and the intendant, both appointed by the king as his official representatives and charged with the functions and control of colonial administration. Together they represented the absolute authority of the king, against which there was no recourse, and thus created a constant source of bitterness for the colonists. The planters hated them for their arrogant, despotic pretensions and were only further frustrated by the special privileges and protection accorded by the Crown to the merchant bourgeoisie.

Alongside the *grands blancs* in city and country were the lower- and middle-class whites who, as plantation managers, *procureurs*, and *économes* in the country, were known as *petits blancs*. In the towns, they occupied positions as lawyers, shopkeepers, retail merchants, grocers, and tradesmen, usually carpenters or masons. While many of the *petits blancs* were descendants of the former seventeenth-century *engagés*, there were also among the urban "small" whites a whole host of vagabonds, petty criminals, debtors, and soldiers-of-fortune who swarmed to Saint Domingue, where, regardless of one's background or origin, the single privilege of race could elevate the most despicable to a position of social respectability.[11] A British soldier who was sent to Saint Domingue some years after the revolution began, spoke of "the necessity the White People are under, of making a pointed difference between the two Colours," and offered these observations: "A white Man how ever low his Situation, in every sense of the Word may be, conceives himself equal to the Richest Man in the Colony . . . in regard to the respect he expects shall be paid him."[12]

It would be an oversimplification, however, to argue, as one historian has done, that despite the social and economic differences that separated the planters from the *petits blancs*, these differences were of relatively minor importance since they were subsumed under the one unifying factor of race prejudice, tying together all the diverse sections of the white population.[13] Race prejudice was undeniably practiced by white society against the mulattoes and the blacks, and by virtue of the common bond of superiority that membership in the white race alone afforded them, the various categories of whites, as diverse in their origins as in their social and political functions, nonetheless formed a distinct and privileged social caste. Their superiority thus extended not only over the entire mass of black slaves—some fifteen times their own number—but, as well, over the *affranchis*, or free persons of color, who constituted an intermediate sector of colonial society but whose numbers, estimated roughly at twenty-seven thousand, nearly equaled that of the whites.[14] There was a universally accepted and a juridically enforced maxim in Saint Domingue to govern race relations. It asserted that "a white is never in the wrong vis-à-vis a black," and it was equally applied to the *affranchis*, most of whom were free mulattoes. [15]

Yet this racial ideology did not produce a coherent and solid white bloc, either before or during the revolution. With the advancement and expansion of Saint Domingue's sugar economy, the *petits blancs* witnessed the progressive closing off of their chances for property ownership, the one criterion that would guarantee their social integration and satisfy their frustrated aspirations.[16] In addition, they suffered increasing competition from the *affranchis* and even the upper-strata slaves for jobs in the trades.[17] More than that, *affranchis* and slaves alike viewed the *petit blanc* as an object of derision, thus further exacerbating the psychological effects of economic insecurity in a society where, without property ownership, entry into the upper echelons was all but impossible. The slaves, those most discerning and candid observers of the society around them, even had a vocabulary to describe the various categories of whites. Only the *grands blancs*, the great sugar planters, were the real whites, the *Blancs-blancs*. The *petit blanc*, the small white who worked for a salary, was little more than a *Blanchet* and a *faux blanc* by comparison; if he were in the militia he might be called a *Blanc-soldat* or perhaps even a *Nègre-blanc*. [18]

Irascible, insolent, with much to lose out on in the socioeconomic structure of Saint Domingue, the *petits blancs* were, in one sense, the most vulnerable and consequently the most volatile element in the white colonial regime. Though they despised the planters as their social superiors, the wealth and prestige of this class nevertheless represented their ultimate and yet unattainable goals. Thus, when interests periodically clashed between the colonial planters and the royal bureaucracy, at times culminating in defiant rebellion, it was among these disaffected elements of the *petits blancs* that the planters readily recruited their support. And equally as bitterly, the colonial planters opposed the metropolitan bourgeoisie, the great merchants and slave traders by whom, because of their exclusive commercial privileges, they felt unjustly exploited. Imbued with feelings of autonomy and of contempt for metropolitan authority, the colonial planters saw themselves as the legitimate heirs to Saint Domingue, as an ennobled race by virtue of their residence in the colony, and they increasingly came to resent the absentee owners of their own class for their affinities with the metropolis. [19]

But beneath these divergent elements were the free mulattoes and free blacks who, because of their color, constituted an intermediary caste between the whites and the slaves. Due to the widespread practice of concubinage by the white masters with their female slaves, followed by eventual grants of freedom to the offspring of such unions, a free colored population emerged at the beginning of the eighteenth century and, by 1789, had increased over fiftyfold to a near-equal balance with the white population. The most dramatic rate of increase, however, occurred in the last two decades of the colonial regime, when the free colored population jumped from a mere 6,000 in 1770 to 27,500 in 1789, nearly twice the increase of the white population for the same period.[20] In fact, in Saint Domingue alone their numbers far exceeded their total in the rest of the French and British West Indies combined.[21] Even more alarming for the whites was that this demographic increase was paralleled by sustained economic growth among the *affranchis*.

If at first the *affranchis* provided competition with the *petits blancs* for jobs in the specialized trades on the plantations, by mid-century and especially after 1763, many had become plantation owners themselves as the rise and rapid expansion of coffee production brought much of the undeveloped mountainous regions of the West and the virtual frontier in the South under cultivation and ownership by the *affranchis*. Through industry, thrift, and a characteristically sober life style, they had made considerable economic strides and were amassing fortunes that rivaled and, at times, even surpassed those of some whites. This, moreover, was becoming disturbingly evident as early as the 1750s, as the colonial administrators then informed the ministry of the marine:

> These men are beginning to fill the colony and it is of the greatest perversion to see them, their numbers continually increasing amongst the whites, with fortunes often greater than those of the whites. . . . Their strict frugality prompting them to place their profits in the bank every year, they accumulate huge capital sums and become arrogant because they are rich, and their arrogance increases in proportion to their wealth. They bid on properties that are for sale in every district and cause their prices to reach such astronomical heights that the whites who have not so much wealth are unable to buy, or else ruin themselves if they do persist. In this manner, in many districts the best land is owned by the half-castes. . . . These coloreds, [moreover], imitate the style of the whites and try to wipe out all memory of their original state. [22]

The administrators' report went on to predict, somewhat hyperbolically, that, should this pattern continue, the mulattoes would even try to contract marriages within the most distinguished white families and, worse, through these marriages tie these families to the slave gangs from which the mothers were taken. [23]

By 1789, the *affranchis* owned one-third of the plantation property, one-quarter of the slaves, and one-quarter of the real estate property in Saint Domingue; in addition, they held a fair position in commerce and in the trades, as well as in the military.[24] Circumstances permitting, a few had even "infiltrated" the almost exclusively *grand blanc* domain of the sugar plantation by becoming managers of the paternal estate upon the father's return to Europe or even inheritors of property upon the father's death.[25] By 1763, at least three hundred white planters were married to women of color in Saint Domingue, in spite of the social aspersions cast upon them as *mésalliés*.[26] The *affranchis* imitated white manners, were often educated in France, and, in turn, sent their own children abroad to be educated. Having become slave-holding plantation owners, they could even employ white contract labor among the *petits blancs*.

Not only did their situation pose a potential threat to the political hegemony of the whites, but because of their color and their free status, the whites saw them as a threat to racial hegemony in the colony and, from there, to the maintenance of slavery itself. The irony of it was that many of the *affranchis* were themselves slaveowners and, if only theoretically, allies of property with the whites.[27] So it was only through repressive social legislation that the whites of Saint Domingue could hope to maintain their privileges and prerogatives against the economic and social encroachments of the *affranchis*. A memoir from the king sent to the intendant and the governor of Martinique in 1777 unequivocally stated the policy of the metropolis concerning the state of the colored population in the French colonies: "The *gens de couleur* are either free or slave: The free are *affranchis* and descendants of *affranchis:* however far removed they may be from their [black] origins, they retain forever the imprint of slavery."[28] This, then, was the general principle preventing any effective assimilation with the whites. By virtue of their racial origins, the *affranchis* were legally defined, for all intents and purposes, as a distinct and subordinate social "caste."

Although restrictions against the social advancement of the *affranchis* date as far back as the early 1720s, the turning point in colonial, as in metropolitan, legislation came after 1763 and accompanied both the economic and demographic expansion of the *affranchis*.[29] By strictly forbidding free persons of color to hold any public office in the colony, to practice law, medicine, pharmacy, or certain privileged trades, such as that of goldsmith,[30] the whites sought to establish insurmountable barriers to frustrate the social and political aspirations of the free coloreds and to preclude all possibility of their assimilation on an equal basis. Yet at the same time, the *affranchis* were required to participate in the defense of the colony, as an ordinance of 1768 made militia duty compulsory for all free mulattoes and free blacks between the ages of fifteen and fifty-five. They were to provide their own uniforms and equipment, were to serve in separate units, and would be commanded by white officers.[31] In addition, a local law-enforcing body, the *maréchaussée*, had been created for the chief purpose of hunting down and capturing runaway slaves, or maroons; it was composed exclusively of *affranchis*, whose superior capabilities in pursuing slave deserters into inaccessible and dangerous mountain retreats were candidly recognized by colonial authorities.[32] By making the composition of the *maréchaussée* exclusively colored, the whites could incidentally reinforce the contempt of the free mulatto for his own black origins and at the same time exploit his affinities to a white slave society, even though it denied him full equality.

The colonists left nothing to circumstance, though, and out of their own fears of slave conspiracy denied the *affranchis* the right to freely assemble in public after 9 P.M. for any reason whatsoever, be it for a wedding, for a public dance, or any other festivity. This was punishable by a fine of three hundred livres for the first offense and the loss of freedom for any subsequent offense. The free blacks also risked losing their freedom if caught sheltering or in any way aiding a fugitive slave. The mulattoes and free blacks were equally forbidden to engage in games of chance and, by the 1770s, to travel to or enter France for any purpose.[33] They were forbidden to take the name of their former master and natural parent. Their inferior status was reinforced by regulations stipulating their mode of dress in the colony, both to degrade and humiliate them and at the same time to prevent assimilation.[34] In short, outside of owning property and slaves, about "the only privilege the whites allowed them," as James wrote, "was the privilege of lending white men money."[35]

If the *affranchis* thought of themselves as equal, deference reminded them that, in social relations with the whites, they were still inferior. Should they invite a white to their house for dinner, they could not sit with that person at the same table. They were obliged by law to submit with utmost respect to the arrogance and contempt which whites not uncommonly displayed toward them.[36] A mulatto who publicly struck a white person in retaliation, in self-defense, or for any other reason could ultimately (even though it rarely happened) be punished by having his right arm cut off.[37] But, "for insults and a premeditated assault" on a white man, one free black was condemned to death by hanging. And since it was imperative to keep free blacks and slaves subordinate, the Crown ordered that the decree be published throughout the colony. A free mulatto of le Cap was sentenced to three years on the public chain gang for having raised his hand against a white man who forcibly tried to remove a slave woman accompanying him along the road. Another free mulatto received the same sentence simply for causing a white man to fall off his chair when he threw a stone that broke the cross bar. On the other hand, a white man of le Cap, having struck a free mulatto and nearly causing him to lose his eye, was simply fined three thousand livres.[38] In spite of their freedom from the institution of slavery, the mulattoes, as the free blacks, never escaped the opprobrium of their origins.

But the great mass of the population consisted of the slaves, and it was upon their backs that the tremendous fortunes of the colonial planters, as

of the French maritime bourgeoisie, were built. It was upon their continuing labor, as slaves, that all this seemingly endless prosperity depended.
By 1789, Saint Domingue boasted well over seven thousand plantations,
over three thousand in indigo, twenty-five hundred in coffee, close to eight
hundred in cotton, with some fifty-odd in cocoa, but the cornerstone of her
economy and the key to her rapid expansion was sugar.[39] If prior to 1690 the
colony had not one sugar plantation, within fifteen years there were already
120, more than 100 of these being established over a mere four-year period
from 1700 to 1704.[40] The first decade of the eighteenth century thus set in
motion a veritable "take-off" period for what would be another eighty-five
years of sustained and unparalleled growth. By mid-century, the number of
sugar plantations had increased fivefold to six hundred and reached its peak
at nearly eight hundred on the eve of the revolution, making the colony by
far the single most important sugar colony of the Caribbean (having long
since surpassed Martinique and Guadeloupe in the Lesser Antilles, as well
as Barbados, in the British West Indies) and certainly one of the greatest
wealth-producing colonies of the world. But the explanation for that wealth
may, in part, be found in the particular requirements of sugar production itself. The cultivation of cane and the multi-stage process of producing sugar
necessitated both a large and a highly diversified labor force.[41] This invariably brought about dramatic increases in the number of slaves imported into
the colony and provided perhaps the greatest impetus to the expansion of
the French slave trade in the eighteenth century. [42]

By comparison, the seventeenth-century slave trade was almost insignificant, supplying the French West Indies with little more than one or two
thousand slaves annually toward the end of the century.[43] Though figures for
the eighteenth century periodically fluctuate, they reached an overall average from 1700 to 1792 of some 14,500 captives per year. In actual numbers,
however, the slave trade had significantly increased after the Seven Years'
War, averaging roughly 26,400 per year from 1764 to 1792, and, in the last
decade of the colonial regime, from 1783 to 1792, some 37,000 slaves per
year. [44]

A highly lucrative business, the slave trade was by no means an autar-
kic economic activity, but a constituent part of a much broader and more
highly diversified system tying together slavery, the colonial trade (including
both colonial imports and their reexportation to foreign markets throughout
Europe), and the slave trade into an interdependent and interlocking web.
In most cases the *armateur*, or outfitter, of a slaving expedition to Africa
was also an importer of colonial commodities, which were loaded in the
islands for the return voyage to France once the captives were sold to colonial planters. In fact, more often than not, colonists made partial payment
for their slaves with colonial products, usually sugar or coffee. According

to official government statistics for 1789, the value of colonial imports to France, primarily sugar and coffee, as well as indigo, cotton, cocoa, and a few hides, had soared to roughly 218 million livres. Although exports from the metropolis to the islands, such as flour, meat, wine, and textiles, totaled 78 million livres by comparison, still, a full two-thirds of the 218 million livres were reexported to the markets of Europe, either in bulk or after having eventually been turned into refined goods. [45]

Bordeaux was without question the center of the French colonial trade. By the end of the Old Regime, the city was furnishing over 50 percent of Saint Domingue's imports from France and by the 1760s already accounted for up to half of all French exports of colonial commodities to Europe.[46] With such a tremendous volume of imports and exports, where "so much wealth provided endless possibilities for enterprising businessmen," there was little reason for Bordeaux merchants to invest directly in the slave trade, which actually existed only as an auxiliary element in the local economy.[47] Yet without slavery and the slave trade to supply the laborers producing the colonial commodities, Bordeaux's role as the center of the French colonial trade would have been diminished considerably. Colonial economic prosperity hinged on sugar, and sugar production, a labor-intensive operation, required massive numbers of slaves. The slave trade was thus fundamental to the triangular system and, in fact, became the cornerstone of the Nantes economy, as it additionally stimulated and directly financed other sectors of economic activity, foremost among which was shipbuilding, but which also included printed textiles, iron works, and sugar refining. [48]

These derivative activities were hardly exclusive to Nantes, however. As in the area of refining, colonial sugar supplied the refineries of Orléans, Dieppe, de Bercy-Paris, Marseilles, and, of course, Bordeaux. In the Bordeaux suburbs alone, some sixteen refineries had been in operation by the mid–eighteenth century and, as early as 1740, were refining a yearly average of fifty shiploads of raw sugar at roughly two hundred tons each.[49] Whereas, by the eve of the revolution, her sister city, Nantes, had become the shipbuilding leader of all French ports in order to meet the needs of the slave trade, for Bordeaux the shipbuilding industry, as that of refining, rapidly flourished in response to her colonial trade.[50] One may safely say, then, that the colonies contributed to the development of French industry while, at the same time, supporting a sizable portion of her international trade, as well. As to the political vitality of the French bourgeoisie on the eve of the revolution, it had, as Jean Jaurès observed, been bolstered by the fortunes generated both directly and indirectly by the slave trade itself: "Sad irony of human history! The fortunes created at Bordeaux, at Nantes, by the slave trade gave to the bourgeoisie that pride which demanded liberty and so contributed to human emancipation." [51]

Perhaps the most important source of wealth for the maritime bourgeoisie, however, lay in the area of finance capital. As most colonists never had sufficient capital to purchase slaves outright, credit was extended to the planter, allowing him to delay or defer his payments over several years. Habitually, colonists simply refused to honor the totality of their obligations, and at least 10 percent of their debt to slavers went regularly unpaid. During the final decade of the Old Regime, the period from 1783 to 1792, the slave-trading debts of colonial planters to the Nantes traders had reached some 45 million livres, much of which, with the outbreak of the Saint Domingue slave revolution, would never get paid.[52] Nonpayment or deferred payment of debts by colonists was actually endemic to their situation and not a particular feature of the end of a regime. One colonial administrator complained in 1733 that "all the colonists owe twice as much as they own. The practice here is that, when they have borrowed, they do not reimburse; when they buy some land or a plantation, they never pay."[53] But if merchants and traders were creditors to the colonial planters (a situation they did not appreciate), they themselves had become debtors in the process.

To offset the colonial debts owed them and their own consequent lack of capital reserve, they borrowed heavily from the huge banking houses of Paris, as well as those of Bordeaux, Nantes, or Marseilles, locally. Many a slave trader finally found himself in the position of having to take over the financially troubled plantation of a debtor colonist, thus becoming concurrently a plantation owner and a buyer of slaves, as well as a supplier of slaves and shipper of colonial raw material. His reliance, if not dependence, upon the Parisian (and often foreign) banks was, on the one hand, reinforced, while, on the other, he began to play an increasingly direct role in the colonial economy and in colonial affairs.[54]

Relations between creole planters and the French merchant bourgeoisie were characteristically marked by deep hostilities and jealousies on both sides. If the merchants saw the colonial planters as a vile and deceiving race of profiteers, unscrupulously defaulting on payments and falsifying both the quality and quantity of their produce for personal gain, the planters hated the merchants for the unfair (as they saw it) privileges bestowed upon them by French mercantile policy. According to the policy known as the Exclusive, dating back to the days of Colbert, "the colonies are founded by and for the Metropolis."[55] That is, to assure maximum economic benefits for the mother country, all manufactured goods consumed by the colonists were imported from France. By the same token, all exports of raw materials from the colony were to be sold exclusively to France and to be carried exclusively aboard French ships. The mercantile policy of the Crown both encouraged and sustained the economic growth of the merchant bourgeoisie while leaving the Saint Domingue planter virtually in a state of political and economic dependence upon the metropolis. The smuggling by planters of cheaper foreign slaves, or even foodstuffs and finished goods, into Saint Domingue was thus far from uncommon and a practice that further envenomed relations between colonists and French metropolitan merchants, many of whom had by now also become absentee owners. If their interests happened to coincide, relations might superficially be cordial, but on the whole, they remained perpetually antagonistic and characteristically hostile. [56]

By 1789 nearly every sector of colonial society was in a state of unrest —slave against master, mulatto against white, "small" white against "big" white, both of the latter, at various times, against the local administration and especially the French bourgeoisie. While alliances might be made among groups against a common enemy, such alliances were occasional and of short duration, to serve only immediate interests. On the eve of the revolution, each group had its own grievances, and each represented particular interests arising out of the specific conditions and contradictions of class and caste, intertwined and confounded as they were by the colonial politics of race.

But once the revolution had opened, it was not the seditious activities of colonial planters seeking independence from French authority, but the great mass of black slaves themselves, who would deliver the decisive death blow to colonial Saint Domingue. When they revolted in full force in 1791 and onward, the whole system, already seriously shaky, crumbled into pieces impossible to put together again. The year 1791 marked the climax of a long and deep-rooted tradition of slave resistance in many forms, some overt, some covert, some individual, and some collective, some even potentially self-destructive. In conjunction with the impact and influence of the French Revolution, which provided the historical conditions for the emergence of a full-scale revolution in Saint Domingue, the more limited scope of traditional slave resistance was thrown wide open. New avenues and alternatives for achieving old goals were now within reach. Even more than by the legislative decrees of France, it was through the obtrusive intervention of their own efforts, their own popular initiative, and often spontaneously organized activities into a complex web of political and military events, that the Saint Domingue slaves won their own freedom and finally became a politically independent nation.

By 1789, two-thirds of the roughly half a million slaves in Saint Domingue were African-born.[57] Over a period of three centuries, Africans had been uprooted by force from their homelands, packed on slave ships, and sold in the Americas to fill a constantly expanding demand for labor in what one writer has called "the most colossal demographic event of modern times," the Atlantic slave trade. [58]

With the slave trade, however, came a rich diversity of African cultures, nations, tribes, languages, religions, classes, customs, all subsumed under the dominant structure of slave society in Saint Domingue. In his *Description . . . de l'isle de Saint-Domingue*, Moreau de Saint-Méry delineated three major regions of Africa from which the slaves of Saint Domingue were successively extracted. The first arrivals in the early sixteenth century came chiefly from the region and outlying areas of Senegal on the upper west coast and were generally of the Islamic faith. From there, European slavers moved southward during the seventeenth and especially eighteenth centuries along the west coast toward the Gulf of Guinea, where they replenished their supplies in human cargo. Here in the Ivory Coast, the Gold Coast (Ghana), and the Slave Coast (roughly, Togo, Benin, and a part of western Nigeria) were to be found some twenty-five nations or tribes, including Dahomeans, Aradas, Hausas, Ibos, Yorubas, Minas, Misérables, and Bourriqui, among many others. A third and equally important regional grouping of slaves came from the kingdoms of the Congo and Angola, south of the equator, and even, to a significant degree after 1773, from Mozambique on the east coast of Africa. In general, one can safely say that by the latter part of the eighteenth century these last two regional groupings, whose belief systems and patterns of thought were essentially animistic, not only represented the vast majority of the slaves introduced into the colony,[59] but also constituted their overall cultural framework, wherein voodoo, that most vital spiritual force in the slave culture of Saint Domingue, derived its distinctive characteristics. [60]

The French observer Hilliard d'Auberteuil estimated that, during the years from 1680 to 1776, over 800,000 slaves had been imported from Africa to Saint Domingue. By the end of that period, when he wrote, there were only 290,000.[61] He went on to say, as did Père Labat for the seventeenth century, that over one-third of the Africans brought to the colony died off within the first few years.[62] Such an excessive mortality rate among the newly arrived slaves was due as much to the psychological shock of becoming a slave, to moral despondency and an inability to rapidly adapt and physically resist the rigors of chattel slavery, as to the grossly inhuman conditions aboard the slave ships and to resulting sicknesses, not the least of which was scurvy. Through his extensive research of plantation papers and colonial correspondence for eighteenth-century Saint Domingue, Debien has found that the mortality rates of newly purchased Africans during the first three to eight years of their induction could—without exaggeration—be generally evaluated at 50 percent, thus confirming the approximation of the eighteenth-century French antislavery advocate Frossard. [63]

The fact was, the slave population of Saint Domingue never reproduced itself, and the reasons lay squarely on the conditions and economic relations of slavery itself. In fact, d'Auberteuil estimated the working life of an average plantation slave who was born in the colony to be little more than fifteen years,[64] and it was certainly no longer than that for creolized Africans who had survived the initial years. Slave mortality, it seems, was a matter of overwork, undernourishment, and the absolutism of the masters.

Slaves were literally worked to death because they were the units of production and, as such, represented an investment that, once amortized, had already yielded its profits. So, once dead, infirm, or otherwise physically unable to continue working, they were replaced by additional investments in new slaves.[65] Indicative of this pattern was the age distribution of slaves on most plantations: the principal age group consisted of slaves between the ages of seventeen or eighteen and thirty-five. Given the disproportionately low fertility rate among slave women, this necessarily required a constant influx of new acquisitions in slaves. [66]

To assure the submission of the slaves and the mastership of the owners, slaves were introduced into the colony and eventually integrated into the plantation labor system within an overall context of social alienation and psychological, as well as physical, violence. Parental and kinship ties were broken; their names were changed; their bodies were branded with red-hot irons to designate their new owners; and the slave who was once a socially integrated member of a structured community in Africa had, in a matter of months, become what has now been termed a "socially dead person," that is, one who no longer had a socially recognized existence, either before law or by custom, outside of the master whose authority was absolute.[67] Given these odds, most slaves had little choice but to submit and hope to survive. Their actual introduction into the labor force, however, followed a short period of acclimatization, usually six to twelve months, during which they were assigned a slave tutor and a small plot of land to begin cultivating; as well, they usually were required to build their own huts for living quarters. This period of transition was supposed to ease the pains of adjustment to the new environment and to the types and intensity of labor demanded of them. However, despite all the preparatory measures taken by the planters, or for that matter because of those inadequately taken, from one-third to one-half of the newly arrived slaves, as we have seen, died off during the first few years. [68]

Those who survived and were fully inducted into the plantation system occupied a variety of positions. In general, slave laborers on all plantations were organized into work groups, or *ateliers,* usually one or two major ones and a smaller one. The first were composed of the strongest and healthiest slaves, both men and women, doing the heaviest and hardest work, such as the tilling and clearing of the soil, digging the ditches and canals, planting and picking on the coffee estates, or cutting the cane on the sugar plantations, as well as the cutting and clearing of trees and extraction of rocks, which were tasks undertaken by the men. These workers were under the direct orders of the driver, or *commandeur*, himself a slave.

In the smaller or secondary *atelier*, then, one would find the less robust: the newly arrived Africans not yet integrated into the regular work force, women in their seventh or eighth month of pregnancy and others who were nursing infants, as well as children between eight and thirteen who were not yet ready for the major *atelier*. Work in these smaller *ateliers* was generally lighter and more varied, such as planting foodstuffs, fertilizing plants, or weeding and clearing dried leaves from the cane. As in the major *ateliers*, however, they too were subject to the direct orders of a *commandeur*.

The often-cited observations of Girod-Chantrans, a Swiss traveller of the time, vividly describe the working conditions of the field slaves on a typical sugar plantation, where

> The slaves numbered roughly one hundred men and women of different ages, all engaged in digging ditches in a cane field [in preparation for the planting of the cane], most of them naked or dressed in rags. The sun beat straight down on their heads; sweat ran from all parts of their bodies. Their arms and legs, worn out by excessive heat, by the weight of their picks and by the resistance of the clayey soil become so hardened that it broke their tools, the slaves neverthe- less made tremendous efforts to overcome all obstacles. A dead silence reigned among them. In their faces, one could see the human suffering and pain they en- dured, but the time for rest had not yet come. The merciless eye of the plantation steward watched over the workers while several foremen, dispersed among the workers and armed with long whips, delivered harsh blows to those who seemed too weary to sustain the pace and were forced to slow down. Men, women, young and old alike—none escaped the crack of the whip if they could not keep up the pace. [69]

By far the most intense utilization of the slaves' labor was on the sugar plantations, where, during the harvest and grinding season, an ordinary workday could easily average eighteen to twenty hours. Because of the nature of sugar production, work on the sugar plantations was virtually nonstop and followed a nearly complete twenty-four-hour schedule.[70] As one historian put it, "the operations of cutting, hauling, grinding, clarification, filtration, evaporation and crystallization had to be carried out in that order, without interruption, simultaneously, and at top speed."[71] Since the processing of the cane once cut had to be completed in a matter of hours lest its yield in juice diminish and spoil, night work was inevitable. For the night shifts, slaves were recruited from the major *atelier* and divided into four sections, the first two working from eight to midnight, and the second two from mid- night until six the next morning.[72] Night work for the first shift naturally followed a full day's work of cutting and hauling in the fields from five or six in the morning until sundown at six or six-thirty in the evening. Equally, work for the second shift of slaves preceded a full twelve-hour workday that ended at six the following evening. Each night shift alternated with the other so as to keep operations uninterrupted. So, during the grinding season, which ran for five to six months, roughly from January to July, many a slave received little more than four hours sleep per day. The only compensation for night work was a slightly better diet and more tafia.

In general, women were used to load the mills for grinding. It was a particularly dangerous task as one could easily lose a finger, a hand, or one's whole arm in the mill wheel, and all the more dangerous since it was part of the night work.[73] Once the juice was extracted, the residue cane, or *bagasse*, later to be used as fuel for the boilers, was gathered and stacked by children and the less vigorous slaves.[74] Once the grinding was done and their shift over, these women and children were then sent back to the fields. Simultaneous with this operation, the boilers (usually arranged in a series of five) were maintained by slaves who stoked the fires from beneath, while several others, specially selected for their capabilities, supervised the whole process from boiling to eventual crystallization. These workers remained at their posts and were separated from the ordinary field slaves, at least for the grinding season, before returning to the fields themselves. All were supervised by a head master, or *maître-sucrier*, usually a white plantation employee but not uncommonly an exceptional black slave. As can be imagined, when the *maître-sucrier* was himself a slave, frictions and jealousies were easily aroused between him and the *commandeur*, the two positions being of relatively equal importance in sugar production and requiring much the same knowledge of soil conditions, watering, fertilization, the health and maturity of the plants, their ripeness when cut, and so forth. In fact, the *maître-sucrier* could often become a *commandeur* and vice versa. [75]

The type of work, however, the rhythm of production, and the intensity of labor in which a slave was involved varied both according to the seasons and the nature of the crop being produced. While the sugar plantations were by far the most labor-intensive, on the coffee plantations, where the rhythm and seasonality of production were quite different, work was no less arduous and the hours just as long. These estates were situated on mountainous slopes in the newer, uncleared and unsettled regions of the colony, where the climate was far cooler and the rains more frequent. Yet this hardly made for healthier living or working conditions for the slaves. Ill-protected against the evening and night chill with inadequate clothing, ill-fed, undernourished, and overworked, the slaves on the coffee plantations suffered a mortality rate that was exceedingly high,[76] especially so since the slaves on these plantations were almost entirely African, many having just arrived. Although the planting and intermittent harvesting of coffee was, by comparison with work on the sugar estates, less routine and rigid and the discipline somewhat less exacting, night work was also a regular feature of the working day, and it followed a full day's harvesting and gleaning. After the evening meal, slaves continued to sort and husk the coffee beans, often until midnight, and sometimes even after. So here, too, the slave was often left with no more than five hours sleep. As on the sugar plantations, labor was divided into *ateliers*, and the workers supervised by a *commandeur*.

The role of the *commandeur* on the plantations was central, for it was upon him that the rhythm of work in the fields depended and under his direct authority that the vast majority of the slaves labored. More often than not, especially toward the end of the colonial period, he was recruited from among the creole slaves and would be a person whose general demeanor projected authority and commanded respect. He would be in his prime, intelligent, one who knew how to execute the orders he received and who in turn was obeyed by those under his command. To enhance his prestige and flatter his ego, he would receive finer clothing than the other slaves at the end of the year, and he was, in general, even better dressed than many a domestic slave.[77] Although he was never led to expect favors gratuitously, neither was he left without a reasonable hope of receiving them. Often he was consulted by the master for advice on purchasing new slaves of a particular nation or on purchasing a former runaway at auction. In a sense, this preferential treatment and these decision-making opportunities created the illusion for the *commandeur* that he was himself a plantation steward.[78] But if his privileged position and authority within the slave hierarchy set him apart from the mass of laborers and cast him in an envious light, on the one hand, it was, on the other, these very same authoritative qualities and daily contact with his white superiors that made the *commandeur* a potential revolutionary leader. As Debien summed it up, he was the life and soul of the plantation.[79] He knew the slaves well—the particular disposition, personality, capabilities, and limitations of each one. So if the smooth functioning and uninterrupted pace of work and production depended on the *commandeur*, so too did the spirit of rebellion and organizational potential for revolutionary activity among the plantation work force. And as we shall see later, much of the success of the August 1791 revolt in the North was due to the pivotal and influential role of the *commandeurs*. Toward the end of the colonial period, in fact, it was not uncommon to find a *commandeur* at the head of an entire *atelier* engaged in collective marronage. [80]

Also in the upper ranks of the slave-labor hierarchy on the plantations were the artisans, or *nègres à talent:* the carpenters, coopers, masons, wheelwrights, cartwrights, loggers, and guardians of the animals, the latter usually being former or "retired" *commandeurs*. And finally, apart from those who labored in the productive process were the domestics. Given their exposure to and contact with white society, they also were instrumental in propagating resistance movements throughout the colonial period, as well as on the eve of the 1791 outbreak.[81] Their rank was visibly enhanced by finer clothing, better food, a far less arduous work schedule than the field laborers and, in general, somewhat better treatment by the masters, whom they often accompanied on trips back to France. But regardless of one's rank or station in slavery, in Saint Domingue a slave was a slave and was at all times subject to the economic vicissitudes of the system. Thus, domestic slave families serving the same master for several generations, or extended families through marriage in the same parish or district, could face the very real possibility of having parental ties indiscriminately broken up should the owner choose to sell his plantation or return to France. On these occasions, domestics were often relegated to the fields by a new owner, and in reaction to their loss in status they might turn fugitive and join the ranks of the maroons. [82]

These, then, were the privileged positions in the slave hierarchy, those that afforded slightly better conditions for certain slaves, almost invariably creole, and that set them apart from the ordinary field hands whom they often despised and considered inferior. Indeed, the daughter of a skilled slave would never entertain the idea of marrying or forming a couple with a field slave.[83] In Saint Domingue, these latter had little or no hope at all of ever advancing.

The lot of the average field slave was, on the whole, one of misery and despair. From the age of fourteen, youths were enrolled in the regular work force of the large plantations, where they continued to labor until the age of sixty. Rare, indeed, was the slave who survived to reach that age. Women in the fields were treated no differently from the men, except for a brief reprieve when pregnant or while nursing a newborn.[84] Herded together in what were known as the *cases à nègres*, or slave quarters, families lived in straw-covered barracks, one next to the other, row upon row, at some distance from the master's house, or *grande case*. On the average, they were no more than twenty-five feet long, twelve feet wide, and fifteen feet high, with one or two partitions in the interior. There were no windows and, with the exception of a single door, no ventilation. Narrow straw cots of a rudimentary sort, only slightly elevated above the bare earth floors, served as beds. Crowded together in these confines, father, mother, and children all slept indiscriminately.

Slaves were awakened at five in the morning by the sound of the *commandeur*'s whistle or by several cracks of his whip or, on the large plantations of over a hundred slaves, by a huge bell. After the recital of perfunctory prayers by the steward, slaves began work in the fields until eight, were allowed to stop for a meager breakfast, and then returned until noon. The midday break lasted until two, when they returned at the crack of the whip

the field until sundown. On many plantations slaves were forced
of the day to gather feed for the draft animals, often having to
considerable distances from the plantation. Finally, firewood had to
be gathered, and dinner, consisting of beans and manioc, or a few potatoes,
but rarely, if ever, any meat or fish, had to be prepared. During the grinding
season on the sugar plantations, slaves then faced what must have seemed
like interminable hours of night work at the mills, or of husking and sorting
on the coffee plantations.

What little time the slave had for rest was consumed by other types of
work. The two hours per day for rest at noon, as well as Sundays and holidays, were granted the slaves by law. And on most plantations, slave families
were allotted a small piece of land on which to grow their food. Cultivation
of their garden, upon which they were more often than not totally dependent
for their subsistence, could be undertaken only on Sundays and holidays,
or in the meager time remaining after preparation of the midday meal. (On
plantations where a piece of land was not provided, slaves were sometimes
required to work Sundays, as well.) By allotting small plots to the slaves for
their own subsistence, the owner freed himself from the cost and responsibility of feeding them; yet these "kitchen gardens," meager as they were and
with as little time as the slaves had to plant and tend to their crops, came
to be seen by the slaves as their own and thus eventually contributed to the
development of a sense, if not of "proprietorship," at least of the firm notion
that the land belonged to those who cultivated it. [85]

It was in the kitchen gardens, as well as in the fields, that slaves acquired
and developed not only certain agricultural skills, but also a knowledge of
the soil and the ability to cultivate new crops. And where their survival depended upon being able to produce their own food and to assure their own
subsistence, their ingenuity, creativity, and resourcefulness were keenly
stimulated and pushed to new limits. As laborers, slaves knew their own
worth. An anecdote cited by de Wimpffen reveals in all its utter simplicity
—and perhaps even with a tinge of naïveté—this self-recognition and self-
affirmation. Preaching from the pulpit in front of a large congregation of
slaves, one priest declared that everything they had came from God. As he
went on to enumerate vegetables, fruits, and all other crops for which they
were indebted and owed thanks to God, an elderly black rose up and shouted
out: "That's mockery, Father Boutin. If I hadn't planted them myself, they
would never have grown." [86]

For those slaves fortunate enough to have produced a small surplus from
their gardens, Sundays and holidays meant market day, and they were
allowed to sell their produce in town, if a town happened to be nearby,
usually at a distance of several miles, if not more, from the plantation. Permission to go into town was not, however, given out gratuitously to whoever

wished to go. Passes were distributed selectively and in rotation, most often to creole slaves and especially to the women, on Saturday night. Those who received a pass were allowed to leave on the following Sunday morning but were required back at sundown, whereupon they were to give up their passes. Naturally, many did not, keeping them or altering the dates for the purposes of trafficking amongst themselves.[87] So the market experience afforded certain opportunities, as did their small gardens, for at least some of the slaves. As well as allowing them to use and develop marketing skills, the market also provided for encounters with slaves from other plantations, for the exchange of news, ideas, and opinions, not to mention for refining their techniques at forging passes.

However, until 1784, the practice of allotting small pieces of land to the slaves for their own cultivation was not a legally recognized system and was not necessarily the rule on all plantations.[88] Where this was the case, the master would be required to supply the minimum food rations stipulated in the Black Code: 2½ pots of manioc and either 2 pounds of salt beef or 3 pounds of fish per week.[89] Rarely, if ever, were *any* of the Code's provisions governing the conditions of the slaves enforced in Saint Domingue. In reality, an average slave's diet provided by the master to sustain an entire day's work amounted to little more than seven or eight boiled potatoes and a bit of water. [90]

Under slavery, it has been written, "all is a question of practice; the will of the master is everything. It is from his will, and his will alone, that the slave may expect misery or well-being."[91] In general, slaves were both underfed and undernourished. It was a common practice for slaves to steal chickens or a few potatoes from the master, even at the risk of severe punishment. One historian notes how a slave woman, for having stolen a duck, received fifty lashes of the whip, had spiced lemon juice rubbed over her wounds, was chained to a post, and remained there to expiate her "crime."[92] M. de Gallifet, one of the wealthiest planters of the North Plain, stated the case bluntly when he wrote in 1702 that "Negroes steal at night because they are not fed by their masters."[93] By 1784, over eighty years later, nothing had changed. The Baron de Saint-Victor, in a prophetic statement, related that "three-quarters of the masters do not feed their slaves and rob almost all of them of the time provided them by law for rest. It is too much, and sooner or later these unfortunates will be driven to the horrors of desperation."[94] The abuses of the planters had reached a point where the Crown found it necessary, the same year, 1784, to reimpose by royal ordinance the provisions of the 1685 Black Code concerning the hours of work, food allotments for slaves, restrictions on punishments, and establishing minimal controls over the inhumanity of the masters. The ordinance now made it a legal obligation of all masters to provide the slaves with small plots exclusively for their personal use, and, in order to protect these kitchen gardens from being utilized to feed an entire *atelier*, the ordinance required that the plantation managers assume this responsibility. [95]

That slaves could be intimidated into submitting to such conditions can only be explained by the use and necessity of both psychological and physical violence by the masters. Just as the slave's existence depended entirely upon the master's will, so there could be no masters without slaves. And to reduce the human spirit to the level of submission required of slaves necessitated a regime of calculated brutality. While the origins of New World slavery were undeniably economic, in its essence slavery was a social relationship of power, and the power of the master over his slaves was almost absolute. On one level, only the sheer terrorism and brute force of the masters could keep the slaves from killing them off. And though slaves occasionally tried this, the balance of power, until the eve of the Saint Domingue revolution, lay in the hands of the white colonists.

It was through terror that the colonists instilled fear in the slaves and through fear that the slaves' labor was motivated. The Baron de Wimpffen, who knew the colony well, nonetheless wrote with a sense of incredulity that some slaves simply could not be made to move in the morning without being whipped.[96] In Saint Domingue, where slavery rapidly assumed a modern capitalistic orientation, where profit was, if not the sole, at least the dominant, motive for owning slaves, and where profit depended not merely upon maintaining a constant flow of production but upon expanding it, the uses and refinements of terror took on ghastly proportions. One is almost tempted to sum up the situation crudely: the greater the need for profits, the greater and more insidious the violence.

Punishment, often surpassing the human imagination in its grotesque refinements of barbarism and torture, was often the order of the day. Only with the advent of the Black Code in 1685 were certain written restrictions placed upon the masters to limit the extent of their brutality. It recognized whipping with a rod or cord as the single right of the master over the slave in administering punishments, though it singularly omitted any limitation on the number of blows. The degree of latitude planters offered themselves is suggested in a statement made by M. de Gallifet, a purportedly humane master but one who, in 1702, nevertheless felt that "any wrongdoing that was not sufficiently punished by one hundred blows of the whip should be handled by the courts."[97] Nominally, the Code left such forms of punishment as torture, mutilation, quartering, hanging, and the like, to the judicial system, while the severity of punishment by whipping was left, for a full century, entirely up to the temperament of the master or, worse, his agent.

It was not until 1784, and again in 1785, one century later, that the number of blows a master could deliver or have delivered by the overseer or the slave driver, was limited to fifty,[98] and this was heralded as an enlightened, humanitarian measure and a step forward in master-slave relations. The Black Code also gave the slave the right to bring a case of outright cruelty or deprivation by a master to the attention of the Crown prosecutor, but pursuance of the complaint was left to the discretion of the prosecutor. In reality, law remained as it had always been, in the hands of the individual slaveholder. The fate of the slaves, and in more than a few cases their life or death, depended rather upon the character and personality of the masters or of their agents, who commonly and consistently flouted the restrictions—odious in themselves—prescribed by the Black Code and subsequent royal legislation.

The barbarism of some masters left little to the imagination. While administering the whip, they would stop, place a burning piece of wood on the slave's buttocks, and then continue, rendering the subsequent blows all the more painful. Common was the practice of pouring pepper, salt, lemon, ashes, or quicklime on the slave's open and bleeding wounds, under the pretext of cauterizing the skin, while at the same time increasing the torture. This method was particularly utilized for interrogating or "putting to the question" slaves suspected of some criminal wrongdoing.[99] It was expressly forbidden by an ordinance of 1712, not only for the "unheard of cruelty [of the treatment] even among the most barbarous nations," but also because "other slaves who have not yet suffered such punishments, intimidated by the example, are taken to desertion in order to escape such inhumanity as this."[100] Other examples exist of slaves being thrown into hot ovens and consumed by fire; or of being tied to a skewer above an open fire, there to roast to death; or of having white-hot slats applied to their ankles and soles of their feet, this being repeated hour after hour. There were masters who would stuff a slave with gunpowder—like a cannon—and blow him to pieces. Women had their sexual parts burned by a smoldering log; others had hot wax splattered over hands, arms, and backs, or boiling cane syrup poured over their heads.

Some preferred the art of direct mutilation. They would hang a slave by the ears, mutilate a leg, pull teeth out, gash open one's side and pour melted lard into the incision, or mutilate genital organs. Still others used the torture of live burial, whereby the slave, in the presence of the rest of the slaves who were forced to bear witness, was made to dig his own grave. Some would have a slave buried up to the neck and the head coated with sugar, leaving it to be devoured by flies, while others managed to invent insidious variations. Less refined cruelties, but none the less horrible, included locking slaves up in barrels, dragging them by horses, making them eat their own excrements and drink their urine. Those slaves who dared to run away faced having a foot cut off or being whipped to death when caught and returned. One young planter even cut the ears of six slaves that his father had given him in such a way as to be able to tell them apart. [101]

One might well argue that the ruthlessly labor-intensive, capitalistic nature of Caribbean slavery necessitated the extraction of maximum labor from the slave in the shortest period of time and that, to do this, the utilization of fear and the creation of an atmosphere of terror were requisite. Yet at the same time, in colonial Saint Domingue there seemed to be an indeterminate line between economic interest, on the one hand, and pure self-indulgent sadism, on the other. Where the one began and the other left off in these cases was hardly clear. Certainly not all masters indulged in such unrestrained excesses of cruelty. There were good ones, and there were bad ones. But the point is not to determine whether slavery was, after all, a good or bad, a moral or an immoral, system. On the average sugar plantation, even comparatively benevolent masters by colonial standards could not protect their slaves from being overworked and underfed, nor for that matter from the occasional whipping. Even here, though, the benevolence masters may have had toward their slaves was more a question of sparing the slaves' health to prolong their profits than one of altruism; in the end, masters still had absolute rights over the slave. And as objects of property, all slaves, even domestics, could be and were indiscriminately sold, bartered, purchased, families at times broken up, wives separated from husbands, mothers and fathers separated from their children. Even though the Black Code prohibited the breakup of slave families in cases of repossession and resale by the owner's creditor, it apparently posed no restrictions on the right of masters to voluntarily sell any one of their slaves as they may have seen fit, and, in any case, it concerned only slave families legally recognized by the church. More than that, the code still considered slaves as belonging to the personal estate of the master and, as such, they would be divided up equally among the inheritors upon the owner's death.[102] Such occurrences were even cause for slaves to poison their master and particularly their master's children, especially when these were "too numerous," for, as one colonist revealed upon learning of these motives, "the slaves would then find themselves all dispersed and forced to abandon father, mother, wife, children, brothers and sisters, relations which effectively are not taken into account. If there were only one or two inheritors, the slaves would not run this risk." [103] Slavery was a system that robbed them of the most basic of all things—their humanity, the recognition before law and before society of their status (and consequent rights) as free, social individuals. [104]

Even on those plantations where slaves were reasonably well cared for by eighteenth-century standards and where masters were benevolent by comparison in their treatment of the slaves, there reigned the imperative element of fear. St. Foäche, one of the largest and wealthiest plantation owners in the colony, makes this clear in his *Instructions* to the managers of his several sugar plantations.[105] The *Instructions* set down basic minimum standards of health care, hygiene, nutrition, and housing for the slaves, as well as specific instructions regarding methods of working the slaves and of administering punishments. Given the excessive indulgence in cruelty of many masters, his guidelines on punishment might even seem humane by comparison. Basically, however, they reveal a highly controlled, highly rationalized sort of madness and underscore the master mentality. Concerned with the smooth and disciplined functioning of the plantation, it was necessary that one develop the "art" of executing punishments:

> Slow punishments make a greater impression than quick or violent ones. Twenty-five lashes of the whip administered in a quarter of an hour, interrupted at intervals to hear the cause which the unfortunates always plead in their defense, and resumed again, continuing in this fashion two or three times, are far more likely to make an impression than fifty lashes administered in five minutes and less a danger to their health. This objective is especially important for serious punishments. Woe to him who punishes with pleasure. He who does not know how to punish is unfit to command. [106]

While defenders of slavery claimed that those masters who indulged in sadistic and barbaric treatment of their slaves were the rare exception in Saint Domingue and were, in any event, socially and politically ostracized by their class, certain cases suggest otherwise. The most blatant and often-cited example is that of the Le Jeune case in 1788.

Le Jeune was a wealthy coffee planter from Plaisance, in the North Plain. He believed that his slaves were being killed off by poison and had put to death four of his slaves who he suspected were responsible. Two other women were mercilessly tortured by fire while being interrogated. Le Jeune thereafter threatened to kill all of his slaves who spoke French if they tried to denounce him before the courts. In defiance of these threats, fourteen of Le Jeune's slaves went to le Cap to register an official complaint against their master's barbaric behavior. Two magistrates of the state went to the plantation to investigate the matter, only to find the allegations of the fourteen confirmed. The two slave women, barely alive, were still in chains, their legs so badly burned they were already decomposing.

All the evidence pointed against Le Jeune, and the case against him was even further strengthened by the subsequent death of the two women. Le Jeune took quick measures to flee before he could be arrested. The fourteen slaves were again called upon to testify and insistently stuck to the letter of their original accusations. Support for Le Jeune came swiftly. Every influential sector of white society was solidly ranged behind him. The concluding remarks of the governor and intendant summed up the case: "It seems, in a word, that the security of the colony depends upon the acquittal of Le Jeune." Not a single judge or magistrate wanted the responsibility of condemning Le Jeune, regardless of the incontrovertible evidence against him. Finally, after a long delay, the judges rendered a negative verdict, acquitting Le Jeune and rendering the case against him null and void. [107]

Was this merely an isolated case? Or was it but one example among a multitude of crimes committed and condoned by the whites against slaves? In the first place, the government of the colony, on principle, rarely intervened in master-slave relations. And as it was highly unlikely that slaveowners would denounce each other, about the only cases heard were those in which a slave's initiative may have caused a master to be charged before the court. In fact, it was only with the royal ordinances of 1784 and 1785, during the last few years of the colonial regime, that slaves were permitted to legally denounce the abuses of a master, overseer, or plantation manager. Even so, slaves' statements were still not received as legal testimony against their own masters and could be used only to clarify circumstances surrounding a case. [108] But if some slaves did respond to the new measures by denouncing their master's brutality, in general, they were still held in fear of punishment and torture if they dared to do so. Le Jeune himself later commented that, far from the fear and equity of the law, "it is the feeling of absolute power the master holds over the slaves' person that prevents them from stabbing the master to death. Remove this brake and the slave will attempt anything." [109] So official cases on record were few. In addition, the dossiers of those cases that did reach the courts were conveniently burned every five years. [110]

The Le Jeune case does, however, provide insight into the class and race interests at stake in Saint Domingue society and reveals the precarious position in which the masters found themselves, a position that necessitated and invariably evoked white solidarity in its defense, especially in the most shocking and incriminating of cases. The obsessive need to protect white supremacy at all costs and to ensure the consequent submission, not only of the slaves, but also of the free colored population, was conversely manifested in a 1784 decree condemning a free black slaveowner. Since the death of his female slave was a direct result of his cruelty, he was to be publicly beaten with a rod by the Executioner of High Justice (a slave whose death penalty had been commuted in exchange for this odious duty), then branded on the right shoulder with the letters GAL and sent to the galleys for three years, during which time he was required to provide proof of his status or be sold as a slave of the state. He was also forbidden ever to own or acquire a slave again. [111] Le Jeune, for his part, was acquitted for crimes committed to a far greater extent. Not only did the Le Jeune affair exonerate the white masters whose inhumanity flew in the face of already inhuman practices and standards, but it gave further proof of the utter futility of slaves' attempts to bring masters to account for their deeds. The Black Code remained as it always had been, a dead letter. The generally accepted and practiced principle in the colony was that a white can never be in the wrong vis-à-vis a black, thus placing supreme authority over the slaves in the hands of the masters and sanctioning this tyranny through the complicity of the legal and judicial system.

The master-slave relationship, however, was a two-sided one. On the one hand, as we have already seen, the master held absolute rights of life and death over the slave and could and did exercise these at will. Existence for many a slave was at times one of total fear—fear for one's entire being, the fear of utter death. But from this state of fear, in which slaves constantly faced the possibility of torture and often the harsh reality of a brutal death, arose a consciousness of one's own self-existence. [112]

Slaves existed in and for themselves, and in this ongoing life-and-death struggle, they developed a sense of their own identity, one inexorably opposed to the very persons upon whom their lives depended. Resistance and protest were therefore both natural and necessary features of slavery. But when one considers the relationship of power upon which the system was built and the overwhelming odds in favor of the master, the human problems involved in the whole phenomenon of slave resistance become far more complex. Open resistance was not always possible, nor even prudent. Thus slaves adapted and accommodated themselves to the situations and circumstances surrounding them at different moments, and measured their resistance in relation to the reasonable or perceived chances of success. [113] Within the system, however, were areas of autonomous slave activity, forms of cultural resistance contributing to a reinforced sense of self-identity and found within the slaves' own popular culture.

At night, or on Sundays or holidays when not working, slaves freely expressed another side of their personality. The Baron de Wimpffen, who took the trouble to observe and to listen to slaves when they were assembled together, away from the master and the plantation steward, remarked with astonishment on the dynamic nature of the slave personality: "One has to hear with what enthusiasm, with what precision of ideas and accuracy of judgment, these creatures, gloomy and taciturn during the day, now squatting before their fire, tell stories, talk, gesticulate, reason, express opinions, approve or condemn both the master and all those around them." [114] Slaves brought with them to the New World their natural and acquired capacities. Numerous slaves considered illiterate by the undiscerning white could read and write their own language and were fully educated in their own culture. [115] The colonist Hilliard d'Auberteuil wrote of them in 1776, affirming that "no human species has more intelligence," after which his book was banned. [116]

Their induction into the New World, however, was also a meeting and blending of cultures, and from this historical situation emerged what came to be the single unifying language of creole, decidedly African in its structure and rhythm, but characteristically European in its lexical dynamics. The genesis and subsequent evolution of this language, assumed to have occurred out of the very early eighteenth-century slave experience in Saint Domingue,[117] thus provided a common linguistic framework for communication among slaves, one into which new African arrivals of diverse ethnic groups and languages could readily be integrated. In fact, through cultural adaptation to their New World setting, slaves had, by the eve of the revolution, acquired an essential unifying tool that enabled both Africans of widely different origins, as well as slaves born in Saint Domingue, to share experiences, exchange views and opinions, communicate their ideas, and even conspire against the master.

But at the same time, slaves expressed their African identity in cultural ways that the sociolinguistic necessities of slavery did not impinge upon, and to which they remained intensely attached. One of the favorite leisure-time activities of slaves, practiced with passion and fervor, was dancing. Despite the rigors and fatigues of slavery and in addition to the repeated prohibitions against nocturnal gatherings (especially if they included slaves from different plantations), in Saint Domingue as in all plantation societies throughout the New World, slaves invariably found the energy to dance, and even to travel several miles if necessary for the occasion.

The *calenda*, the most popular dance, involved young and old alike, even small children barely able to walk.[118] Moreau de Saint-Méry remarked that one actually had to see this dance performed to believe how lively, how animated, and yet how rigorously measured and graceful it was.[119] The orchestra consisted of two types of drums, the smaller of the two called a *bamboula*, along with numerous gourds filled with pebbles or grains of corn for accompaniment. The *banza*, a primitive type of violin with four strings, completed the arrangement. Women, gathered round in a circle, responded in chorus to the "call," an improvised phrase or song forcefully delivered by one or two singers, after which both men and women would enter the circle in pairs, to begin dancing and, in succession, continue almost indefinitely into the night.

Another dance, as evenly measured as the calenda but distinctively lascivious, was the *chica*, of West African origin and practiced generally throughout the Caribbean.[120] Describing the steps and the bodily movements of the dancers, male and female, Moreau depicts the chica as "a kind of struggle where every ruse of love and every means of triumph are brought into action: fear, hope, disdain, tenderness, caprice, pleasure, refusal, frenzy, evasion, ecstasy, prostration; all has its own language in this dance." [121] The impression it created was so powerful, in the author's words, that whether African or creole, no blacks ever saw this dance performed without experiencing great emotion, lest they be taken for having lost their last spark of sensitivity. [122]

The various dances in which slaves so voraciously indulged had their origins in Africa and were a fundamental part of the cultural heritage they brought with them to the colony where, upon contact with the European cultures, they evolved to what they are today. Common to all slave dances was the vital and pivotal role of both the drum and the drummer to animate and govern the elaboration of these dances. Also of African origin was their "call-response" structure and the distinctive group formation within which each performer could individualize his or her contribution, thereby displaying unique talents and agility. The group formation of these dances also assured the uninterrupted duration of the festivities well into the night, as dancers successively replaced one another upon the slightest sign of fatigue.[123] But more than this, the various dances served as cultural ties uniting all those of common origin: "Each nation displayed its own originality, and the dancers, eager to sustain the prestige of their respective nations, would solicit the approval of the spectators in its favor." [124] So closely felt were the cultural ties that a dancer of a different nation was sometimes seen as an intruder by those present and not particularly welcomed by them. The naturalist Descourtiltz related during his stay in Saint Domingue how one Ibo dancer had desperately offered gifts of tafia, a bit of money, even his last few chickens to be received into an Arada gathering in the Artibonite valley; with each attempt the poor man was invariably rejected. [125]

But not all dances were secular. Voodoo, both a sacred dance and a religion, was expressly forbidden in the French colonies, and from the very beginning, the colonists tried in vain to crush it.[126] And not only was the strict practice of voodoo forbidden to slaves, but severe restrictions were also imposed on the calendas, which sometimes served as a cover for voodoo gatherings. Père Labat observed that

> they have passed laws in the islands to prevent the calendas, not only because of the indecent and lascivious postures which make up this dance, but especially to prevent too many blacks from assembling and who, finding themselves thus gathered together in joy and usually inebriated, are capable of revolts, insurrections or raids. But in spite of these laws and all of the precautions the masters take, it is almost impossible to suppress [the dances], because, of all the diversions, this is the one which [the slaves] enjoy the most and to which they are the most sensitive. [127]

In fact more than one planter often found it necessary to give in to so vital an element in the slaves' culture and at least tacitly tolerate the dances.

Voodoo had not only survived, but had evolved under slavery for over two hundred years and had become, by the eve of the revolution, a far more volatile and formidable force than in the early days. As a cult, however, it was practiced and sustained in secrecy, and new adepts were admitted only through the strictly ordered ritual of initiation. Among the initiated, then, voodoo served to bind more closely the loose psychological ties arising out of the common experience of organized plantation labor and the material conditions of life under slavery, raising these to a form of collective consciousness. [128]

One dance that held a particularly prominent place in the overall practice of voodoo in Saint Domingue was the *danse à Don Pèdre*, introduced into the colony around 1768 and bearing the name of its originator.[129] Coming from the Spanish part of the island, Don Pèdre established his cult at Petit-Goâve, in the South Province, which served as a base from which to propagate his influence throughout the colony.[130] The dance was far more violent in its movements than other voodoo dances. With eyes fixed downward while drinking tafia, reputedly mixed with gunpowder, the dancers would enter into a state of frenzy, producing what observers described as epileptic-like contortions, and would continue dancing until near or total exhaustion.[131] During the ceremony a pact was made among all participants, committing them to secrecy, solidarity, and the vow of vengeance. [132]

[margin note: VOODOO AS REL.]

Voodoo, however, was more than merely a ceremonial dance bent on vengeance. It was a religion and, as such, played a vital role in the daily lives and general world view of its adherents. During the ceremonies, slaves often called upon the various gods, or *loa*, for spiritual comfort, guidance, protection from misfortune, and cures for their sicknesses, as well as vengeance against their oppressors.[133] The French anthropologist Alfred Métraux relates, in the words of a present-day Haitian peasant woman, a statement *[margin note: ASK FOR SAME THINGS WE ASK OF GOD]* that sums up for him what voodoo devotees expect from their gods: "The *loa* love us, protect us and watch over us. They show us what is happening to our relatives living far away, and they tell us what medicines will do us good when we are sick. If we are hungry, they appear to us in a dream and say: 'Don't despair, you will soon earn some money,' and the money comes."[134] Métraux hastens to suggest that "she might, however, have added: The *loa* inform us of the plots being hatched by our enemies."[135]

Although Métraux's study is based on twentieth-century practices in Haiti, it nevertheless provides keen insights into a religion whose basic elements have largely remained unaltered and which occupied such an important place in the lives of most slaves. It has the further advantage of treating voodoo from a purely anthropological vantage point, thus removing it from the romanticized and denigrating category of "fanaticism," "orgiastic frenzy," "collective hysteria," or just plain superstition, to which it was relegated by almost all seventeenth- and eighteenth-century observers.

In a voodoo ceremony, dancing plays not only a prominent, but an essential, role as a ritualistic act and is carried out in precise rhythm to the drumbeats, which govern the steps and movements of the dancers. The drums themselves are a religious symbol and are viewed as the very vessel of a deity. The drumbeats, in unified interaction with the dancers, thus evoke numerous families of gods and release certain "mystic forces" which are be-lieved to "work" on those who are summoned. The climax of the ceremony occurs with the blood sacrifice, wherein a goat or fowl is offered to the *loa.* The killing is preceded by a ritualistic act embracing both divination and communion, after which a sacred type of food or drink is given to the ani-mal. If consumed, it is deemed acceptable to the gods, and those making the sacrifice attempt to identify themselves with it or to " 'infuse' their own bodies with the mystic powers invested in it." The blood is collected in a gourd and tasted by the *houngan,* or priest, and then successively by the assisting *hounsi,* or "servants of the gods." [136]

Communication between the gods and mortals is then established through the phenomenon of possession which "is nothing more than the descent of a god or spirit come to take possession of a chosen person. . . . The god uses the body of a man or a woman to manifest himself to his worshippers, share their amusements, make known his wishes or his will, wreak ven-geance or express gratitude, as the case may be." [137] The possessed thus becomes both the vessel and the instrument of the god, through which the latter expresses his or her personality. Possession is therefore a fundamental element in the religious experience of the initiated. Moreover, "[it] is a con-trolled phenomenon obeying precise rules . . . [and] every god is expected to appear in his turn when the devotees summon him by songs in his honor." [138] The psychological implications of possession for the Haitian peasant, as for the slave living under dehumanized conditions and the terror of brutal punishments, are profound: "The very real satisfaction to be gained by a poor peasant woman who becomes the vessel of a god and is able to parade about in silken dresses acknowledging marks of respect from the crowd has not been sufficiently underlined by studies of possession as a phenomenon. *What a release for repressed bitterness and prisoned hatred!*" (italics mine) [139]

While voodoo constituted for the slave a unique and autonomous cul-tural form, it would nevertheless be wrong to assume that its development and proliferation in Saint Domingue occurred independently of other influ-ences. All religious practice, except for Catholicism, was outlawed in the colony, and in accordance, all slaves were to be baptized in the Catholic church. However, the religious, as well as the educational, instruction of the slaves was never seriously or widely undertaken, either by the masters or by the church. Thus, superficially, many of the ritualistic aspects of Catholi-cism appeared in voodoo, but consciously adapted and reinterpreted by the slaves to accord with their own religious beliefs. [140] In this way, Catholicism

[Handwritten margin notes: DANCING IS VITAL; RITUALS OF VOODOO; TALKING W/ GODS THRU POSS.; RELEASE FROM CRUEL TREATMENT; CATH. REL. ONLY; REINT. CATH. x VOODOO]

served as a kind of mask, or façade, behind which their own beliefs and practices could flourish. One might even say that, under the Black Code, the prohibition to practice voodoo and the alternate obligation of nominal membership in the Catholic church provided "an external structure for the voodoo consciousness, a consciousness which arose out of slavery itself." [141]

Similarly, slave burials were often an occasion for the expression of African ways. The Black Code not only obliged masters to have their slaves baptized in the Catholic religion but also to provide for their burial in church cemeteries, though in designated sections. Given the generalized disregard and neglect of cemeteries in Saint Domingue, coupled with their frequent displacements and relocations, slaves eventually came to appropriate for themselves the sites of cemeteries abandoned by the whites. [142] There they came at night to bury their dead. Moreau de Saint-Méry relates one such case, among many others, in the South: "[At Aquin] can still be seen what is said to be the ruins of the [old] chapel. A cross was noticed there not so long ago. A superstition, the grounds for which are difficult to imagine, has led the slaves of the Aquin parish to bury their fellow companions there. All attempts to make them bring the dead to the present cemetery have been in vain; they would wait for night to fall to elude surveillance. In the end, we were wise enough not to make of these circumstances an object of religious persecution." [143] It is evident here that Moreau's use of the term "religious persecution" refers not to Catholicism but to the slaves' own religion. He depicts a typical funeral procession in the South, where "the African slaves gather together in a large crowd to bring their [deceased] companions to the cemetery. The women, preceding the corpse, sing and clap their hands while the men follow. A slave accompanies the corpse with a bamboula on which he strikes, once and again, a mournful note." [144]

Paradoxically, the once-communal cemeteries now abandoned by the whites had become the "privileged" sanctuary for African slaves to freely continue their own religious practices and cultural ways concerning the dead, while the funeral ceremonies themselves served as an occasion for slaves to gather together in traditional celebration. [145] And like the voodoo dances, slave funeral ceremonies, when they did occur, were at least tacitly tolerated by the colonists, though expressly forbidden by law.

Despite rigid prohibitions, voodoo was indeed one of the few areas of totally autonomous activity for the African slaves. As a religion and a vital spiritual force, it was a source of psychological liberation in that it enabled them to express and reaffirm that self-existence they objectively recognized through their own labor (and of which they were subjectively conscious through the daily realities of coercion and fear). Voodoo further enabled the slaves to break away psychologically from the very real and concrete chains of slavery and to see themselves as independent beings; in short, it

gave them a sense of human dignity and enabled them to survive. Indeed the sheer tenacity and vigor with which slaves worshiped their gods and danced in their honor—in spite of the risks, in spite of incredibly long and physically exacting hours of labor during the day and often half the night— eloquently attest to voodoo as a driving force of resistance in the daily lives of the slaves.

But insofar as voodoo was a means of self-expression and of psychological or cathartic release from material oppression, the slaves' acquired consciousness as autonomous beings remained stoically imprisoned within themselves as they invariably faced their oppressors the next day. It was only when slaves were able at various times to translate that consciousness into active rebellion and, finally, into the life-and-death struggle of revolution aimed at the total destruction of their masters and of slavery, that emancipation could and did become reality. For self-hatred turned outward, the drive to affirm one's own existence and the urge to destroy the oppressor were as fundamental a part of the slaves' daily existence as were submission and accommodation in appearance.

2

Slave Resistance

Through repression and terror the white masters managed to erect a system of social control to contain and regiment the half million black slaves whose labor created their wealth, but they could not annihilate the slave's human spirit.

Slave resistance to the brutality and human degradation of the system took many forms, not all of them overt, and some of them even self-destructive. Similarly, not all slaves resisted to the same degree or in the same ways, depending upon their place in the ranks of slavery, their treatment as a slave, their cultural background or, simply, their individual level of tolerance and capacity to endure. It was well known, for example, that Ibo slaves were more inclined to suicide, even collectively, as a response to slavery than slaves of other nations. Of the Ibos, Moreau de Saint-Méry wrote that they had to be closely watched, as "feelings of chagrin or the slightest dissatisfaction pushes them to suicide, the idea of which, far from terrifying them, seems rather to offer something alluring because they believe in the transmigration of souls."[1]

Suicide, however, was certainly not limited to the Ibos. One reads time and again throughout the literature how slaves often preferred death to a lifetime of slavery. In the words of d'Auberteuil: "The greatest dangers and even death do not frighten the Negroes. They are more courageous than men subjected to slavery ought to be. They appear insensible amidst torment and are inclined to suicide."[2] Or, in the nearly exasperated tone of the second captain of a slave ship leaving Mozambique: "The blacks, an impossible race, prefer death to slavery."[3]

In response to those who sought to justify the slave trade by claiming that they were saving the blacks from a life of hunger, misery, and mutual destruction in primitive Africa, a white colonist, himself creole, remarked with astonishment:

If the blacks were so undernourished and so miserable [in Africa] . . . how is it that they are so well-proportioned, strong and in such vigorous health when they arrive in the colonies? And how is it that at the end of one year here, their health diminishes, they become weak, thin and unrecognizable—a state from which, if they do not die, they never completely recover? . . . Likewise, if the blacks were so miserable and without feeling in their native land, why are they driven by despair to commit suicide, one of the chief reasons for which they are so scrupulously kept in chains on the boats? . . . How is it, then, that their yearning for freedom is so insatiable?[4]

Indeed, the first instance of resistance, and of suicide as resistance, occurred aboard these slave ships, most often while still at port, in the initial stage of what was to become for most a long and tortuous journey toward a life of perpetual bondage in the colonies. For those unable to escape before being boarded as captives, suicide was a fatal affirmation of their refusal to accept the conditions of bondage imposed on them. One trader cautioned: "The moment one has completed one's trade and loaded the Negroes on the ship, one must set sail. The reason for this is that the slaves have such a love for their land that they despair to see that they are leaving it forever, and they die from sadness. I have heard merchants who participate in this commerce affirm that more Negroes die before leaving port than during the voyage."[5]

While some captives succeeded in throwing themselves into the sea, often with chains still attached, others would knock their heads against the ship or hold their breath until they suffocated; still others would attempt to starve themselves aboard the ships, hoping to die before the end of the voyage. To force recalcitrant slaves to eat, some ship captains would have the slaves' lips burned by hot charcoal; others would try to make them swallow the coals if they persisted. To set an example, one captain even reportedly went to the extreme of having molten lead poured into the mouths of those who stubbornly refused all food.[6] In another instance, a young African girl of sixteen, having been taken captive aboard a slave ship, was so profoundly affected that she categorically refused everything given her to eat. In a short time her physical and moral condition deteriorated to the point where death was imminent. The captain, concerned chiefly with the loss of potential profit that her death would incur, had her returned to land to be cared for until the boat was ready to depart. Upon seeing once again her native village and friends, upon reexperiencing her former state of freedom, she rapidly regained her health. When, however, she learned that she was to be taken back aboard the ship, she killed herself.[7]

Once sold and introduced into the plantation system, slaves continued to resist individually and collectively by means of suicide. Death was seen not only as a liberation from the extreme conditions of slavery but, according to popular African beliefs, as a means of escape permitting the dead to return to their native land.[8] However, feelings of despair or, conversely, of outraged dignity and pride were not the only factors provoking suicide. By the beginning of the eighteenth century, contemporary observers became aware of a calculated motive on the part of slaves who committed suicide either individually or collectively to inflict serious economic damage, if not not ruin, upon the master. Regarding slave suicides, Père Labat wrote in 1701: "They destroy themselves, they off-handedly slit their throats for trivial reasons, but most often, they do this to cause damage to their masters."[9] M. de Gallifet, one of the wealthiest slaveholders in the North Plain, also observed the same motive: "Last night a slave choked himself to death with his tongue while his master was having him whipped. This happens quite often, as there are slaves who are desperate enough to kill themselves in order to inflict loss upon their masters."[10] As a means of resistance, then, suicide was also an offensive measure that could go beyond purely personal considerations and, in the same blow, aim at the economic base of the planter.

Slave women often resorted to abortion and even infanticide as a form of resistance rather than permit their children to grow up under the abomination of slavery. D'Auberteuil, himself a colonial planter and a slaveowner, criticized the tyranny of the system that pushed women to commit acts of abortion and spoke of the slaves' self-destructive acts in these terms: "If they see the earth as a place of torment and pain, is it not those who are dearest to them who will be the first to be sacrificed by their deadly compassion?"[11] In cases of infanticide, the death of the child usually resulted from a sickness referred to by contemporaries as *mal de mâchoire*, or lockjaw [tetanus], a sickness that struck only newborn babies and only those delivered by black midwives. Invariably, death occurred within the first few days. One slave woman from the Rossignol-Desdunes plantation in the district of Artibonite admitted having poisoned or killed in this manner over seventy children in order to spare them the pains of slavery.[12] Although other considerations may have played an additional role in the motivation of such acts—vengeance against a master for cruel treatment, the desire to inflict pain upon a master when the slave child was in fact his own, jealousy, retribution—in all instances, the net result was the near decimation of a potential work force.[13]

Equally as characteristic of slave resistance, however, was its opposite, outwardly aggressive or assertive, rather than self-destructive, nature. One slave captain complained before arriving to unload his captive cargo: "The older ones are uncontrollable; they turn fugitive. Not only are they of little use in the colony, but they are even dangerous."[14] Aboard this particular ship they broke out in revolt. Armed revolts were actually not unusual during the first stages of captivity and, in fact, occurred far more frequently aboard slave ships along the African coast or during the voyage than in the colony itself. The sheer nonchalance with which they are often treated or passingly referred to in ships' registers may strongly suggest that slave revolts in these situations were indeed commonplace occurrences and, in the opinion of a recent historian of the French slave trade, were even "expected and accepted as integral parts of the triangle."[15]

But if slave revolts were far more recurrent aboard the ships at harbor and during the voyages than in Saint Domingue itself, it may be that, outside of desperate and propitious revolt at the one end, or suicide by diverse means at the other, alternative modes of resistance aboard ship were few and far between. An organized slave society no doubt afforded more varied, and perhaps even more effective, long-term ways and means of resisting or protesting one's conditions than open revolt. Significantly, the revolts and conspiracies to revolt that did occur in Saint Domingue were nearly all situated in a relatively early period of the colony's economic and sociopolitical development, the very first one occurring in 1522 while the island was still under exclusive Spanish rule.[16] Within the twenty-five years between 1679 and 1704, four other armed conspiracies had been planned by slaves in different parts of French Saint Domingue, all aimed at the massacre and annihilation of their white masters.[17] In the end, however, they were localized affairs that the authorities quickly crushed, and so collective armed revolt remained at this time a limited form of slave resistance with minimal chances of success. With the one notable exception of the Makandal conspiracy in 1757, no other organized slave revolt was conceived before the revolution in 1791.[18] But then the conspiracy of 1757, as well as the revolt of 1791, which dramatically opened the black revolution, occurred within a context substantially different from that of the earlier revolts. The revolt that was planned by Makandal in the North, and which subsequently was to have spread to "all corners of the colony," was both conceived and organized in marronnage. Also, some evidence exists to suggest that marronage may indeed have contributed to the basic groundwork and general form of the massive outbreak of 1791.[19]

Of the many and diverse forms of resistance, marronage proved in the end to be the most viable and certainly the most consistent. From the very beginning of the colony under Spanish rule, throughout its long history under the French, until the abolition of slavery in 1793–94, slaves defied the system that denied them the most essential of social and human rights: the right to be a free person. They claimed that right in marronage. But it was not until 1791 that this form of resistance, having by this time acquired a distinctively collective characteristic, would converge with the volatile political climate of the time and with the opening of a revolution that would eventually guarantee that right. That marronage had become an explosive revolutionary force in 1791 was due as much to the global context of revolutionary events as to the persistent traditions of resistance which, necessarily, remained narrower in scope.

Prior to the revolution, colonial observers who bothered to question the motives of slaves who left the plantation to eke out an existence for themselves in the mountains or in other secluded, inaccessible areas, or on the fringes of plantation society where they risked being recaptured, almost invariably invoked undernourishment, cruel treatment, or overwork as the chief causes; in short, the living and working conditions of slavery. While all of these factors contributed to the slaves' decision to escape, it leaves the question unanswered as to why reputedly humane masters often had as many fugitives as the cruel ones.[20] For the planters to voluntarily accede that fugitive slaves had fled to become free persons, that they had the ability to consciously and materially negate the condition of perpetual bondage imposed upon them by slavery, would be to undermine the ideological foundations of slavery itself. More than that, such an admission would require both a fundamental reevaluation and a consequent rearrangement of the entire economic base of their wealth and power, thus jeopardizing the viability of the slave system to which their own survival was irrevocably tied. No ruling class does this gratuitously. They convinced themselves, rather, that it was merely a recurrent manpower problem, which in part it was.

On the other hand, contemporary literature and administrative correspondence (especially in the two decades preceding the revolution) reveal a tendency, both implicit and explicit, to see in marronage not only the individual will of the slave to be a free person, but a force that, if left unchecked, threatened to destroy the colony. In an extract from the register of the Upper Council of le Cap, one finds this statement, written in 1767: "The slave . . . , inconstant by nature and capable of comparing his present state with that to which he aspires, is incessantly inclined toward marronage. *It is his ability to think,* and not the instinct of domestic animals who flee a cruel master in the hope of bettering their condition, that compels him to flee. That which appears to offer him a happier state, that which facilitates his inconstance, is the path which he will embrace" (italics mine).[21] Or, a memoir of 1775 on the state of the maroons in Saint Domingue that declares that

> marronage, or the desertion of the black slaves in our colonies since they were founded, has always been regarded as one of the possible causes of their destruction. . . . The Minister should be informed that there are inaccessible or reputedly inaccessible areas in different sections of our colony which serve as retreat and shelter for maroons; it is in the mountains and in the forests that these tribes of slaves establish themselves and multiply, invading the plains from time to time, spreading alarm and always causing great damage to the inhabitants. [22]

Of the maroons, Père Charlevoix wrote earlier that "once they see that they will die, it matters little how they will die, and the least success renders them practically invincible."[23] On the one hand, the colonists tried, if not to eliminate, at least to control, marronage through a long series of rigorous punitive laws, even the death penalty. On the other hand, some planters preferred a more humane treatment of their slaves. Regardless of the measures taken, and in spite of them, marronage persisted as a means of resisting slavery.

It was practiced in a variety of ways and involved slav
tions, the creole elite as well as the African field laborer.[24]
of the maroons were men, on an average between the ages
thirty-five, thus in their prime. Although they were more
merous as the women in the slave population of Saint D.....
nonetheless a significant proportion of women (estimated at 15 to 20 percent)
among the maroons, in addition to young children and even an occasional
aged slave. [25]

Marronage was practiced both collectively and individually, in small
groups as well as in larger established communities, in organized armed
bands or by slaves as free persons with a trade in the urban centers. When
slaves left the plantations, they left with no knowledge of what their future
would be, nor did they know how long their marronage would last, nor
whether they would be recaptured. While some may have fled to escape punishment or cruel treatment and returned in a plea for clemency, others had
made a consciously planned and determined break from slavery, from the
master and the plantation regime, and were prepared to face the unknown.
They carried out their escape with the bare minimum of clothing and food,
often taking with them a few tools, a horse, a mule, or a canoe and, not
uncommonly, arms of some sort. Rarely, if ever, did the African-born slave
live in marronage alone. Many went off to join other slaves already established and subsisting in bands in the heavily wooded mountains, often living
in entrenched camps closed off by walls of woven liana and surrounded
by ditches of some twelve to fifteen feet deep and eight or ten feet wide,
lined at the bottom with sharpened stakes.[26] Others, fortunate enough to find
some long-abandoned piece of property in an isolated region, attempted to
assure their survival off the land. Once established, some even risked their
newly acquired freedom by going back to the plantation at night to secure
the escape of their wives or children, left behind under circumstances that
rendered impossible the collective flight of the family. [27]

The most frequent refuge for the field slave was in the Spanish part of
the island, the colony of Santo Domingo, or in the extensive range of mountains in the South, extending eastward to form the border between the two
colonies. Here, since the beginnings of slavery, slaves had formed permanent and collective maroon communities. The very first of these communities was, in fact, established in the eastern Bahoruco mountains by the
last survivors of the indigenous Arawaks, brutally massacred, enslaved, and
finally exterminated under the genocidal practices of the Spanish.[28] Within
the perimeters of these mountains, of which Bahoruco comprised only the
eastern limits, other well-known maroon communities existed, notably in
the southern region of Plymouth, which provided asylum for the periodic
marronage of diverse groups of slaves, and in Maniel, stretching from the

.ern limits of Jacmel, in the South, and extending well into the Span-
.n part of the island.[29] In the case of the Maniel maroons, the authorities
of Saint Domingue had attempted, since the beginning of the eighteenth
century, to reach an accord with the Spanish for the return of the fugitives
from the French colony and to join efforts in capturing and dispersing the
maroons along the border, all without much success. In 1785, the French
authorities finally comprehended the futility of their aims and yielded. A
peace treaty was signed granting pardon and according independence to the
remaining maroons. Each family would receive a small plot of land and provisions for eight months to assure their subsistence until their farms became
productive. [30]

In addition to these long-established and well-known communities, other
bands in various parts of the colony, smaller in number and perhaps lesser
known, waged similar struggles throughout the colonial era in defense of
their precariously acquired freedom. Establishing themselves in the forests
or in the thickly wooded foothills of the mountains, they maintained a marginal but independent existence. They, too, had their chosen leaders whose
decisions governed the organization and functioning of the group. When
conditions no longer permitted them to subsist off the land, it became necessary for them to descend at night upon neighboring plantations in organized
raids, pillaging, ransacking, sometimes even devastating the plantation to
secure food, animals, additional arms, or other necessary supplies for their
survival. These marauding maroon bands often created such terror as to
cause certain planters in relatively isolated areas to sell out or simply to
abandon their holdings.

In 1705, the Upper Council of Léogane published an official report on the
movement and activities of the maroons in the South:

> They gather together in the woods and live there exempt from service to their
> masters without any other leader but one elected among them; others, under
> cover of the cane fields by day, wait at night to rob those who travel along the
> main roads, and go from plantation to plantation to steal farm animals to feed
> themselves, hiding in the living quarters of their friends who, ordinarily, partici-
> pate in their thefts and who, aware of the goings on in the master's house, advise
> the fugitives so that they can take the necessary precautions to steal without
> getting caught. [31]

Two years later a special body, later reinstated permanently as the *maréchaussée*, in which the *affranchis* would be required to serve, was created in
the North to hunt down and capture fugitive slaves.

It was precisely the aggressive and intrepid aspects of marronage that
necessitated, from the beginning of slavery, the adoption of repressive and
punitive measures to eliminate what many contemporaries came to consider
a continual plague and a danger to the security of the colony.[32] The first

comprehensive legislation dealing with marronage appeared in the Black Code of 1685. Slaves of different plantations were now forbidden to assemble together, be it in celebration of a marriage, to organize a calenda, or for any reason whatsoever, under punishment of the whip or the burning brand of the *fleur de lys*. For those who persisted, it could mean death. Slaves were forbidden to carry anything that might be construed as a weapon or to circulate without a written pass from the master. A fugitive slave in flight up to one month from the date of his reported escape would have his ears cut off and the *fleur de lys* branded on one shoulder. If his flight should span another month, he would be hamstrung, in addition, and the *fleur de lys* stamped on the other shoulder. After that, the punishment was death. Any *affranchi* providing asylum to a fugitive slave was fined three hundred livres in sugar for each day of protection given. An *affranchi* offering shelter to a fugitive or in any way aiding a slave in committing thefts, or in becoming a maroon, could lose his freedom and be sold into slavery along with his family.[33] Planters were now permitted to shoot on sight any slave they believed to be a fugitive, a provision that incidentally caused innocent slaves mistaken for fugitives to be recklessly killed. [34]

In 1741, following a maroon attack on the town of Mirebalais, additional punishments for marronage were imposed. Captured fugitives were put in public chain gangs for a specified period of time, sometimes for life. Two years later, the punishment for maroons caught with arms of any kind was death.[35] In spite of these restrictions, as well as subsequent ordinances of similar consequence, marronage remained a well-entrenched mode of resistance to slavery. In fact, official estimates in 1751 had brought the number of French slaves living in marronage in the Spanish colony alone to nearly three thousand.[36] The administrators of the colony passed a new ordinance in 1767. The *affranchis* were now forbidden to purchase arms or munitions without the express permission of the Crown prosecutor. The attempt was clearly made to cut off all sales of arms between the free persons of color and the maroons, and thereby control the problem.[37] Yet during the two decades before the massive slave revolt of 1791, while the planters themselves seemed relatively imperturbable, colonial correspondence, official reports, and administrative ordinances continued to underscore the threat of marronage to the general security of the colony, as new groups and new maroon leaders successively emerged.

But this type of collective marronage, of fugitive slaves living in small groups, forming armed bands or even large, organized communities, constituted only one of its aspects. It predominantly involved the African-born, non-creole field slaves and certainly characterized its more openly aggressive form. The domestic slave, on the other hand, profited from the numerous avenues of escape available to those slaves whose particular position in the plantation system afforded them greater mobility and freedom of movement than that of the field slave.

Many took advantage of the situation when sent by the master on a daytime errand, and never came back. Others, having learned to read and write, fabricated their own passes indicating that they were on an errand for the master. The practice had become so common that it was nearly impossible for the authorities to distinguish, at the marketplace, in the streets, at the crossroads, between the free blacks and those who, using passes to escape from the plantation, gave themselves out to be free. In 1764 the Chamber of Agriculture of Port-au-Prince proposed, as a control measure, that all legitimately free blacks fourteen years of age and over be forced to wear a standardized medallion indicating their name and the nature of their enfranchisement.[38] To escape detection, some slaves would carefully change names; most were dressed in their best clothing to project the outward appearance of a free black. Some even pushed their audacity to the extreme and attached a pair of stolen pistols in fine holsters onto the saddle of a stolen horse as a surer guarantee that they would be recognized as a free black, especially since slaves were forbidden to own or ride a horse.[39] They fabricated false documents of enfranchisement, baptismal certificates, or any other type of attestation to legitimize their assumed status.[40] Others, having stolen a horse or mule upon leaving the plantation, would travel considerable distances to reach an isolated town or bourg where they were unknown, sell the animals, and establish themselves in the community as free. Unless pure chance should bring the master or a neighbor to the area for some unwonted reason, it was nearly impossible for the fugitive to be discovered. Moreover, his security was further safeguarded by the fact that the masters, upon discovering the flight of a slave, generally assumed that the slave had taken refuge in Spanish territory, without considering the possibility of other regions within the colony.[41] Thus, once having established himself for two or three years in a given town, working and living as a free black, the slave was accepted by the community as free, and his status thereafter remained unquestioned. For example: "A hard-working slave will pass from this region to that of Port-au-Prince; for greater security he can take a name more closely resembling that of a free black . . . he will work at his trade; at the end of a few years he will marry, have children; and there you have a whole family which has become free through the effrontery of its head and yet which has no other rights than those usurped by a plausible tongue."[42]

If circumstances should arise that might cause a slave to be detected, he was prepared to move on to another area, take on another identity, and establish himself elsewhere. Some may have succeeded indefinitely, and of these there is obviously no record. But most managed to remain in marronage undetected for at least a few, if not a considerable, number of years.[43] So by ingenuity, intelligence, audacity, skill, and cunning, the fugitive slave's freedom became a fait accompli.

Engendered by the social and economic relations of slavery itself, marronage had become an irreversible feature of Saint Domingue slave society. But it was not endemic nor was it unique to Saint Domingue. Marronage existed in all New World slave societies and was generally characterized by certain common features, at least in regard to the armed communities or bands of fugitive slaves. Among these, of course, were the inaccessibility of their settlements, their highly efficient skill at guerrilla warfare, the harsh discipline required by their military organization, and a partial dependence upon colonial society and the plantations for recruits, arms, ammunition, food, or other supplies. The armed settlements of maroons in the Blue Mountains of Jamaica, the Central and South American *palenques* in Colombia, Mexico, and Cuba, the *cumbe* of Venezuela, the maroon societies of bush Negroes in Dutch Guyana, or the famous Brazilian *quilombos*, all displayed these common factors at various stages.[44] In several cases, the most notable being in Jamaica and Dutch Guyana, but also in Colombia and Mexico, the inability of the ruling authorities to destroy these movements eventually led them to seek a truce with the maroons by means of treaty. In each instance, the maroons were guaranteed their freedom in exchange for no longer accepting fugitives into their communities and for aiding the authorities in hunting them down. It was consequently at that point that marronage became marginalized in relation to the plantation slaves and relatively innocuous in relation to the existing social and political structures of those particular slave societies. In other societies such as Brazil, the *quilombos*—even the famous Palmares state that spanned the entire seventeenth century—were ultimately defeated by government troops after years of armed resistance.[45] Eventually (at least in the case of Brazil), marronage came to be replaced in the nineteenth century by slave revolt as the more characteristic form of resistance. [46]

In Saint Domingue, however, marronage persisted long after the few seventeenth- and early eighteenth-century revolts and was never wholly eradicated nor diminished through submission to the government as a viable means of resisting slavery. Even in the one case of Maniel, where the maroons negotiated with the authorities who desired peace, they never compromised their precarious independence when the time came for them to settle on the land offered them within French territory. They were convinced, and in the end perhaps rightly so, that the French wanted to lure them back only to destroy them. [47]

As a constant reality, then, the impact of marronage upon the slaves could be felt in a number of ways. First, the mere existence of fugitive slaves in a plantation slavery society offered an alternative, although a treacherous one, to accommodation and perpetual submission. It meant that avenues of escape did exist—perhaps they were no less perilous than life under slavery, in any case—and whether or not the individual slave decided to resort to them was as much a matter of choice as the force of circumstance. Marronage offered no guarantees, but its continued existence in colonial society was testimony that slavery was not an irrevocably closed system. Second, a contingent relationship necessarily developed between the fugitives and their plantation counterparts, who often sheltered them, gave them food, helped them steal for provisions, and, aware of the goings-on in the master's house, could advise and warn them.[48] Reciprocally, the impact of armed maroons who audaciously raided nearby plantations and occasionally even attacked white colonists, forcing them to organize night vigils, could be highly disruptive of the plantation slaves.[49] Although it was strictly forbidden for slaves to carry arms of any sort, exception was made by the colonial administrators for the slave *commandeurs*, "in order to defend the slaves' quarters and keep guard of their animals and crops against the outrages of the maroons."[50]

If a certain complicity, tacit or otherwise, existed between the fugitive and the plantation slaves, it also existed between the fugitive and the free blacks. A royal ordinance of 1705 revealed that the punishments established in the Black Code of 1685 "against free blacks who facilitate the means by which slaves may become maroons or commit acts of theft did not stop them from sheltering such maroons in their homes, from concealing their thefts and sharing the booty with them." Consequently, any free black who committed one of these acts "would lose his freedom and be sold into slavery along with his immediate residing family." The profits, with the exception of one-third reserved for the informer when there was one, would go to the Crown.[51] And so, here again, one finds evidence of reciprocal relations between two sectors of the black population, the one not so far removed from slavery itself. Through repressive and discriminatory legislation, the free coloreds were to serve as a buffer to protect white supremacy and buttress the slave system, but their mere presence as free persons in colonial slave society could also facilitate avenues of marronage and flight for slaves. Conversely, however, the repercussions of this contact with fugitive slaves could drastically influence both the status and social conditions of the free blacks, who themselves risked becoming slaves.[52]

In this vein, one ought perhaps to be cautious of succumbing to the tendency to classify the maroons as a type of separate entity that existed entirely outside of the system. While this seems to have been the case with the Maniel maroons on the Spanish border, it did not exclusively characterize marronage within the colony. The maroons, one ought to remember, were still slaves and, when caught, were subject to the laws and practices governing slavery. Though they existed on the fringes of the plantations, they were nontheless an integral element of slave society generally. Thus to see them simply as a distinct or separate group might be to suppose that fugitive slaves, once punished, were never reintegrated into the plantation amongst the others, or that they never repeated their acts of defiance to turn fugitive again, or that the hard-working and apparently accommodating plantation slave who stayed on to bide his time never turned fugitive himself. Significant relations did exist between maroons and other elements of the larger society, and it is perhaps from this dynamic that the practical consequences of marronage and, ultimately, its potential for popular revolutionary organization and activity in Saint Domingue might best be understood.

Similarly, reciprocal relations existed between marronage as a mode of slave resistance, in itself, and other forms of resistance for which marronage provided conditions that allowed these to pervade. Among them was voodoo. As one of the first collective forms of resistance, it was both a cultural and, in its practical applications, a politically ideological force. Since it was severely outlawed in the colony and therefore forced into clandestinity,[53] its development and proliferation were reinforced in the general context of marronage. The maroon leaders of African origin were almost without exception either voodoo priests or, at least, voodoo devotees.[54] And, of course, the case has generally been made for the perpetuation, or at least reconstitution within a New World context, of African ways in marronage.

Characteristically, it was in the voodoo ceremonies that African traditions: language, dance, religion, world view, and medicine were all evident. Indeed, the words of the sacramental voodoo hymns were almost all, if not exclusively, of African origin.[55] In a sense, then, the various African languages constituted in themselves a form of cultural protest against the colonial order, as well (as we have seen) as a means of reinforcing a self-consciousness and a cultural identity independent of the white masters. Voodoo as generally practiced in Saint Domingue (and especially its linguistic diversity) constituted, in effect, a broad synthesis of the various religious beliefs and practices of all the African nations forming the slave population.[56] One of the most famous voodoo hymns, chanted in unison for the initiation of a neophyte, according to Moreau de Saint-Méry, is the following:

Eh! eh! Bomba, hen! hen!
Canga bafio té
Canga moune dé lé
Canga do ki la
Canga li[57]

It is of Congolese origin; more specifically it is in the Kikongo language and might be translated this way:

! Mbumba [rainbow spirit = serpent]
the BaFioti [a coastal African slave-trading people]
the whites [i.e., Europeans]
Tie up the witches
Tie them. [58]

The significance not only of the words but of the levels of meaning is to be found both within the African society and culture of the Kongo, or Bakongo, and the New World setting of Saint Domingue. For if, as Moreau de Saint-Méry observed, the incantation was used for the initiation of a neophyte, then it may pertinently involve the creation of a *nkisi* charm, whereby one symbolically "ties up," or gathers together, the enumerated powers by tying a string around the combined elements. Mbumba may be Mbumba Luangu, the rainbow serpent invoked in adoration in the coastal Kongo initiation society, Khimba.[59] Bafioti, meaning "the coastal people," more than likely referred to the coastal Fioti, who were slave traders that hunted down and captured people of the Kongo interior to trade them as slaves to the Europeans, or the white man, the Mundele. The Fioti were thus feared and believed capable of using their powers, not the least of which was witchcraft.[60] And so, the tying up of the *ndoki*, or witches, may refer as much to these slave traders, the Fioti, as to any other person believed to be an evil spirit causing hardship, taking other people's goods, making animals disappear, making the earth sterile, killing in mysterious ways, or, more pertinently, being responsible for the slaves' bondage. [61]

By the eve of the 1791 slave revolt in the North, in a changing context of war and armed slave rebellion, it may perhaps not be too presumptive to infer an even more literal connotation to the "tying up" of the white man, as in the physical act of capturing and tying up the enemy, and thereby conquering those powers. But in the context of slavery, the chant was generally used to initiate a newcomer into the rite of Saint Dominguean voodoo, and in this sense it was most certainly an invocation of protection from the dreaded powers ranged against the slaves. Here, then, we find a culturally specific Congolese ritual contained within an overall religious structure with rules, procedures, hierarchy, and general principles that Moreau himself distinctly described as Dahomean, or more generally, Arada.[62] Among the most highly structured of African animistic religions, Dahomean Vodu thus provided an existing substructure in Saint Domingue within which the religious, cultural, and linguistic traditions of the diverse African nations successively found a place and effectively contributed to its evolution. Moreover, it was precisely through the dispersion of nations among different plantations in the colonial era (and through intermarriages later in the Haitian period) that other cults influenced and enriched the content of voodoo, the overall structure of which remained Dahomean. [63]

By the eve of the revolution the Congolese were certainly among the most numerous of the ethnic groupings composing the African-born slave population, and although reputedly well-adjusted to slavery, they constituted the predominant nation among the maroons.[64] Their preponderance by the end of the colonial period also helps explain the considerable cultural input of this grouping into a religion embraced and informed by the ethnically diverse African slave masses.[65] It was precisely this pluralistic nature of Saint Dominguean voodoo and its disinclination to separate into ethnic cults, as was the case in Brazil, for example, that allowed it to function as a far-reaching collective force. Not surprisingly, it was from the voodoo tradition that the African-born maroon leaders generally emerged. Almost exclusively, if not voodoo priests, they were at least fervent voodoo devotees of one rite or another, whether rada, congo, or petro.[66] And so, a popular religion on the one hand, voodoo constituted, on the other, an important organizational tool for resistance. It facilitated secret meetings, as well as the initiation and the adherence of slaves of diverse origins, provided a network of communication between slaves of different plantations who gathered clandestinely to participate in the ceremonies, and secured the pledge of solidarity and secrecy of those involved in plots against the masters. Describing the inside goings-on of a colonial voodoo ceremony, Moreau de Saint-Méry writes:

> They propose plans, they decide upon steps to be taken, they prescribe actions that the *Vaudoux* priestess always sanctions with the will of [their] God, and they are actions that do not so habitually have the public order and tranquility as object. A new oath, just as abominable as the first one, requires each one to remain silent on what has transpired, to concur on what has been concluded, and sometimes a vase, containing the still-warm blood of a goat, will seal on the lips of the participants the promise to suffer death rather than reveal anything, and even to administer death to whomever may forget that he had solemnly bound himself to the oath. [67]

And of the powerful influence the voodoo high priests held over the members:

> One can hardly believe the extent of dependence in which the *Vaudoux* chiefs hold the members of the sect. There is not one of these who would not prefer the worst of everything to the misfortunes that threaten him if he does not assiduously attend the meetings, if he does not undiscerningly comply with what *Vaudoux* demands of him. . . . In a word, nothing is more dangerous in every respect than this cult of *Vaudoux*, founded on the extravagant notion—but one which can become a terrifying weapon—that the ministers of the being decorated by this name know all and can do all. [68]

By far the most extraordinary and awesome of these prerevolutionary voodoo maroon leaders was François Makandal. According to a contempo-

source, he was born in "Guinea" into an illustrious family that under-
took his education at a very early age. He was supposedly brought up in the
Moslem religion and apparently had an excellent command of Arabic. As
a young man he possessed a remarkably inquisitive mind and, introduced
to the arts, displayed a keen interest in music, painting, and sculpture,
while having acquired a considerable knowledge of tropical medicine, despite his young age.[69] Very little else is known about his background, for at
the age of twelve he was captured as a prisoner of war, sold as a common
slave to the European traders, and shipped to Saint Domingue.[70] Here he
was sold again, this time to Lenormand de Mézy in the district of Limbé,
whose plantations were among the largest and wealthiest in the North. (It
was, incidentally, at another of Lenormand's plantations in Morne Rouge
that the plans for the August 1791 revolt were drawn up less than fifty years
later.) According to one version, Makandal turned fugitive after his hand
was amputated, having caught it in the machinery of the sugar mill while
working the night shift.[71] Another, however, attributes his marronage to the
consequences of a dispute between himself and his master over a young and
beautiful Negress. Apparently Makandal's master had, out of vengeance,
ordered him to receive fifty lashes of the whip, whereupon Makandal refused this humiliation and precipitously took to the woods.[72] Here he began
his long and notorious career, one that spanned nearly eighteen years, as a
prerevolutionary maroon leader.

Operating from his mountain retreat during these years, he carefully built
an extensive network of resistance with agents, as one account goes, in
nearly all points of the colony.[73] Whether the extent of his machinations
actually reached these limits is questionable; it is certain, however, that his
influence covered the better part of the North province. His ultimate weapon
was poison. Having acquired considerable knowledge of herb medicine, a
talent that his master recognized very early, he instructed his followers in its
uses and developed, according to the above account, an "open school of this
execrable art."[74] Effectually, he chose his followers from among those slaves
(and probably some free blacks, as well) known in the colonies as *pacotilleurs* and who were engaged in dealing and selling petty merchandise and
trifles from Europe in the slaves' quarters.[75] It was, as another source relates, "among these *pacotilleurs* that Makandal's disciples and most trusted
partisans were to be found, and, above all, it was they whom he used for the
good or the evil that he wished to accomplish."[76]

His qualities of leadership, his sense of organization, his stature as a
religious cult leader, his eloquence as an orator, not only rivaled that of
the European orators of the day, but surpassed it in strength and vigor,
affording him an immeasurable influence and command over the slaves in
his following. Every contemporary account of Makandal substantiates this

point.[77] One of these suggests that he was at the head of a band of fifty-some maroons,[78] while another claims that, together with his two chief associates, Mayombé and Teysselo, Makandal had assembled "a considerable number of maroons." Moreover, on the summit of their nearly inaccessible mountain retreat, "they had their women, their children, and well-cultivated farms; sometimes armed bands of these brigands descended at Makandal's orders to spread terror and ravage the plantations of the neighboring plains, or to extinguish those who had disobeyed the prophet."[79] Having persuaded many a slave that it was he whom the Creator had sent to carry out the destruction of the whites and to liberate his people, Makandal was thus able to extract not only the most unyielding allegiance from his fugitive followers, but to extend his influence over vast numbers of slaves on the plantations of the whole North Plain region.

Here, a few considerations may be posed concerning marronage in the New World context, and in Saint Domingue particularly. At a first glance, one may be inclined to interpret this case of prerevolutionary marronage as one of the many "restorationist" movements of traditional slave resistance, given the messianic style of leadership espoused by Makandal, as well as the existence of a fairly settled community of followers in apparent withdrawal from slave society.[80] Even more, Makandal's conspiratorial movement in the 1750s was not yet a part of that "bourgeois, democratic revolutionary wave" sweeping through the Age of Revolution in the late eighteenth century. Yet, as a maroon leader, Makandal did not restrict or marginalize his activities exclusively outside the plantation system, nor did he attempt, in the isolation of wooded mountain retreats, to create an independent, socially and politically organized Afro-Caribbean community, as was evidently the case with the Bahoruco and Maniel maroons on the eastern border, or as in other Latin American and West Indian colonies. Rather, marronage became the organizational vehicle, drawing nonetheless upon existing African beliefs and practices, religious animism, and herb medicine, for building a resistance movement aimed at nothing less than the destruction of the white masters and of slavery. Significantly, he had adepts and followers within slave society and within the parameters of the plantation system who, as *pacotilleurs*, as domestic slaves on an errand, or as "occasional" maroons, actively procured and distributed various poisons, potions, and other "remedies." Here, then, was a case of a maroon band with a formidable leader operating in a permanent state of marronage, but one that extended itself, at the same time, to set afoot a vast movement of resistance. It was a type of marronage that differed qualitatively from that practiced by other Saint Dominguean maroon bands or communities in terms of its organization, its infiltration into the plantation system for the recruitment of slave allies and adherents,[81] and in terms of its overall goal.

In this vein, the observations of de Vaissière appear singularly lucid: "Macandal was more than simply a leader of maroon bands. Not that he disdained the pillaging and ransacking of plantations, or the theft of cattle and other ordinary exploits of fugitive slaves; but he seemed at the same time to have sensed the possibility of creating out of marronage a center of organized black resistance against the whites."[82] More than that, he had a solid understanding of the racial origins and development of Saint Domingue, as well as their broader implications. To illustrate this before a large gathering of slaves, he had a vase full of water brought to him, in which he placed three scarves—one yellow, one white, and one black. Pulling out the yellow scarf first, he told his listeners: "This represents the original inhabitants of Saint Domingue. They were yellow." "These," he said, pulling out the white scarf, "are the present inhabitants. Here, finally, are those who will remain masters of the island; it is the black scarf."[83]

For the first few years, he remained completely unknown to the white masters (except his own who, after a number of years, most likely gave him up for dead) and, with extraordinary audacity, went from plantation to plantation to proselytize and stir up the zeal of his partisans, often under cover of the anonymity afforded by calendas and other nocturnal slave gatherings or festivities. During the next twelve years of marronage, he and his followers pursued their ultimate plan with a constancy and ingenuity, as one report goes, that "one would almost be tempted to admire."[84] Finally, the day and the hour were set when the water of all the houses in le Cap was to be poisoned. Within the core of his band he had disciplined agents—captains, lieutenants, and various other officers—operating and organizing on the plantations. He knew the names of every slave on each plantation who supported and participated in his movement. He had an exact list of those slaves who, once the poison had struck panic throughout the town, were to organize in contingents from le Cap and spread out into the countryside to massacre the whites. [85]

The aim was to overthrow the white regime, whereby the blacks would become the new masters of Saint Domingue. It was the first real attempt in the long history of slave resistance at disciplined, organized revolt aiming not only at the destruction of the white masters and of slavery, but at the political notion of independence, albeit historically premature and rhetorically expressed in messianic overtones. The final goals of the conspiracy were not achieved, and unfortunately we have no way of knowing what the outcome might have been. It was, ironically, an inopportune and unfortunate carelessness on the part of Makandal that led to his capture.[86] He managed to maneuver a spectacular but short-lived escape and was promptly recaptured when dogs were finally sent upon his trail. He was summarily tried and burned at the stake.

But for many blacks, Makandal was still alive and would return some day to fulfill his prophecies.[87] For others, his memory was sufficient to nourish the long and bitter struggle that would one day lead to their emancipation. As a legendary figure, his name became identified with almost all forms of fetishism, with poisoning, sorcery, and slave dances. Thereafter, the *houngan*, or voodoo priests, were often referred to as "makandals"; to possess certain powers or simply to practice voodoo was to be a "makandal"; his name was ascribed to certain voodoo dances; voodoo talismans were thereafter often referred to as "makandals" and were strictly forbidden. [88]

Who were the slaves who followed Makandal, who joined him in marronage, who poisoned their masters and members of their family, who poisoned other slaves that could not be trusted? We know from one source that Makandal recruited some of his closest agents from among the *pacotilleurs* who would buy and resell trinkets and sundries in the slaves' quarters. The 1757 prison record for le Cap indicates the names and status (slave or free black) of the accused but does not indicate their slave rank (domestic, *commandeur*, artisan, field worker); and while the names of their masters are given in most cases, their specific plantations of residence and their ages are rarely and only sporadically given. However, certain indications revealed in a letter, dated 24 June 1758 and written from le Cap, suggest that the majority of those arrested after Makandal were in fact house slaves: "We are alarmed to discover that almost all the guilty are those who work in the master's house and in whom was placed the greatest confidence— the coachman, the cook and other domestics at our disposition. . . . Note that all of the guilty ones are highly priced slaves, and even at four to five thousand livres each, they are not spared."[89]

To these can be added a considerable proportion of free blacks, arrested either for acts of poisoning or, most frequently, for the composing, trafficking, or distributing of poison to the slaves. The November 1757 prison report for le Cap, drawn up two months prior to Makandal's capture, indicates eighteen prisoners arrested on charges relating specifically to poison. Of these, twelve were slaves and six were free blacks.[90] Other evidence suggests that free blacks, who were only one step removed from slavery but who enjoyed a far greater freedom of movement than their compatriots in slavery, often acted either as intermediaries between the fugitive maroons and the plantation slaves, or as direct agents in distributing poison to the slaves. Some of them had access to drugs kept by pharmacists and doctors in the colony. Hilliard d'Auberteuil mentions an apothecary whose property and supplies were sold at auction upon his death. Among the possessions sold were arsenic and other drugs. A free black purchased certain quantities of these and had more purchased by others. According to d'Auberteuil, he worked in liaison with Makandal and was himself a distributor of poison. [91]

Among those arrested for crimes relating to poison was Assam, a young slave woman belonging to the planter M. Vallet of la Souffrière, and Pompée, a free black and farmer on the plantation of Sieur Deseuttres [des Gentres?], who served as intermediary. The official interrogation of Assam, dated 27 September 1757, offers certain insights into the attitudes and motives, as well as the methods used by slaves in their covert undertakings.[92] Upon reading and evaluating the interrogation, it seems clearly evident, in spite of her protests to the contrary, that Assam knew full well it was a death-inducing potion she administered to two slaves of the plantation who had fallen ill and finally died shortly after her treatments. Originally, she told her master she would be able to obtain a remedy to cure their illness but needed a pass for at least a day. Pompée directed her to the quarters of a slave named Jean on the Laplaine plantation at Limbé. There she met several other Negresses who had evidently come for the same purpose. Jean asked her to stay for four or five days; this would give him enough time to collect the herbs he needed and to prepare the concoction, which he did in her presence: sage, mixed with an egg yolk and boiler scrapings, into which was mixed *pois puants*, blue verbena, and wheat herb. These were all boiled together and a black powder added. Before Assam left his quarters, Jean drew some blood from her shoulder, rubbed the cut with gunpowder, and scraped the blood off with a knife, placing it in a piece of ram's horn, which he then put in his pocket.[93] Upon returning, Assam administered this remedy to the sick slaves, but far from alleviating their illness, she precipitated their death. Then, so as not to be caught with the substance in her possession, Assam threw away her concoction, though insisting all the while that it was a "good remedy" Jean had given her.

Further, her reactions to Pompée's condemnatory attitudes toward the white masters and even his offer to purchase her freedom were, in the face of her interrogators, nominally negative. She declared that she had nothing against the whites and got along well with her master. On the whole, it is doubtful she was sincere in her declarations. But was she lying in a plea for clemency? Was she lying to conceal names and information? Or was she a willing and conscious participant in the use of poison, who, at the same time, found herself unable to overcome a certain inner ambivalence? Thus caught in torment, facing torture and fearing for her total being, did she feel inclined to express a sympathy toward her master?[94] During her trial in December 1757 it was only as she was being terrorized with burning laths that she agreed to tell all she knew, not wanting to "suffer the fire twice." At this point, she finally divulged the names of some fifty accomplices, both men and women, admitted to having poisoned three of her master's children whom she had nursed, as well as a certain number of slaves on his plantation, and, according to the same source, provided the means by which the authorities were able to arrest Makandal, "who was their leader." [95] Finally, she was accused of twice having administered poison to her own master. [96]

M. Courtin, the seneschal of le Cap, had spent two days and two nights with Assam to extract information from her. During this time, she also declared that the Jesuit priest Father Duquesnoy, a *curé des nègres* charged with the religious instruction of slaves, had come to visit her in prison for confession. He had forbidden her, under punishment of eternal damnation, to reveal the names of her accomplices, advising her that it was far better to endure the torments that could be inflicted upon her rather than succumb to the whites and risk the torments of eternal damnation. This type of tacit complicity was not entirely untypical of the Jesuits. Some even provided protection and asylum for maroons. [97] But the reputation the Jesuits had acquired for appearing to justify marronage and other acts of resistance to grossly inhuman treatment by masters and overseers, not the least of which was poisoning, was due chiefly to the individual acts of certain priests in defense of the slaves. Though inoffensive in themselves, such acts could, by implication, be deemed highly subversive and thereby send shock waves through the white slaveholding community. Father Boutin, a *curé des nègres*, gave a "solemn" religious burial to a Negress accused and hanged for poisoning. To spare other slaves from inevitable torture, Father Duquesnoy effectively offered spiritual absolution to Assam if she withheld the names of her accomplices. Another Jesuit, in Guadeloupe, protested the execution of slaves who were only reputedly, but not proven to be, guilty. At le Cap, the Jesuits were reproached by the Upper Council for fostering too close a contact with the slaves, in general, and with their own, in particular, whom they designated as "servants" rather than slaves. [98] The order was suppressed by royal edict in 1764 after having been expelled from the colony in 1763 on charges of "being in complicity with the slaves." [99]

As an official body, however, the Catholic church generally worked hand in hand with the white masters and the colonial administration. In the slave community, its institutional role was in fact one of utter domination and spiritual terror aimed at breaking the slaves' spirit of rebellion and liberation. By virtue of a special regulation issued by the French government and addressed to the priests of the French colonies, slaves who committed acts of marronage, abortion, poisoning, or arson were threatened by the priests with being refused the sacraments of the church, with excommunication, and eternal damnation. In addition, the regulations ordered the priests to deliver specially prescribed sermons to these slaves, designed to infuse them with a sense of worthlessness and self-hatred for their acts. [100] Voodoo, on the other hand, provided slaves with amulets and talismans believed to protect the holder against any harm while committing an act of resistance that was justified by this religion. Because voodoo was practiced clandestinely, it not only provided an important vehicle for resistance, but also helped to create and sustain an atmosphere of terror that tended at times to lock the planter in a state of psychological insecurity, if not paranoia.

Whether the poisons that slaves obtained and used with such alarming proficiency were actually toxic herbal potions derived from certain plants and prepared by African blacks who held the knowledge and highly guarded secrets of herb medicine; or whether they were simply compositions of an arsenic base, disguised by the presence of various colonial herbal substances, remained for the colonists a matter of dispute.[101] What is more significant, however, in the context of voodoo and marronage, is the impact the use of poison had upon the colonial mentality, at times producing collective panic and hysteria among the white population. Thus, in addition to the countless fatalities resulting from the use of poison as a weapon of slave resistance, this practice contributed greatly toward maintaining the master class in a state of fear from which there appeared to be little effective recourse. Through the uses and abuses of poison, the slaves themselves placed the masters in a position of uncertainty and dependence, for, in the final count, their economic survival, as well as their own life or death, were matters that could equally be determined by those they oppressed. As a social relationship of forces, power in the hands of the Saint Dominguean colonists was never totally absolute, nor were the slaves ever totally victims. It was a double-edged sword that could just as easily turn against the master, and often did. Gabriel Debien even accedes that it was possible the slaves using poison had as their aim "to dominate their master, to make him suffer the supreme humiliation of his ruin; it was a hidden power they had, but one close at hand." [102]

To what degree, then, were the colonists' fears justified? The correspondence of local administrative officials gives some indication as to the extent of popular involvement in the use of poison. In the words of du Millet, lieutenant-judge of Port-de-Paix, situated at a considerable distance from le Cap along the northern coast of the colony:

> This colony is swarming with slaves, so-called soothsayers and sorcerers who poison and who, for a long time, have conceived the plan of insensibly wiping out all the whites. . . . These blacks are of a sect or a new kind of religion formed by two leaders, old Negroes, who for many long years have been fugitive and whose names are Macandal and Tassereau: These two sectarians have fortunately been arrested . . . , but unfortunately they have a considerable number of sectarians and disciples; there are presently over two hundred in the prisons of le Cap: We have roughly a dozen in those of Port-de-Paix since instructions have been delivered a fortnight ago, and twenty-two more have been denounced; and I have reason to believe that those who remain to be discovered in the various quarters of this department are equal in number to those at le Cap. [103]

Another letter, written two months later from le Cap, in June 1758, reveals that, since the execution of Makandal, four or five were burned at the stake every month. Already twenty-four slaves, both men and women, and three free blacks had suffered the same punishment. The author goes on to state that

> as soon as they are put to questioning, the *maréchaussée* arrests nine or ten others as declared accomplices. Thus the number of criminals increases in proportion as one is executed. . . . There are now 140 accused in prison.
>
> Of the blacks who have been executed, some have admitted to killing by poison thirty to forty whites, even their masters, their wives, their children; others, two to three hundred slaves belonging to various masters.
>
> There are some planters who had fifty to sixty slaves working on their plantation. In less than two weeks, they had only four or five remaining, and sometimes not even one. I know many who have had this misfortune befall them. [104]

What was particularly alarming was that "for every one unfortunate that [Makandal] instructed, a hundred more can likewise be instructed." [105] Another letter, written the same month, states that

> there are hardly any slaves, especially those of the nations from the Gold Coast, who in our colonies do not have knowledge of various plants containing poisons or the necessary elements with which to compose them. There have always been those who have used this knowledge, but for two or three years the practice had become so common in the North that, in addition to a very large number of whites who . . . have perished by poison, one can add at least six to seven thousand slaves who were destroyed by this wretched practice. . . . A considerable number of accused still remain in the prisons of le Cap, as well as those of Fort Dauphin and Port-de-Paix. [106]

What becomes strikingly evident from these reports, then, is the generalized state of shock in which the colonial authorities, and many a planter, found themselves. On the one hand, such shocking revelations may indeed have stimulated the masters' fears, while these fears, with a cumulative effect, may then have prompted excessive slave arrests and executions to provide the masters with a desperate sense of security, regardless of the cost. And so in this vein, in the fundamental relationship between master and slave, what the masters believed their slaves capable of doing, what they thought the slaves could and would do, was equally as important as that which the slaves actually did or did not bring about through poison. And yet, they learned exceedingly little from this whole episode. Had they heeded their own fears over what could have happened in 1758, instead of psychologically displacing them through both a literal and a figurative witch hunt, thus erecting a precarious sense of security, they may well have been better prepared and less incredulous and dumbfounded over what did happen in 1791.

Unfortunately any systematic, quantitative social study of the Makandal conspiracy and the "epidemic" wave of poisonings surrounding the event is all but impossible. The evidence, when it does exist, is far too fragmentary, and we must rely upon the colonial correspondence and administrative reports for the elements with which to construct an interpretation. Given the torture tactics used in extracting confessions from suspected slaves, one may justifiably raise questions as to whether all of those arrested and executed were actually guilty; whether the numbers of slaves having perished by poison, reaching into the hundreds by one report and the thousands by another, were accurate; whether the numbers of slaves incarcerated in colonial prisons were exact. But that these massive arrests may have served more to assuage the fears that gripped the masters than to actually punish the guilty ones need not obviate the fact that the fears were themselves perpetrated, in the first instance, by the homicidal activities of at least some of the slaves. And then, one may also assume that there were a good number of slaves and free blacks who used or distributed poisons and who were never caught or identified.

Yet in the end, Makandal and his followers did not succeed in exterminating the whites nor in becoming "masters of the island," a fact that led some observers to conclude that these never were the clear intentions of the slaves who engaged in acts of poisoning. Rather, the failure of the conspiracy prompted them to interpret such acts purely in terms of individual interest: vengeance, jealousy, reduction of the work load, infliction of economic loss on a master, elimination of inheritance rights by poisoning the master's children and thus preventing the breakup of their own families,[107] or the hastening of the day of emancipation provided in the master's testament. As we have already seen in the general correspondence of the period, acts of poisoning were as often inflicted upon other slaves as upon the masters. In many of these cases, however, slaves aimed at damaging the master financially, at reducing the size of his work force to prevent the expansion of his operations, and thereby to exert a measure of control over their own working and living conditions under slavery. In a letter addressed by a colonist to the Comte de Langeron, these motives are clear:

> The hatred which slavery aroused in them against us has given rise to extraordinary thoughts of vengeance, the sad effects of which we have suffered in seeing three-quarters of our laborers perish from sicknesses of a cause unknown even to doctors. When we discovered who the followers of Macandal were, they admitted that they had put to death a large number of whites and an even larger number of blacks, and that the only reason they did this was to restrict their masters to a small number of slaves in order to prevent them from undertaking production that would cause them to be overworked. [108]

To this end, many acts of poisoning were carried out against plantation work animals, as well as against other slaves or against the master and his family.[109] Additionally, slaves who could not be trusted with the secrets of these homicidal endeavors were among the first to fall victim to the poisons used by fellow slaves.

As to the personal desire for freedom on the part of slaves who individually committed acts of poisoning against their masters, sufficient evidence exists to reveal the conscious and deliberate nature of such acts. A letter from the interim intendancy at le Cap, dated 13 January 1758, just a week before Makandal's execution, revealed the motive of four slaves, three women and one man, who poisoned their masters. These slaves were tempted by the "expectation of enjoying their freedom sooner than they could have hoped for in the testament that their masters had left, and that is what prompted them to cut short their masters' lives by poisoning them."[110] In a similar vein, Pompée had told the Negress Assam that when the whites live too long, the slaves who were waiting for their freedom gave the masters drugs to make them die sooner, that many free blacks had gained their freedom this way and that she should do the same.[111] In the opinion of the intendants, the practice of granting freedom by testament would, if left unchecked, lead to the destruction of the colony. The problem, then, could be remedied only by passing a law that, except in the case of a slave noted for "distinguished services," would annul all future acts of liberty granted to slaves by testament.[112] In yet another letter, written only a month earlier, additional evidence of the desire for personal freedom in the poisoning of masters is provided, but the blame for this widespread practice is placed upon the decadence of colonial lifestyles: creole women afraid to die with the reputation of being poor if they did not provide for the emancipation of their slaves; or the concubinage of the masters with their Negress slaves, eventually assuring the freedom of the latter. Thus, given the promises of freedom that were "lavishly accorded by the masters," many slaves were prompted to poison them and become free by virtue of their testament. [113]

Individual acts of poisoning, then, could be motivated by diverse factors, but whatever the motive, the consequences of such acts struck at the economic base of the slave system. However, the fact that individual instances of poisoning occurred for individual reasons on a more or less wide scale does not necessarily exclude the motive of collective liberation in the Makandal conspiracy, nor does it undermine the material objectives of the revolt. Yet the historical relationship between the generalized social phenomenon of slave poisonings and sorcery, as cited by various colonists throughout the North Province, and the actual 1757 political conspiracy of Makandal, remains for the historian a conjectural one. One can argue, however, that these poisonings were all acts of sustained resistance against the nature of slavery and the colonial order, and as such contributed to the creation of a state of fear, uncertainty, and even paranoia and hysteria within the master class. It was, after all, only toward the end of some eighteen-odd years of clandestine maroon activity to build a slave network, to distribute these poisons, instruct a following, and establish trusted contacts on the plantations throughout the North Plain that Makandal could actually organize an effective slave underground and crystallize a precise plan of attack.

One letter, written from le Cap and dated 8 November 1758, suggests even after the arrest and execution of Makandal and the other leaders, along with hundreds of their followers, that the operations and plans for revolt had still not entirely been crushed: "The principal leaders of these rebels have been burned and, of late, eight others have been arrested at the source which supplies water to the military barracks; their plan was to inject poison in the canal that carries the water to the fountain and thereby kill off the troops who proved to be the only obstacle holding them back and preventing them from exterminating the whites."[114] So the evidence seems to indicate that, however loose or rudimentary the Makandal affair may have been, it was neither a spontaneous eruption nor was it only blind terrorism, but rather a deliberately organized plan of revolt that appears to have taken concrete form within a concurrent context of widespread, often unexplained, poisonings that he and his followers had done much to create.

Indeed, by 1757, the use of poison had become a generally established practice among many slaves, and they carried out their acts with impunity: "What alarms us further is to see how little these unfortunates are touched by the fate of those that are executed and how little an impression their punishment makes upon them."[115] The reporter gives as an example the case of one master from Limbé who had obtained a writ from the judge allowing the execution of the accused slaves belonging to him to take place on his plantation. Three days after the execution, the commanding officer, M. de Gondy, went to the plantation with a contingent of fifteen whites. Three of M. de Gondy's slaves found the means to poison the whole contingent. As they began vomiting, an antidote was promptly administered, and they were saved. The three slaves were arrested and executed. Other contemporary observations further attest to the intrepidity with which slaves continued to resist. M. de Rochefort wrote that "the very day scheduled for the greatest number of executions of [Makandal's] accomplices, other domestic slaves were poisoning their masters and guests."[116] Another relates: "In fact, the frequent punishments and torture which their compatriots suffer before their eyes creates no fear in them whatsoever, and it must be said that the victims endure the most cruel torments with an unequalled steadfastness, appearing on the scaffold and at the stake with ferocious courage and tranquility."[117]

Moreover, slaves who administered poison often did so in a highly calculated manner. Of the poisons used, some were so dangerous and so violent
that when given to dogs, they inflicted immediate death. Others had a much
slower effect, causing the victim to languish five to six months before finally
dying. Some slaves would consciously administer small doses of poison in
their master's food or drink as an initial warning. If the master's cruelty
persisted, the doses could be increased and finally induce death. [118]

Makandal's final plan was a premature attempt at revolution. The com-
ponent elements comprising its general framework were those found within
the material and historical parameters of mid-eighteenth-century slave society in Saint Domingue: poison, voodoo, marronage.[119] It was nevertheless
a forecast of what would come in full force some thirty years later. It sig-
naled what had become an incipient movement among the masses, at this
stage fragmentary and incohesive and not yet conscious of its revolutionary
potential, but one that tended toward the eventual destruction of slavery and
one whose avowed goal, despite the messianic overtones and African outlook of its leaders, was nonetheless the independence and mastery of Saint
Domingue.

Concurrently, within this general context, another widespread, almost
"epidemic," use of poison was uncovered around May 1757 in the regions
of le Cap and Fort Dauphin, only eight months prior to Makandal's capture.
The first arrest was made on the Lavaud plantation, where countless numbers of slaves had perished within an astonishingly short period of time,
and where Lavaud and his wife were left in a hopelessly languishing state of
health. Again, it was a domestic slave, Médor, who was suspected as chief
perpetrator of the poisonings.[120] It is probable that Médor had established
formal links with Makandal, and the documentary evidence available certainly suggests this.[121] However, following his arrest, Médor killed himself
before he could be brought to the tribunal for more extensive questioning.
His role as a leader behind the poisonings on the Lavaud plantation, however, facilitated by his position as a domestic, certainly places him within
the overall scheme of poisonings generally attributed to Makandal and his
accomplices from as far as Port-de-Paix at the one end, to Fort Dauphin
at the other. It is also certain that he and Makandal operated at the same
time, within and around the same geographic base of le Cap–Fort Dauphin,
and shared a common vision of emancipation. Inherent in that vision was
the belief in its imminence and the necessity of an eventual confrontation
with the whites. Médor's final declaration, situated at an undefined point
between the hyperbolic and the prophetic, nevertheless sheds light on the
attitudes and motives of many a slave who used poison as a means of resistance: "If slaves commit acts of poisoning, they do it in order to obtain
their freedom. . . . There is also a secret among them which can only lead

to the destruction of the colony, of which the whites are totally unaware and of which the free blacks are the principal cause, using all possible means to increase their numbers in order to be in a position to confront the whites whenever necessary." [122] Indeed, had not the free black Pompée advised the slave Assam to obtain her own freedom by poisoning her master?

With the onslaught of arrests, interrogations, and executions following the Makandal affair, colonial opinion tended to discount the existence of an organized plot or even a general tendency among the slaves toward liberation and the eventual extermination of the masters. [123] Yet the impact of the whole affair upon the colonial mentality and upon subsequent legislation suggests at least that the white masters' fears of continuing slave resistance were nonetheless real and not necessarily without due cause. In fact, the repercussions of the Makandal affair, as those of the Le Jeune case in a similar fashion, may actually tell us as much about the master mentality in Saint Domingue as about slave activities relating to poison per se.

On 11 March 1758, two months after Makandal's execution, the Upper Council of le Cap declared illegal the fabrication or distribution of "makandals," or talismans, as well as the casting of evil spells, under the pretext that these constituted a profanation of holy artifacts. [124] The same ordinance equally forbade slaves to compose or to distribute any sort of remedy to other slaves without the master's permission. Another ordinance of 7 April 1758 prohibited any slave ceremony involving a death prayer for one of the members. The prohibition against "makandals" was also extended to free blacks and mulattoes. For the slaves, prohibitions were reinforced against bearing arms, the sale of foodstuffs in the towns, and assemblies after 7 P.M., even in churches. A free black providing asylum to a fugitive slave would, along with his entire resident family, lose his freedom. A further act of the Upper Council of le Cap ordered in 1761 that churches be closed after sundown and between noon and two o'clock—the periods accorded slaves for their free time. As well, the activities of the *curés des nègres* were severely circumscribed in an attempt to minimize their direct contact with the slaves. [125] All *affranchis*, whether black or mulatto, were forbidden to wear sword, saber, or *manchette* unless they were members of the *maréchaussée*. [126]

In the end, the Makandal affair was not simply an isolated episode in the history of slave resistance. On the one hand, 1758 marked the climax of slave resistance by means of poison, facilitated by marronage (especially of the chief leaders) and reinforced by the powerful influences of colonial voodoo. But the use of poison as a weapon against slavery hardly began, nor did it end, here. Throughout the eighteenth century, planters were periodically plagued by the ravages of poison on their plantations, and if they believed they had rid themselves of the problem with the wave of executions and repressive legislation after Makandal's death, they proved singularly shortsighted. [127]

During the 1760s, it became clear that actually only a minority of the slaves who engaged in poisoning, or who were believed to have done so, had been eliminated. Cabon relates that during this period, some plantations had even been decimated due to massive executions of suspected slaves.[128] As the poisonings continued, the general feeling was that the principal culprits, as well as the rest of their leaders, remained untouched by the combined campaigns of planters and administrators to torture, to inflict a multitude of cruelties, to burn alive suspected slaves from whom they attempted to extract confessions and denunciations of accomplices. One legislator wrote that "[p]unishment by fire to which the criminals have been condemned is totally incapable of frightening them, of making them admit to their crimes and of preventing those who wish to imitate them from continuing the intrigues of their secret undertakings."[129] While some colonists suggested suppressing grants of freedom by testament altogether, others proposed their retention, but only in very special cases, thus keeping alive the illusory hope of eventual freedom in order to maintain the docility and obedience of slaves. A few of the more enlightened minds proposed humane treatment and sufficient food as a palliative to stimulate respect among slaves for their masters, all to little avail.

If by the 1780s, however, the wave of poisonings that had seemingly swept the North in the 1750s had finally subsided, the sporadic use of poison as a means of resisting slavery continued to be noted: in 1777, for example, the slave Jacques, belonging to Corbières, arrested for having poisoned over one hundred of his master's animals in eight months; in 1781, an apothecary arrested for selling a lethal drug to a slave who poisoned himself; or in 1784, the Negress Elizabeth, called Zabeau, arrested for attempting to poison her master by introducing emetic substances in his food and drink.[130] In fact, the administrators found it necessary in 1780 to issue an ordinance reinforcing half a dozen previous ones concerning restrictions on the sale of poisons and other dangerous drugs in the colony. In addition, the 1780 ordinance made it illegal for free persons of color, as well as slaves, to compose or distribute a remedy of any sort and in any form, or to undertake the cure of sick persons.[131] The notoriously cruel Nicolas Le Jeune related in 1788, just three years before the massive slave revolt in the North Plain, that his father had lost through poison over four hundred slaves in twenty-five years, and fifty-two more in only six months. In less than two years, he himself had lost forty-seven slaves and thirty mules. [132]

During the 1770s and 1780s, however, at least in the Fort Dauphin region in the North, more overtly violent forms of resistance seemed to replace the covert schemes of poison as a retaliatory arm. The outright murder and assassination of a master or other whites, plotted by small groups of half a dozen slaves, or even by individual slaves, were noted in 1776, 1779, and 1784. Here, in the cases of group-led assassinations, the slaves leading the plots occupied the higher ranks of slave society: a miller and a coachman, a *commandeur*, sailors, and a quarteroon (no doubt a domestic).[133] As well, the 1770s witnessed the emergence of armed maroon bands ravaging plantations and throwing "the whole district of Fort Dauphin into a state of alarm."[134] Noël, the leader of one of these, had assembled "a considerable number of slaves around him, and notably several *commandeurs* of different *ateliers*"; his intrepidity even "terrified the *gens de couleur* to the point where they no longer dared confront him," and a ransom was therefore issued.[135] Even more formidable, it seems, was the armed band led by Thélémaque Canga, seconded by Isaac and by Pirrhus Candide, numbering some three hundred.[136] Though the interpretation of the evidence has led to much controversy, the impression still remains that, on the whole, marronage was probably increasing during the decade or so preceding the revolution. As well, collective marronage involving groups of slaves and even entire *ateliers*, sometimes headed by the *commandeur*, was not an unusual occurrence after 1784. [137]

Undercurrents of thought forecasting a change were expressed in both the slave and the white communities. Perhaps unconsciously foreseeing the black revolution that would break out among the masses eight years later, M. de Rouvray, a colonial planter and brigadier in the royal army, observed in 1783 that "a slave colony is as a city threatened by attack; we are treading on powder kegs."[138] Again, by 1786, some slaves were spreading the concept of independence.

In the North, the mulatto Jérôme, called Poteau, and his black companion, Télémaque, inspired by the contemporary vogue of mesmerism, were holding clandestine nightly assemblies that drew large crowds, usually numbering up to two hundred slaves from the plantations around Marmelade. The two leaders distributed iron bars and other cabalistic objects while preaching independence and instructing others in the same practice.[139] Jérôme and Télémaque were arrested and sentenced to the galleys for life in December 1787. The presiding magistrate believed that this public punishment "would prove once and for all the impotence of their practices" and the empty powers of their talismans "to protect them from the punishments which justice must always deal out for brazen-faced charlatanism."[140] What this magistrate did not see, or did not want to see, wrote Cabon, was that these superstitious practices had gone beyond the limits of what the colonists deemed the narrow consciousness of the slaves, to attain the concept of an independence embracing perhaps even the entire race. [141]

Slave resistance had spanned several centuries and was expressed or carried out by the slaves in many ways. Partial revolts, conspiracies, plots to kill the master, suicide, infanticide, voodoo, poisonings, marronage with its long and diverse history, all bore witness to the slaves' human spirit and capacity to assert an independent will. If undercurrents of a consciousness harboring the eventual destruction of slavery and the master class had become evident in the half-decade or so before the revolution, it was not until 1791 that this consciousness became substantively collective, when, beginning in the North, entire plantations of slaves deserted in rapid succession to join what had become a massive revolutionary army. And what was unique about this slave revolt, in addition to its highly disciplined and broadly based organization, was the widespread (and alarming) extent of popular participation and support. Although somewhat fragmentary, there is even evidence to suggest that, in fact, a few of the early leaders of the revolt, notably Boukman and Jean-François, had an acquired experience of popular marronage. [142]

For nearly three years, between 1789 and 1791, the slaves of Saint Domingue witnessed the revolts of the propertied classes. The white colonists began by claiming their rights and demanding the abolition of the economic and commercial restrictions laid upon them by the Ancien Régime. They were followed by the *affranchis*, who demanded an equal footing with the whites. New forces had burst open in the colony. Talk of "liberty, equality, and fraternity" fell upon the receptive ears of domestic slaves, who interpreted these slogans in their own way as they perfunctorily served their white masters. One colonist writes in 1789: "What preoccupies us the most at this time are the menaces of a revolt. . . . Our slaves have already held assemblies in one part of the colony with threats of wanting to destroy all the whites and to become masters of the colony." [143] Another lucidly observes: "Everyone has made a habit of arming himself and of grouping together to patrol the roads and the large savannas. These precautions seem to make an impression on the slaves, but the work is going badly, and it is easy to perceive that something is being conspired and will break out in mutiny on one plantation: This will be the signal for all the others." [144]

It was the French Revolution that provided the opportunity for that revolt.

3
The Coming of the Black Revolution

O nce news of the convocation of the Estates General was announced in 1788, colonists in Saint Domingue, as well as absentee planters in France, began rapidly organizing committees and clubs, thus establishing a network of communication between these spontaneously formed bodies as they set out to determine how best to make their claims and grievances known to the national assembly that would convene the following year.

In Saint Domingue, the aristocratic planters of the North were the first to take the initiative. During 1788 a small party had coalesced around the issue of colonial representation in the Estates General and by August had formed, illegally and with the utmost secrecy, a committee to propagate its views and rally support among the planters of the outlying parishes. This committee, along with the propaganda emanating from the Chamber of Agriculture in le Cap, had sparked the creation of similar committees in the two other provinces. They were all actively engaged in preparing official lists of grievances, or *cahiers*, as well as the eventual election of deputies who would present these claims and specific interests to the Estates General.

They wanted an end to what they called "ministerial despotism" and reserved for themselves alone the right to legislate on the internal structure and administration of the island. The governor and intendant were to become mere figureheads representing the king and would fall under the influence and control of colonial authority. They wanted an end to the prohibitive measures of the Exclusive and demanded the right of free trade and the opening of colonial ports to merchant ships of other countries, especially for the unrestricted importation of grain and slaves. Land distribution, jurisprudence, finances, legislation—these were all matters that for the colonists could best be decided upon by themselves. By declaring that only the colony could act in its own best interests, they saw themselves not as subjects of the French Crown, but rather as a French province, distinctively different from the others by virtue of climate, agriculture, the specific nature of its slave-based economy, and the particularity of its social and racial structure.

Their aim was to stabilize and to increase their colonial possessions and productivity, and for this they explicitly excluded the mulattoes and free blacks from the primary electoral assemblies. By the end of the year, they had elected their own deputies to France in the belief that the members of the Estates General, because of their unfamiliarity with the specific needs of the colonies and general ignorance of colonial affairs, would accept them as experts and, with little debate, adopt whatever they proposed. They were themselves unaware, however, of attitudes prevalent among some of the more enlightened leaders of the revolutionary movement in France, who, influenced by the ideas of the *philosophes*, depicted the slave-owning colonists as a "breed of political leeches and violators of human dignity."[1]

[margin note: FR. REV. SUPPORTED SLAVES + DISLIKED OWNERS]

The colonists had not yet even obtained the right of representation. Since their petitions for admission into the Estates General had already been rejected by the king and the royal bureaucracy, and subsequently by the nobility, their last refuge was in the Third Estate, which by June had come to the forefront of the revolution in France. Assembled in the Tennis Court at Versailles, the Third Estate had declared itself the nation, the true representatives of the people, and swore, as a body, never to disperse. Almost all the colonial deputies had also participated in this oath, and in the general euphoria and enthusiasm that surrounded the event, the Third Estate recognized the principle of colonial representation.

Given the wealth and economic importance of Saint Domingue to France, the provisional deputies brazenly requested twenty colonial representatives. At this point Mirabeau, a liberal bourgeois and member of the French abolitionist society, the Amis des Noirs, indignantly intervened and maintained that the principles of proportional representation followed in France allowed the colony only four deputies. Moreover, he continued, with biting irony: "You want representation in proportion to the number of inhabitants. But have the blacks and free persons of color competed in the elections? The free blacks are property owners and taxpayers. Yet they could not vote. And, as to the slaves, either they are men or they are not; if the colonists consider them to be men, let them free them and make them eligible for seats; if not, have we, in proportioning the number of deputies to the population of France, taken into account the number of our horses and mules?"[2] A compromise was reached, and the colony was allowed six deputies.

[margin note: SPEECH AG. SLAVERY]

Colonial representation in a metropolitan assembly was an audacious innovation. It was contrary to the established theory of mercantilism and had never before been granted by a European power. In essence, the idea of colonial representation embodied the general principle of "no taxation without representation" over which the North American colonies had already fought a war for independence. It was a victory for the Saint Domingue deputies, but a precarious one for which they would in the end pay dearly. Without realizing it, the colonists had seriously compromised their future and their fortunes by demanding representation in a parliamentary body in revolution. They were caught in the trap of their own ambitions and would

[margin note: DOOMED THEMSELVES]

now have to find a way to separate their own private interests from those of France, from the principles guiding the revolution and embraced in the Declaration of the Rights of Man and Citizen, which proclaimed that "all men are born and remain free and equal in their rights."

At the same time as the white deputies from Saint Domingue were seeking admission to the Estates General, the mulattoes residing in Paris had organized a parallel movement for representation under the leadership of Julien Raimond. Their cause was hopeless in the colony since they were excluded from the electoral assemblies. In Paris, at least, they had allies, and with the help of the Amis des Noirs, whose leading spokesman, Abbé Grégoire, was a member of the Constituent Assembly, they were allowed to present their case in October. The assembly was hard-pressed to make a decision, but remained ideologically consistent with its own revolutionary principles and declared that no part of the nation would ever claim its rights in vain before the elected assembly of the French people. The mulattoes had also succeeded in obtaining a recommendation from the Credentials Committee, of which Grégoire was a member, for two representatives.[3] Their cause was filled with new hopes. Yet reaction and fear were now stronger than ever among the white colonial forces.

The Massiac Club, a group of notable and influential colonists in Paris, had already organized themselves in opposition to colonial representation. They had foreseen the imminent dangers of the whole debate. Officially founded in August 1789, they had set themselves the task of coordinating a system of pressure to block the aspirations of the pro-representation party.[4] They strongly contested the powers of the six deputies who had already been admitted provisionally, as the question of mulatto representation began taking on wider proportions. It was, incidentally, to the absentee planters of the Massiac Club that the mulattoes first addressed their petitions, seeking at least some support from their allies in property. By intrigue and intimidation, the members of the club, now in alliance with the colonial deputies, attempted at every opportunity to suspend all discussion of colonial affairs and prevent the reemergence of the mulatto question in the National Assembly.[5] Thus, Grégoire's recommendations were never heard.

By now, events in Saint Domingue had taken their own course. News from France was slow in coming, and the colonists had already taken the initiative of electing district and provincial assemblies months before the arrival of the convocation orders promised by the minister of the marine. The Provincial Assembly of the North accused Peynier, the governor, of hiding the orders, and began stealing ministerial mail. Peynier was forced to act and finally decided to issue the orders of convocation. The general colonial assembly was to be located at Léogane. This only infuriated the provincial assembly further, as it meant to retain control of the revolution in the North and began delegating itself both legislative and executive powers in the name of the colony.

The *gens de couleur*, as free persons and as property owners, continued to demand full and equal rights of citizenship with the whites. They were richer, more numerous, and far more militant than elsewhere in the French West Indies. In Saint Domingue, they outnumbered the whites in the South and constituted an equivalent force in the West. The planters, aware of the activities of the mulatto delegation in Paris, became increasingly fearful and determined at all costs to undermine their movement. They kept the mulattoes under strict surveillance, issued curfews, and tried to intimidate them through arrogance and brutality. If they allowed the free persons of color to vote and hold office, it would, they believed, open the way to, and encourage, insurrection among the slaves. It would be the end of white supremacy and of their fortunes.

At le Cap, they had already executed one mulatto, Lacombe, for having submitted a petition to the Provincial Assembly of the North requesting political rights for free persons of color. In November, a white, Ferrand de Baudières, seneschal of Petit Goâve, had written a similar petition. He was arrested at his residence, dragged through the streets, and brutally killed by a furious mob of *petits blancs* who cut off his head and paraded it through the town on a pike. At Aquin, Labadie, an elderly, respectable mulatto and close friend of Raimond, was suspected of having in his possession a copy of the petition that prompted the death of de Baudières. Shot down at his home, he was then tied to a horse and left to be dragged to death, though his life was spared by the intervention and aid of his slaves and some neighbors. A notary at Petite-Rivière nearly missed being killed for having drawn up a petition claiming the political and civil rights of the mulattoes and free blacks. [6]

By February 1790 the planters began organizing elections for the new colonial assembly. Rejecting the instructions of the minister La Luzerne, they decided upon Saint Marc as the site of the assembly and, in a special ordinance issued by the provincial assemblies, explicitly excluded the mulattoes and free blacks from the primary electoral committees. By the end of March, the deputies from the three provinces met in Saint Marc and on 14 April, avoiding any reference to their colonial status, declared themselves the General Assembly of Saint Domingue.

While all this was going on in the colony, the National Assembly in France had not yet determined the official constitutional status of the colonies. The Saint Domingue deputies realized they could not introduce measures concerning the colony without reopening the debate on the mulatto question. Conscious of the precarious position in which they now found themselves, a deputy from Martinique, de Curt, proposed in November 1789 the creation of a special Colonial Committee in order to remove all colonial questions from the floor of the assembly, where debate would merely focus troublesome attention and publicity upon the racial interests of the planters.

The committee was to be composed of an equal number of colonists and wealthy port merchants, whose role would be, among others, to present a plan for a constitution of the colonies. Strong opposition came at this point from Abbé Grégoire. In his speech on 3 December, he maintained that the question of a constitution for the colonies could not be considered so long as the question of the rights of the free persons of color had not been settled.[7] It was an issue that had plagued the colonial deputies from the very moment they had begun agitating for representation in Paris. In spite of Grégoire's efforts to settle the mulatto question first, and in view of the recent events in the colony, the proposal for a colonial committee was accepted on 2 March 1790. Although only two colonists and two port merchants were named to the committee, the other eight, including Barnave, who was chosen to head the committee, were solid supporters and allies of the colonists, as of the merchant bourgeoisie, and susceptible to the influence and manipulation of the Massiac Club.[8]

The committee had less than one week to come up with a constitutional plan for the colonies. Drawing from work that had already been under way in the Massiac Club, Barnave submitted his report to the National Assembly on 8 March. The report officially recognized the already-existing assemblies in Saint Domingue, authorized each colony to submit its own proposals for a constitution, and finally, aiming at the Amis des Noirs, declared guilty of crime against the nation anyone attempting to undermine or to incite agitation against the interests of the colonists.[9] Not a word was mentioned on the burning question of mulatto rights. By sanctioning the already-elected assemblies, which excluded the mulattoes, the decision as to who was and who was not a citizen was left entirely to the prejudices and dispositions of the white planters.

The report quelled the fears of the colonists as it gave nearly complete local autonomy to the colonies, reassured the maritime bourgeoisie by postponing revisions of the Exclusive, thus avoiding any mention whatsoever of the slave trade, and left only a glimmer of hope for the mulattoes. The assembly received Barnave's proposals, incomplete as they were, with an overwhelming ovation, raucously subverting all discussion. The vote was taken and the report of 8 March approved by what was, for the liberal opposition, an extortionate majority.

The instructions that followed, outlining the application of the 8 March decree, gave full legislative powers to the Colonial Assembly, which by now was acting in the colony as a miniature Constituent Assembly, but whose laws, in spite of its declared intentions to circumvent the National Assembly, still needed the approval of the latter and the perfunctory sanction of the king.[10] The Colonial Assembly was free to propose modifications of the commercial relations between the colony and France and, in short, would hold virtual sovereignty over its internal regime. But the instructions remained ambiguous on the explosive question of the political rights of mulattoes and free blacks. Article 4 merely stated that the right to vote and hold office be accorded to all persons twenty-five years of age who owned property or paid the requisite amount of taxes, and who fulfilled a two-year residence requirement.

Virulent opposition came both from the colonial deputies and from the pro-mulatto forces led by Grégoire. Were not the mulattoes and free blacks persons? Did they not own property and pay taxes? Grégoire demanded a clarification of Article 4. He understood the word *persons* to mean mulattoes and free blacks, as well, and insisted that they be expressly included in the wording. The colonial deputies wanted Article 4 suppressed altogether, or else rewritten to specifically exclude mulattoes and free blacks. The assembly refused to face the issue, closed the debate, and dispatched the instructions, along with their inherent ambiguity, to the colony.

The news of the 8 March decree and the instructions of the twenty-eighth did not arrive until the end of May. In the meantime, the assembly at Saint Marc had already assumed supreme legislative authority in the colony, declared itself permanent, and had begun a thorough reorganization of the colony's administrative structure. On 28 May, it issued a decree serving as the constitutional basis of the colony. The decree declared that if urgency dictated, its laws, as those of the National Assembly in France, were subject only to the sanction of the king. Moreover, any law passed by the National Assembly on affairs of common interest between the colony and France were subject to colonial veto. Henceforth, Saint Domingue was to be a federative ally rather than a subject of the French government.[11] By the same decree, it suspended all functions of the colonial deputies in the National Assembly, who were now to be no more than commissioners charged with presenting its decrees for official sanction.[12] In July, it passed a law contravening the Exclusive to open up the ports for the unrestricted importation of certain foodstuffs.

In the face of this insurrectionary activity, which had gone far beyond the moderate intentions of the 8 March decree, and which seemed to be driving the colony toward virtual independence, the governor issued a proclamation denouncing the General Assembly as a traitor to the nation and amassed his troops to dissolve it by force. Saint Domingue was now divided into two distinct camps. On the right were the *pompons blancs*, the royalists, and all those who had occupied military or administrative posts in the colony. The Provincial Assembly of the North, dominated by the wealthy aristocratic planters and commercial bourgeoisie, believed the Saint Marc assembly had gone too far for its own good and for the good of the colony. They recalled their deputies, sided for the time being with the royalists, and aimed to regain control of the revolution. On the left were the patriots, or the *pompons rouges*, who supported the constitutional reforms of the Saint Marc assembly and for whom the revolution had opened up certain avenues of advancement. Both sides bid for the support of the mulattoes, extending hypocritical overtures and promises to win them over.

The Saint Marc assembly rebutted the governor's denunciation by declaring Peynier a traitor, as well as the officers of his staff, and issued a call to arms of all citizens. The Provincial Assembly of the North offered its services to the governor. It was decided that Colonel de Mauduit would leave Port-au-Prince on 5 August with his royalist regiment to collaborate with de Vincent, commander of the forces in the North; both would converge at Saint Marc and force the assembly to dissolve. Upon the arrival of the troops, a twenty-four-hour ultimatum was issued. The assembly was left defenseless and faced certain defeat. The eighty-five remaining members took advantage of the presence of a ship, the *Léopard*, docked in the Port-au-Prince harbor, and with the aid of a sympathetic crew who maneuvered it to Saint Marc, all eighty-five jumped aboard, sailed to France, and tried to plea for justice in the National Assembly.

In France, the mulattoes had attempted ever since the adoption of the 8 March decree to obtain a clarification of their rights implied in Article 4, but with no success. De Joly, a lawyer and member of the Amis des Noirs, intervened on their behalf to solicit an explanation from the Colonial Committee, which remained noncommittal. The National Assembly had effectively washed its hands of the whole problem by delegating to the Colonial Assembly the sole initiative for its constitution and its laws governing the status of persons.

It was clear that the aspirations of the mulattoes were now a lost cause in France. Vincent Ogé, a close friend and colleague of Raimond, understood this. He had already made it known to Barnave and the Colonial Committee that if the whites persisted in refusing to recognize persons of color as free citizens, he would force them, by arms if necessary, to recognize their rights. The activities and agitation of the mulattoes in Paris had caused the colonists' fears to reach an unprecedented stage. The Massiac Club issued directives to all the major ports, advising ship captains to refuse passage to any person of color leaving for Saint Domingue. In spite of these measures, Ogé managed to escape. He went first to England, where he was secretly received and aided by the abolitionist leader Thomas Clarkson. With an advance of thirty pounds, he left for the United States, purchased some arms, and arrived in Saint Domingue on 21 October. [13]

When the planters of the Saint Marc assembly had received news of the March decrees, along with the equivocal provisions of Article 4, they vowed that they would never accord political rights to a "bastard and degenerate race" and expressly excluded them from the primary assemblies.[14] When a group of mulattoes appeared before the Provincial Assembly of the South at les Cayes to request a clarification of their rights, they were told that "nothing can destroy nor even alter the line of demarcation which both nature and our institutions have irrevocably fixed between you and your benefactors." The assembly further warned them against taking any action that would be "incompatible with the state of subordination in which you must continually remain."[15] The new colonial assembly prescribed by the March decrees had been elected without a single mulatto or free black vote.

Ogé's plan upon arriving in Saint Domingue was to secure by force the application of these decrees for his people. Having managed to elude the police, who had been warned of his arrival, he went on to Dondon where he had family and friends, and there organized a common front of *gens de couleur* against the forces of white supremacy. Among his supporters were his brother, Jacques, and Jean-Baptiste Chavannes, a close friend and associate who had already proven his military abilities as a soldier in the North American war for independence. With an armed following of over two hundred men, including some free blacks, they advanced to Grande-Rivière, joined with additional forces to take over the city, and disarmed the white population without incident. Ogé then dispatched letters to the governor, to de Vincent, and to the Provincial Assembly of the North. In the letters, he demanded the just application of the March decrees, stated that they would proceed to elect their own representatives and, if thwarted in their endeavors, would meet force with force.[16] The Provincial Assembly immediately countered their demands by sending its forces to defeat the insurgents. Vastly outnumbered and overpowered, they were forced to disband. Ogé and a number of his companions fled to Spanish territory, whence they were soon extradited.

The trial did not take place until February 1791, when, on the twenty-fifth, Ogé and Chavannes were both sentenced to a merciless death. They were led by the executioner to the parish church where, with a cord around their necks and on bended knee, they were to repent their "crimes," after which their bodies were tied to a wheel and broken on a scaffold where they died—opposite the execution place for whites. As a reminder of the written and unwritten laws of white supremacy for all to see, their heads were cut off and exposed on stakes, Ogé's on the road leading to Dondon, and Chavanne's on the one leading to Grande-Rivière. Two days later Ogé's brother, along with some twenty-one others, were also condemned to death, and thirteen more sentenced the following month to the galleys for life. Such were the consequences of the ambiguous March decrees designed to leave to the colonists "the merit and option of exercising an act of generosity toward mulattoes and free blacks, an act which would inspire in them sentiments of affection and gratitude and establish the most perfect harmony among the different classes composing the population." [17]

In France, the National Assembly listened to the patriotic protests of the deputies who had arrived the previous September from Saint Marc. They claimed to be a democratically elected body and the legitimate representatives of the entire colony, but they constituted only a minority of the original 212 members. As an assembly, they had lost all credibility. The Massiac Club remained neutral, as did the colonial deputies, whose powers they themselves had stripped, while the National Assembly turned a deaf ear. Its decree of 20 September 1790 made it illegal for the eighty-five to leave France until further notice. On 12 October, it declared the dissolution of the Saint Marc assembly, promised future elections, and, at the same time, reaffirmed the exclusive right of the colonies to initiate legislation on the state of free persons of color. For the moment all did not seem lost, at least for the colonists.

However, by November, news had arrived of similar unrest in Martinique, while in Saint Domingue, Ogé and his companions had organized and led the mulattoes into open revolt. Determined to reassert its authority over the colonies and to reestablish order, the National Assembly voted on the twenty-ninth to send additional troops to the colonies, to be accompanied by civil commissioners, and suspended, as it did for Saint Domingue in October, those assemblies in rebellion against French authority. These resolutions, however, were definitively adopted only in February 1791. The National Assembly had already rescinded its right to legislate on the political status of the mulattoes by its decrees of March and October 1790, and the promised instructions for the future Saint Domingue assembly were still unwritten as news arrived of Ogé's martyrdom.

Grégoire was bitterly attacked by the colonists who held him personally responsible for the revolt, and who wanted legal proceedings brought against him. In March and April, the eighty-five members of the defunct colonial legislature were admitted before the National Assembly, where they repented their insubordination, declared they never sought independence, and affirmed their submission to the laws of France. The whole debate was once again opened and thrown on the floor of the National Assembly. It was now forced to deal with the issue that it had refused to confront a year earlier by adopting the contradictory decrees of March.

The report of the Colonial Committee was presented on 7 May, but it contained nothing new, and merely reasserted under another form colonial jurisdiction over the mulatto question. In the heated debate that ensued,

Grégoire took the stand to demand an adjournment; the opposition called for an immediate vote but was defeated. When the debates resumed on the eleventh, it was Robespierre who laid the issue squarely before the members of the assembly. The colonial supporters were undermining the very foundation of those principles upon which their own rights and liberties were founded. If the colonies were to be preserved at the price of submitting to colonial threats by adopting legislation contrary to the most basic principles of humanity, then they should perish: "We will sacrifice to the colonial deputies neither the nation nor the colonies nor the whole of humanity. . . . I ask the Assembly to declare that the free persons of color be allowed to enjoy the rights of voting citizens." [18] The question was settled on 15 May. Political rights were granted only to those persons of color born of free parents. The existing colonial assemblies, which excluded mulattoes and free blacks, were to remain; those persons of color born of free parents and possessing the requisite qualifications could be admitted to all future assemblies. It was in fact a conservative measure that enfranchised only a small minority of the mulattoes and free blacks in Saint Domingue.

The colonists were infuriated. The deputies, the members of the Colonial Committee, the Massiac Club—all forgot their former differences and joined forces to organize a united front to subvert the application of the 15 May decree. By July, the legislative powers of the colony were reinstated. Most of the colonists in France had by now returned to Saint Domingue, where they were fortified by the planters in a common front of white solidarity and white supremacy. The governor, Blanchelande, managed to postpone the arrival of the civil commissioners, and elections were held that summer for the new colonial assembly without the participation of those newly enfranchised by the 15 May law. Nearly all of the eighty-five deputies of the former Saint Marc legislature, pardoned in June by the National Assembly, had returned to the colony and were reelected.

But it was not the few hundred mulattoes and free blacks included in the law that the planters feared. The entire social and economic structure of the colony, slavery itself, and the precious fortunes tied to it were at stake. To allow even a few mulattoes to vote would immediately open the whole question of those mulattoes still in slavery or born of only one free parent, and from there the abolition of slavery would be but one step away. The new colonial assembly opened at Léogane on 1 August, and within a fortnight the black revolution had begun.

The slaves had depended neither upon France nor upon the success or failure of the mulatto struggle. They were organizing for something that did not figure in any of the political debates, either in France or in the colony. But for the past three years they had witnessed the events, the agitation, the revolutionary and counterrevolutionary ferment that was throwing the colony into disarray. When news of the French Revolution reached the colony, slaves heard talk of liberty and equality, and they interpreted these ideals in their own way. Domestics listened to their masters argue over independence, while they perfunctorily served them their meals and drinks. Some had even traveled to France with masters who could not do without their servants. They were exposed to new ideas, to the principles upon which that revolution was being built, and they carried this experience back with them. In the ports, newly arrived French soldiers brought news of the recent events in France and spoke of them with great enthusiasm. Sailors aboard the merchant ships did the same as they worked side by side with the slaves, loading and unloading cargo in the harbors. [19]

NEWS OF OTHER REBEL + DROUGHT

News had arrived in the fall of 1789 of a slave uprising in Martinique. At the end of that year, plantations everywhere in Saint Domingue were afflicted by a devastating drought; the hardest hit by the famine were the slaves, left largely to shift for themselves to find food. Marronage seemed to be increasing, becoming potentially more dangerous, and slaves far more audacious.[20] On some plantations (as we have seen in Chapter 2), an entire *atelier* had deserted along with its *commandeur*, himself a slave. In October of that year, one plantation manager wrote the owner that his slaves were beginning to let things go to their heads: "The sight of the cockade is giving them ideas, and even more, the news from France which is flaunted indiscreetly." Another observer wrote: "Many [slaves] imagine that the king has granted their freedom and that it is their master who does not want to consent to it. Your plantation [in Jean-Rabel] has subjects who can only be restrained by fear of punishments. . . . One must lend a deaf ear and pretend not to hear what they are saying to avoid a general uprising."[21] They saw the whites lynch and torture mulattoes, free blacks, and white sympathizers alike, for daring to advocate the civil rights of free persons of color. When Ogé and his followers had taken up arms to secure those rights, many slaves had come spontaneously to offer their aid. They witnessed once again the merciless justice of the white authorities.

REBEL

MET IN WOODS ALOT

During the months of June and July, just preceding the massive outbreak of violence in the North, the slaves of several plantations in the Cul-de-Sac plain near Port-au-Prince left the fields and began holding frequent gatherings in the woods. Those of the Fortin-Bellantien plantation near Croix-des-Bouquets had assassinated their *commandeur*, whom they considered overly loyal to the whites and therefore dangerously untrustworthy. As was so often the case, the predispositions of the *commandeur* toward rebellion on the one hand, or loyalty on the other, proved central in the launching of a conspiracy. And if he could not be trusted in the eyes of the conspirators, he would have to be eliminated, lest he turn other slaves against them. So once the Fortin-Bellantien conspirators had rid themselves of their dangerous superior, they

LEADER WAS PICKED CAREFULLY

deserted en masse during the night to assemble in the woods. At the same time, groups of slaves from five nearby plantations, numbering roughly fifty in all, and this time including a *commandeur*, in addition to the entire *ateliers* of two other plantations, were reported maroon. The following day, as the *maréchaussée* arrived, accompanied by neighboring planters to break up the meetings, the slaves resisted with unrestrained courage and determination. Thirteen were captured and a number of others mortally wounded. Some sixty of them, armed with rifles and machetes, had retreated to the coast but were pursued by the *maréchaussée*, who took one of their leaders and killed a second. Eight other leaders had been executed, as well; two of them were broken alive on a scaffold, and six were hanged.

The planters and the authorities believed that an example such as this one would bring the rest of the slaves, who had dispersed, back to the masters from whom they would presumably seek pardon and thereby avoid the tragic fate of their leaders. But, as one colonist wrote, "We have not yet seen any of them come forward." [22]

The planters were forced to increase their surveillance over the slaves, organize nightly patrols, and search the slave cabins for arms. In spite of these measures, slaves managed to communicate and consort with those of other plantations in the districts. The domestic slaves, largely outside the plantation itself, were in continual contact with whites and consequently in the best position to receive and disseminate information. At the market place, in the port towns, at the crossroads, they spoke with one another, exchanged ideas and information, overheard the discussions and arguments of the whites, and communicated what they knew, either directly or through contacts, to their black compatriots in the fields.

The whole structure of colonial Saint Domingue was rapidly being transformed. The traditional antagonisms and hostilities between the planters and the bureaucracy had reached their peak and were now fought out in the open. The planters, as a class, were recklessly divided amongst themselves in the early days of 1788. They wanted certain reforms, but were uncertain as to how they should proceed. It was a small minority of the planters of the North that took the lead and pushed for representation in France, and it was the same planters whose troops joined the counterrevolutionary royalist forces a year later to smash the patriot legislature at Saint Marc. The "small" whites had deserted their former allies of convenience, the royal bureaucrats, and now sided with the planters to lynch and kill mulattoes and free blacks, whose aspirations and energies were unleashed by a revolution the planters themselves had begun and could no longer control.

The colony had never been in such a state of social and administrative chaos. Not only was the old colonial regime shattered to pieces, the governor and the bureaucracy stripped of their former powers, the prerogatives of the merchant bourgeoisie dismantled with the opening of the ports, but the new regime had no centralized power. Authority shifted regionally back and forth between the Provincial Assembly of the North and the Colonial Assembly in the West, each attempting to concentrate control in its own hands and in its own interests.

Planters were far too preoccupied with these problems to worry much about the effects their words and actions might have upon their slaves. They had come to Saint Domingue to make a fortune out of slavery, and they saw no reason for things to change. Although a few might have foreseen the dangers that lay ahead, most generally assumed that slavery was as inviolable as it was enduring. It had lasted for over two hundred years. Slave rebellions had occurred in the past, and marronage had been a constant plague. But the revolts were always isolated affairs, and maroon bands were invariably defeated along with their leaders. For the planters, there was no reason to believe that slave activity was any different from what it had been in the past.

They would soon learn, but only by the raging flames that within hours reduced their magnificent plantations to ashes, how wrong they were.

PART TWO
Revolts of 1791

4

Slaves in the North

The insurrection that broke out in August 1791 was by no means a spontaneous or unmediated event. The slaves in the North had been consciously preparing and organizing themselves for weeks before that fateful night of 22 August, which marked the beginning of the end of one of the greatest wealth-producing slave colonies the world had ever known—the pearl of the Antilles, as it was extravagantly called.

On Sundays, slave representatives from the major plantations would meet clandestinely to lay the plans for the general insurrection, but it was on the night of the fourteenth, one week before the actual outbreak, that the final scheme was drawn up and the instructions given out. Numbering some two hundred in all, consisting of "two delegates each from all the plantations of Port-Margot, Limbé, Acul, Petite-Anse, Limonade, Plaine du Nord, Quartier-Morin, Morne-Rouge, etc., etc." covering the entire central region of the North Province, they were assembled to fix the date for the revolt that had been in the planning for some time.[1] They met at the Lenormand de Mézy plantation in Morne-Rouge, and all of the delegates were upper-strata slaves in whom the masters had placed their confidence, most of them *commandeurs* whose influence and authority over the field slaves were undoubtedly considerable. Upon a given signal, the plantations would be systematically set aflame, and a generalized slave insurrection set afoot. To dissipate any hesitation or equivocation the assembled conspirators may have had, a statement was read by an unknown mulatto or quarteroon to the effect that the king and the National Assembly in France had decreed three free days per week for every slave, as well as the abolition of the whip as a form of punishment. They were told that it was the white masters and the colonial authorities who refused to consent and that royalist troops were on their way from France to execute the decree by force. The news was of course false, but it represented the nearest thing to freedom the slaves had ever known, and it served as a rallying point around which to galvanize the aspirations of the slaves, to solidify and channel these into open rebellion.

Although the majority of the delegates agreed in principle that they should await the arrival of these royalist troops, the slave representatives from some of the plantations in Limbé and Acul insisted upon instigating the war against

whites at whatever cost, with or without the troops. In the end, they
early agreed to begin the revolt that very night, but then went back on this
decision as they considered it inopportune to carry out, on the spot, a general insurrection for which the plans had been finalized only that evening.
The majority of the slaves had thus decided to wait, and the date was fixed
for the twenty-second.

The early leaders forming the core of this movement were Boukman Dutty,
Jeannot Bullet, Jean-François, and Georges Biassou. The first two, according to one source, were to take charge of the initial stages of the movement,
while Jean-François and Biassou were to take over first and second command of the insurrection once under way. Toussaint Louverture, who would
emerge as supreme leader of the revolution years later, served, inauspi-
ciously at this point, as the link between these leaders and the system,
carefully dissimulating his actual participation.[2] Although he remained on
the Bréda plantation, where he served as coachman for the manager, Bayon
de Libertas, he had by now already been a free black, or *affranchi*, for well
over a decade.[3] With a pass signed by the governor, Toussaint was thus permitted to circulate freely and to frequent other plantations; but he was also
in communication with influential elements of the royalist faction who hoped
to profit from, and who even helped stimulate, the brewing slave insurrection by invoking a common cause—the defense of the king, who had, they
rumored, granted the slaves three free days per week. Once they had used
the slave insurrection to defeat the rival patriot faction, once power was restored in royalist hands and the king securely on the throne of France, the
blacks, they no doubt believed, could then be persuaded by their leaders to
return to the plantations and be duped back into slavery. Undeniably, links
between the slave leaders and certain royalists in the early stages were important, but for the latter to have assumed that the slave insurrection would,
in the end, amount to little more than a traditional jacquerie was, in the
unmitigated context of impending revolution and imperial wars, to make a
profoundly grave mistake.[4]

Of the leaders, it was Boukman who was to give the signal for the revolt.
He had been a *commandeur* and later a coachman on the Clément plantation, among the first to go up in flames once the revolt began. While his
experience as *commandeur* provided him with certain organizational and
leadership qualities, the post as coachman no doubt enabled him to follow the ongoing political developments in the colony, as well as to facilitate
communication links and establish contacts among the slaves of different
plantations. Reputedly, Boukman was also a voodoo priest and, as such,
exercised an undisputed influence and command over his followers, who
knew him as "Zamba" Boukman. His authority was only enhanced by the
overpowering impression projected by his gigantic size.[5]

Once the conspirators had reached agreement on the date, set for the twenty-second, the accord was solemnized by a voodoo ceremony held in a thickly wooded area known as Bois-Caïman, not far from the Lenormand plantation.[6] According to most accounts, the ceremony was officiated by Boukman and a voodoo high priestess, an old African woman "with strange eyes and bristly hair," just as terrifying as her counterpart.[7] Amidst raging streaks of lightning and violent bursts of thunder, as the account goes, accompanied by high winds and the torrential rains of the storm that had broken out that night, the high priestess raised her knife to kill a sacrificial pig, the blood of which was passed round for all to partake. As she began to invoke the deities, Boukman rose to deliver an impassioned oration to the assembled slaves. It was, in essence, a call to arms:

> The Good Lord who created the sun which gives us light from above, who rouses the sea and makes the thunder roar—listen well, all of you—this god, hidden in the clouds, watches us. He sees all that the white man does. The god of the white man calls him to commit crimes; our god asks only good works of us. But this god who is so good orders revenge! He will direct our hands; he will aid us. Throw away the image of the god of the whites who thirsts for our tears and listen to the voice of liberty which speaks in the hearts of all of us. [8]

Couté la liberté li palé nan coeur nous tous: "Listen to the voice of liberty which speaks in the hearts of all of us." It was a refrain that would later recur under Boukman's leadership during the early days of the insurrection as he would exhort the insurgent slaves under his command to attack. [9]

The story of this ceremony has long since passed into legend, rendering all the more difficult the separation of actual fact from the elaborated mythology that later developed around the event.[10] Contemporary evidence is sparse; in fact, there is no mention of it at all in the archival documents that recount the conspiracy and are based largely on the testimony of a few slaves. But then, given the imperative of utmost secrecy in voodoo ceremonies, it is hardly surprising that no detailed contemporaneous accounts exist. This hardly justifies, on the other hand, dismissing the various accounts that do exist as pure historical fabrication. In fact, certain nineteenth-century Haitian family papers clearly identify one of the participants in the Bois-Caïman ceremony as Cécile Fatiman (that family member's own grandmother), a green-eyed mulatto woman with long silken black hair, the daughter of a Corsican prince and an African woman. She was herself a *mambo*, a voodoo high priestess. [11]

But in the absence of additional detailed documentation, many questions may still be raised concerning this event. Did all of the Morne-Rouge slave delegates participate in the Bois-Caïman ritual ceremony? Or conversely, were the participants in the Bois-Caïman ceremony the same individuals as those whose political views were expressed at the Morne-Rouge assembly earlier that evening? Certainly Boukman, as one of the chief leaders of the revolt and the orator who delivered the Bois-Caïman speech, would have been present at both. Here then, the often-assumed antipathy of elite creole slaves toward voodoo, and toward African-born slaves practicing it, may be brought into question as well. All or nearly all of the slave delegates were from the upper ranks of slave society usually filled by creole slaves. Cécile Fatiman, though a creole mulattress, was nonetheless a *mambo*. But was she actually the officiating priestess described quite dissimilarly in the one account as "an old negress with strange eyes and bristly hair"? As to so many questions pertaining to clandestine slave practices and activities in Saint Domingue before and during the revolution, where hard scientific evidence is intrinsically lacking, the answers will necessarily remain conjectural ones. What we can safely say, however, is first, that the Bois-Caïman ceremony did historically occur following the Morne-Rouge assembly; second, that the oration delivered was authentically Boukman's and that the ceremony was, after all, a voodoo event.

Even more important, though, is the historical significance of the 14 August assemblies, and this can be viewed on both an ideological and a political level. First, the Morne-Rouge gathering was a thoroughly organized affair and constituted in every sense a revolutionary political assembly, where issues were discussed, points of view and differing strategies presented, where a final agreement was reached, and a call to arms issued. That agreement was then confirmed and solemnized during the ritual ceremony at Bois-Caïman by a blood pact (and the symbolic drinking of the blood is mentioned in the one contemporary account of Dalmas) that committed the participants to utmost secrecy, solidarity, and a vow of revenge.[12] In this sense, voodoo provided a medium for the political organization of the slaves, as well as an ideological force, both of which contributed directly to the success of what became a virtual blitzkrieg attack on the plantations across the province.

Equally as controversial in relation to the general framework and early stages of the conspiracy is the role of marronage. Whether the August revolt was actually planned and organized in marronage, or rather by slaves in privileged positions within the plantation system, will no doubt remain a matter of dispute. What is probably closer to the truth is that the two elements worked hand in hand. Some evidence suggests that Jean-François was a maroon at the outset of the revolt and that Boukman was chronically maroon.[13] The report of the civil commissioner Roume states that "for several weeks slave delegations had assembled on Sundays to work out together the plans for this destructive project."[14] As these slave delegations all came from different plantations throughout the North, from "Port-Margot, Limbé, Acul, Petite-Anse, Limonade, Plaine du Nord, Quartier-Morin, Morne-Rouge, etc. etc.," attendance at the meetings would have necessitated some sort of fairly regular *petit* marronage, unless of course each and every one of them had a Sunday pass.[15] Even so, passes were notoriously forged by even minimally literate slaves.

On the other hand, it is known that Toussaint was in close communication with Jean-François, Biassou, and Boukman even as he remained on his plantation and did not officially join the ranks until nearly three months later. We also have the statement (referred to below) of the Desgrieux slave *commandeur* revealing that coachmen, domestics, and other trusted slaves of the surrounding plantations, in addition to the *commandeurs*, were involved in the conspiracy.[16] Or, the statement of an old Gallifet slave, Ignace, who was "distinguished from the other slaves by his exemption from any sort of work," who held the secret of the conspiracy for a long time and who had received instructions from a free black, one of those sentenced *in absentia* in the Ogé affair.[17] In fact, another of the core ringleaders was Jean-Baptiste Cap, a free black said to be possessed of substantial income and property. [18]

An incredibly vast network had been set afoot and facilitated by the interaction of several elements. These were African, as well as creole, and included the dynamics of marronage, as well as the subversive activities of *commandeurs* and of house slaves, and even a restricted segment of the free blacks (Toussaint was himself a free black), whose mobility and closer relationship to white society afforded them access to news and information on the political situation. To separate any one element from the others, as if they are by nature mutually exclusive, will invariably leave the vital questions about the revolutionary organization and capacities of these black masses perpetually unanswered.

The 14 August conspiracy was an ingenious plan, and it would have been perfect were it not for the premature activities of a few slaves in the Limbé district, who either misunderstood the final instructions or who impatiently insisted, in spite of the accord, upon beginning the revolt before the designated date. On 16 August, two days after the Morne-Rouge affair, some slaves were caught setting fire to one of the buildings on the Chabaud estate, in which the bagasse, or straw residue of the sugar cane, was stored. One of them, armed with a saber, was the *commandeur* from the Desgrieux plantation. A physical battle ensued, and, though wounded, the slave was arrested, put into irons, and interrogated. Upon questioning, he revealed that the *commandeurs*, coachmen, domestics, and other slaves whom the masters trusted from the neighboring plantations had formed a conspiracy to burn the plantations down and kill off all the whites. He named as leaders a certain number of slaves from the Desgrieux plantation, four from the Flaville plantation in Acul, and Paul, a *commandeur* on the Blin plantation in Limbé. [19]

Upon confirming the declaration of the Desgrieux *commandeur*, the municipal authorities of Limbé issued a warning of the impending danger to the planters of the district and suggested to the manager of the Flaville estate that he apprehend those of his slaves who were denounced by name. Incredulous and unsuspecting, the Flaville manager convoked his slaves and offered his own head in exchange if the denunciations of the Desgrieux *commandeur* proved true. They all categorically denied any truth to the *commandeur*'s statement, as did Paul Blin, who was also questioned and who also replied that the accusation brought against him was "false and slanderous," that, filled with gratitude for the continual benevolence of his master, one would never see him involved in plots hatched against the whites or their property. A few days later (on the twentieth) another conspirator, a mulatto slave, François, from the Chapotin estate was arrested and put to questioning for his part as accomplice to the arson committed at the Chabaud plantation. It was he who finally revealed the details of the Morne-Rouge assembly on the fourteenth.[20] The following day the cook from the Desgrieux plantation was also to be arrested as one of the named conspirators, whereupon he managed to escape and went off to warn Paul Blin; together they joined the other ringleaders to prepare "the iron and the torch" for the execution of their dreadful projects. The general insurrection broke out on the following night as scheduled. [21]

At ten o'clock, the slaves of the Flaville-Turpin estate in Acul, under the direction of one Auguste, deserted en masse to make their way to the Clément plantation, where they joined Boukman and combined their forces with the rest of the slaves there. Their numbers reinforced, they immediately set out to the Tremes estate; having narrowly missed the resident carpenter with their bullets, they took him prisoner and proceeded to the Noé plantation, where a dozen or so of these slaves had killed the refiner and his apprentice, as well as the manager. The only whites spared were the doctor and his wife, whose services they deemed might prove to be of great value to them.[22] By midnight the entire plantation was aflame, and the revolt had effectively begun.[23] The troops, by now consisting of the slaves from the Turpin-Flaville, Clément, and Noé plantations, returned with the three prisoners to the Clément estate, methodically assassinated M. Clément and his refiner, and left the prisoners there under guard. Armed with torches, guns, sabers, and whatever makeshift weapons they were able to contrive, they continued their devastation as they carried the revolt to the surrounding plantations. By six o'clock the next morning, both the Molines and Flaville plantations were totally destroyed, along with all of the white personnel; of all the plantations in the Acul district, only on two did some of the slaves refrain for the time being from participating in the revolt. [24]

From Acul, these slaves proceeded westward that same morning, the twenty-third, toward the immediately adjacent Limbé district, augmenting their forces, by now close to two thousand,[25] as they moved from plantation to plantation and established military camps on each one as they took it over. One horrified colonist wrote at this point that "one can count as many rebel camps as there were plantations."[26] Making their way into Limbé via the Saint-Michel plantation, they were immediately joined by large numbers of slaves in the district where the premature beginnings of this insurrection had been seen a week earlier. Within these few hours, the finest sugar plantations of Saint Domingue were literally devoured by flames. A resident merchant of le Cap remarked how, "like the effect of epidemical disease," the example set by slaves on one plantation communicated itself throughout the quarter of Limbé, and "in a few hours that immensely rich and flourishing country exhibited one vast scene of horror and devastation."[27] Nor was there much tolerance in these crucial hours for slaves, and especially *commandeurs*, who hesitated or who offered opposition, for "wherever they have committed their ravages," the writer notes, "[the practice was] to seduce or oblige the Negroes on different plantations to join their party. . . . Those who discovered a reluctance or [who] refused to follow and assist in their designs [if they could not escape] were cut to pieces."[28]

Continuing westward, the slaves attacked Port-Margot in the early evening of the twenty-fourth, hitting at least four plantations, and by the twenty-fifth the entire plain of this district had been decimated. The slaves took care to destroy, as they did from the very beginning and would continue to do throughout the first weeks of the revolution, not only the cane fields, but also the manufacturing installations, sugar mills, tools and other farm equipment, storage bins, and slave quarters; in short, every material manifestation of their existence under slavery and its means of exploitation. Insufficiently armed and totally unprepared, the planters could do little to oppose the rebels, and nothing to stop the fires that lasted for three days. The residents of Port-Margot had believed for a long time that their slaves had had no part in the revolt, "but almost all the *ateliers* in the lower quarter ended up participating in it."[29] Coordinating their forces with insurgent slaves of the plantations situated in the hills and mountainous region bordering on Limbé and Plaisance, they completed their near-total destruction of the parish, leaving only the central area intact.[30]

As these slaves attempted to penetrate Plaisance on the twenty-fifth, they met with armed resistance, the first they had encountered, from a group of inhabitants who managed to drive them back into the Limbé plain, whereupon they divided up and returned by two different routes the following day.[31] Having terrorized the inhabitants upon their reentry, having pillaged and then burned dozens of plantations, they took possession of the Ravine Champagne, where they set up military outposts and fortified their troops.

Here, they held out for over three weeks while the planters, disorganized and
badly armed, having already suffered serious casualties, awaited aid from
the neighboring parishes. Yet whatever aid the whites managed to muster
remained insufficient, for when strategically encircled or militarily overpowered, the slaves would disband and retreat into the mountains, only to attack
again at different points with replenished and reorganized troops. [32]

At the very moment that these slaves were carrying out their depreda-
tions and defending their positions to the west of Acul, which appeared to
have been the center, or hub, from which the revolt would spread in all
directions, slaves in the parishes to the east rose, torch in hand, with equal
coordination and purpose. The movement of the revolt was indeed advancing
like wildfire, and within these first few days, from the twenty-second to the
twenty-fifth, the plantations of the Petite-Anse, Quartier-Morin, and Plaine
du Nord parishes surrounding le Cap, as well as those of Limonade, all to the
east of Acul, went up in flames as swiftly and as methodically as had those to
the west.[33] The slaves on one of the Gallifet estates in Petite-Anse, however,
had prematurely begun to revolt either on the twentieth or the twenty-first
by attempting to assassinate the manager, M. Mossut.[34] That it was on the
smallest of the three, on La Gossette, that this incident occurred is hardly
surprising. Of Gallifet's three sugar plantations, it was here that the slaves'
conditions were harshest;[35] in fact, two years earlier, in 1789, twenty of these
slaves had organized a "strike," or work stoppage, in the form of collective
marronage, by remaining in the woods for two months in order to have the
commandeur removed.[36] The account of the incidents from 20 to 24 August,
presented by Dalmas, offers a small glimpse at some of the logistical difficulties involved in actually carrying through and strategically coordinating
each part of the revolt. Particular circumstances over which the slaves had
no control, such as the presence of key white personnel on the specified day,
or other factors, like the degree of accord or dissidence between the *commandeur* and the slaves, or the role of the domestics, or simply the degree
of impatience among the slaves, varied from one plantation to another.

For a reason that is unclear, the slaves at La Gossette had decided to
begin before those in Limbé and Acul, and some twenty of them (no doubt
some of the same who had deserted in protest in 1789) attempted to kill
the manager during the night of his return from le Cap on the twentieth or
twenty-first. It was also on the twentieth and twenty-first that two of the key
conspirators, the slave François and the Desgrieux cook, were arrested in
Limbé, and while the latter got away, François was taken to le Cap, put to
question, and revealed a major conspiracy afoot. The La Gossette slaves, if
they had gotten word of the arrests, may have deemed it unsafe to wait any
longer. Whatever the case, their attempt on M. Mossut's life was unsuccessful, and the *procureur*, M. Odeluc, along with several other whites from the

main plantation, came to investigate. The *commandeur*, Blaise, who was the instigator of the assassination attempt, had already fled to warn the other leaders on the main plantation, La Grande Place, for when Odeluc returned there later that night, he found the gate wide open and the lock broken: "It was the work of the leader of the revolt who, seeing that the attempt at La Gossette had failed, ran with all his might to hold off the other conspirators." Several fires had, however, already broken out in the immediate area. The Gallifet slaves did not move until Boukman's band, or a section of it, arrived from Limbé on the twenty-fourth. Dalmas relates that, on the night of the twenty-third, the rebel bands, "leaving the Plaine du Nord parish behind them," entered Petite-Anse and began their attack, not on the Gallifet, but on the Choiseuil plantation. From there they advanced on the Pères de la Charité, Bongars, and Clericy plantations, killing the managers and setting the bagasse sheds ablaze, after which they entered the Quartier-Morin parish. Here, according to Dalmas, they met with some resistance from several *ateliers* who were opposed to the revolt, and then retreated en masse to La Gossette. It was here that Odeluc had concentrated the few forces of whites available who, upon sight of the band, fled, leaving Odeluc prey to his own assassin, his trusted coachman, Philibert. As Odeluc pleaded for his life and reminded Philibert that he had always been kind to him, the coachman replied: "That is true, but I have promised to kill you," and then did so.[37] By the twenty-fourth, the insurgents had already established themselves at Gallifet to form a major military camp.[38] Effectually, on the twenty-fourth, as two deputies who had hastily been dispatched by Governor Blanchelande to solicit military aid from the United States prepared to sail, "the village of Petite-Anse had [already] been destroyed, and the light of the flames was visible in the night in the town."[39]

Earlier that day, while the insurgents had begun to penetrate Quartier-Morin, a battalion of citizen-volunteers set out around noon to contain them. While Dalmas claimed, on the one hand, that the slaves of Quartier-Morin "displayed as much disdain and horror toward the rebels as they did zeal and attachment for their masters" and pushed them back,[40] a participant in the volunteer battalion provides quite a different picture. He writes, on the twenty-fourth:

> Having arrived at the Quartier-Morin, which had yet received no injury, we saw the fire upon the plantation Choiseuil [the other one being in Petite-Anse], which is at the foot of Morin. We ran on towards the place, at the rate of three leagues in two hours. We were made to perform bad manoeuvres; our commander got drunk, and 5 or 600 negroes who were there got clear by flight. Arrived at the plantation we found the overseer killed, his body mangled, and marks of teeth on several parts. A few negroes remained with about 40 negro women; we killed 8 or 10 of the number and the remainder got off.[41]

The following day, the twenty-fifth, he writes that all, or nearly all, was ablaze in the parish.[42] On four plantations (perhaps those to which Dalmas referred) the slaves did not take part, but, the observer informs, in less than two weeks they "who hitherto had remained quiet, yesterday [5 September] revolted, in the engagement at Petite-Anse, and joined the body of insurgents."[43]

What these two apparently contradictory accounts appear to indicate, then, is the dispersion of the insurgents into diverse bands that must have struck several places at once upon their entry into the parish on the twenty-fourth. At a few plantations, they were pushed back by recalcitrant slaves, while at others, such as Choiseuil, where they had amassed some five to six hundred cohorts, they obviously enjoyed the complicity of the *ateliers*. In fact, this seems to have been the general pattern of the revolt from the beginning, as the one or two thousand that they were on the first day split into bands to attack the designated plantations, automatically increasing their numbers as well as their strategic superiority. By midnight, the conflagration had already spread to neighboring Limonade, and almost simultaneously, on the twenty-fifth, the Plaine du Nord parish was hit. In this latter parish, situated directly between Acul and Petite-Anse (and apparently circumvented on the twenty-fourth), rebel slaves arrived at the Robillard plantation and, joined by most of Robillard's *atelier*, began by assassinating the *commandeur*, who had refused to take part in the rebellion. What followed was a scene typical of those produced on plantation after plantation during these first days of insurrection. The rebels set fire to Robillard's three bagasse sheds, as well as the boiler house, the curing house, the mill house, and all of the cane fields. Thirteen of his boilers had been sledged to pieces, along with the rest of the sugar manufacturing equipment, including the mill. In addition to Robillard's own house, they burned down the lodgings of the cooper, the carpenter, and the *commandeur* whom they had just killed. "In a word," wrote Robillard, "all that was left of my property was part of the shed for the hand trucks which the brigands spared along with two large tables to take their meals. Everything, all the other buildings, all my furniture, as well, were totally consumed by flames." And once they had achieved their destruction, they set up a military camp, having spared their own quarters for the purpose.[44]

What appears to emerge from these accounts, then, is a brilliantly organized and strategically maneuvered plan of revolt that, had it succeeded in its entirety, conceivably would have enabled the slaves to very rapidly take possession of the entire North Province. For within three days, by the twenty-fifth, once all of the major parishes concentrated in the upper North Plain region had been hit and communication links between them severed,[45] a junction was to take place between insurgent bands from these areas surrounding le Cap and fellow rebels in the capital. (See Map 2.)

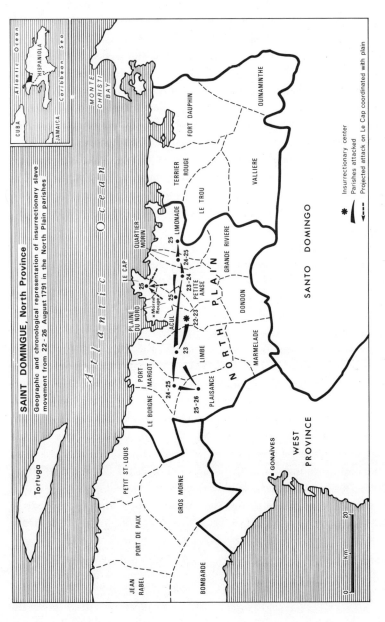

Map 2. *Saint Domingue, North Province:*
Geographic and chronological representation of insurrectionary slave
movement, 22–26 August 1791.
(Map by Lucien J. Goupil.)

The very first rumors of a plan to burn the capital were uncovered on the twenty-second, immediately prior to the outbreak of violence in Acul and Limbé. Writing to the minister of the marine a little over a week after the insurrection began, Blanchelande relates that, having been invited by the Provincial Assembly of the North on the twenty-second to hear the declarations of various persons arrested the day before, "I was convinced that a conspiracy had been formed, in particular against the city of le Cap, without being able to determine precisely whether it was fomented by whites, mulattoes, or free blacks, or, even yet, by the slaves."[46] Then, referring to the sequence of events as they did in part unfold, Blanchelande goes on to say, "There was some talk of setting fire, on the night of that day [the twenty-second], to the plantations neighboring around le Cap; fire would then break out in this city and would serve as the signal to assassinate the whites."[47] As the revolt in Acul grew awesome in dimensions, as *ateliers* from one plantation to another joined the revolt in succession, fear for the defense of le Cap, whose inhabitants included some eight to ten thousand male slaves, caused Blanchelande to recall the detachment he had sent out early on the twenty-third to aid the planters of Acul.[48] Le Cap was now the seat of colonial government and already sheltered a good number of whites who had managed to escape the vengeance and fury of their slaves. Fears of a conspiracy were confirmed as, wrote Blanchelande, "we had successively discovered and continue daily to discover plots that prove that the revolt is combined between the slaves of the city and those of the plains; we have therefore established permanent surveillance to prevent the first sign of fire here in the city which would soon develop into a general conflagration."[49]

Other indications that the burning of le Cap was an integral part of the original strategy are revealed in various letters of colonists and other residents writing at the moment the events were occurring. Mme. de Rouvray, whose husband, the marquis de Rouvray, had commanded a part of the military operations against the rebels, wrote to their son-in-law of the insurrection that had just burst open. She relates that it was because of the impatience of the Desgrieux *atelier*, "more ferocious than the others," and which began to revolt several days before the intended date, that the measures conceived by the others "to burn le Cap, the plantations, and to massacre the whites all at the same time," were broken. The impetuous and premature activities of the Desgrieux slaves had apparently given the planters of the surrounding parishes enough time to become informed of the revolt, and, though some of them managed to escape the carnage, nothing could save their plantations from the rebel torches.[50]

From another resident we learn that, after the first plantations had been set ablaze on the twenty-fourth and a score of whites assassinated, "the rebels dispersed and then came up to set fire to the city. They have been repelled and, in spite of their rage to advance on the city, we are certain their attempts will be in vain as it is guarded by the camp at Haut du Cap, which is the only point through which the rebels can penetrate the city."[51] According to another report, after the slaves had revolted on the Chabaud plantation in Limbé, "they advanced toward le Cap, and most of the slaves on the plantations along the way joined them. . . . The rebels marched without stopping and came within two miles of le Cap; we believe they were that night already 1,500 strong."[52] A resident merchant of le Cap also states that "on the 25th, the band from Limbé advanced into this neighborhood."[53] Another writes on 26 August: "Since the 23rd every entrance to the city and every part of the neighborhood has been guarded with the greatest care. For these two days past, a camp of 300 men has been formed in the upper part of the city. The negroes are at a distance of one league, and frequently approach in numbers to bid defiance. Many of them are killed by our cannon. They, notwithstanding, come up unarmed."[54]

Finally, confirmation that the conspiracy against le Cap (coordinated with the revolt in the plains) had been scheduled for the twenty-fifth was obtained, when, because of concentrated security around le Cap, an attempt was made at the end of the month, on the thirtieth and thirty-first, to take the upper part of the city.[55] An anonymous observer, having kept a journal account of the disturbances, relates: "Yesterday [on the thirtieth] some indications of a conspiracy had been discovered; several negroes have been taken and confined, some executed. It appears that the plot is to set fire to the city in 400 houses at once, to butcher the whites, and to take the city in the night by escalade. It appears that the revolted negroes have chiefs in town and who correspond with those in the plains."[56] Referring to this discovery on 30–31 August of the renewed plot against le Cap, another writes that "thousands of these scoundrels are going to fall under the iron hand of justice."[57] One of them, sentenced to be broken on the wheel, was the free black Jean-Baptiste Cap, an organizer and key leader of the insurrection. In fact, as it was the practice of the insurgents to elect titular heads, a king and queen whom "they treated with great respect" in each quarter that they occupied, Jean-Baptiste Cap had been chosen as "King of Limbé and Port-Margot."[58] It was as he incited the slaves on one plantation immediately outside the city of le Cap to revolt that he was denounced by its *commandeur*, seized, and interrogated, no doubt under severe physical duress.[59] From him the authorities learned that "in the night of the 25th [August] all the negroes in the plain were to attack the city in different parts; to be seconded by the negroes in the city, who were to set fire to it in several parts at once."[60] He further declared that "in every workshop in the city there were negroes concerned in the plot."[61] For logistical reasons and tightened security around the capital, it seems the plan had been postponed to the end of August.

It was on this occasion, the first of three unsuccessful attempts to capture le Cap,[62] that Boukman was cited leading the band of insurgents, by now close to fifteen thousand, that had come to lay siege to the capital.[63] The citing of Boukman is referred to in an account compiled from letters written by the nuns of the Communauté des Religieuses Filles de Notre-Dame du Cap-Français (an educational order for young girls in the colony) as they witnessed, from the window of their convent, the events that were occurring.[64] They spoke of a former pupil, a mulattress later known as the princess Améthyste, head of a company of Amazons; she had been initiated into the voodoo cult and had inveigled a good number of her companions to follow.[65] They would leave the convent at night to participate in ritual dances to the African chant, the words of which, inexplicable to the whites, were (as we saw earlier) an invocation to the rainbow serpent, Mbumba, for protection against the evil powers of the "white man," the "slavetraders," and the "witches."[66] The schoolmistresses noticed a certain agitation among the Negresses that increased particularly after they sang this round, adopted to the exclusion of all others. The reason for this agitation, as Adolphe Cabon remarks in his comments on the narrative, became clear when "at the end of August 1791, le Cap faced the uprising of Boukman, the fires on the plantations at the edge of the city, and the devastation of the plain. From the convent, the nuns saw the insurgents at the gates of le Cap, heard their death cries, witnessed their dances; they felt the terror that had struck the soul of the whites upon hearing of the massacres and destruction that were carried out in the countryside."[67] The narrator of the account relates that the king of the voodoo cult had just declared war on the colonists; they were marching to the assault on the cities and had come to lay siege to le Cap: "Amidst the rebels was Zamba Boukman inciting them to attack the barracks and the convent, which lodged a good number of young girls and other colonists." Then, in what amounts to a paraphrase of Boukman's Bois-Caïman oration, the writer notes how Boukman, "in his poetic improvisations, reminded the insurgents that the whites were damned by God because they were the oppressors of the slaves, whom they crushed without pity, and [how] he ended each refrain with these words: '*Couté la liberté li palé coeur nous tous.*' "[68]

The relationship between voodoo and the insurrection, or the spirit of insurrection, is certainly not a gratuitous one, nor is it, on the other hand, entirely intangible. The "Eh! eh! Mbumba" voodoo invocation dated back to at least the mid–eighteenth century in colonial Saint Domingue, when, as part of the initiation ceremony for a neophyte, it was a call for protection against the dreaded forces of those who had enslaved them and, as such, a form of cultural and spiritual protest against the horrors of their New World environment. On the eve of the slave insurrection, however, in the midst of what would be a difficult and dangerous liberation struggle to actually rid themselves of their enslavers, the incantation certainly must have taken on a more specific, a more political if still fetishistic, meaning, for the individual rebel would need now, more than ever before, a great deal of protection and, perhaps even more, luck in the annihilative endeavors that lay ahead. Similarly, Boukman's Bois-Caïman oration—by no means a voodoo incantation in its strictest sense—may nonetheless have been an exhortation for the slaves to rely on the governing forces of the Supreme Being found within nearly all African animistic religions, as opposed to the "false" Christian God of the whites. In other words, they must draw from within themselves, from their own beliefs, and their belief in themselves, for success.

Though the colonists managed to spare le Cap from destruction by the rebel armies, there was nothing they could do to save the plantations. One colonist wrote from le Cap: "We had learned . . . that a large attack was afoot, but how could we ever have known that there reigned among these men, so numerous and formerly so passive, such a concerted accord that everything was carried out exactly as was declared?"[69] Another wrote that "the revolt had been too sudden, too vast and too well-planned for it to seem possible to stop it or even to moderate its ravages."[70] The several frantic dispatches that were sent off to Jamaica, Cuba, Santo Domingo, and the United States for military aid were, with the single exception of a plea for assistance from a few American ships and crew at harbor, to no avail.[71] Finally, they accepted the offer of a body of mulattoes and free blacks in le Cap to take up arms and assist the whites in fighting the slaves. Within eight days, the slaves had devastated seven parishes and completely destroyed 184 sugar plantations throughout the northern province; in less than one month, the count rose to over 200, to which would be added nearly 1,200 coffee plantations.[72] An early estimate placed the loss in productive value for the sugar plantations alone at nearly forty million livres.[73] By September, all of the plantations within fifty miles either side of le Cap had been reduced to ashes and smoke; twenty-three of the twenty-seven parishes were in ruins, and the other four would fall in a matter of days.[74]

If during the first few days of the revolt the slaves were roughly ten to fifteen hundred strong, perhaps even two thousand by one account dated 23 August, their numbers continued to swell with astonishing rapidity as they were joined by masses of slaves that deserted or were otherwise swept from their plantations, one after another, throughout the countryside.[75] On 24–25 August, by the time de Touzard, commander of the local militia, arrived at the Dufour and Latour plantations in Acul, where the slaves appeared to have concentrated a part of their forces just two days after the revolt began, their numbers here had already reached three to four thousand.[76] Indeed, by a report of the twenty-seventh, "they are now reckoned ten thousand strong, divided into three armies, of whom seven or eight hundred are on horse-

back, and tolerably well armed; the remainder are almost without arms." [77]
And though at first their losses were heavy by conventional standards, "their
numbers," wrote one colonist, "unfortunately increase one hundred fold in
proportion." [78] In less than two weeks, the original core of ten to fifteen hundred had increased over tenfold to fifteen, some claimed twenty, thousand,
one-third of them fully equipped with rifles and ammunition pilfered from
the plantations, the rest armed with sabers, knives, farm implements, and
a whole host of other contrivances that served them as weapons. Fear and
panic among the whites spread almost as rapidly as the insurrection itself,
causing some to believe that there were, at this point, as many as forty or
fifty thousand slaves in revolt, a number the rebels did, however, achieve
by late September or early October, and the number may even have reached
close to eighty thousand toward the end of November. [79] The total number of
slaves in the North Province was roughly one hundred seventy thousand. [80]

Here then, within the initial lightning stage of the insurrection, within the
first eight to ten days, were fifteen thousand slaves (a number that continued
to multiply) who had deserted their plantations, by will or by force, or by
the sheer thrust and compulsion of events purposefully set in motion by the
activities of a revolutionary core. Had this phenomenon occurred anywhere
else but revolutionary Saint Domingue, it quite reasonably would have been
called a maroon war, and under the colonial regime of Saint Domingue,
the colonists characteristically would have designated these slave troops as
marauding, ravaging maroon bands with their chosen leaders. But if the maroon wars that broke out in Jamaica and elsewhere had occurred in a context
of revolution, had they assumed the same magnitude and degree of political complexity, the circuitous question of whether the slaves were maroons
or revolutionary rebels, or some combination of both, would no doubt have
played its role in the historiography of slave rebellion in these plantation
societies as well. It should be sufficient to say, as one sociologist of slavery
has so lucidly pointed out, that all armed slave rebellion necessarily takes
on a maroon dimension. [81] Here in Saint Domingue, the whole situation had
radically changed; the colonial context in which colonists could try to reassure themselves by seeing armed maroon bands as entities outside of the
plantations—troublesome, to be sure, but not enough to threaten the foundations and institutional viability of slavery—had now fallen into a million
pieces and reposed, literally, on little more than a pile of ashes.

In this whole process, caught up in the web of events that were taking
place, many slaves became maroons by deserting their plantations, perhaps
having killed the master, the overseer, or even their own *commandeur*, perhaps having set fire to a cane field or a shed. Once maroon, they then found
themselves in an irreversible position with little choice but to defend their
lives with arms. The transformation of the fugitive slave or deserter into a

hardened, armed rebel, fighting for freedom, is one that occurred, no doubt to varying degrees, within the consciousness of each individual slave; but also, this transformation was accelerated by collective rebellion in a context of revolutionary social and political upheaval.

The example of some slaves on the Vaudreuil plantation in the Plaine du Nord parish, just prior to the outbreak, may provide a small glimpse into these very elusive circumstances. Situated at Morne-Rouge, it was very near the Lenormand plantation where the 14 August conspiratorial gathering had first taken place.[82] Around the twentieth, at about the same time as a few of the Limbé conspirators were being arrested and interrogated, and just before the revolt prematurely broke out at Gallifet's estates, the *commandeur* at Vaudreuil was caught setting fire to a part of the cane field. Apparently the slaves here were divided in their support for the insurrection that was to take place. Seeing the manager in battle with the *commandeur*, some of the slaves came to the aid of the manager and caught the *commandeur*, who, according to one letter, revealed that he had been influenced by a free mulatto; but then, according to another letter, twenty-eight of the Vaudreuil slaves had also gone maroon. Three of them were captured in Limbé and revealed the conspiracy. [83]

Here one may ask whether the Vaudreuil maroons were actually involved in the revolt, as was the *commandeur*, or whether, having knowledge of the conspiracy, they ran away to flee the impending destruction. If the latter had been the case, however, there would have been no need to flee since they would have had the support of the rest of the *atelier*, as well as the protection of the manager, whom the other slaves had just saved. More likely, they were in complicity with the *commandeur*, and, as he had just been apprehended with the aid of the other slaves, their own turn undoubtedly would be next. One may also find it significant that at least three of them ran away to Limbé, where the insurrection was to break out. Once having become maroons, though, it was now only a matter of days before the other twenty-five would be swept along into the larger body of insurgent slaves as a constituent part. It is perhaps at this conjuncture that slave deserters, who in ordinary times were called maroons or fugitives (and up to this point still are by their unsuspecting masters), become, by the very nature of the circumstances, insurrectionaries, brigands, and rebels. They had in fact embarked on a collective struggle never before waged in such a manner, or on such a scale, by colonial slaves anywhere, and their activities were now inscribed within an irreversible revolutionary situation. The real significance of their movement, in the early days as well as throughout the revolution, was the profound impact of self-mobilization, of the popular organization and the obtrusive intervention of these slaves—on a massive scale—on a revolutionary process already several years in motion.

During those first weeks of revolution, the slaves destroyed the whites and their property with much the same ruthlessness and cruelty that they had suffered for so many years at the hands of their masters. The scenes of horror and bloodshed on the plantations, as whites hopelessly tried to defend themselves or, at best, to flee from the unleashed terror and rage of their former slaves, were only too reminiscent of the brutality that the slaves themselves had endured under the plantation regime. Yet as atrocious as they were, these acts of vengeance were surprisingly moderate, in the opinion of one of the best-known historians of that revolution, compared with the cold-blooded, grotesque savagery and sadistically calculated torture committed by their oppressors throughout the past.[84] These were impassioned acts of revenge, of retribution, and were relatively short-lived. [85]

Amidst the violence and fury of the August days, there were some slaves whose sense of decency and range of human understanding nevertheless stood apart from the all-consuming force of collective vengeance. A frequently cited example is that of a slave who was himself implicated in the revolt but who risked, and later lost, his own life to save those of two colonists, M. and Mme. Baillon, and their family. The slave was Paul Blin; he was, as we know, a *commandeur* and one of the original conspirators. He had also become one of the leading generals.[86] According to one account presented in the 30 November address to the National Assembly, the black nurse of M. and Mme. Baillon, who resided with their daughter and son-in-law on their plantation, warned them that there was not a minute to lose and offered to accompany them in their flight. This nurse was Paul Blin's wife, and it was she who secured the food for her master and mistress. Paul, for his part, had promised to find them a canoe, but when they came to the spot where it was to be, it turned out to be nothing more than a dilapidated skiff with neither oars nor mast, and no one to navigate it. As Paul's wife reproached him for the manner in which he fulfilled his promises, he answered that he merely provided this means of escape as a death preferable to that which the rebels had prepared for these unfortunates, and that it was the best he could do.

A somewhat different version of the account, related by Bryan Edwards, has it that the slave, Paul, after leading the Baillon couple safely into the woods, left to join the revolt and made frequent trips between the rebel camp and the white fugitives, providing them with food, a canoe, then a boat. He came back once again to lead them through the woods to Port-Margot where, after nineteen days of various hardships, they would finally be able to make their way to le Cap, and then took leave of them forever.[87] In all probability Paul Blin was present at the Morne-Rouge assembly and, had he participated in the Bois-Caïman ceremony, as well, no doubt would have committed himself to the sacred vow of vengeance so essential to the success of the revolt.[88] The remarkable sense of humanity on the part of Blin, conveyed in the Edwards account, may also be due to the influence, persuasion, and solicitations of his wife who, as a woman, led him to confront the struggle within himself—the inner struggle of any individual engaged in violent revolution—between his devotion and responsibility to the cause he had undertaken (especially as a high-ranking chief in Limbé) and his sentiments toward those near him, but who were unavoidably part of the enemy class. [89]

The uncontrolled explosions of vengeance and suppressed hatred that marked the beginning of the revolution constituted, however, only a temporary stage. Once expiated, these destructive energies were progressively channeled into military strategy, tactical maneuvers, and political alliances as the slaves gained territory and began to stabilize their positions. They had no experience in the use of military weaponry, and though their losses in the early engagements were heavy,[90] they learned quickly enough. A le Cap resident who participated in the militia observed how, "in the beginning of the insurrection, the negroes made their attacks with much irregularity and confusion, and their weapons were mostly their instruments of labor, but . . . they now come on in regular bodies, and a considerable part of them are well armed with muskets, swords, etc., which they have taken and purchased."[91] They would ransack the plantations for money, precious metals, furniture, clothing, sacks of coffee, sugar, and indigo, for any article of value they could place their hands on, in order to equip their army or to trade with the Spaniards for additional guns and ammunition. In this respect, as well as in discipline, in the opinion of the militia recruit, they were growing more formidable.[92] When they repelled an attack by the whites on one of their outposts, they would make off with cannons and other equipment left behind with which to wage their struggle.

During these first months, the blacks continued to defend their positions across the province through tactical guerilla warfare. They retreated into the hills when it was to their advantage, organized their forces for counterattacks, and often continued to burn and ravage the nearby plantations in reprisal. Previous to Governor Blanchelande's attack on one of their fortified encampments at the Gallifet and d'Agoult estates, they were a full six thousand, two-thirds of whom had secretly retreated during the night before his two columns had even arrived. Though Blanchelande reported to the minister of the marine that he had taken possession of the two plantations within an hour's time and with only one wounded, the report of a militia volunteer revealed otherwise: "It began at five in the morning and they gained possession at nine." The free mulattoes and Negroes, most of them mounted, had entered first, and as orders had been given to take no prisoners, a horrible carnage ensued. The slaughter finished at two.[93] Of the one hundred or so that Blanchelande claimed were killed in the encounter, however, no distinction was made between the women, children, and the aged, who were all indiscriminately butchered, and those insurgents actually bearing arms. In fact, the vast majority of the two thousand rebels who remained had, in their turn, also taken flight through the cane and thicket. The pillaging then began, and Blanchelande "found it impossible to continue my expedition to turn it to any greater advantage."[94] Though white troops often had the military advantage, they generally "thought it imprudent, in small bodies," in the words of one observer, "to pursue their advantage," once the insurgents had dispersed in their retreat.[95] From the Gallifet camp, the rebels had rejoined a body of eight to ten thousand encamped at Morne-Rouge just outside le Cap.[96]

One general described their tactics and sense of military organization in this way:

> They established themselves nearly everywhere on the lower cliffs and on the slopes of high mountains to be within better range of their incursions into the plains, and to keep the rear well protected. For this, they always had behind them nearly inaccessible summits or gorges that they were perfectly familiar with. They established communication links between their positions in such a way that they were able mutually to come to each other's aid whenever we partially attacked them. They have surveillance posts and designated rendezvous positions.[97]

These were maroon tactics, and they were utilized and refined in much the same way by maroons in other Caribbean colonies where resistance had turned to actual warfare.

What the slaves lacked in military hardware they compensated for with ruse and ingenuity. They camouflaged traps, fabricated poisoned arrows, feigned cease-fires to lure the enemy into ambush, disguised tree trunks as cannons, and threw obstructions of one kind or another into the roads to hamper advancing troops; in short, any means they could invent to psychologically disorient, frighten, demoralize, or otherwise generally confuse the European units in order to defend their own positions.[98] On their flag was inscribed a motto calling for death to all whites. They marched to African martial music and would begin an engagement with considerable order and firmness, crying out victory. But they would retreat in what whites could only understand as "confused precipitation."[99] To disperse a prodigious body of slaves advancing on le Cap, Blanchelande's troops had "fired three times, but without the least effect," as each man had devised for himself a kind of light mattress stuffed with cotton as a vest to prevent the bullets from penetrating, "and thus stood the fire without shewing any signs of fear," as one observer noted.[100]

When caught by their pursuers, they could convincingly invoke past affective ties with whites during the old plantation days in a plea for pardon, as did one slave who claimed to be the loving godson of his assailant's mother. Taken off-guard by these sentiments, the pursuer dismounted as the slave, meanwhile, recharged his gun, shot, and narrowly missed his opponent. Even then, he claimed he had not seen correctly and loved his godmother's son too much to kill him. But when contradicted by witnesses who had seen the entire incident, he admitted: "Master, I know that is true. It is the Devil who gets inside of this body of mine." Though his fate was sealed as he was bound to a tree to be shot, he furiously reviled his captors through laughter, song, and joke, and jeered at them in mockery. He gave the signal for his own execution with neither fear nor complaint. In the end, the contents of his pockets revealed more about the mentality, the beliefs, the unarticulated ideals, and fighting spirit of the slaves than any grandiloquent declaration their leaders might make to the colonial whites about emancipation and "liberty or death." In one of his pockets, the slave's captor relates, "we found pamphlets printed in France [claiming] the Rights of Man; in his vest pocket was a large packet of tinder and phosphate of lime. On his chest he had a little sack full of hair, herbs, bits of bone, which they call a fetish . . . and it was, no doubt, because of this amulet, that our man had the intrepidity which the philosophers call Stoicism." [101]

The slaves were organized in bands, as European armies were organized in regiments, and although interband rivalry and divisions were not uncommon, the internal discipline of each band or camp was maintained with an iron hand by the individual leaders. In the camps, the least sign of insubordination or slightest evidence of uncertainty was often met with unimaginably harsh treatment and, on occasion, even death. [102] In the first weeks, their main camps were concentrated westwardly in Limbé, Morne-Rouge, and at Gallifet in Petite-Anse. Following the Gallifet defeat in September, major strongholds had already formed, by October, in the eastward districts of Grande-Rivière and Dondon; [103] by November, Fort-Dauphin and Ouinaminthe at the eastern extremity of the province near the Spanish border, where participation of the free coloreds was particularly evident, were under rebel control. [104] It was under the military command of Jean-Baptiste Marc, a free black, seconded by Cézar, a recently emancipated free black, that they gained control of Ouinaminthe. Jean-Baptiste Marc, in particular, was described as one who ruled with the air of an army general (and who was also well known in Fort-Dauphin for thievery). [105] Through intrigue, skillful duplicity, and brilliant maneuvering, they had feigned desertion from the rebels and allied themselves with government forces under de Touzard, who graciously supplied them with as much military armament as they needed or requested, allowing them to hold complete control for over three months. De Touzard had nothing but praise for Cézar, whom he credited with having saved the entire district from the "brigands," and he promised to write the Colonial Assembly to recommend that he receive a handsome recompense for his services. Cézar absconded to Dondon, having first taken the precaution of hiding three of the best cannons in the cane fields. Within two days, he was back fighting with his black comrades in the attack on Marmelade.[106] Shortly thereafter, Jean-Baptiste Marc, having obtained replenished munitions to fight a few brigands, turned on the garrison and converged with rebel forces who took control of the district. [107]

For the time being, the blacks had allied with the counterrevolutionary royalists, a segment of the clergy, and to some extent with the mulattoes, but in none of these cases were they directed or controlled by their allies of convenience.[108] In the rebel camps in the east, where the free colored population of the North was concentrated,[109] mulattoes nearly always occupied inferior positions. Blanchelande, writing to the minister of the marine, observed that the mulattoes of le Trou and Grande-Rivière, who had joined the rebel slaves, "have no authority over them; their leaders are all chosen from among the blacks, and not one from the *gens de couleur.*"[110] A prisoner of war in Jean-François's camp at Grande-Rivière stated that, although there were many armed mulattoes amongst the black rebels, in general they were scrupulously surveyed. One of them, Desprès, had even been suspected of collaboration with the whites and of preventing the capture of Fort-Dauphin where he had resided. Biassou issued orders on 23 December to have him killed.[111] If the royalists, for their part, tacitly supported and supplied the black forces, they believed they could use the slave insurrection to destabilize the colony to their advantage, defeat the patriot faction, and restore the Ancien Régime. And when it was all over, the slaves would passively go back to their plantations as before. What they did not see was that the black insurrection had leaders and a raison d'être of its own.

The revolution had, in fact, produced hundreds of local leaders, for the most part obscure ones, slaves as well as free blacks like Jean-Baptiste Marc or Cézar, who held military posts on the plantations, organized raids, and maneuvered with France's enemies, with royalists and Spaniards, for ammunition, military supplies, and protection. Certainly the most revered of the early leaders, however, was Boukman. In November, during an attack by the Cap regiment in the Acul plain, he was killed, the first of the original leaders to fall, while defending a rebel post at Fond Bleu.[112] Upon his death, it was Jean-François and Biassou who would coordinate the activities and assume the direction of the New World's first colonial liberation struggle of its kind. Jean-François now officially assumed the rank and responsibility of general, while Biassou, as lieutenant-general, was second in command, and Jeannot in charge of the black troops in the east.

As a political leader, Jean-François was ambitious; as a general, he was

outwardly pompous and unabashedly flaunted his ego by decorating his uniform with an abundant assortment of medals and other impressive military
trinkets, not the least among them being the Cross of Saint-Louis. Yet he
was a man of exceptional intelligence for one who had spent the greater part
of his life as a slave; he was highly respected and especially well liked by
the mulattoes and free blacks under his command, as well as by the "better
subjects" among the slaves.[113] Biassou was of a far more fiery disposition.
He was, according to Madiou, a fervent voodoo adept and kept himself surrounded by *houngans*, from whom he frequently sought advice.[114] He was
impulsive and forever ready, at the first sign of personal insult or political
deception on the part of his white enemies, to take revenge on the prisoners
in his camp. He would have killed them all were it not for the judicious
interventions of Jean-François or Toussaint, who at this stage served as Biassou's secretary and as physician of the black army.[115] Jeannot, as well as
being commander in the east, had also received the title of judge, giving
him undisputed authority over the life or death of the prisoners.[116] He was
a man of insatiable vengeance who thrived on torturing the white prisoners
in as barbaric and heinous a manner as that of those masters who knew no
bounds.[117] His tyranny did not stop here, but extended equally to the blacks
under his command. Following a crushing defeat in Limbé by the combined
forces under General Blanchelande, Jeannot immediately suspected treason, and Paul Blin was the victim. Knowing that he had helped some white
masters to escape, Jeannot had him burned alive on the nefarious pretext
that he had removed the bullets from their cartridges. [118]

By November, the political situation in the colony had changed with the
arrival of the civil commissioners from France. Negotiations would soon be
under way between the rebel leaders and the French representatives. Upon
being informed of Jeannot's excesses, Jean-François, a man of humanity in
spite of his arrogance, and possessing a sense of common decency, was revolted by such atrocities. He also realized that this executioner was a danger
and a liability to their revolution; more than that, his uncontrolled barbarism could seriously jeopardize their imminent negotiations with the white
authorities. The black general had Jeannot tried and gave him a military
execution at about the same time that the whites, who had killed Boukman
in battle, cut his head off and garishly exposed it on a stake at the public
square in le Cap with the inscription: "The head of Boukman, leader of the
rebels." [119]

News of Boukman's death had in fact produced a profound effect in the
rebel camps. There the slave leaders went into mourning and ordered solemn
services to be held in honor of their deeply revered comrade.[120] But within
the ranks of the slaves, the immediate reaction was quite different; their
only wish was to assassinate, on the spot, every white prisoner to atone for

their leader's death. Finally, they turned the event to their own advantage, extolled their abilities and successes on the battlefield, derided the whites for their cowardice, and celebrated with a calenda lasting three days. [121]

A far more serious differentiation between the mentality of the mass of slave rebels and that of their chief leaders, however, evidenced itself during the period of negotiations that had brought about a temporary cease-fire, as well as a set of demands formulated by Jean-François and Biassou. It was under these circumstances that the first signs of division appeared between the aims of those who had become the official leaders of the revolution, and the aspirations of the black masses. Together they had practically annihilated an entire province; that they were fighting to free themselves can hardly be denied. But neither Jean-François nor Biassou, nor even Toussaint for that matter, knew what to do at this point. While Toussaint mediated and kept the peace within their camp, the difficult and unfortunate responsibility of officially representing the revolutionary slave masses in negotiation with French authorities fell to Jean-François.

The whole scope of the revolution, only three months under way but rapidly taking on wider and graver proportions, had gone far beyond his capacities as the political leader of a people engaged in revolutionary struggle. To negotiate the outright abolition of slavery would be absurd; no ruling class ever negotiates away the economic foundation of its own power. Jean-François knew this as well as anyone. When asked about the real causes of the insurrection by one of his white prisoners—it was M. Gros, a le Cap lawyer who had served as the general's personal secretary—Jean-François eventually answered, after brushing earlier questions aside, "that they have not taken up arms to obtain a liberty which, even if the whites chose to grant it, would be for them nothing more than a fatal and venimous gift, but at least they hoped for an amelioration of their condition." [122]

Gros published an account of his captivity shortly thereafter, in which he relates somewhat differently that, while refusing to explain himself categorically, Jean-François nevertheless gave as his reply to this question:

> It is not I who have installed myself as general over the slaves. Those who had the power to do so have invested me with this title: in taking up arms, I never claimed to be fighting for general emancipation which I know to be an illusory dream, as much in terms of France's need for the colonies as the danger involved in procuring for these uncivilized hordes a right that would become infinitely dangerous for them, and that would indubitably lead to the annihilation of the colony. [Moreover], if the owners had all stayed on their plantations, perhaps the revolution may never have occurred. [123]

Following this statement, the slave leader unleashed his animosity toward the *procureurs* and *économes*, and wanted included as a fundamental article of their demands that these men should no longer exist in Saint Domingue. [124]

In spite of his personal respect for Gros, he was nevertheless speaking to the enemy. Moreover, he knew he would eventually have to answer to the French authorities for the tremendous devastation of property and lives they had already committed. It was now an impossible situation in which the one plausible alternative may have been to blame it all on the royalists, while putting forward a reasonably limited set of demands for themselves. Under the circumstances, the best Jean-François could do was to demand, by dispatching a formal address to the Colonial Assembly with de Touzard as mediator, an unconditional amnesty for all slaves who had participated in the revolt, freedom for fifty of the leaders and several hundred of their officers, as well as an amelioration of conditions for the slaves (the abolition of the whip and the *cachot* as forms of punishment). In exchange for this, he promised to use his influence over the slaves to encourage them to return to their respective plantations and agreed to deliver the remaining prisoners, on the condition that his wife, who was held prisoner by the whites in le Cap, also be released. Although personally opposed to these limited demands, Biassou finally agreed to subscribe to them, but demanded, as well, the release of his own family. To charge Jean-François with the deliberate and cold-blooded betrayal of his people at this stage in the revolution, however, may perhaps be too premature a judgment. The events of a revolution barely three months under way, but with rapidly broadening dimensions, hardly afforded him the political experience and fortitude of character necessary to see his way through at this point. Yet someone had to do something, and Jean-François was the only one in a position to decide. [125]

Among the prominent leaders, it was now Biassou, the fiery and impassioned voodoo adept who, in his more impulsive moments, best incarnated the aspirations and mentality of the insurgent slaves. The black masses had furiously burned and ransacked the plantations for money and other necessary goods, thrusting the whites aside, retorting that "they did not give a damn about the manager or any other white, that they would take what they pleased, that they were not Ogé." [126] When they learned of the death of Boukman, they, like Biassou, had been enraged to the point of threatening to massacre all the white prisoners. [127] In the camps, the black troops and local officers, already irritated by the long delay in the Colonial Assembly's response to the address their leaders had sent, by now over two weeks past, were determined to continue the war when they learned that de Touzard, commander of the white troops at Fort-Dauphin, had broken the temporary cease-fire to attack several of their camps. But they were under strict orders to refrain from all hostilities. [128] They became increasingly suspicious of the frequent contacts Jean-François and Biassou were having with various whites and swore they would exterminate all the whites, and even their own leaders, if these men dared to come to terms with the authorities. [129] Having gotten nowhere with the Colonial Assembly, the slave leaders had now turned to the newly arrived civil commissioners to be heard. The black troops soon learned of the impending negotiations and, near one camp, had assembled themselves and "appeared ready to break by force any negotiation that would conduce their return to the plantations."[130] Of these slaves, Gros remarked that "it is useful to point out to those who are so good natured as to believe their slaves are being forcibly detained and that their [real] dispositions are peaceful ones, that, out of a hundred of these, generally speaking, if there are four whose intentions are good, it would be a lot; all of them, rather, breathe forth nothing but the total destruction of the whites."[131]

At the Gallifet camp in Grande-Rivière, the slave troops and especially their commander, Jean-Baptiste Godard, openly affirmed that the civil commissioners were representatives without any power and without a mandate, that it was not the king who had sent them, and that if they proposed peace, it was to trick them into submission before killing them all off.[132] It was not the whole truth, but it was not too far from it. Some of them even began murmuring that it was all because of the mulattoes that their leaders had entered into relations with the whites of le Cap.[133] If a few of the white prisoners tried to convince these slaves that their revolt was pure folly, that the king had never granted them three free days per week, and that only the Colonial Assembly could legislate on such matters, they pretended not to listen and said that the government would give them what they wanted or they would continue the war to the bitter end. Abbé de la Porte tried to frighten them by describing the might and power of the combined forces of France, Spain, and Britain, and all the other kingdoms of Europe that would unite to exterminate them if they did not give up their arms and go back to the plantations, but his words, as he said, went in at one ear and out at the other.[134]

The proclamation of 28 September 1791, decreed by the National Assembly of France and sanctioned by the king, granted amnesty to all free persons in Saint Domingue charged with "acts of revolution." Biassou received a copy of it and had it read to his troops, who could not have cared less. They wanted war and "*bout à blancs*"—an end to the whites. Most of all, they wanted their three free days per week, and as for the other three days, they would see about those in due course.[135] At this point Toussaint rose, demanded that the proclamation be reread, and delivered such a moving speech in creole that the slaves' attitudes suddenly changed to the point where they were willing to go back to their various plantations if that was what their leaders wanted.[136] Already Toussaint's qualities of leadership were beginning to take shape, and he knew more than anyone else what they really wanted. He had been discreetly involved in the 14 August affair from the very beginning and carefully observed all that went on before finally deciding in November to join with Biassou and Jean-François. Once the agreement was reached to surrender their prisoners, Toussaint accompanied the prisoners as escort to the bar of the Colonial Assembly.

But for the mass of armed slaves, this also meant their return to the plantations. They were now violently opposed to any settlement whatsoever with the whites, and, at the Tannerie camp along the way to the site designated for the exchange of prisoners, they besieged the delegation with sabers and threats of sending all their heads off to le Cap, swearing vehemently against peace and against their own generals.[137] "We were convinced this time of a great truth," wrote Gros, "that the slave would never return to his duties but by constraint and by his partial destruction."[138] It was the uninstructed mass of slaves, and not their leaders, who saw so clearly what was at stake, regardless of the cost. And if the price they were ready to pay was high, it was no greater than the human suffering they had already endured.

The Colonial Assembly disdainfully refused to accede to any one of their leaders' demands (except for a nominal agreement on the release of Jean-François's wife), even after the number of requested emancipations was reduced by Toussaint himself from four hundred to sixty.[139] He returned to their camp and told the slaves what they already knew. There was nothing to be gained, neither from the civil commissioners nor from the Assembly. Jean-François convoked his council, and it was unanimously decided to continue the war, to finish the destruction of what they had begun.[140]

The slaves in Jean-François's band began on 15 January by attacking and recapturing the district of Ouinaminthe. On 22–23 January, the slaves under Biassou attacked le Cap to secure ammunition and to replenish their diminished resources. It would be another two years, however, before Toussaint would emerge as the one to give clear, vigorous, and decisive direction to the profoundly felt aspirations of these slave masses who had killed their masters and burned the plantations to be free.

5

The Mulattoes and the Free Blacks

The slaves in the West and the South at this time had not, like their compatriots in the North, yet emerged as a collective force, independently organized by their own leaders and with self-defined goals and perspectives. The political situation in these two provinces was dominated, on the one hand, by the activities of the mulattoes and free blacks to obtain the civil and political rights guaranteed them by the 15 May decree and, on the other, by the attendant intensification of divisions and hostilities between the contending factions within the white ruling class. It was, ironically, in the absence of such massive slave revolt as overwhelmed the North and threatened to destroy that province's economy and social foundations, that the struggles of the various parties in the West and South became increasingly acute, rapidly turning to violence and then, inevitably, to open warfare.[1] For the slaves, neither the stakes nor the alternatives were nearly as clear as they were in the North, where insurgent blacks had taken the lead and remained in the forefront of the revolution, where the free mulattoes were comparatively few, and where some free blacks actually supported and helped organize the provincewide insurrectionary movement. In the West and South, it was a three-way war in which the whites, divided in opposing camps between the patriot autonomists and the wealthy, counterrevolutionary, conservative planters, were literally destroying themselves, and in which the free coloreds were fighting for political equality and legal ratification of their rights. None of these groups represented the interests of the slaves, but they would each in turn use slave unrest to further their own aims by enrolling the slaves, under various pretenses and promises of freedom. Out of this confusion and conflict, in which slaves participated in arms (doubtless with notions of their own), but in which they were also fighting and killing one another, they would learn soon enough that their emancipation depended ultimately upon their own efforts and the capabilities of their own leaders.

Since July, the free coloreds had been organizing meetings and assemblies in an effort to break the intransigence of the government and to secure their right to participate in the elections of that summer. The white planters, with Blanchelande on their side, had done everything in their power to sabotage the application of the May decree, and the new Colonial Assembly was,

as planned, elected without a single mulatto or free-black vote. The whites
had extolled the dangers of extending full rights of citizenship to the mulattoes and free blacks by claiming that, since civil equality would remove the
"inalterable" and "insurmountable" barrier of color separating them from
whites, it would thus destroy the buffer separating master and slave and open
the way for slaves to seek an end to their subjection, as well. The aversion
of slave rebellion and the maintenance of slavery therefore depended, they
argued, upon the continued subordination of the free coloreds. But once
slave insurrection had already broken out in the North, the mulattoes and
free blacks in the West and South, using the same justification of containing
slave rebellion, argued that only if they obtained their full rights peaceably
could the slaves in these two provinces be kept tranquil and the maintenance of slavery guaranteed.[2] So, although both the free coloreds and whites
claimed the same motive for fighting each other—to avoid slave rebellion—
the foundations of slavery, either way, reposed on thin ice.

In August, the mulattoes and free blacks held a mass political assembly
in Mirebalais, where they elected as their president and leading spokesman
Pierre Pinchinat, a man of outstanding political talent and finesse who, like
many others of his caste, had been formally educated in France.[3] A council
of forty delegates was also created with full powers to represent their claims,
either by formal address or by direct delegation, before the National Assembly in France, the king, the colonial assemblies, the governor-general and,
upon their arrival, the civil commissioners. Moreover, they swore upon the
last drop of their blood to protect the elected representatives against any
attack or harassment while exercising their functions. [4]

Upon hearing of this assembly and the position it had taken, some of
the local whites tried to incite opposition among the free persons of color
not included in the May decree. When this failed, they resorted to their
habitual tactics of intimidation and lynching to block the execution of the
law. On 11 August, the council of forty sent to Blanchelande a copy of their
constituted aims, along with a judicious and respectful letter recognizing
him as the sole legal authority in the colony, reminding him of the harsh
injustices they had already suffered, and requesting, for the peace and prosperity of the colony, that he execute the 15 May law in its entirety. On the
twenty-second, as the slaves in the North began to set their torches to the
plantations and to massacre their masters, Blanchelande sent his reply to
the mulattoes in the West. In the letter, he made clear his disapproval of
their conduct and especially of their "illicit" assembly and deliberations.
His reply further ordered them to dissolve, to return to their homes and wait
peacefully and patiently. In due time, their white benefactors would decide
upon their future condition. [5]

The anger and frustration of the mulattoes were further exacerbated by

[Handwritten marginal notes: "...ITY WOULD RUIN SLAVE-MASTER REL.S" "THREATEN TO MAKE SLAVES REVOLT" "DIDN'T CARE ABOUT SLAVES THO?"]

the additional news of violent assaults, arbitrary arrests, and killings that were being committed by the whites against their compatriots in Port-au-Prince. A general assembly was immediately called and a second letter sent to Blanchelande, this time declaring their intention to arm themselves and to take responsibility for their collective security.[6] Meanwhile, the mulattoes in Port-au-Prince had organized themselves and had remained in constant communication with those of Mirebalais, with whom they now joined forces to establish a camp in the Charbonnière mountains outside Port-au-Prince, there to devise a common plan of action.

Their military leaders were Bauvais and Riguad. Born in Port-au-Prince, Bauvais, like Pinchinat, had received the privilege of an education in France, where he spent his early years as a collegian.[7] He returned to the colony to teach until the revolution, during the course of which he served the cause of his people with a steadfast and impeccable character.[8] Rigaud, born in les Cayes in the South and educated at Bordeaux, was the most prominent of the mulatto leaders. He had learned the trade of goldsmith in France and practiced it in the colony, but his real vocation was military. He was a trained and experienced soldier, who had already proven his military capabilities as a volunteer in the French army under the Comte d'Estaing during the North American war for independence. Like Bauvais, he had fought at Savannah.[9] Now, as commander of the mulatto forces in the South, he joined with Bauvais and Pinchinat.

Lambert, a free black born in Martinique, was placed second in command of the army in the West. In addition, there were nearly three hundred slaves from the Cul-de-Sac plain known as the *Suisses*, or auxiliaries, who were incorporated into their ranks. Among these were the Fortin-Bellantien and other slaves who, in their own interests, had deserted their plantations earlier in July to form independent gatherings in the woods. Having remained in marronage after they were attacked, they now joined the mulattoes who armed them and promised them their freedom, which was their evident motive for rising in July.[10] Also among the *Suisses* were a number of black and mulatto domestic slaves recently armed by their masters to fight the *affranchis;* they also had deserted to join the confederates.[11]

In the meantime, the white patriots in Port-au-Prince were amassing their forces in armed opposition to the mulattoes. They had already launched one attack against them,[12] but were severely defeated and quickly dispersed. Now, a group of sailors, adventurers, mercenaries, and other déclassé elements, organized under the name of *flibustiers*, combined with a contingent of the national guard in Port-au-Prince and set out on 2 September with cannon and other artillery to crush the mulatto army in the Charbonnière mountains.[13] Earlier, the mulattoes had received word of the military pressures being mounted against them at Port-au-Prince and decided to move their camp beyond the Cul-de-Sac plain. As the confederate army of mulattoes, free blacks, and *Suisses* neared Croix-des-Bouquets, they were attacked by the troops from Port-au-Prince, whereupon they set fire to the Pernier plantation, blocking off any possible escape route for their aggressors, and, with a few rounds of well-aimed shots, totally decimated the enemy troops.

At this point Hanus de Jumécourt, a wealthy conservative planter at the head of a group of white royalists in Croix-des-Bouquets, proposed an alliance with the mulattoes. Jumécourt, himself a member of the former Saint Marc assembly, had deserted that party when it decided in the summer of 1790 to stage its mini-revolt and jump aboard the *Léopard* to plead its case in France. The royalists, bitterly opposed to the Saint Marc patriots who now dominated Port-au-Prince, hoped to use the support and capabilities of the mulattoes to defeat a common enemy and then reestablish the Ancien Régime. The confederates wanted neither a return to the old regime nor the continuation of the present one as it stood. Bauvais and Pinchinat had repeatedly sworn an unyielding respect for France and her laws in all their dealings with the colonial authorities; however, their one political imperative was to conquer their rights, and to do this they needed troops, arms, and allies, even if these were royalist.

On 7 September, a concordat was signed between the confederates and the two municipalities of Croix-des-Bouquets and Mirebalais. Both sides agreed to abide by the duly-sanctioned laws and decrees of the French National Assembly; the antipatriot whites therefore accepted unconditionally the execution of the 15 May legislation.[14] The municipality of Port-au-Prince, having already suffered two crushing defeats by the mulatto army— and a third with the signing of this concordat—became even more alarmed by reports of mounting insubordination among the slaves on the plantations. Several plantations around the city had already been burned, and rumors were spreading of a slave conspiracy to burn the city itself.[15] Under these circumstances, the municipality sent a commission to Croix-des-Bouquets to negotiate with the mulattoes.

On 11 September, a second concordat was signed between the confederates and Port-au-Prince which, in addition to confirming the earlier accord, went even further by guaranteeing political equality for all free persons of color, regardless of the status of their parents. So the 15 May decree would be executed in advance of its arrival in the colony. Primary electoral assemblies would be held in conformity with Article 4 of the March 1790 law. The concordat also guaranteed their right to elect deputies to the Colonial Assembly, recognized the illegality of the municipal and provincial assemblies, annulled all prohibitions and sentences rendered against them, and guaranteed freedom of the press. The confederates would remain armed until these articles were executed, but both sides would proceed to an immediate exchange of prisoners.[16] A few days later, the municipality of Saint Marc signed a similar accord with the mulattoes and free blacks.

Yet no sooner were the 11 September agreements signed than certain factions within the patriot party began to subvert them. Caradeux, commander of the national guard in the West, the Provincial Assembly, and diverse groups of white citizens in Port-au-Prince refused to acquiesce in the concordat. The Colonial Assembly, the municipality of Port-au-Prince, as well as the Provincial Assembly of the West, had already sent requests to Jamaica for military aid; shipment of the food supplies stipulated in the concordat and destined for the confederates at Croix-des-Bouquets was also blocked. Caradeux demanded as a condition for negotiation with the mulattoes and free blacks that they support his project for independence. It was an obvious trap, and the mulattoes refused.

Blanchelande, whose weak and malleable personality in politics was indeed among his most outstanding features as governor, fell prey to the pressures and manipulations of the patriots and refused to sanction the 11 September concordat. In the wake of the slave revolt sweeping the North, the Colonial Assembly had originally revoked its unconditional refusal to accept mulatto rights. Now, informed of what was happening in the West, the assembly declared it would openly oppose the 15 May decree upon its arrival. Blanchelande issued a proclamation ordering all persons of color who had taken up arms to disperse, return to thier respective districts, and help defend the common cause by putting down insurgent slaves. He ended by reminding them of the respect and obedience they owed to the militia, the national guard, and other all-white law enforcing bodies. Jumécourt publicly protested the proclamation, and Blanchelande, persuaded in the end that the maintenance of a colored armed corps may be a more effective means of preventing generalized slave insurrection, later retracted the proclamation.[17] But the entire administration of the colony was now in shambles and its government politically bankrupt, making one inept decision after another. The civil commissioners, whose job was to restore order and a proper respect for the laws of France, had not yet arrived. At this point power belonged to any group or party strong enough to seize it or, more pertinently, to obtain it through political deceit and manipulation.

By now the confederate army was nearly four thousand strong, not counting the white royalists and the several hundred *Suisses*, whose tremendous courage in battle proved to be a precious mainstay of the rebel forces.[18] Already several parishes in the South had signed similar concordats with the insurgent mulattoes of that province. The authorities in the West were all the more frightened as they received reports of the progress and devastation of the slave revolt in the North that continued to spread at an alarming pace. In the West, the slaves were becoming dangerously rebellious. Some had taken up arms in open rebellion, while others deserted to join the confederates.[19] Although the mass of the slaves had not yet entered the revolution as a collective, autonomous force, they nonetheless remained in a constant state of agitation and unrest. The free coloreds were by no means abolitionist, and it was not their avowed intention to facilitate the road to slave emancipation by provoking insurrection among the slaves. But their earlier argument that the whites' treatment of Ogé and the whole question of political equality for mulattoes and free blacks had contributed to the slave revolt in the North, now seemed to be more singularly ominous here in the West and the South.[20] Already, a contingent of the national guard had been sent to Léogane in anticipation of a possible slave uprising. Some twenty-five slaves accused of stirring up the plantations around the area had been arrested and thrown into prison. The slaves from the various plantations organized to demand their release. The municipality refused and, with the protection of the national guard, proceeded to execute the arrested slaves.[21] Toward the end of September, the Port-au-Prince authorities arbitrarily arrested and hanged a few slaves nearly every day. [22]

The whites had no alternative now but to come to terms with the mulattoes on a provincewide basis. While the patriot factions in Port-au-Prince were still maneuvering to subvert the September concordat, a commission from Croix-des-Bouquets arrived to convince the municipality of the importance of respecting the agreement it had signed. The envoys brought back only a vicious and bloodthirsty reply. Caradeux, who had been violently opposed to the concordat from the beginning, made another unsuccessful bid to the mulattoes—acceptance of their demands in exchange for acceptance of independence. When the mulattoes sent a delegation to Port-au-Prince requesting the food supplies promised them in the concordat, the soldiers, the "small" whites, and other city rabble, always ready to lynch and harass the mulattoes, rose up in the streets against them. They proposed that the municipality hang them and send the others bullets in place of bread.[23] The city was in a state of near-total anarchy.

Finally, on 17 October a meeting of the commune assembly was held at Port-au-Prince, and delegates were chosen to meet with the mulattoes to work out a new agreement. On the nineteenth, representatives of the province's fourteen parishes met with the confederates on the Damien plantation near Croix-des-Bouquets, and after three days of negotiations, both parties signed a new treaty. All of the provisions of the 11 September concordat were renewed. The local all-white police forces were to be dissolved immediately, and a new militia formed, irrespective of racial origins. Although new municipal elections would not be held until the following month, the mulattoes and free blacks could send delegates to these bodies immediately, and armed with full powers. The Provincial Assembly was to be dissolved without delay; as well, all of the parishes of the West were to recall their deputies from the Colonial Assembly and request its dissolution; two new battalions of the national guard, composed only of persons of color, were to be formed; finally, the mutually signed agreements would be sent to the National Assembly for approval and to the king for sanction.[24] The following day, the whites, mulattoes, free blacks, and the *Suisses* all marched into Port-au-Prince to celebrate the new accords with military festivities, and, to solemnize the occasion, a Te Deum was sung at the main church.

While things seemed for the moment to have reached a stage of concilia- tion and at least temporary tranquility, there remained two problems. The first was an immediate one—the *Suisses;* the second, an imminent one of which the colonists were not yet aware, was that the National Assembly in France had just passed a new law that, in light of the recent outbreaks in the colony, rescinded the 15 May decree.

As for the *Suisses*, there was no mention of them anywhere in the con- cordat. They had fought as equals alongside the mulattoes and their allies, the royalists. They had been promised their freedom and believed, as did most of the mulattoes, that the provisions of the concordat at least implic- itly included them, as well.[25] For the municipality of Port-au-Prince, the mere presence of the *Suisses* meant trouble. They had marched into Port-au- Prince as an integral part of the confederate army to join in the festivities along with everyone else; so when the slaves on some of the plantations saw their black comrades in arms pass by, their reaction nearly provoked a general uprising.[26] Slaves around this area were already agitated and, to an increasing degree, rebellious; insubordination and talk of revolt were now becoming rampant among the slaves of the city, and especially among the domestics. [27]

The white authorities of Port-au-Prince had initially considered sending the *Suisses* back into slavery on their respective plantations. Realizing, how- ever, the effect that this would have produced upon the other slaves, they maneuvered to have the *Suisses* deported from the colony and shipped to the coast of Guatemala, "where even the devil could not have survived."[28] They were to be given three months' provisions and a few tools with which to keep themselves alive. When the *Suisses* got word of this perfidious plan, a few managed to escape, but the rest, over 240, were sent off to meet their fate. Instead of taking the *Suisses* to Guatemala, whence the mulattoes could possibly have rescued them, the captain of the ship, under the pretext of bad weather, sailed to Jamaica, where he dumped them along the shore. The Jamaican government, wishing to unburden itself of all responsibility for this unwonted human cargo, sent the *Suisses* back to le Cap. When they ar- rived, the authorities in Port-au-Prince proposed to have them all sentenced to death. Finally, the Colonial Assembly had them put in chains and left them to die aboard a ship in the Môle Saint-Nicolas harbor at the western extremity of the North province. Sixty of the strongest and healthiest among the *Suisses* were brutally murdered, their heads cut off and thrown to the sea.[29] The rest died of starvation and sickness, with the exception of about twenty, who were spared and sent back by the whites to the West to convince the blacks that the mulattoes had betrayed them.

A few of the local mulatto leaders in the South had foreseen that the whites would use an affair such as this one to prejudice the blacks against them, and had already written to Pinchinat opposing, at all costs, the deportation of the *Suisses*.[30] And in general, most of the mulatto and free black leaders were opposed to the deportation of their slave allies. But their own interests were not at stake here, and the freedom of a few hundred slaves was not an issue over which they were politically prepared to reopen armed hostilities. They did, nevertheless, present numerous proposals for alternative solutions, each categorically rejected by the whites. Finally Bauvais, Pinchinat, Rigaud, and Lambert, as well, in the interest of peace and the preservation of their newly won rights under the concordat, surrendered their position. Their concession was, in the end, a grave and inexcusable mistake. The concordat had been signed by the whites as no more than a temporary measure; with no military reinforcements, they had little chance of defeating the confederate army and made a bid for time. Before long, the Provincial Assembly, Caradeux, and one Praloto, a Maltese deserter, profiteer, agitator against the mulattoes, and now head of the national guard artillery, all began maneuvering to break the treaty.

To further inflame the situation, news of a new law, the 24 September decree, had just arrived from France. The decree was pushed through the National Assembly by Barnave, the Massiac Club, and the remaining members of the old Saint Marc assembly, and rescinded that of 15 May, once again leaving the political status of the free persons of color in the hands of the colonial assemblies.[31] News of its adoption had in fact arrived just as the October concordat was concluded, and by now most of the parishes in the West had already recalled their deputies from the Provincial Assembly in anticipation of the new elections prescribed by the concordat. A few remaining members, however, refused to acquiesce and swore, as a legislative body, to remain in permanent session and to obey no other law than that of armed resistance.[32] At the same time, the situation in Port-au-Prince had taken another turn. The date for the ratification of the concordat by this municipality had been set for 21 November. On that day the vote was taken, and by noon three of the four municipal sections had voted almost unanimously in favor of ratification. This meant near-total ruin for the patriot faction, which sought only to subvert the concordat by whatever means or pretext it could find.[33]

Once the vote was known, a quarrel broke out in the streets between a black member of the confederate army, Scapin, a former drummer of the National Guard who had joined the confederates, and one of Praloto's men. To provoke the incident, the latter had insulted Scapin, who returned in kind, and the quarrel rapidly turned into a street brawl. The *maréchaussée* arrived on the spot, arrested Scapin, and took him directly to the municipal authorities, all of this in contravention of the treaty the city had just ratified.[34] The mulatto representatives vigorously protested these arbitrary and illegal procedures and provided proof that the black was, in fact, a free citizen, only to learn that he had already been tried summarily by the military and hanged from a lamp-post.[35] The mulattoes were furious, and their indignation reached the breaking point when they saw another of Praloto's men approach the town hall in front of which they were still gathered. They demanded of him an explanation for the travesty of justice that had just occurred; he lashed back with an arrogant, menacing reply and was shot down.[36] This was all the patriots needed to declare the concordat null and void and to reopen armed aggression against the mulattoes. Caradeux and Praloto lost no time in advancing their troops toward the mulatto headquarters, where they opened fire. The mulattoes were considerably outnumbered as most of them had already returned to the countryside following the October celebrations. Taken by surprise and overpowered by the whites, they were forced back into their quarters after two hours of sustained but unsuccessful defense and made their retreat through the mountains toward Croix-des-Bouquets that night.

Next morning, however, fire broke out in several parts of the city simultaneously, and particularly in the affluent commercial districts. Within a few hours, the whole of Port-au-Prince was in a state of total chaos. Praloto and his gang of profiteers plundered and ransacked the homes of rich whites as the panic-stricken occupants hurriedly fled for their lives. On the pretext that the blacks might be accessory to the conflagration, they began indiscriminately to murder black and mulatto women and children, and the few aged or infirm who still remained in the city.[37] As the fire spread swiftly from one section of the city to another, a crowd of over eighty mulatto women and children fled toward the shore, seeking shelter aboard the boats in the harbor. Praloto opened fire on them with cannons, and all would have perished were it not for the timely aid of a charitable individual who directed them along another route.[38] Port-au-Prince had become one huge scene of horror and devastation. The fires lasted nearly forty-eight hours, and within the first twenty-four, all but four of the lucrative merchant houses along the bay, rue des Capitaines, were consumed by flames. When it was over, two-thirds of the city had been completely destroyed and the value in damages and financial losses estimated at some 500 million livres. [39]

Until now, the mulattoes had acted with considerable moderation and restraint in their struggle for political rights, but this last betrayal by the patriots had broken the limits of their forbearance. Not only had they deliberately and violently subverted the concordat, but France, as well, had supplanted the 15 May decree with that of 24 September to place legislative jurisdiction over the political status of citizens back in the hands of the colonial assemblies. If the September decree was to forestall civil disorder in the colony by closing off or postponing the liberalization of rights for mulattoes and free blacks (limited as the 15 May decree was), it in fact produced the opposite effect. In the present context, with the hard-won concordat broken and the 15 May decree removed, mulattoes and free blacks were completely despoiled of any legal protection over their civil rights; as to their own physical security, they would have to depend entirely upon themselves. From this point on, it was open warfare. At Croix-des-Bouquets, where they had retreated to reorganize their forces, one of their leaders, Chanlatte, issued a call to arms. The tone was violent, filled with vengeance and rage. Anyone who wavered or hesitated to march in the defense of their cause was declared suspect and guilty of treason. The proclamation called upon all compatriots of color to gather arms, war munitions, and provisions, to unite and rally under a common banner, and to annihilate the upholders of prejudice and inequality, who for so long had caused them so much suffering.[40] They were to prepare for the siege of Port-au-Prince.

Following the shock of the 22 November incidents in Port-au-Prince, the mulattoes and free blacks of Jacmel, who had remained on good terms with the whites since the concordat, now began organizing themselves in armed defense, as well, whereupon the whites attacked and drove them out of the city. In Léogane, the mulattoes and their royalist allies had already taken over control of the city's government when Rigaud marched through from the South to join with Bauvais and Pinchinat at Croix-des-Bouquets.

Parallel to and simultaneous with these movements was that of Romaine Rivière, a free black or *griffe* (offspring of a mulatto and a black) of Spanish origin.[41] He had organized in armed rebellion a considerable number of slaves from the area surrounding Léogane and Jacmel, where insurrectionary currents had already emerged on several plantations. It was, according to one contemporary account, on his own plantation at Trou Coffy, in a nearly inaccessible mountain retreat near Léogane, that they established their military camp.[42] He appeared to be a shaman. His cult, however, was as dubious as it was bizarre. Having set up quarters in an abandoned church, he preached mass before an inverted cross and, saber in hand, instructed the slaves that God was black and that the whites all had to be killed.[43] He promised them their freedom, indeed, told them the king had already freed them, but that the masters refused to acquiesce. He guaranteed them certain victory over their enemies, from whose bullets they would be protected. One source even claimed that his real intention, once the whites were defeated, was to become king of Saint Domingue.[44] He called himself Romaine-la-prophétesse, claimed to be inspired by the Holy Spirit and in direct communication with the Virgin Mary, his godmother, who answered his solicitations in writing.[45] He was, nonetheless, married to a mulattress and was a "respectable" father of two children.

A self-styled prophet who also practiced herb medicine, he no doubt was seen in the eyes of many a slave to be endowed with some sort of supernatural power. Yet in all of the documentation surrounding these events, not one reference to this leader can be found that even vaguely suggests genuine African voodoo practices, unless his were in some way peculiar to cults in the Spanish colonies. It is possible that he adopted a shamanistic pretense to reinforce his influence and augment his numbers. This, in any event, was the opinion of the civil commissioner Saint-Léger.[46] And it is true, as a leader of slave resistance, his influence over his following was as undisputed as that of any voodoo leader using the rallying powers of religion for political ends. As a free black, an *homme de couleur libre*, however, he certainly represented a far left-wing fringe that would eventually jeopardize the credibility of his fellow confederates of Léogane and Jacmel, who had formed an alliance with him, causing them later to break off their ties with Romaine. Whatever his personal motives, the overall impact of Romaine's movement resulted in a total destabilization of the slave population in this region and, worse, in the arming and enrolling of slaves in a war against their masters.

Since September, he and his band had terrorized the planters of the entire region between Léogane and Jacmel. Periodically descending from their well-situated mountain retreat at Trou Coffy, they raided, pillaged, and ransacked the nearby plantations for additional provisions and recruits, killed off the masters and other white personnel, reminded the slaves on the plantations that the king had freed them, and incited them, by armed force if necessary, to join their band, rapidly approaching several thousand in number.[47] A number of devastating attacks were launched against the city of Jacmel itself, one of these reportedly involving some thirteen thousand, as Romaine and his army of slaves joined forces with the mulattoes who had been driven out of there by force earlier in November.[48] Romaine and his troops, continually increasing in numbers and now allied, as well, with the mulatto and free-black confederates of Léogane, seized control of this city and the outlying areas under its jurisdiction. Villars, a member of the royalist faction, was named mayor, and on 31 December a peace treaty was signed with the whites who, having already suffered tremendous losses, could no longer sustain even minimal resistance. By virtue of this treaty, wrote one Léogane resident, "we have recognized [Romaine] as commander of all the assembled citizens. In this capacity, he issues orders to all whites and persons of color . . . , and it is by virtue of his orders alone that the slaves work and are led to abandon their masters' plantations to join the camp that he established near Jacmel." [49]

Under cover of the treaty, Romaine and his troops in fact continued their subversive activities virtually unopposed, spreading insurrection throughout the countryside from one plantation to the next. They would gain proselytes by liberating those slaves detained in prison or condemned by their masters to chains, and by threatening to kill, and sometimes even killing, those slaves who would remain loyal to their masters.[50] The white residents of Léogane had all been disarmed and were now virtual prisoners. During the raids on the plantations, the rebels had seized horses, mules, cows, and whatever other work animals they could lay their hands on, while sabotaging sugar mills and plantation equipment. Production had ceased; all communication and transportation routes were blocked off, and the port closed. In addition, the whites were required to send munitions, clothing, and food supplies to Camp Bizoton, near Port-au-Prince, where Riguad and his army were stationed. The city was helpless, and famine now began to take its toll. The civil commissioners having finally arrived at the end of November, the citizens of Léogane, despite the blacks, did manage to get a petition through to Saint-Léger with a desperate plea for aid. He transmitted the petition to the Provincial Assembly, which replied, adding derision to its habitual condescension, that surely the commissioner's wisdom would provide him with the means which the Assembly lacked![51]

Such was the Saint Domingue to which the civil commissioners, the official representatives of France and the National Assembly, were to restore some semblance of order and tranquility. Stripped of all effective authority by the colonial and provincial assemblies which jealously concentrated power in their own hands, the commissioners were reduced to little more than titular ambassadors from the mother country. By the time they arrived, not only had insurgent slaves destroyed and taken control of most of the North, the concordats had been broken, Port-au-Prince reduced to ashes, and the struggle of the mulattoes and free blacks for political equality pushed forward into open warfare, in which slaves in the West and South were now participating, as well. And so with no effectual opposition, Romaine and his allies maintained control of Léogane and the surrounding region until the following spring, during which time the slaves continued to desert in alarming numbers. By February, not a single white was left on the plantations in the area. [52]

In the South, the struggle of the mulattoes and free blacks had been co-ordinated and integrally linked with that of their compatriots in the rest of the colony from the very early beginnings, in 1788–89, of the movement for political equality, and subsequent events in 1791 followed a roughly parallel course. With the news of the first concordat at Croix-des-Bouquets in September, the mulattoes and free blacks of les Cayes and Torbeck, in the South, demanded of the municipal authorities a similar treaty to implement and safeguard the rights accorded them by the 15 May decree; in the event of a refusal they threatened to provoke a general slave insurrection.[53] Fearing a repetition of the troubles that beset the West, the two municipalities acquiesced, and a number of others followed suit. By November, the Provincial Assembly of the South had accepted a provincewide concordat modeled on the one in the West, a concordat which for the whites was merely a temporary agreement signed out of fear, and one that they had few intentions of keeping.[54] They needed a mere pretext to break it, and when, as in the West, a quarrel broke out between a white and a mulatto in les Cayes, the whites recommenced their traditional hostilities and aggression against the mulattoes, forcing them to leave the city. They retreated en masse to the Prou plantation, owned by a free mulatto, where they formed a camp in the mountainous region behind the Plaine-du-Fond. From there they marched on to Saint Louis, joined with the mulattoes and free blacks of Cavaillon and Saint Louis d'Aquin, disarmed the whites, and took over the city of Saint Louis.[55] Here they learned of the November events at Port-au-Prince and of the massacres committed by Praloto and his party against their comrades of color. At Aquin, Rigaud's brother issued a call to arms. Like the proclamation of Chanlatte in the West, it called for vengeance. In spite of the recent concordat, there was no security to be found anywhere. The proclamation urged mulattoes and free blacks to leave the cities and, at the least sign of aggression, to arm and organize themselves, to kill, pillage, and burn if need be. They must fly in aid to the cause of their slaughtered brothers. [56]

If anything, hostilities between the free coloreds and the whites in the South tended to assume a degree of rapacity that was at least partially attenuated in the West by the counterbalancing influence of wealthy conservative whites, allied in convenience with the free coloreds against patriot machinations. In the South, as Robert Stein has shown, the relative absence of a large class of wealthy white planters precluded the possibility of an *affranchi*-royalist alliance as had been helpful in the West in bringing about the concordats. Lacking this "moderating" *grand blanc* element, then, the South witnessed the struggles between two relatively equal groups in which massacres, lynchings, and acts of retribution were commonplace, and in which both sides readily invoked arguments about averting slave insurrection in order to further their own ends.[57] In either case, social upheaval and slave rebellion, in one form or another, were almost inevitable.

The mulattoes and free blacks had indeed used these arguments in the early days of the Ogé rebellion when they had, with circumspection, shunned slave participation in the revolt. However, if the tranquility of the slaves in the South and West depended upon the peaceable accession to political equality of the mulattoes and free blacks, it was only to the extent that, should they not obtain civil equality through negotiation, the evolution of the struggles may well turn into open warfare. This would then provide the conditions that were lacking for the slaves in the South and West to promote their own aims. And in this sense, the mulattoes were mistaken (as events eventually proved) if they believed they could ultimately manipulate the slaves as marionettes in an increasingly complex web of power struggles.

Earlier in 1790, the mulattoes had feared that slave enrollment during the Ogé rebellion would jeopardize their movement for civil rights and perhaps even permit white colonists to cast emancipationist aspersions upon them; thus they refused slave support. Now, however, with rampant slave insurrection ravaging the North and their own struggle pushed incessantly toward civil warfare, they actively engaged rebellious slaves into their own ranks. But if these slaves fought alongside the mulattoes and free blacks, it was in many cases with hopes and unarticulated aims of their own. Romaine Rivière notwithstanding, no indigenous slave leaders had yet emerged from the masses to coordinate and organize, as they did in the North, their independent struggle for emancipation. In the West, slave participation had begun with the incorpation of the Croix-des-Bouquets maroons, who had armed themselves and deserted their plantations in July just prior to the outbreak of slave insurrection in the North. In August, they were joined by a group of slaves who had deserted the white planters, by whom they had been armed to fight the mulattoes. These slaves, collectively known as the *Suisses* and numbering a few hundred, were the first to have joined the confederate ranks and, with goals of their own in mind, to fight a common adversary. In general, however, throughout the summer and early fall, most of the slaves in the West and the South, although agitated, restless, and often dangerously insubordinate, did not flock in great numbers to join the mulattoes and free blacks, but were reticent and chose, for the moment, to remain on the plantations. And given the treatment meted out to the *Suisses*, their reticence was well placed. However, the November events in Port-au-Prince had dramatically accelerated the mulatto and free-black movement in both the West and the South, and had pushed the situation into openly declared warfare. It was under these circumstances that slaves increasingly became involved in armed struggle, and on both sides.

Following the Port-au-Prince massacre and similar occurrences in the South, the recruitment methods of mulattoes and free blacks on the plantations became proportionately more rapacious and violent. Slaves were told, on the one hand, that they were free and that they must no longer work for the whites; they were to join the mulattoes and free blacks, from whom they would henceforth take orders and arms. On plantations where confederate troops wished to establish a military camp, they might burn the slaves' quarters and steal their belongings, or seize and cut to pieces the whip of the *commandeur*, who was to convince the other slaves they must follow. If the *commandeur* refused, he was shot.[58] These tactics were not necessarily systematic, nor were they necessarily practiced by all mulattoes and free blacks in every parish. But there is ample evidence of these occurences in the correspondence and official reports, as well as in declarations made by slaves themselves, to conclude that they were far from uncommon.

The reactions of the slaves witnessing these events were mixed. In the first place, these men were not their own leaders, but they were promising them their freedom, and many a slave no doubt genuinely seized the opportunity to join the ranks of the confederate army where, as equals in arms, they took as an accomplished fact the freedom they were promised. For other slaves, as in the case of André, *commandeur* on one of the Laborde estates near les Cayes in the South, attachment to the master cost them their lives. André belonged to the third and most recently established of the three Laborde plantations. He was forty, a creole slave, and second *commandeur* on this plantation, formed in 1775 when the owner purchased the creolized *atelier* from the Champigny estate to which André belonged.[59] As was so often the case, one of the influential factors determining whether the slaves would rebel or remain loyal seems, here again, to have hinged on the pivotal role of the *commandeur* and his relationship to the slaves in his charge.[60] In this case, however, the scales were tipped toward the side of the master. When a brigade of mulattoes and free blacks came and threatened to kill the Laborde *commandeur* if he did not unite with them to turn the slaves to revolt, he told them they were all vile brigands and that he would never follow them; nothing could shake the loyalty he felt toward the whites. Moreover, he had a master and, even though he did not know him, would nevertheless remain faithful. Finally, he told them they need not bother killing him, then removed a revolver from under his vest, placed it to his head, and shot himself.[61] The manager, Delelocque, wrote of André in a letter to Laborde in January: "This slave is generally regretted, and you have lost a very valuable subject. The province wants to free his family."[62] Following these incidents, slaves from all three of Laborde's plantations offered to join the whites to fight the mulattoes.[63]

Horrible atrocities were committed on both sides. The whites cut off the heads of their mulatto prisoners and sent them to the Provincial Assembly; mulattoes caught with arms in hand were tortured and even burned alive.[64] The mulattoes retaliated in kind.[65] The Provincial Assembly and the municipalities of the South had repeatedly requested the Colonial Assembly to send troops and provisions to defend the province, always to no avail. In desperation, they freed their own slaves. At Jérémie, where the whites were in a position of strength and where, in October, they had disarmed the mulattoes and free blacks, they reportedly herded scores of mulattoes onto boats infested with smallpox, under the nefarious pretext of sheltering them against these armed slaves who would otherwise massacre them because of the atrocities the mulattoes had committed. [66]

The decision of the whites to arm their slaves was a perilous one that they would come to regret. In colonial times, the institution of slavery was reinforced by the rule of white supremacy and the existence of an intermediary caste of mulattoes and free blacks who, because of their racial origins, were to remain inferior in status and serve as an immutable barrier between the slave and the white master. Now, in the midst of revolution, that barrier had rapidly and violently broken down. One colonist, writing from les Cayes earlier in July 1791, had foreseen this eventuality: "It is feared that the slaves, seeing that the mulattoes and free blacks will have gained [their rights] by insurrection will themselves come to regard insurrection not only as the means by which to be freed of slavery, but as the most sacred of their duties." [67] Here the argument of averting slave insurrection was expressed again, this time by a white colonist apprehending the dangers of acquiescing in the free coloreds' demands for equality, especially as those demands were taking the form of open rebellion. By now, the white planters of the South had little choice, and to fight the mulattoes and free blacks they had only their slaves. On 25 December, a free day for the slaves and one on which marronage habitually plagued the masters, the Provincial Assembly approved a decree from the towns of Torbeck and les Cayes to arm one-tenth of their slaves to defend the whites and fight the mulattoes and free blacks. [68] Also to be fought were rebel slaves who had already deserted their plantations to join the mulatto camps in the mountains when the November truce was broken in the South. By the end of December, the slaves on the plantations between the Grande and the Salée rivers had risen, and in less than two months, slave participation throughout that province became a generalized occurence. From Cavaillon, across the Plaine-du-Fond, to Tiburon and Cap Dame-Marie at the western extremity of the province, as well as around Jérémie and Petit Trou, slaves were abandoning the plantation to join mulattoes and free blacks in arms against a common enemy. [69]

So slaves in the South were now fighting each other in enemy camps, and at the same time were acquiring valuable military skills and political experience. Here was a situation in which slaves were either freed or promised their freedom by others to help wage an armed struggle that, in either case,

ENDED UP KILLING OWN PEOPLE.

did not aim at their own liberation, but rather more significantly caused them to kill each other. It was only a matter of time before they would break with both sides to lead an independent struggle, organized in their own interests, on their own terms, and directed by their own popular leaders. In this, the slaves of the Plaine-du-Fond in the area around les Cayes and Torbeck had taken the lead.

WOULD FORM
OWN INDEP
ORG.

PART THREE
The South

6
Port-Salut to Les Platons

In January 1791, nearly seven months prior to the outbreak of the massive slave revolt in the North, the slaves of Port-Salut in the region around les Cayes had already begun to organize an insurrectionary movement. It was not as widespread geographically nor as tightly organized and as highly disciplined as the movement that broke out in the North, where voodoo played a politically instrumental role in its preparation and execution. It marked a beginning, however, and their demands were the same as those put forward later that year by the slaves at Morne-Rouge.

On 24 January, a band of some two hundred, armed with pistols, machetes, lances, sticks, and other makeshift weapons, had gathered together and set off to visit the plantations, one after another, in the area of Port-Salut. Their purpose was to agitate, to propagandize, to incite, and even force other slaves to join them. It was at this time that the mulattoes had organized themselves to defend and demand the application of the political rights they believed were granted them in the March decree of 1790. They told the slaves they were also going to fight the whites to obtain three free days per week for the slaves, whereupon those of the Plaine-du-Fond offered to join them. At this stage, however, the mulattoes refused the slaves' support on the pretext that if they did so, worse might befall the slaves. The converse, however, was probably closer to the truth. Actually, it was not so much slave participation that they feared as the consequences, which might well lead to a generalized slave rebellion. The mulattoes were fighting, after all, for political rights, not the abolition of slavery, an issue with which they, as even the Amis des Noirs in France, were never conspicuously or forcefully involved. Thus, they told the slaves they must act on their own behalf.

So when those of Port-Salut got word of all this, they chose leaders from amongst themselves to represent the slaves on the plantations of each district. On 24–25 January, they held a nocturnal meeting to fix "the date, the hour, and the moment" when the leaders would, in the name of the slaves they represented on each plantation, demand of their masters three free days per week. This would occur simultaneously in each district. If the masters refused, the revolt would begin. It was during that night, 24–25 January, that they set out with arms in hand to gain additional recruits and even (as did the Fortin-Bellantien maroons of the Croix-des-Bouquets movement later that year) carried off by force the *commandeur* of one plantation, along with three other slaves. Among the slaves in this band of insurgents were those from the plantations where the district leaders and other ringleaders were to be found.[1] Unfortunately, the conspiracy was discovered and the leaders arrested and sentenced.

[margin: DIDN'T FOLLOW THRU]

A few observations ought to be made at this point. The first is that the conspiracy was initiated and organized by the slaves themselves, and although it ran parallel to the movement of the mulattoes and free blacks for political rights, these slaves were neither directed nor controlled by them. If they offered to join them in early 1791, they did so as an independent force and with motives directly concerning themselves, as slaves. While the rumor that the king had decreed three free days per week for the slaves circulated throughout the colony, the slaves of Port-Salut accepted it as fact and demanded its application as a right. In other words, they were no longer to be exclusively the property of their masters.

[margin: SLAVES OWN REV WERE INDEP FORCE]

By the summer of that year, the mulatto revolt began to take on wider and graver proportions in the face of a common front of white colonists opposed to the application of the more explicit 15 May decree. By September, it had reached the stage of open, armed rebellion, and now the mulattoes actively solicited the support of the black slaves, sometimes promising them freedom, other times, three free days per week, or even, in some instances, the sharing of colonial profits once the whites were eliminated—anything to get the slaves to join their ranks.[2] In general, they were convinced that once they had obtained their rights and come to an accord with the whites, they would then be able to deal with the blacks and send them back to the plantations. It was out of this struggle, in which the slaves participated as armed equals, that the independent slave movement for emancipation emerged. The origins of that movement, however, lay in the Port-Salut conspiracy.

[margin: MUL. NEEDED SLAVE SUPPORT BUT PLANNED TO PUT BLKS BACK ON PLANTS.]

The insurgent slaves of the North, under Jean-François and Biassou, had meanwhile consolidated their position and established military rule in the district of Grande-Rivière. In the West, the confederates had seized Port-au-Prince, cut its water supply, and blocked all access to incoming food supplies. The arrival in the colony of the 24 September decree rescinding that of 15 May had not helped their cause, and tended only to strengthen the whites' resistance to the concordats. Nevertheless, the confederates were prepared to submit and to negotiate a conciliatory agreement upon the arrival in Port-au-Prince of the civil commissioner, Saint-Léger. For the time being, hostilities had ceased. The confederates dispersed and retreated to the areas beyond the Cul-de-Sac plain, but left one post at Croix-des-Bouquets should further trouble break out.

Saint-Léger then set out for Léogane, where Romaine and his troops were still in control. The mulattoes there had come to regret their initial alliance with this self-styled prophet and religious zealot, whose reign of terror had gone beyond their control and now merely cast discredit upon their cause.[3] Since the Colonial Assembly had already refused Saint-Léger's request for troops, the commissioner thus turned for military support to the mulattoes and free blacks, the only sector of colonial society still respecting the laws of France. By mid-March, an expedition was organized, and Romaine's band totally dispersed. During this time, however, Caradeux's patriot forces in Port-au-Prince had been maneuvering to prepare a counterattack. On the false pretext of putting down a slave rebellion in the plain, the Port-au-Prince regiment, headed by a contingent of blacks that Praloto imprudently armed, set out on 22 March to take over Croix-des-Bouquets. As the troops advanced, the planters fled, and their plantations naturally fell prey to the ravages of the armed slaves.

In less than two weeks, a general insurrection of ten to fifteen thousand slaves broke out in the entire Cul-de-Sac plain. The confederates had managed to gain the support of a young slave leader, Hyacinthe. Although he was only twenty-two years old, he was already a revered voodoo leader who had gained the confidence and respect of the slaves throughout the region. Armed only with pointed sticks, knives, machetes, and various farm implements as weapons, the blacks marched on Croix-des-Bouquets in the thousands, defying the onslaughts of cannon and artillery fire. Hyacinthe carried with him a talisman made of horsehair, which he waved before his troops to protect them and to reinforce their defiance and determination, crying: "Forward! Don't be afraid; it's only water coming out of the cannon." French observers related with incredulity how they would throw themselves directly onto the cannon, stick their arms into the mouth, shout to the others, "Come, come; I've got it," but would inevitably be blown to pieces. In great masses, they advanced over the dead bodies of their comrades, and finally began fighting hand to hand with Praloto's men and the national guard, forcing them to abandon their post and to retreat to Port-au-Prince. [4]

This massive mobilization of slaves had sparked further slave insurrections around Mirebalais, Arcahaye, Petite-Rivière, Verettes, and Saint Marc. The slaves of nearly half the province were now in armed rebellion. To restore order to the province, Saint-Léger immediately tried to work out a peace settlement with Pinchinat, who demanded the absolute submission of the Port-au-Prince faction and the dissolution of the Provincial Assembly. He told Saint-Léger what Bauvais later confirmed in his own words to Roume: "We were never the dupes of the white cockade; we had to conquer our rights and we needed auxiliaries. Even if the devil had presented himself, we would have enrolled him. These gentlemen offered themselves to us and we used them while letting them believe they were using us."[5]

Saint-Léger flew straightaway to France to inform the government of the situation in the colony. Mirbeck had left a few days earlier. So long as the patriot faction continued to agitate, the confederates would use the slave insurrections as a counterweight, without realizing that, in fact, the slaves were revolting for themselves. Roume was scheduled to leave as well, but, primed by a member of the Colonial Assembly, suspected a royalist plot and decided to stay in an effort to suppress it. At the end of May, news arrived from France of the 4 April decree restoring the rights of the mulattoes and free blacks that had been rescinded by the decree of 24 September. They had won a major victory and could now frankly admit their allegiance to France.

For the slaves, however, this stage signified the real beginning of their own struggles; they now had to be disarmed and returned to the plantations. Blanchelande and the civil commissioner worked out an agreement with the slaves whereby 100 of the popular leaders from Croix-des-Bouquets and 144 from Arcahaye were granted freedom on condition that they serve for five years in the local militia to survey and maintain order on the plantations. Hyacinthe was appointed captain of the Croix-des-Bouquets contingent.[6] Encouraged by his success in the West, Blanchelande then set out for the South, where a group of planters from the municipalities comprising the district of Grande-Anse had formed an independent confederation to openly oppose the 4 April decree. At the same time as he sought to enforce the submission of the whites to the new law, he hoped to regain the confidence of the mulattoes and free blacks and use their forces to help defeat the revolt of the slaves in the North, who by now controlled the entire eastern section of that province.[7] The situation in the South, however, proved far more difficult for Blanchelande to handle than that in the West, and would before long seal his doom.

In the meantime, Saint-Léger had sent Rigaud to the South to work out a plan similar to the one in the West for the disarmament of the insurgent slaves in this province. The 4 April decree had brought about a temporary rapprochement between the mulattoes and the whites in most of the South and a cessation of hostilities between the two groups. The slaves, however, armed by the mulattoes who promised them their freedom, took advantage of their position, refused to surrender their arms, and organized themselves in opposition to the various proclamations ordering them to return to their respective plantations.[8] By June, shortly after the arrival in the colony of the April decree, a considerable number of slaves in the Plaine-du-Fond were still armed and intended to remain so until they obtained their freedom. Whether armed by the mulattoes or by the whites, their experience on the battlefields and in the military camps had transformed them. They had fought as equals and now considered themselves free. One colonist wrote that the slave, employed in the military camps to serve one side or the other, "has lost the habit of working, and it is thus that he got accustomed to thinking."[9]

True enough. These slaves were now thinking and planning for their own future. To return to the plantation and work as they had in the past under the regimen of slavery would be impossible. A new stage had been reached, and it was up to them to carry it further. When Rigaud met with the white authorities in the South, he argued that to preserve the peace and to carry out the disarmament of the slaves, the Provincial Assembly must accord freedom to those who had fought within their ranks. Thiballier, the commander of the army in the South, refused. The law ordered him to get the slaves back onto the plantations; it did not authorize him to grant them freedom. [10]

Toward the beginning of July, two of their leaders, Armand, a *commandeur* from the Bérault plantation, and Martial, known as Maréchal, from the Pemerle estate, descended from their camps upon the request of Thiballier to meet with their masters. When they arrived—Armand in modest attire and Martial in uniform, complete with epaulets, saber, and a set of pistols —their masters welcomed them.[11] They tried to persuade the two leaders to give up their arms, use their influence over the rest of the slaves to do likewise, and return to the good graces of their benefactors. That Armand was one of the principal leaders of this movement left Bérault in a stupor. Writing to his agent in Bordeaux, he stated: "The general of these rebels is my slave Armand who after twenty-five years of service with me never had any more grievances against me than I against him. Two weeks before the horrors began, I gave him my word that he would receive his freedom." [12] No doubt Bérault was serious in his offer and, were it not for the revolution, probably would have freed Armand at a later date, or perhaps in his will. But to have offered it at this juncture was little more than political bribery. After twenty-five years, he, like others who knew Armand, was fully aware of the respect and influence this leader held, not only among the slaves of his own plantation, but among those of the entire Plaine-du-Fond, as well.[13] In any event, Armand had no interest at this point in saving his own skin at the expense of those he represented.

Before returning to their respective camps, he and Martial presented their demands to Thiballier. As in the early days of the revolt in the North, they demanded the freedom of three hundred of their leaders, three free days per week for every slave (as in the Port-Salut conspiracy), and the abolition of the whip as a means of punishment.[14] It should be noted here that, during these early struggles, the slaves never demanded outright the abolition of slavery, but rather, as we have seen, freedom for a certain number of them and three free days per week for all slaves, thus proceeding tactically and by stages. In the North, Toussaint, Jean-François, and Biassou had made similar demands during their negotiations with the civil commissioners and the Colonial Assembly. As a tactic, however, these demands created a new set of circumstances in the midst of changing political conditions and eventually did contribute, among other important factors, to general emancipation. [15]

Though the demands were limited ones, the white authorities categorically refused to negotiate with rebel slaves, as they did in the North, and rejected their demands, once again pleading for their return to the plantations. At this point, Armand retreated with his armed followers to establish a military camp in the region of Platons, one of the highest and most inaccessible mountain chains in the colony.[16] Martial rejoined his band to form a camp in the hills of Boucan Tuffy near Plymouth. Attacked and pushed back by the surrounding planters, they set out across the Plaine-de-Fond to combine forces with Armand.[17] In addition to these two leaders were Jacques Formon and Félix, both military camp commanders at Platons, as well as another slave, named Bernard.[18] A considerable number of minor leaders, including Bertrand, the slave of M. Perrigny, a wealthy, conservative planter from Torbeck, were in charge of the revolutionary bands.[19] Their numbers increased daily, along with their courage and audacity as they carried out frequent descents upon the plantations in the area to gather additional armaments and recruits. By the end of July, they were over four thousand strong. [20]

Prior to the military encampment of these slave leaders, the municipality of Jérémie had expelled from its district, in April or May, a contingent of three to four hundred armed slaves who had fought alongside the mulattoes and free blacks in the confederate army. Driven out, they marched on foot until they reached Camp Gérard, near Platons, where they joined with eight hundred other armed slaves, not including the two companies of Armand and Martial.[21] Although Thiballier claimed that orders had been issued to have them disarmed and returned to Jérémie, it is almost certain that they combined with the other rebels at Platons. [22]

Additional forces came from the plantations in the immediate region around les Cayes. From the beginning of the armed struggle of the mulattoes and free blacks, most of the planters had fled the countryside to take refuge in les Cayes, the principal city of the South, thus leaving the slaves who remained on the plantations unattended and without surveillance. One colonist, M. Gaujon, stated that upon returning to his plantation in mid-July after the promulgation of the 4 April decree, he found several armed slaves from other plantations. Among them was one Joseph Cupidon, who had been visiting Gaujon's slaves daily and preaching revolt in their quarters. Cupidon was disarmed by M. Gaujon, but he was not arrested as he insisted that he was a free black. Instead, the colonist himself was arrested and charged with having disarmed a free citizen of color, even though Cupidon was known to be a slave. When Gaujon returned to his plantation, his slaves, formerly loyal and obedient, now told him: "So, they arrested you for having disarmed a black slave; we will do the same to you if you try to force us to work." The next day, fifteen of them deserted and joined the rebel bands at Platons. [23]

At the same time, the Provincial Assembly of the South wrote to the Colonial Assembly, stating that during the retreat of Armand and Martial to Platons, several whites had been assassinated along the way and that already "partial fires have broken out on various plantations in the parish of Torbeck."[24] In fact, as Blanchelande arrived in the South on 20 July, the slaves of the entire southern region from Tiburon to les Cayes were deserting and rising in armed rebellion. The South was left practically defenseless, and the few troops it had were dying like flies under the rigors of a merciless climate that left them vulnerable to sickness, disease, and constant fatigue.[25] What troops the colonial government had were concentrated in the North, and reinforcements from France were still months away as slaves continued to burn and pillage the plantations along the southern coast to the Port-Salut peninsula. Here, too, another band of rebel slaves had begun insurrectionary activities.[26] At their head was Dominique Duhard, one of the district slave leaders of the Port-Salut conspiracy in January 1791.[27] At that time, Dominique had been arrested, whipped, branded, and sentenced to the galleys for life. He managed to escape, however, and now led the revolt at Marche-à-Terre in the region of Port-Salut. [28]

By this time, the majority of the planters saw in Blanchelande their only hope for saving what was left of their property and slaves. Upon his arrival in les Cayes on 23 July, the planters immediately demanded that he organize an expedition against the insurgents, whose forces were concentrated in the mountains around Trois-Rivières and Platons. Strong opposition to this proposal came, however, from the wealthier, more conservative planters who, along with Blanchelande, Thiballier, and Rigaud, insisted upon the futility of a general expedition with inadequate troops and munitions against bands of guerilla slaves. Experience had proved that, even if the rebels could temporarily be defeated and pushed back, they invariably set fire to surrounding plantations on their retreat. Believing a conciliatory approach more effective than a badly equipped expedition, Blanchelande set off on the twenty-fifth with a small delegation, including Thiballier and Rigaud, to meet with Armand and Martial. The two leaders persisted in their original demands for the freedom of three hundred of their leaders, in addition to three free days per week for every slave.[29] Blanchelande promised all of them amnesty, in spite of the destruction of property and lives they had already committed, if they would lay down their arms and return to their respective plantations. Armand and Martial requested an extra day to discuss the situation amongst themselves and to formulate a reply. The response came on the twenty-seventh, as four plantations went up in flames and a number of colonists were assassinated.[30] On the twenty-ninth, a violent storm broke out. Roughly two thousand strong, the slaves seized the opportunity and attacked the Bérault plantation, now one of the colonists' major military camps.[31] By the time Blanchelande arrived at the Bérault post with reinforcements, all was aflame. The slaves had already divided themselves into small contingents to make simultaneous attacks on the plantations of the Torbeck region, whose slaves they incited to join them. Those few who refused were killed. [32]

Upon apprehending the incendiary aims of Armand and his band, the slave Jean-Baptiste, second *commandeur* of the Bérault plantation, asked Armand in astonishment how he could bring himself to burn the plantation of his master. Armand replied: "At le Cap, the slaves did not leave a single structure standing; the same must happen here in the Plaine-du-Fond."[33] That day, all but one-tenth of the Bérault slaves deserted, along with hundreds of others in the plain. As they made their retreat, fourteen of the finest plantations were reduced to ashes. [34]

While Blanchelande was still trying to muster forces, a mulatto brought the reply Armand had promised him on the twenty-fifth. It was an ultimatum, already written in fire and blood, calling once again for the immediate and unconditional freedom of three hundred of their leaders.[35] The general had no choice now but to organize an expedition against them. For nearly a week he argued with the colonists over the composition of the troops as the slaves continued, day by day, to burn and ravage other plantations around Torbeck, les Cayes, and in the Plaine-du-Fond.[36] He finally came up with three columns of troops and an additional regiment of mulattoes to be led by Rigaud. On 4 August, as they were preparing to set out for Platons, rebel slaves, torch in hand, descended upon Port-Salut from all four sides; not a single plantation was left. The reserve contingent stationed at les Cotteaux to the west hurriedly abandoned camp, leaving their munitions behind. [37]

Blanchelande had made the mistake of rendering public his plans for the attack so as (he claimed) not to be considered a traitor should he fail.[38] The divisions and hostilities amongst the colonists deepened, and Blanchelande was now rapidly losing the confidence of those he was supposed to be leading. Under these conditions, the slaves could hardly have failed to get word of the plans, and they organized themselves accordingly. Skillfully setting one ambush after another, they successfully pushed back each column as it advanced along the mountainous cliffs, thereby destroying the coordination of the attack and creating total confusion and disorder among the troops. To trick Blanchelande, Armand sent out on 7 August a young envoy from his camp with a white flag and a message that he wished to negotiate. The conference lasted two hours and proved to be a tactic to prevent Blanchelande from reinforcing his retreating columns.[39] By now, night had fallen; in the morning he learned of the total defeat of all his forces. Over two hundred had been killed, nearly as many by the frequent avalanches of falling rocks and other hazards of a treacherous and unfamiliar terrain as were lost in battle, without counting the wounded or the prisoners. [40]

On the eighth, Blanchelande returned to les Cayes with his dilapidated army, having left behind two cannons and a considerable quantity of munitions and arms. The residents held him personally responsible for the disaster and, among other charges, accused him of collaboration with the slaves, of favoritism toward the mulattoes, and of having executed a counter-revolutionary plot. In his defense, the general castigated them for their egotism, their factionalism, their intransigence regarding the slaves' original demands which, he claimed, if granted would have brought the slaves back into submission and restored tranquility to the South. On the tenth, under a barrage of insults and cries for vengeance, Blanchelande set sail for le Cap, whence he was later deported to France.

For the next two days the slaves continued to attack several plantations in the plain. The colonist M. Moullin wrote: "Sixty-two of my slaves have revolted. And on 12 August, an unforgettable day, over five hundred of the rebels descended upon my plantation, torch in hand, and burned everything."[41] By the following day, however, the slaves' incendiary activities had generally ceased, and it was they who took the initiative of reopening negotiations with the provincial authorities. They sent as envoy one of their prisoners who brought with him the slaves' proposals. They now demanded the general emancipation of the entire band at Platons and three free days per week for every slave. The assembly was hard pressed to come to a decision and sent the prisoner, accompanied by a few of its own delegates, back to Platons. When they returned to les Cayes, they reported that the slave leaders had reduced their demands to the liberation of only four hundred slaves. As a token of their sincerity, they also offered to surrender nine hundred good rifles and to induce the other slaves to return to their plantations.

The assembly deliberated for days. To grant the freedom of even one rebel slave, they argued, would be to condone armed insurrection, set an example for other slaves to follow, and would lead to the end of slavery and the total ruin of the colony. While some colonists proposed freeing a portion of the slaves armed to defend the masters against the confederates, Rigaud proposed freedom for an equal number of slaves armed by the whites but who had deserted their posts and joined the confederates. These slaves, he suggested, should be enrolled in a special militia to police the countryside. The planters repeated their blank refusal; so once more no decision was made. [42]

On the sixteenth, they sent another delegation to confer with the rebel leaders, who impatiently demanded once again the general emancipation of the band and, even more, territorial rights to the entire Platons region. Since the provincial authorities refused to negotiate seriously with a band of rebel slaves, Armand was now willing to allow Rigaud to negotiate with the whites on their behalf. The rank and file protested. Félix, one of their popular leaders, intervened and told Armand: "You don't know what you're doing!"[43] Indeed, had not Rigaud led an armed contingent of mulattoes against them just a week earlier? Were not his hands tied by the very interests he and his caste represented? Already, Rigaud was losing the confidence of these slaves, who apprehended a possible betrayal. Armand then made their position clear: their munitions were plentiful; they had no idea, he claimed, where or from whom the arms were coming, or why. Nor did it matter. If they did not receive a reply to their new demands by the following day, they would descend upon les Cayes and burn the city down.[44] In desperation, the assembly agreed to free seven hundred of the slaves armed by the mulattoes. They would be enrolled in contingents of one hundred to survey and maintain order among the slaves on the plantations.

However, there were a number of problems with this solution. First of all, the seven hundred represented only a select few of those armed by the mulattoes and a tiny minority of the four to five thousand slaves at Platons who rebelled collectively to free themselves. Many had been armed by the whites and therefore were not included in the number. Many more had not been armed by either party but had deserted to join the revolt as active and equal participants.[45] Armand may have been aware of these difficulties when he had demanded, on two occasions, the unconditional emancipation of the entire group. Of the 700 who were granted freedom, only 350–400 accepted. The rest refused to accept a piece of paper signed by Rigaud in the name of the Provincial Assembly stating that they were free. They knew that under colonial law the only valid statement of emancipation was one signed by the master.[46] The affidavits signed by Rigaud were, of course, legal. But for these slaves, freedom was not something they could be tricked into accepting to serve the interests of those in power. In times of revolution, when dominating interests shift from one faction to another, circumspection becomes imperative. These slaves understood this in their own way, and half of those designated for emancipation rejected the act emanating from the provincial legislature, an act, they felt, that might later be rescinded. This was their first lesson in revolutionary politics and one that would serve them well in the future. Thus, they chose to remain at Platons and cast their lot with the others, who were prepared to fight to the bitter end.

It should be said, however, that the decision to accept or reject Rigaud's offer of emancipation, under the auspices of the Provincial Assembly, was purely an individual one that each slave had to make for himself. In one case, two slaves of M. Lafosse, Grégoire and Vendôme, were on the list of seven hundred. Vendôme accepted and was put in charge of a company. Grégoire, sixteen years of age, was supposed to serve in Vendôme's company, but "he did not want to be free on Rigaud's terms." Although Vendôme accepted, he was nevertheless known in the area to be an incorrigible rogue.[47] Moreover, the Lafosse plantation had harbored some of the ringleaders of the Port-Salut conspiracy a year ago.[48] That Vendôme had suddenly become "rehabilitated" overnight and so submissively grateful for his freedom that he would now sincerely serve the interests of the masters, is highly improbable. Similarly, among the 350-odd other slaves who accepted Rigaud's offer, there were those who would (and did) use this position covertly to further the revolt.

By mid-September, the repercussions of their revolt had already spread beyond the Plaine-du-Fond to the region of Petit-Trou and Anse-à-Veau along the northern coast of the province. The slaves here were demanding nothing more nor less than what had been granted the slaves at Platons.[49] Delaval, a colonial deputy from the South, foresaw this eventuality when he wrote on 8 September that if the treaty proposed by the Provincial Assembly were signed (as it was), the colony would be ruined: "For, if we reward with freedom those who have burned our plantations and massacred our people, the slaves who have hitherto remained loyal will do likewise in order to receive the same benefit. Then nothing more can be said: the whites must perish."[50]

Throughout the following months, the slave forces at Platons continued to increase. The planter who in August had lost sixty-two of his slaves wrote to a friend concerning the state of her brothers' plantation: "Twenty-six of their best slaves, both men and women, have deserted to follow the rebels."[51] On the Nicolaï plantation, forty-one slaves had deserted, most of them to join with the insurgents at Platons. Two others had been killed during one of their attacks on the colonists' outpost at Camp Prou; three had already received freedom following their August victory; a fourth, Mathurin, had also been offered freedom but apparently refused it, as the *procureur* listed him as among the Nicolaï slaves in insurrection at Platons. Only one returned.[52] Another colonist wrote, "[Your slave] Hazor, his wife, and his two children are among the insurgents," while yet another lamented, "All of my slaves are with the rebels."[53] Statements such as these were far from atypical among the planters throughout the plain.

Although most of the slaves from the three Laborde estates had proclaimed their unyielding loyalty to their master and to the whites by refusing to join the mulattoes and free blacks in armed rebellion a year earlier, a considerable number of them from the first, and the largest, of the three plantations now joined the other slaves in arms. The *procureur* François

Lavignolle listed 120 as being "in a state of insurrection."[54] He explained the greater degree of stability and fewer desertions on the other two by the fact that these were chiefly composed of older and of creole slaves. The older ones, "already inured to slavery, did not allow themselves to be dazzled by this momentary victory of the rebels, while the creoles, naturally more attached to their masters who raised them from a tender age, preferred in general their primitive condition [of slavery] to the illusory hopes that have led so many others astray." On the other hand, on the first of Laborde's plantations, it was chiefly the Africans of the Gold Coast, who, "not having yet acquired the principles of servitude and whose favorite passion in Guinea was war and pillage," were now involved as rebel runaways.[55] Paradoxically, however, if creolization may have been a forceful factor in deterring some slaves from rebelling, as in the case of Laborde's other two plantations, it could, for other slaves, be an important factor in determining and developing qualities of independent slave leadership. It was, after all, Armand, the trusted and loyal *commandeur* of Bérault, who after twenty-five years of service to his master, led the Platons insurrection and negotiated specific terms for freedom with the authorities.

In the midst of a situation that was by now beyond their control, the colonists attempted through increased brutality and harsher punishments to deter their remaining slaves from joining the insurrection. In November, the entire *atelier* on one planter's estate rose in revolt and assassinated their master. The national guard stationed at Camp Gérard was called in to smash the rebellion. Hoping to set an example and to intimidate other slaves who might be inclined to do the same, they slashed to pieces those they were able to capture; among these were four from the one Laborde plantation that had counted 120 insurgents.[56] Such measures, however, produced little effect upon the slaves and only seemed to reinforce their determination. Two absolutely unmanageable slaves of an absentee owner were sentenced by his *procureur* to the public chain gang. One of them, Jouan, was transferred with the slave to whom he was chained and sent to a hospital where additional workers were needed. He and his companion, though in chains, both succeeded in escaping and joined the rebel forces in the mountains. [57]

As their numbers grew, so too did their audacity. They descended by several thousands upon the various plantations that the colonists had transformed into military camps, in order to secure additional munitions and weaponry with which to replenish their diminishing arsenal and reinforce their position. Given the plantation tradition of Sundays and holidays as free days for their own activities and occupations, they chose these times to carry out their raids and "had absolutely no faith in any other days but these."[58] When they advanced, they split into groups of three or four hundred to encircle the camp, while shouting as their war cry: "*Coupé tête à li; coupé bras à li; coupé jambe à li; amaré li*" (Cut this one's head off; cut that one's arm off; cut the other's leg off; tie him up).[59] The slaves took what materials they had and improvised, using pots filled with stones to creat a tumultuous, frightening racket as they surprise-attacked, heightening the effect by blowing simultaneously into pieces of reed. Though they were unable to capture any of the major posts and often suffered losses in the hundreds, they managed as best they could. They applied their knowledge of herbs and other plants and began fabricating poisoned arrows.[60] When they retreated from an attack, they pilfered the plantations along the way for whatever supplies they could lay their hands on and set the cane fields ablaze. They pretended to be civic-minded, told the planters their horses and livestock were needed for public service, and carried them off to the mountains. [61]

The slaves who for the time being remained on the plantations became increasingly rebellious. The planter who, before, could keep his slaves in line with just one overseer, now needed two or three.[62] It did not take much to drive into rebellion those who, until now, had been hesitant. One *procureur* wrote: "Your slave, Cézar, left two months ago, and I have not heard from him since. . . . I think he had a quarrel with [the overseer] who, at his patience's end, gave him two or three blows with a cord. . . . But Cézar had been wavering for quite some time, and since a considerable number of domestics from les Cayes left thereafter, [Cézar] no doubt joined his friends in the city to leave with them."[63] A *procureur* advised a resident planter in France against acquiring another plantation in the area unless at a bargain price, for "it would take but a spark to make the slaves [there] desert. . . . Among them are a lot of incorrigible troublemakers, including some from the city who will undoubtedly incite the others to revolt."[64]

Most slaves remaining on the plantations simply stopped working altogether. On all but a few of the plantations from les Cayes to les Anglais, the slave labor force was practically nonexistent. In fact, before the end of the year, only six or seven plantations in the entire plain were operating; even on these, half the slaves were gone and the sugar cane crop so thoroughly ruined that the most they could produce was a low-grade syrup, and very little at that.[65] As the majority of the planters fled to les Cayes or to the various military camps for protection against the insurgent bands of black guerillas, their slaves, for the most part unsupervised, were left in a position advantageous to revolt.[66] On one plantation whose owner had been killed, the slaves remaining were involuntarily swept along into the revolt.[67] By the end of the year, the slaves had burned over one-third of the plantations in the province and had massacred an equal proportion of the colonists.[68] The magnificent Plaine-des-Cayes, comprising nearly one hundred sugar plantations, was totally destroyed; not a single one was left intact.[69] Planters began to pool their few slaves and other remaining resources in a desperate attempt to combine operations with their neighbors.[70] Some even rented out their slaves who had been left idle. [71]

The planters were financially and morally ruined. Credit was virtually nonexistent and was often replaced with bartering.[72] Many colonists considered themselves fortunate just to get out of this wretched colony with their lives and a shirt on their backs. Already, over half of the six thousand troops sent by France to restore order throughout the colony had perished from the ravages of a tropical climate and endemic sicknesses reaching epidemic proportions.[73] "This is the graveyard of the French; here one dies off like flies," wrote one army volunteer.[74] This war was unlike anything the whites had ever known in Europe: "Here one does not take prisoners of war; so many captured, so many slashed to pieces. Another reason is that we are not accustomed like the slave to climbing the cliffs, and the heat constrains us a great deal."[75] The slaves resisted the climate; they were accustomed to living on very little and could sustain a long day's work with a few potatoes, a banana, and a bit of water. They were familiar with the heavily wooded, mountainous terrain of Platons, and climbed its dangerously sharp precipices and gorges with remarkable agility. They were elusive, and, through stealth and wile, mentally disoriented the European soldiers: "In this war which is more like brigandage, we kill without seeing the enemy; under cover of the brush, they come as near as a pistol's range without even being seen."[76]

The colonist Solon de Bénech, a wealthy sugar planter from les Cotteaux, had suffered the fate of a hundred others. His plantation was completely burned out, and 90 percent of his slaves had deserted.[77] Among these insurgents was Gilles Bénech. Nicknamed *petit malice* for his cunning and craft at dissimulating his thoughts and acts, Gilles later became one of the most renowned and steadfast maroon leaders of the South. He had become a principal leader at Platons, alongside Armand, Martial, Jacques Formon, and the others, and held command over one of the major camps. [78]

These, then, were the slaves and their leaders who, encamped at Platons, now constituted an immense, socially and militarily organized maroon community of ten to twelve thousand people.[79] An irreversible transformation had occurred in the lives of these slaves. In less than a year, many of them had traveled the distance from obedient servant to armed auxiliary of mulattoes and free blacks in a movement that was not of their own making, finally to emerge as agents of their own freedom, and on their own footing. Many more were swept into the struggle by the sheer rapidity of events and the unequivocal nature of the circumstances. And it is true, violent revolutions leave precious little room for vacillators. Here at Platons, they would begin life anew. They had taken possession of the region, had fought for it with their lives, and were now resolved to stay. The population had settled on the summit, where Armand, Martial, and Jacques held their camps in close proximity, while Gilles's lay at a short distance from the three. They protected themselves by carefully constructing entrenchments of earth or rock, below which were precipices reaching down three thousand feet or more.[80] Here the slaves built homes for themselves. Each camp had eight to nine hundred dwellings, thus prompting one astonished soldier to report: "There are as many cabins here as there are houses in les Cayes."[81] They constructed two infirmaries for the sick. The soil permitting, they began to plant crops and stockpile their food supplies.[82] It seems they had even begun a rudimentary type of civil government, as they called their newly acquired territory the Kingdom of Platons, and chose for themselves a titular ruler whom they designated as king. [83]

At this point, a few observations might be appropriate concerning marronage and its relationship to the revolution. Although it may be argued by some that, once the slave insurrections broke out in 1791 and after, one can no longer justifiably define these slaves as maroons and must see things as did the colonists, who now spoke in terms of insurgents and rebels. That they were not exactly the type of fugitives who would readily have been identified as maroon in the colonial past is obvious, but that colonial past was now practically shattered, and the slaves were striving, in the process, for basic changes in their condition. That they had become both maroons and insurgents, that insurgency may in turn have provoked other slaves to desert as maroons and join them in arms, seems much closer to describing these circumstances as they were unfolding.

On another level, a rather unfortunate bifurcation of marronage in New World slave societies into African (i.e., "backward-looking") and modern (i.e., "revolutionary") categories has been suggested. When strictly applied to the case of the Saint Domingue revolution, however, it runs the risk of oversimplifying a highly fluid, rapidly changing, and richly diverse situation. The Platons rebellion is only one case in point. This massive assembly of slaves may indeed appear to be one of those movements that, by definition, could fall into a "restorationist" category, as a historically backward-looking maroon settlement seeking to restore African ways while attempting to escape slave society. Yet when more fully examined, this category is little more satisfying than the one that denies they were maroons at all.

If we consider their initial demands for the freedom of three hundred of their leaders, for three free days per week for all slaves, and the abolition of the whip, then we are faced with a situation in which insurgent maroons, independently organized in inaccessible mountain retreats and armed in their defense, are negotiating, not for their withdrawal from slavery, but for manifest changes in its nature and form.[84] In this sense, the Platons leaders represented the slaves of the Plaine-du-Fond collectively, but they were

doing so as leaders of a massive maroon settlement and, for the moment at
least, from a more balanced position of power within the paramaters of a
volatile revolutionary situation. As maroon leaders, they were now directly
inscribed in a revolutionary process that eventually did lead to general emancipation. Moreover, the seven hundred enfranchisements that were granted
were hardly taken in the vein of self-concerned political opportunism, or
escapism. Half of those freed in this way refused (as we have seen) the terms
of their enfranchisement; among the others were many who later used their
freedom to continue agitating amongst their companions on the plantations.[85]
The majority of the Platons maroons not only stayed on, but also remained
in close military and political contact, not to mention their various kinship
ties, with these latter.

Finally, even though Armand demanded freedom for the entire band at
one or two points and territorial rights to the area they occupied, it hardly
meant they were seeking isolated status or political independence. This
would have been impossible to defend as such—and he undoubtedly knew
it, too—in the midst of revolutionary tumult. In fact, full territorial rights
to the Platons were not among their first demands, but were rather thrust
forward out of exasperation when they realized their negotiations with the
colonial authorities were leading to a dead end. Also, more generally, territorial rights might be seen as a deceptively simple expression of the con-
viction that the land belongs to those who have conquered it and to those
who labor it. Here, then, were some ten thousand slaves, not all of them
armed warriors, but families and children, as well, who were fighting with
maroon tactics, living and organizing themselves as a maroon society with
discernably "restorationist" characteristics, but who were squarely involved
in one of the modern world's first anticolonial liberation struggles. Needless
to say, these times were radically different from those surrounding the 1785
treaty agreements that granted independence to the Maniel maroons and,
thereafter, freedom from colonial attack.

At the end of November 1792, as the planters of les Cayes and Torbeck
were preparing elections for a new municipal government in conformity with
the 4 April decree, they had relaxed troop surveillance over the plain. The
slaves at Platons took advantage of the situation. They knew, as well, that the
colonists were planning to organize a second offensive against them. On
the twenty-ninth, two armed bands of a few hundred each descended upon
the several plantations around Torbeck with the aim of taking as prisoner,
or killing if necessary, as many whites as possible. One of the bands, led
by Bertrand, went to the Perrigny estate, where over fifty slaves had already
deserted; some twenty of these were with Bertrand at that moment. On the
pretext that they wished to surrender, Bertrand held a short conference with
his former master, the substance of which is unknown. It seems, however,

that Bertrand's aim was to verify the news of a new attack and to extract from Perrigny additional information.[86] While Bertrand was conversing with Perrigny, some of the other slaves captured and bound the resident physician, M. Philibert, along with three others, who nonetheless managed to escape by the skin of their teeth. They would have assassinated Philibert were it not for the judicious intervention of Bertrand, who wanted him alive, first, to take care of Martial's wounds at Platons and second, as a prisoner whom they could use as an emissary. They returned the following night after having visited several nearby plantations to propagandize and gain recruits, this time using neither force nor intimidation, but simply ordering those who wished to remain to stop working. [87]

Two weeks had elapsed when Armand and Martial sent Philibert back with a message addressed to the planters of the entire province. First, they stated that they had been misled by the mulattoes, who armed them against their masters, who used them for their own purposes, and who, as soon as their rights were won, hunted them down as fiercely as did the whites. In this the slave leaders were absolutely right, but it was also a tactic. In their message, they invited the white planters to evacuate the plain so that they could settle their score with the mulattoes, after which they would make arrangements with the whites concerning their return to work on the plantations. [88]

But the fundamental question was not simply one of race. The mulattoes, as the whites, were slave-holding property owners, and they were (as we know) more numerous than the whites in the South. The slaves were beginning to see clearly that the mulatto owners were no less a class enemy than their white masters. In fact, one of the most striking features concerning the ethnic origins of the Saint Domingue slave population in the South is the near-total absence of mulatto slaves.[89] What this means is that the free population here was overwhelmingly mulatto or white, with the mulattoes slightly in the majority, while the slave, or nonfree, population was almost exclusively black, either creole or African. Predictably, not one piece of evidence has been found (by the present writer) in the voluminous documentation covering the period from July 1792 to January 1793 of any mulattoes —whether slave or free—amongst the Platons insurgents, neither in the fighting ranks nor within the leadership. More striking, however, is the absence of any free blacks among the insurgents and, as compared to the North, their relatively smaller proportion within the free colored population generally. One almost has the impression that, on the whole, the free blacks in the South were only slightly more significant among the free coloreds than were the mulattoes among the slaves. Certainly it is an aspect of the province's social demography that deserves closer scrutiny than it has yet received, for if at least some free blacks played an important collaborative role in the planning and execution of the insurrection in the North, it was not the case at Platons. In the South, free-black participation was manifested exclusively alongside the free mulattoes (and in secondary roles) in the struggles for political equality. Such demographic peculiarities as we find in the South may in part, then, help to explain why at times class issues take on the seemingly rhetorical nature of black versus mulatto (especially after emancipation, when the mulattoes assumed political control and the blacks, by and large, remained on the plantations in subservient conditions), and why race and class become such sharply defined categories. Generally, the two categories reflect a demographic dichotomy in which blacks invariably composed the laboring masses as slaves and plantation workers, or, as free laborers, were found in the menial trades and occupations, while the mulattoes, if not owners of property, nevertheless represented the liberal professions and privileged trades. [90]

So when Armand and Martial told the whites they wanted to settle their score with the mulattoes, this was no doubt true. They had pillaged and burned the property of the mulatto masters, and had even assassinated a few,[91] as they had done to the whites, but, on the other hand, that they now intended to return to their white masters, even under what could be no more than a spurious agreement to improve their conditions, was absurd.[92] By telling the whites to evacuate the plain, they were more plausibly appealing to the race prejudice of the whites as a means by which to challenge the material foundations of their oppression, first by attacking the remaining property of the whites, and then by "settling their score" with the mulattoes.

In a similar vein, the adamant refusal of the white colonists to heed the slaves' message and evacuate had little to do with the 4 April decree and the fact that they were now obliged to respect mulatto rights. Race prejudice against the mulattoes was still prevalent, in spite of the law, but in times of crisis, such prejudices invariably become submerged, and are subsumed by the economic necessities of the ruling class to preserve its property relations, and therefore its survival. Whether they liked it or not, the mulattoes, as fellow property owners, were their economic allies in slavery. The whole system was at stake, and they categorically refused to negotiate with rebel slaves. One colonist had already stated the case explicitly: "There can be no agriculture in Saint Domingue without slavery; we did not go to fetch half a million savage slaves off the coast of Africa to bring them to the colony as French citizens."[93] It was going to be a war to the finish. Either the slaves would win and the structure of that society and the nature of its economic and human relations would be transformed, or the struggle would result in the mutual destruction of both sides. The colonists knew this, as well as the slaves, but they could hardly afford to admit it.

Polverel, the new civil commissioner in charge of the West and the South, had arrived at the end of December. The slaves offered for the last time to negotiate, requesting specifically Polverel and Rigaud as representatives. Polverel reassured the colonists that he recognized only two categories of persons in Saint Domingue—free citizens and slaves. He told the slave emissaries that neither he nor Rigaud would negotiate with a band of rebels, but that if they wished to descend from the mountains in small groups and surrender their arms, he would assure them all an unconditional pardon by the powers invested in him. He tried to convince the authorities of les Cayes that the best policy in dealing with these slaves was one of clemency, that since they were already suffering from hunger and sickness and no longer had sufficient arms to defend themselves, they would be forced to come back. The colonists would not hear of it. Even if they granted the slaves a pardon, they would work submissively for three or four months, by which time the troops would be removed, and then would recommence their activities, exterminate the planters, and become masters of the island. This was not a war between two moderate or reasonable powers, in which differences could be settled by treaties or agreements; it was a war to the end, the quintessential struggle between master and rebel slave. Such was the opinion of the distinguished Club des Cayes. [94]

The inevitable clash of opposing forces, as succinctly expressed in the words of a Plaisance (slightly northeast of les Cayes) coffee planter, was now at hand: "Barbarians, brigands who have been armed against us, vile slaves, rebels, your agitations do not frighten me. It is true you have caused a great number of my friends to perish. I will follow them cold-bloodedly into the grave, and I swear that you will see all my blood flow before I consent to your freedom, because your slavery, my fortune, and my happiness are inseparable." [95] Polverel found himself in the same situation as Blanchelande in August, with no alternative but to order a general attack against the insurgent slaves. Colonel Harty, a staunch, trustworthy republican, was placed in command of the expedition. The colonists agreed to wait, however, until after the New Year, when in colonial days fugitive slaves traditionally returned and masters traditionally pardoned them. They knew it would be futile, and they were right. Not a single slave returned. [96] On 9 January, Harty set out with an expeditionary army of nearly two thousand troops, including a strong contingent of two hundred black slaves, armed by their masters and led by the ex-slave Jean Kina. [97]

The slaves at Platons were badly armed but defended themselves until the last possible moment. They prepared ambushes to push back the advancing troops; they stretched their munitions supply by mixing coals with the powder; in a final attempt, they stuffed to the brim one of their only two cannons with cartridges, grapeshot, cannonballs, bullets, whatever they had left. When it became clear that they could not defeat the enemy troops, the slaves swiftly abandoned their camps; Gilles, having provided the fiercest resistance, was the last to evacuate. At this point, expecting to destroy Armand and Martial's camps, all four columns marched to the attack on the thirteenth. The previous day, however, the two leaders had spoken to the slaves, informing them of the situation. They were going to evacuate in small groups that night and retreat higher up into the mountains at Macaya. Those who chose to follow would join them. Those who chose to remain in the woods or to return to their plantations were free to do so.[98] A few hundred of them—mostly women, children, the aged, and the sick—unable to flee or perhaps expecting some sign of humanity on the part of the troops, stayed behind. They were brutally massacred to the very last one, their heads cut off and their bodies slashed to pieces as the women fought ferociously to protect their children. [99]

The colonists celebrated this event as a tremendous victory. Among the more astute, however, the realities of the situation were all too apparent. The core of the insurgent slave movement, including the ablest, best-trained, and most determined slaves, as well as their principal leaders, was still intact. One colonist estimated their numbers at over three thousand.[100] A considerable portion of the slaves had divided themselves into bands and remained as maroons around the plantations of the area, while others, perhaps even an equal number, returned to their masters seeking pardon.[101] But the planters who received their slaves without administering merciless, and quite often mortal, punishments were few. Generally, the attitude of the planters was to sacrifice those who came back and, whatever the cost, to make an example of them in order to prevent the rest from rebelling. [102]

For the time being, there reigned a semblance of calm, but the vast majority of the planters would never be able to restore their devastated properties and ruined fortunes. One colonist summed up the situation this way: "The enemy we must destroy in order to restore calm in the colony is too numerous and their means of defense too great for us to ever bring them back into submission; whichever way things turn out, our ruin is total. If we do not defeat and destroy the rebel slaves, we will all end up being slaughtered by these monsters, and by destroying them we destroy our fortunes. For it is in these slaves that our fortunes exist." [103] For three quarters of the planters, the most pressing desire was to leave. A soldier, reporting home to his mother after the expedition, wrote of these rebel slaves: "They come and treat us as if we were the brigands and tell us: '*nous après tandé zaute*,' which is to say, 'we had expected you, and we will cut off your heads to the last man; this land is not for you; it is for us.'"[104] Those slaves who retreated and remained in the mountains had formed a new camp, midway between Platons and Macaya, from which the leaders surveyed their remaining troops, waiting and watching for a new opportunity to strike.

7

The Blacks React to Freedom

No major expedition was ever carried out against the Platons maroons during the months following the January attack. Although plans for a third, and presumably final, expedition were in the making, those plans never materialized.[1] All the principal leaders—Armand, Martial, Gilles Bénech, Jacques Forman, and Bernard—as well as a number of minor leaders, including Félix and Bertrand, remained at Macaya in armed camps with their fellow insurrectionists to defend their hard-won but free existence. News of a new outbreak in the Cul-de-Sac plain had diverted the projected expedition, and Polverel was forced to send the Aube regiment commanded by colonel Harty to the West, thus depriving the South of its only significant military force.[2]

The arrival in the colony of the new civil commission in September 1792, with powers to enforce the 4 April decree throughout the colony and to establish the equality of all free citizens, had created new problems and posed a direct threat to both the royalist and the patriot factions.[3] The royalists were convinced that, having proclaimed equality, the French government, now strongly influenced by the Jacobin group in the National Convention, would hasten to proclaim general emancipation, thereby bringing about the destruction of the colonists and their property.[4] The patriots, on the other side, suspected that they, too, would fall under the stern surveillance of the commissioners for their secessionist aims. Whether royalist or patriot, both parties had a vested interest in overthrowing national authority in the colony. Borel, an influential member of the patriot faction and former deputy to the Colonial Assembly, made the first move. He held a conference with Jumécourt and proposed a coalition with the royalists, their former archenemies.

Since the insurrection of March 1792, the slaves of the Cul-de-Sac plain had remained relatively tranquil under the influence and command of Hyacinthe. By the end of January 1793, however, two new insurrections had broken out: one among the independent maroons of Bahoruco, who descended upon the area of Fond-Parisien; the other, in the region of Crochus just outside the Cul-de-Sac plain, was led by another insurgent band leader, Jean Pineau.[5] The insurrections were secretly incited by Hyacinthe, and once they broke out, each factional party sought to profit from them to the detriment of the other. Because of Jumécourt's association with Hyacinthe, Borel accused the Croix-des-Bouquets mayor of collaboration with rebel slaves and had him arrested as a counterrevolutionary. This had been Borel's covert plan from the very beginning, and he was now in complete control of the Cul-de-Sac plain, as well as of Port-au-Prince. [6]

Through an excessive display of revolutionary patriotism, Borel planned to use the civil commissioners to have the royalists arrested and deported, then to manipulate public agitation against the commissioners themselves in order to overthrow French national authority in the colony. To ensure the success of these Machiavellian plans, the patriot faction had already entered into secret negotiations with Britain who, by virtue of its 1 February declaration of war, was now a confirmed enemy of France and the revolution. [7] Aware of Borel's seditious aims, Polverel and Sonthonax organized an armed march on Port-au-Prince at the beginning of April. The city eventually surrendered; Borel fled and took refuge in Jamaica.

Having pacified the West and reestablished government authority, for the time being at least, the civil commissioners were now beset with new troubles that were breaking out in the North. Galbaud, sent from France to replace Blanchelande as official governor-general, arrived in le Cap at the beginning of May. The civil commissioners had originally planned to leave the West for Grande-Anse in the South, still in open rebellion against the 4 April decree and now rapidly solidifying its ties with the British. The arrival of Galbaud in the North, combined with the enthusiastic welcome he received from the counterrevolutionary whites of le Cap, had diverted these plans, and they therefore left Rigaud and Pinchinat in charge of the Grande-Anse mission. When they arrived in le Cap, they held a conference with Galbaud and, on the pretext of an irregularity in his nomination, dismissed him and his staff from their functions and put them on a ship bound for France. [8]

But in the harbor were a number of ships, some of them carrying a few hundred political prisoners who had been arrested and deported from Port-au-Prince after the Borel affair. As they, too, were prisoners of Sonthonax and Polverel, they joined with Galbaud and his brother to gain the sympathy of the sailors, about two thousand strong. On 20 June, they made an armed landing, captured the main arsenal, and then attacked the government offices, forcing Sonthonax and Polverel to flee for protection to the Bréda plantation outside le Cap. [9] The national guard having joined the attack, the mulattoes were called to the defense, but it was impossible for them to maintain order. Every street had become a virtual battlefield. The prisons were opened, and the prisoners, most of them rebel slaves, joined in the defense, along with over ten thousand black slaves of le Cap, who by now had armed as best they could and were actively engaged. [10] Terror and panic spread like wildfire as the women and children desperately tried to escape; atrocities and pillaging were committed on both sides. Without additional military support, the authority of the government, as well as le Cap itself, would be doomed.

Over ten thousand slaves in le Cap were now in open revolt. The black rebel armies under Jean-François and Biassou occupied nearly all the North province from Port-de-Paix to Fort-Dauphin under the protection of Spain, who, one month after the declaration of war against England, had also entered the war as France's enemy. It now seemed that the salvation of the colony depended directly upon winning over these slaves to the side of the republic. So the commissioners, in their desperation, took a great step. On 21 June, the day of their retreat to Bréda, the civil commissioners issued a proclamation guaranteeing freedom and the full rights of French citizenship to all slaves who would fight to defend France against her enemies, be they foreign or domestic.[11] One group of insurgent slaves, encamped in the hills outside le Cap and led by the maroon leader Pierrot, responded to the call. Over three thousand strong, they presented themselves before the commissioners, took the oath of allegiance to France, and the next day descended upon the capital like an avalanche, forcing Galbaud and his men into retreat. But by now fire had broken out and was rapidly spreading, finally consuming two-thirds of the city. The scene was like that in Port-au-Prince in November 1791. The white colonists were literally destroying each other just as their factional power struggles would destroy the colony.

On the twenty-seventh, Sonthonax and Polverel returned to le Cap, a city in near-total ruin and without defense. For the most part, the insurgent slaves remained skeptical of the commissioners' offer of freedom, even of their right to pronounce freedom in the name of France. Many who had participated in the defense of le Cap returned shortly after to rejoin the bands in the hills, and it was only with great difficulty that the commissioners retained the support of Pierrot, whom they had named general.[12] While most of the other maroon leaders preferred the independence they had acquired at the head of their bands, a certain number were won over by the commissioners' promises after the Cap disaster. Apparently abandoning the banner of Spain, monarchy, and royalism, Macaya, Pierrot's lieutenant; Barthélemy, who was in command of Limbé and Port-Margot and who was also among the first insurgent leaders of the August 1791 revolt with Boukman and Biassou;[13] Zephirin, in command of Port-de-Paix; Pierre-Michel; Paul Lafrance, and a few others, all adopted for the moment the flag of the republic.[14] Among them, only Pierrot, Pierre-Michel, and Paul Lafrance remained.[15]

To win over Biassou, the civil commissioners played upon the growing jealousy between him and Jean-François, who held a higher command and received greater favors from their Spanish protectors, but with no success.[16]

They tried again, using Macaya as intermediary. Macaya never returned, reaffirming his fundamental adherence to royalism, while Jean-François and Biassou delivered a joint response on 28 June. They reminded the civil commissioners that in 1791 they were fighting for their rights and for the king. Receiving no aid at that time, they had no choice but to ally with the Spanish.[17] A week later they reiterated their position and stated that only when the French should have restored their king could they recognize the civil commissioners.[18] The refusal of the rebel leaders to accept the commissioners' offer can be understood on two grounds. First, royalism was certainly more consistent with the type of government that African-born slaves would be most inclined to recognize, and in defense of which they would feel least circumspect. Under the circumstances, how could they see the commissioners as representing anything but a regicidal nation? And second, how could they know that the commissioners were actually invested with undisputed governmental powers, habitually held only by kings, to issue a proclamation freeing large numbers of enslaved subjects? Under the Crown of Spain, they were convinced their freedom was valid. Why, then, should they exchange what they already had for freedom under the risky and ambiguous circumstances that the republican commissioners presented? In fact, to gain the confidence of the white colonists upon their arrival, had not the commissioners proclaimed their support of slavery and publicly affirmed that they recognized only two categories of persons in Saint Domingue: free citizens without regard to color, and slaves?[19] Now they were telling the slaves that only republican France could guarantee their freedom, that they must therefore abandon their royalist protectors who sought only to defeat the revolutionary egalitarian principles that France intended to extend to them, as well.

The last hope for Sonthonax and Polverel resided in Toussaint. He had joined Biassou's band in the early days of the revolution as his secretary and as physician of the black army. When war broke out with Spain in March 1793, Toussaint formalized his alliance with that government, but as an independent leader with no more than five to six hundred well-chosen troops. Early in June, however, just prior to the Cap catastrophe, Toussaint had written to General Laveaux, chief commander of the republican forces in the North, offering his support for France against her enemies on the one condition that full amnesty and general emancipation be proclaimed. This was, of course, refused, and Toussaint remained with the Spanish for nearly another full year.[20]

Almost three-quarters of the colonial whites had abandoned France and chosen the side of the foreign powers. The mulattoes, having won a tremendous victory after the defeat of the Port-au-Prince factions earlier that year, had received a considerable number of preeminent appointments, both in the government and in the military, and became the chief protégés of the civil commissioners. Now they, too, began to desert France and join the counterrevolution, abandoning their posts to the enemy powers. With the exception of Rigaud, Bauvais, and Pinchinat, who each remained faithful to the republic, most of the mulattoes in the West were furious over the increasing number of manumissions being granted the slaves by Sonthonax and Polverel. After the incidents in the Cul-de-Sac plain, the commissioners had freed those slaves from Port-au-Prince and Jacmel who were armed by Borel, as well as a certain number armed by the whites in the South.[21] It was no longer even necessary for these armed slaves to negotiate their freedom; Polverel recognized that it would be dangerous to send them back to their plantations, and thus pronounced their freedom outright. They would be enrolled for the defense of the republic in what was to be called the Legion of Equality. From 21 June on, any slave wishing to join the republican army would be free. On 11 July, freedom was extended to their present or future wives and children, who would otherwise still be slaves. [22]

Among those freed after the Cul-de-Sac insurrections was a slave named Jean Guyambois. With the aid of his brother, François, he had established communication with Jean-François and Biassou to gain their adherence to a plan for the restoration of peace. Guyambois, the chief architect of the plan, Jean-François, and Biassou would rule Saint Domingue as a triumvirate; the Spanish would cede certain territories; universal freedom of the slaves would be proclaimed; Guyambois, as military leader, would enforce the distribution of property to the blacks, who would assume the payment of debts to their new creditors. All of this would occur without shedding a single drop of blood. Once the necessary accords were reached with Jean-François and Biassou, Guyambois convoked a commune assembly meeting at Petite-Rivière in the Artibonite valley, and the whites unanimously supported the plan in the name of peace. [23]

Polverel arrived in the West only to learn of the concluded plans, in which the district of Mirebalais had also participated. He immediately had the Guyambois brothers put under arrest and the municipal decrees sanctioning the plan revoked. But it was too late now for anything short of a proclamation by the commissioners decreeing the universal emancipation of the slaves. The situation was becoming increasingly critical by the day. In the North, M. Artaud, one of the wealthiest planters in the colony, with over one thousand slaves, told Sonthonax what his own slaves had made clear to him: only universal freedom could spare the whites from being totally annihilated.[24] So now whites and slaves, alike, were pushing for emancipation, though with differing interests at stake.[25] Finally, on 29 August, Sonthonax proclaimed the abolition of slavery in the North.

The progression toward general emancipation in Saint Domingue has been interpreted diversely by historians who, to varying degrees, may emphasize the impetus and impact of recurring slave insurrection (beginning with the August 1791 revolt) upon the course of events; or the profoundly felt and long-cherished ideal of general liberty that was so prophetically espoused and ineluctably pursued to its end by Toussaint Louverture (even though, after the 29 August promulgation he remained under the banner of Spain and royalism); or, on the other side, the revolutionary ideology and character of the civil commissioner, Sonthonax, who boldly put his emancipationist principles to practice by declaring slavery abolished; or, in the immediate situation of the summer 1793 (following the declarations of war against Britain and Spain), the political and military necessity of freeing the slaves to save the colony. No doubt all of these factors came in to play, and in the absence of any one of them, general emancipation as it was achieved in 1793–94 may have taken quite a different course.

In his recent historical biography of Sonthonax, Robert Stein attributes responsibility and credit for general emancipation chiefly to the radical abolitionism of the civil commissioner, radical in the sense that, within the long tradition of antislavery thought from the seventeenth to the mid-nineteenth century, Sonthonax uniquely stood out as a nongradualist and a practical innovator, and that he was. But even revolutionaries cannot bring about farsighted change by the force of their ideas alone. If, however, Sonthonax was not merely reacting to a difficult situation or making a calculated move in issuing his 29 August declaration but, as Stein argues, was fulfilling the promise of a long line of abolitionist thought, still, without the particular historical conjuncture that existed in 1793, Sonthonax's idealism could not have gone very far in practice. Sonthonax seems almost to have been weaving his way in and out of a constantly changing web of events, rapidly seizing each occasion that presented itself to further manumissions in the colony, until the only logical conclusion would be the practical fulfillment of his philosophical goal to end slavery.

What is missing, however, in Stein's well-argued interpretation of Sonthonax's 29 August proclamation ending slavery in the North, "the most radical step of the Haitian Revolution and perhaps even of the French Revolution," is some sense of the slaves themselves. They are never really brought into view: "Sonthonax took [the step] alone and without hesitation."[26] Indeed he did. Yet one has the impression that abolition for the slaves was something that was being accomplished over the top of their heads, and single-handedly, by Sonthonax. Circumstances allowed and even encouraged Sonthonax to take that step (as Stein recognizes), but the slaves had greatly contributed, by their own revolutionary activities, to the creation of those circumstances. Were it not that a significant portion of them had already effectively freed themselves in the North and had, along with others, been engaged massively and militarily in armed insurrection throughout the colony for a full two years (often in enemy camps, at that), Sonthonax's proclamation may have fallen into something of a void, and his justification would have been rather thin for freeing them *universally*, simply to fight France's enemies. In the end, both the slaves and Sonthonax cherished the same goal, and to a certain extent each needed the other. Through a combination of historical circumstances, in which the presence in Saint Domingue of a radically principled agent of the French Revolution imposed itself upon ongoing events that the slaves themselves had helped precipitate since August 1791, the process toward a parliamentary abolition of slavery was set in motion. And, by a twist of historical irony, if the existence of the colony for the metropolis had previously depended upon the absolute maintenance of slavery, its salvation for revolutionary France now depended precisely upon freeing those very slaves and making them French citizens. Certainly Sonthonax facilitated and hastened the realization of general emancipation; yet, one wonders whether, with or without Sonthonax, the ending of slavery in Saint Domingue may not, in the final analysis, have been a foregone conclusion. Still, however, no other political figure, not Polverel nor even Robespierre, was willing or saw the need to go as far and as fast as Sonthonax in precipitating general emancipation in Saint Domingue, thereby ensuring the parliamentary abolition of slavery.

Up to the 29 August declaration, the progression toward general emancipation in the South had taken a somewhat similar course and, as was the strategy of the slaves, for their part, was carried out in stages. On 25 July, Polverel and Sonthonax had issued a proclamation according freedom to slaves who fought in the defense of the republic. It began by recognizing that the insurgent slaves of the South, by virtue of their military experience and long-established practice of warfare, were the most capable of fighting France's enemies. The manumissions granted by the Provincial Assembly to the insurgents at Platons were confirmed. All the slaves from les Cayes, Torbeck, Marche-à-Terre, and Tiburon, who were armed by their masters of both colors, were also freed, as well as those who had been armed by the municipalities of Jérémie, Cayemittes, and the surrounding towns to serve the counterrevolution. Amnesty and freedom were granted to the slaves who were still armed to conquer that freedom and who would deliver their arms, "including Armand, Martial, Jacques Formon, Gilles Bénech, and the other leaders."

As these new soldiers had to prove themselves worthy of French citizenship, their freedom was dependent upon two conditions. First, they were to be enrolled into legions or companies to fight with courage and devotion for France. Second, the war effort necessitated a disciplined, organized population of agricultural workers. Therefore, as an "indispensable duty," they would have to make the rest of the slaves return to their respective plantations and use appropriate methods to maintain their subordination and the regularity of their work. The wives and children of these new citizen-soldiers would also be free, and a vague promise was made to ameliorate the conditions of the slave workers. [27]

Rigaud had already organized some twelve hundred newly freed blacks into "legions of equality" and hoped, with the 25 July decree, to double that number by winning over the bulk of insurgents still at Macaya. When the slave leaders there got word of this proclamation, they sent representatives on their behalf to inform Rigaud that they were, on the whole, satisfied with these conditions.[28] Most of them would become company captains and, though they accepted the government's offer of conditional freedom, it was not entirely without reserve, a certain measure of distrust and, as for Jacques Formon, open defiance.[29] He alone among the leaders remained consistently loyal to the original goals of their revolutionary struggle, though he would later pay for it with his life. Rigaud referred to him as the most uncompromising of the leaders: "Under the pretext of carrying out the orders I gave him to make all of the slaves from Macaya come down and return to work, he would visit various plantations and play the Tartuffe, delivering speeches to the slaves, telling them to work and not to go up into the mountains anymore. I have been assured that those under his command have incited them to do just the opposite."[30] Of the other leaders, Armand, Bernard, Martial, and Gilles seemed the most inclined to conform to the conditions of freedom offered them.

However, the majority of these insurgents destined to return to the plantations as slaves were furious over this turn of events by which they felt themselves betrayed. They reproached their leaders for acquiescing in the government's offer and, at one point, had even taken Armand and Gilles as prisoner. When they finally did descend, they promised to be submissive and obedient upon their return to work, but instead continued to pillage and ransack the plantations, many of them by now abandoned, and here and there even proceeded to disarm a white planter.[31] Also during this time, the number of fugitives in les Cayes jail who were not claimed by their masters, listed as *nègres épaves*, increased by near-geometric proportions. Among these were two *nègres épaves* who had passed themselves off as freed slaves enrolled in the legion.[32] Given the disposition of these insurgents, Rigaud was forced to postpone the expedition against British-occupied Grande-Anse, for "they will inevitably take advantage of the absence of regular troops to agitate, stir up the other slaves, and pillage everything; all would then be lost."[33]

By September, most of them had come down from Macaya but remained in camps throughout the plain, as was their mode of organization in the mountains. Jacques Formon, still distrustful of, and distrusted by, Rigaud, held the strongest forces, with four to five hundred well-armed slaves in his band.[34] In November, Polverel summoned him to account for his open resistance: "You refuse to obey Rigaud, to serve under the banner of the republic! Well then, leave with your band; we will fight you, and the judgement of war will decide between you and us."[35] Formon left and forged his retreat back into the mountains. Pursued and captured by Rigaud, he was then arrested, given a military trial, and shot.[36]

As late as December, there were still groups of slaves encamped at Macaya or on the abandoned plantations in the Platons region, some of them armed. In addition to these was another company, composed of blacks of the Moco nation and commanded by Chérit, a fellow national.[37] To induce them to submit, Petit, the commander at Camp Périn, sent a black envoy of their nation to speak with Chérit who, highly suspicious, requested that he first be sent a bottle of tafia and some tobacco. When he received these articles, he gave the messenger a rifle to deliver to Petit and, as proof that this messenger was actually sent by the commander on Polverel's orders, demanded that Petit do likewise. During this time, two other bands from the region of Plymouth had set out to attack Camp Périn, but finding this impracticable, made their way to Macaya, where they sought the aid of Chérit and his company for a combined attack. Wearing the red cockade of the republican forces and identifying themselves as part of Jean Kina's company, they were rejected by Chérit, who categorically refused to have anything to do with them and sent them away.[38] Although Jean Kina had joined the Legion of Equality to fight in the name of France, he had already shown his rectionary colors during the first expedition against Jérémie.[39] Chérit's refusal to accept Kina's men, however, had little to do with the political ideologies of republicanism or royalism. The overriding factor was that this black soldier and his men, newly freed slaves that they were, had vigorously attacked them at Platons as part of Colonel Harty's army during the January campaign, forcing them to retreat to Macaya where survival required the maximum of human endurance. In fact, it had been said that the military success of that attack was due chiefly to this awesome Jean Kina and his contingent.[40]

These, then, were the attitudes and this the mentality of the insurgent slaves and their leaders, who had taken up arms in massive revolt to unburden themselves of slavery, who had forged their own freedom independently through marronage, and who had fought with their lives to defend it. Their freedom was sanctioned by the civil commissioners when they agreed to join in the defense of France against her enemies, and they now formed the rank and file of the French army. They did not have the powerful Spanish allies that their black rebel counterparts did in the North. Their choices were limited, and if they agreed to accept the government's proposal of freedom, most did so reluctantly and with a good deal of circumspection. Within the ranks of the legion, they continued to resist. Rigaud complained, only two weeks after the 25 July proclamation, that these new citizens "were still given over to committing acts unworthy of their new condition; they spread themselves out over the plantations, attempting to destroy citizens' property."[41] The *légionnaires*, as they were called, were chronically being arrested and sent to les Cayes jail.[42] Insubordination, refusal to obey orders, agitation, horse thievery, and desertion—all were forms of resistance that characterized the mood and temperament of the newly emancipated black soldier.

By first freeing the black warriors, Polverel was moving toward an eventual proclamation of general emancipation. His conception of emancipation, however, was radically different from that of his colleague in the North. Whereas Sonthonax had proclaimed the immediate abolition of slavery, Polverel was convinced that it could only successfully be achieved gradually, by stages. Two days prior to Sonthonax's proclamation of 29 August, Polverel had declared free those slaves on the sequestered plantations in the West belonging to émigré planters and deportees; in addition, all remaining insurgent maroons, including those of the Bahoruco, were also freed, as were those that had already joined the legion as warriors for France.

At this point he was totally unaware of the proclamation Sonthonax was about to publish. Having unofficially received word of it early in September, his immediate reaction, bordering on utter disbelief, was to question the legality of such an act: "Did you, or did you not proclaim general emancipation in the North? Were you free not to do so? Is the approbation of a single commune assembly in a parish [le Cap] where there are practically no owners left, sufficient to justify an act of this importance for the entire province of the North, an act of which the repercussions could be terrible for the whole colony? I do not know . . . but I fear the worst."[43] Already, the proclamation was beginning to circulate throughout the West. New slave insurrections had begun in the bordering areas of the North, spreading rapidly through the West into parts of the South before the 29 August proclamation was even issued.[44] Nearly half of the slaves in the West were already free. Were it not for Sonthonax's initiative, it would have taken Polverel at least another six months before proclaiming freedom for the rest.[45] He was now left with no other choice but to declare general emancipation, and he had no time to lose.

On 21 September 1793, the first anniversary of the French republic, Polverel invited the planters of the West to follow his example of 27 August and to proclaim the freedom of their own slaves, thus combining the principles of the French Revolution with general emancipation. If the force of events in the colony had driven Polverel to take this stand, the manner in which he concluded the abolition of slavery was dictated by his unshakable respect for the sacred rights of property. The acts of manumission would be signed voluntarily by the planters, and to facilitate this procedure Polverel set up open registers for them to sign in every parish throughout the province. Under these circumstances, and with no other alternative, the planters acquiesced.

The status of the slaves in the South, however, remained undefined. Delpech, as secretary to the civil commission, had been named civil commissioner of the South to alleviate the burden placed on Polverel by Ailhaud's resignation. His reaction to Sonthonax's proclamation was even more conservative than Polverel's. While hemming and hawing over the legalities of abolition, the authority of a delegate of France to impose such a measure, and over the established rights of the colonial regime and the individual property rights of the colonists, he refused to make a decision until a tripartite conference could be held to work out a uniform policy for the colony.[46] The question was settled by his death on the twenty-seventh. Having already taken concrete steps toward general emancipation in the West, Polverel was, to say the least, relieved. In a laconic reference to Delpech's death, Polverel wrote Sonthonax: "I miss [Delpech] because he was an honest man and a good citizen, but he died a month too late."[47] On 10 October, three days after his arrival in the South, Polverel's system was established there as in the West, but it still affected only the slaves of the abandoned plantations and those who had chosen to enroll in the army.

Comparing his system of emancipation with that of Sonthonax in the North, he had previously spoken in these terms to the slaves in the West:

> [Sonthonax] has given you freedom without property, or rather, with one-third of the revenues of the land which is devastated, without installations, without lodging. [He has given you freedom] without the means by which to make the land productive; and I have given you liberty, either with land under production or the means with which to promptly regenerate those lands that have been devastated. He has given no property rights to those of your brothers who are armed in the defense of the colony. . . . I have given the right of co-ownership to those who fight while you cultivate.[48]

The so-called property rights that Polverel envisaged for the emancipated blacks existed, however, more in theory than in fact. In the first place, they were restricted to the slaves of the sequestered plantations and to the warriors, collectively, and did not yet include the slaves on the plantations where the owner was present.[49] In reaction to Polverel's proposed distribution of land and revenues between these agricultural workers and the warriors, one colonist, arguing from a proslavery position, criticized it as "pure sophism," as illusory in any time and age, premature and full of anarchical principles tending toward the destruction of all property rights: "All at one stroke, Polverel has given these slaves freedom, equality, property rights, and the rights of French citizenship." [50] In fact, once universal emancipation was declared in the South and the West (on 31 October) and a *système portionnaire* established by Polverel for all plantation workers, the difficult and complicated notion of co-ownership was simply dropped. [51] His conception of emancipation, bound as it was to the legal abstraction of property, scarcely meant any more to the ex-slaves, from their point of view, than to the outraged colonist who saw it as pure folly. In reality, their "property rights" consisted in regimented, or unfree, wage-labor, as they were bound to their respective plantations and forced to continue working for their former masters as before. The plantations would remain undivided; the whip as a form of punishment was abolished and would be replaced by a future penal code; a detailed work code systematically delineating the specific hours and conditions of work, as well as the proportional salaries of the workers, would also be forthcoming and would be retroactive to 21 September. [52] On 31 October slavery itself was abolished and the Rights of Man now proclaimed universally in the South and West, as in the North, but the work codes did not come for another four and a half months.

It was during this period of transition from slavery to a semi-wage, semi-sharecropping labor system—accompanied in its first stages by administrative chaos, by little or no surveillance on the sequestered plantations, with production in a state of abandon, and with an inconsistent application of regulations existing only in tentative form—that the black workers outrightly expressed their own attitudes toward this freedom. Brief as it was, this period (from October 1793 to roughly April-May 1794 following publication of the codes) offers a unique opportunity to discern, through their acts of resistance to the new system and thus from their own vantage point, what that freedom meant to them.

How, then, did they react to their new state of freedom? In the preamble to his 7 February proclamation on wage allocations and distribution of agricultural produce between the owners and the laborers, Polverel reminded the black workers of the "errors" they had committed during the first months following their emancipation. [53] On some plantations, they took advantage of the absence of the owner and the relative state of abandon in which he left his plantation to expand the size of the small lots, or kitchen gardens, provided them under slavery for subsistence. Thus, they began cultivating portions of the plantation property as their own. They helped themselves to the uncultivated fruit of the land such as wood, fodder, and other products that grew spontaneously and that existed abundantly in a natural state. They helped themselves to the plantation rations and sold what they could at the market. They freely used the horses and mules belonging to the plantation, both for personal pleasure and to carry their stolen goods to market. On some plantations the workers had, in effect, taken over the land for their own purposes. As they were organized in brigades, each group would cultivate that portion of the land assigned to it, and the workers would then sell the products that were superfluous to their needs. The problems for the administration were even more acute on the plantations that had been sequestered from the émigré planters. In the parish of les Cotteaux, a group of blacks had settled themselves on the abandoned Condé plantation. There they cut down and burned the coffee grove to build houses for themselves in its place.[54] Now that they were free, it seemed only logical that the land they had labored upon for so long should rightfully be disposed of as they themselves saw fit.

On those plantations where the owner or a manager was present and where a somewhat regular work schedule was imposed, the most persistent of the workers' demands was the five-day working week. Under slavery, their only free day other than holidays was Sunday. They now expected that to change and refused to work as if they were slaves, from sunup to sundown, six days per week. It was true they could no longer be whipped, mutilated, or tortured, as they had been in the past, for the work code now placed well-defined restrictions on the extent of authority a former owner could exercise over his workers. In fact, by way of plantation assemblies, the slaves apparently even had some voice in nominating their managers and *commandeurs* (who now received the less offensive title of *conducteur*).[55] But to get the blacks to work, managers now had to replace the whip with the force of persuasion. Whereas under slavery the slaves were the object of the master's property rights and had, at best, only the illusory incentive of an eventual grant of freedom by a humane owner, the blacks were now legally free persons and were given a minimal pay incentive to increase production and, theoretically at least, their peculium, or personal possessions, as well. One of the innovations of Polverel's system was the creation of administrative councils on which the skilled laborers could preside and participate in decisions on the running of operations.[56] What actual weight their opinions carried at the meetings, however, is questionable, and the decisions of the administrative council, to be executed by the *conducteurs*, were not (as we shall see) always to the satisfaction of the field workers.

So although the mode of production and consequently the set of social and economic relations prevalent under slavery had been altered, and the locus of power shifted, the change actually had little effect upon the mentality and predispositions of the black workers. They were still legally bound to the plantations of their former masters and now subject to the specific regulations imposed by the government. In reaction, they often refused to work altogether; they would arrive in the fields late in the morning and quit early in the evening. When they did work, their work was slack and un-productive. They resisted the new system as they had resisted slavery—in marronage, a term now replaced by a more innocuous one, vagrancy.

The women, too, were protesting and were demanding equal pay for equal work. As slaves, they had worked in the fields under the same conditions as the men. Now, as laborers receiving a recompense, their role was no different and, excepting pregnancy and childbirth, they were subject to the same regulations as their male co-workers but received only two-thirds the pay: Why should we receive less pay than the men? Do we come to work later than they? Do we leave earlier? They might have added: Do we not re-ceive the same punishments as the men for refusing to work? Simply stated, the women saw themselves as individual and equal workers. Moreover, they were not fighting the men but, rather, the new system and its inequalities. The men evidently raised no objections to these demands, for Polverel had to try to convince them otherwise: "It is not against the owner; it is against yourselves, against their men, that the women formulate these exaggerated pretensions. They do not want any consideration to be given to the inequality of strength that nature has placed between them and the men, to the habitual and periodic infirmities, to the intervals of rest which their pregnancies, their childbirth, their nursing, oblige them to take." [57] Appealing to male pride in an effort to put these women in their "proper place," Polverel went on to say: "These men whose advantageous portion of the revenues they covet, work, save, and desire money only to be able to lavish it on their women. Africans, if you want to make your women listen to reason, listen to reason yourselves." [58]

Polverel could explain these diverse forms of resistance only by assuming that the owners, the former masters, as well as the managers, continued to treat the workers like slaves. He claimed that some presented a false inter-pretation of his proclamations or administered them wrongly,[59] that others told the workers the commissioner did not have the authority to free them and that their freedom would only be short-lived. In a few instances Polverel may have been right. Two days after his arrival in the South, one owner, Vernet, had assembled his slaves and told them that if they thought they were free, they were mistaken. The civil commissioner, he told them, was deceiving them by promising them freedom since only he, their owner, could validly grant it. (This was three weeks prior to the universal abolition of slavery, when only the slaves of the sequestered plantations and the warriors had been freed.) And though they had chosen a *commandeur* (the word was Ver-net's), Gabriel, Vernet refused to recognize him and threatened to have him hanged. When Gabriel, accompanied by three members of the legion (in-cluding Jacques Formon), reported this to Polverel, the commissioner went to the Vernet estate to investigate the matter. On being questioned, the assembled workers all concurred with the statement made by Gabriel although, they said, Vernet's wife told them they would, indeed, by freed by Polverel.[60] Neither the correspondence nor the prison records for this period, however, indicate that incidents as this one were in any way a widespread or common practice. With the counterrevolution now operating in full force throughout the colony, there is no reason to assume that Polverel would have been lax in pursuing recalcitrant planters trying to undermine potential black allegiance to the republic. In fact, he reminded the Vernet workers that if their statements were true, Vernet was a lost man.[61] He believed, in any event, that with his new work code he would be able to enlighten the workers as to their true interests. Once properly understood, the work code would create harmony between them and the owners, both parties being engaged in a collective enterprise, each having specific duties and responsibilities, the whole being based on a hierarchy of labor and the unequal distribution of wealth.

Article 23 of the work code, finally promulgated in early February, instructed the owners or the managers of each plantation to read and explain intelligibly to the assembled workers and *conducteurs* both the preamble and the articles concerning the work expected of them, as well as the allocated earnings due to them. This collective allocation of one-third of the plantation revenue would be based solely upon an arduous six-day work week. But when the question was put to them in accordance with Article 23, a good number persisted in demanding the five-day work week; that is, one day per week for themselves in addition to Sunday. In this case, their collective revenues would be cut by one half. If they decided upon two or more free days per week (in addition to Sunday), they would get nothing at all and would be removed, by force if necessary, from the plantation. Unfortunately, the official reports of the decisions made by the plantation workers throughout the Plaine-des-Cayes are rather few in number. However, those that do exist for the parish of Cavaillon, outside the Plaine-des-Cayes, indicate that in one case in three the black workers adamantly insisted upon a five-day work week, reserving Saturday for themselves, even after they were reminded that their earnings would be reduced to one-sixth. Some of them stated they would render their decision only to the military commander or to Polverel.[62]

Naturally one cannot hope to make any statistically precise generalizations as to worker attitudes toward the six-day week in this part of the province based on the reports of one parish. The type of plantation, the specific nature and intensity of the labor required, and perhaps, as well, the extent of creolization in an *atelier*, are all factors that might influence the decisions of the workers on the number of days they would want to work. However, on la Haye plantation in the Plaine-du-Fond, an area with the highest concentration of sugar plantations, the workers had originally decided upon a five-and-a-half-day work week. It was explained to them, though, that instead of one-third of the net revenues, they would now receive only three-elevenths. The workers then said that they were mistaken when they opted for a half-day off and that, since "a lot of other plantations were operating on five days per week," they, too, wanted an extra full free day and chose Thursday.[63] Based on the evidence available (even though it is fragmentary), it seems that the five-day work week was not an uncommon or untypical desire, at least among the black workers in this middle region of the South, an area where insurrectionary activity was, from the very beginning of the revolution, particularly prominent.

Following the publication of the 7 February work code and the 28 February regulations on the policing of the plantations, the black workers continued to resist in great numbers and in a variety of ways. Under the 28 February police code for plantation workers, the most common form of punishment was imprisonment and forced labor on public works without pay for a specific length of time, depending upon the offense. For example, in cases of disobedience or refusal to carry out the orders of one's superior, the sentence for a field worker was one month and, for a secondary *conducteur*, two months. If the orders were not carried out because of simple negligence, and not because of a formal refusal, the punishments in each case were reduced by a half. If a subordinate threatened his or her superior, either verbally or by gesture, he or she would be condemned to a two-month sentence; for the same offense, a secondary *conducteur* would receive four months. In the case of an armed threat, the punishments were tripled. Any worker or subordinate *conducteur* who carried out a threat by striking the head *conducteur* was dismissed for the rest of the year from the plantation, arrested, and tried under the civil penal code. If the majority of the workers on a plantation were guilty of any one of the above misdeeds, the entire work force would be dismissed and replaced by the owner with day laborers.[64]

In cases of theft, the guilty person was required to pay into the plantation treasury the value of the stolen goods; in addition, he or she would pay the same value a second time, as a fine, half of which was given to the informer, the other half to the government. If the products stolen were from the rations storehouse or were among the uncultivated, spontaneous fruits of the land, the fines would be evaluated at the potential market value of the products. For stealing or "borrowing" an animal, the thief would be required to pay a certain sum per day until the animal was returned, the fine depending upon the animal's utility. As in the case of ordinary thievery, a second fine was imposed and paid to the informer and the government. Damage to any form of plantation property was subject to the same punishments as for theft.

Naturally, plantation workers who resisted the regulations of the work code never had sufficient funds to cover their fines. Thus, they were thrown into prison to labor without pay on public works until such time as their potential, or hypothetical, earnings would equal the amount they owed. If after this they repeated an offense, they would be removed from the plantation, declared unworthy of participating in the plantation community, imprisoned, and sentenced to public works without pay for one year. [65]

In spite of these coercive regulations, incentives, and punishments, many black workers persisted in their refusal to submit to a system of regimented labor, by which they were still the exploited objects of property relations. As could be expected, the most widespread form of resistance revealed in the scattered prison lists and other administrative registers was the refusal to work, usually practiced by individual workers or groups of workers in varying numbers, and occasionally even by entire plantation labor forces.[66] In an attempt to abscond from work or to lighten the work load, they were often caught breaking up or damaging the sugar cane. For the same motives, they continually deserted their assigned plantation to attach themselves to another where, depending upon the type of plantation, the nature of the work required might be less arduous. Or simply, they would leave for another plantation, there to find friends or to hide out and not work at all. [67]

While some remained errant in various regions throughout the plain, others sought refuge in the military camps in the hills and mountainous areas where they could be sheltered by their black comrades in the legion. In a letter to Salomon, the military commander of les Cayes, Sonthonax gave orders to have three runaway workers from the Collet plantation arrested and sentenced to public works: "I have been told that you might be able to find them in the cabin of a *légionnaire* named Zamore, formerly belonging to the Collet plantation."[68] Some workers, as we saw earlier, were even audacious enough to pass themselves off as *légionnaires*.[69] Petit, commander at Camp Périn, wrote to ask Polverel to designate a plantation for over fifty workers who had tried to infiltrate the ranks of two companies, specifying that the plantation should be a safe distance from the camp.[70] In less than two weeks, he wrote to Polverel again, stating that he had arrested, and was sending back, twenty-nine black soldiers from the same two companies to be reintegrated into the plantations: "It is absolutely necessary that they be uprooted from the military milieu." [71]

On most plantations, insubordination was more often the rule than the exception. The hierarchy of labor established under slavery and perpetuated by the work code placed the *conducteur* in a position of direct authority and influence over the workers in his charge, and, as we know, his role in relation to them was a pivotal one. Thus production on the one hand, or insubordination and resistance on the other, generally hinged upon the inclinations and predispositions of the *conducteur*, as well as the strength of his influence over the workers. In some cases, the relationship between the *conducteur* and the workers might be one of solidarity. For example, on the sequestered Champtois plantation in the Plaine-du-Fond, indolence, refusal to work, and insubordination among the workers were seriously hindering production. Polverel sent Petit to visit the plantation and arrest the agitators. Having assembled the workers, he discovered that the *conducteur* was absent and sent one of his soldiers to bring him back from the nearby plantation where he had spent the night. Petit demanded that the *conducteur* denounce on the spot the six worst troublemakers. The *conducteur* refused to name a single one and was arrested, along with four others who were finally singled out by the second *conducteur*. [72]

On the other hand, as an authority figure responsible for executing the orders of his superiors or the decisions of the administrative council, the *conducteur* was often taken to task by dissenting workers. Sometimes worker insubordination was the direct result of the *conducteur*'s either surpassing his authority or being forced by the manager-steward to mistreat his charges.[73] In many instances, however, workers simply refused to obey the legitimate orders of the *conducteur* and usually accompanied their refusal with verbal threats and slanderous insults; a few even backed up their threats with arms. Nearly every plantation throughout the plain had agitators and proselytizers of this sort, and one or two sufficed to disrupt the already irregular rhythm of work. [74]

On the sugar plantations, the most vociferous and resolute type of protest was the refusal of night work. On the Coderc plantation, two female workers ordered by the administrative council to work the night shift categorically refused; one of the women, Guittone, threatened the *conducteur*, adding insult to injury, and told him that if there were any night work to be done, he would have to do it alone.[75] The manager of the third Laborde plantation complained of the same problem: "The workers categorically refuse to operate the mills at night; they arrive in the fields no earlier than eight or nine o'clock in the morning, in very few numbers at that, and do very little work per day." [76] Yet it was here on the third Laborde plantation that the black workers had registered the greatest degree of satisfaction up to the outbreak of the revolution, and even during its early stages. [77]

Even more illustrative of workers' attitudes toward night work, however, was the case of one Joseph Ibo, a sugar worker on the Gallais plantation. Joseph discreetly broke into a meeting of the administrative council, and, as the manager, Rostand, began reading his proposal for night work, he started gnashing his teeth and caused such a disturbance that Rostand was forced to stop reading. As he castigated Joseph for his insolence, the latter replied sardonically that he had a bad toothache. Furious, Rostand told him he had no business being at the meeting in the first place and that, if he disapproved of the proposal, he could leave. Joseph refused to leave, continued to disrupt the meeting, and, upon Rostand's repeated order to leave, lashed back: "Yes, I'm your slave." The manager tried to tell him there were no more slaves in Saint Domingue when Joseph pulled out a huge knife, threatening to strike him down; he would have succeeded were it not for the intervention of a few of the workers on the council. As they escorted him out, Joseph swore he would sell everything he had, up to his last chicken, to see Rostand dead. [78]

Theft of plantation products continued to be a problem. In addition to the natural products of the land, the workers stole surplus goods such as syrup, sugar, coffee, or indigo to sell at the market, either for their own benefit or, in some cases, for the benefit of other workers not engaged on their plantation. They would steal a horse or a mule belonging to the plantation, would try to pass it off as their own, and sell it to the first buyer. At other times, they simply "borrowed" an animal with which to transport and peddle their goods. [79]

In his preface to the work code, Polverel tried to convince the ex-slaves that, as "co-recipients" of the plantation products, their small kitchen gardens were now superfluous to their needs. As he did not want to remove them altogether, he restricted the size of their lots to what it had been under slavery, thirty paces by twenty paces each. The manager-steward, on the other hand, was allotted for his personal use an area three times that of the individual worker, in addition to his regular salary.[80] The inequality in favor of the plantation bookkeeper, perhaps combined with a long-standing resentment, pushed the workers at the Mercy estate to exact revenge on the steward. This latter, Poulain, wrote to Polverel to determine the proper measures to take against both the *conducteurs* and the workers, who persistently, if not purposely, left their pigs out of their pens at night; the pigs, naturally, ravaged and completely devoured his garden. [81]

Among the workers sentenced to public works for their misdeeds, prison escapes and subsequent flights into hiding were not uncommon.[82] Other such workers were sometimes openly supported by the solidarity of their co-workers who, considering that their comrades had sufficiently purged their sentences, presented themselves before the jailer to petition their release. This was the case with Guittone, one of the two female workers on the Coderc plantation who had adamantly refused night work and slandered the *conducteur;* her fellow workers felt that her loss of pay for one month was sufficient.[83] Or, from the second Laborde plantation, the petitioners promised that if their co-workers were released, they would try to make sure they remained on good behavior and, if they did not, would send them back. [84]

So the newly enfranchised slaves expressed through their acts what they thought of Polverel's type of freedom, of his work code and of the new regime, and from these acts one can begin to see, in a small way, how they wished to define their lives and their future as free citizens. They were no longer slaves and, as workers, they now earned a small retribution; yet the new regime had brought about no fundamental change in their relationship to the land nor to the products of their labor. The land did not belong to them. Polverel had made that explicitly clear in his 7 February proclamation. So when they took over abandoned plantations or cleared away a coffee grove to build homes for themselves, and when they took surplus crops to market and started using portions of the plantation land to expand their own minimal plots, they were merely taking and appropriating for themselves what they felt rightly belonged to them by virtue of their unrequited labor under slavery. This attitude was, as we have seen earlier, most vigorously expressed by slaves while defending the Platons region they had conquered with arms only the year before: "This land is not for you; it is for us," was their attitude in face of the "white brigands" who had come to attack them. Now, they would work, and would work perseveringly, but only if it meant that they had an independent and an undisputed claim to the land they cultivated, to their own labor, and to the fruits of their labor. For better or worse, this was how they felt, and neither Polverel nor Sonthonax, nor even Toussaint Louverture, could ever substantially change that mentality. Polverel now told them point-blank: "This land does not belong to you. It belongs to those who purchased it [or] who inherited it from the original owners"; in other words, to their former masters. [85]

Polverel tried to impress upon them that, left to themselves, they would end up plundering the land, leaving it barren and unproductive; they would end up killing off all the owners and then would begin struggling with one another for the means of survival. They would then be sufficiently divided amongst themselves and would fall prey to the first foreign power that sought to put them back in chains. Polverel used this sort of exaggerated bribery to get the ex-slaves back to work and to keep the system from collapsing. This contradiction between the aspirations of the newly freed black laborers and the harsh realities imposed by the system had generated certain patterns of resistance and had, in fact, stimulated a sense of solidarity. When the workers pillaged the plantation rations, they used their own methods of dividing them up; if they sold stolen surplus, it was often for the benefit of other workers. They covered up for one another, organized themselves to obtain the release of a co-worker from prison; they sheltered their comrades who had run away or who were being pursued. And if disobedience and flagrant insubordination toward one's superior were common, the incidence of *conducteurs* being arrested along with groups of workers in their charge was equally common, despite the increased severity of their sentences. [86]

Among the former slave leaders of the Platons insurrection, many had become company captains, either in the Legion of Equality or in the local militia units that were created to police the countryside and maintain the subordination of the black workers to the new work regime. But workers and soldiers often carried out acts of resistance in mutual complicity. Sometimes, imprisoned workers would escape under the dissimulating eye of the black militia guards responsible for their surveillance.[87] As we have already seen, it was not uncommon for a *légionnaire* to provide shelter for fugitive workers. At the same time, the *légionnaires* could be found agitating amongst the plantation workers: Beauregard, military commander of Cavaillon, wrote to Polverel concerning the effect of his 28 February proclamation on the plantations he visited. He discovered several workers who, having disrupted the working order on their own plantations, had taken cover on various others. Along with these agitators, he found two deserters from the Legion "who serve as models of indolence for the rest. It would be impossible for me to depict the new order of things without making mention of the runaways, and I would not be surprised at all, citizen commissioner, if before long the runaways follow one another with the same rapidity as in the days of despotism. That, effectively, is the success of the regenerating principles of liberty, equality and humanity."[88] Nicolas, a dragoon in the Legion of Equality, was arrested in early April and sentenced to public works without pay "until all the plantation workers in the parish of Baynet return to an orderly, disciplined work routine." On the same day, thirty-one workers, including the two *conducteurs* from La Cour plantation in Baynet, were arrested along with Nicolas. [89]

Forced labor on public works, however, was not always a form of direct punishment. Plantation workers could often be called upon to leave the fields and report for *corvée* duty, lasting anywhere from a few days to an entire week. The black officers and soldiers in the legion were responsible for delivering the orders issued by their superiors for the enumerated workers from each plantation. The blacks often resisted this additional form of forced labor by not reporting for *corvée* duty at all or by reporting for only a part of the required length of time. Toward the end of January, an equal number of men and women from the Bourdet plantation—30 in all—were slated for public works for the week of the twentieth. They never showed up once. In the same week, 23 more, ordered from the Raynaud-Charpentier plantation, did not report for duty until Friday. And, having already missed four days' work, they did not appear until ten o'clock, well after their mid-morning meal. In both of these cases, the plantation *conducteurs* evaded their obligations as much as the workers did.[90] The *légionnaires*, who were supposed to deliver the work orders to the plantation managers, sometimes covertly aided the blacks in absconding from their required duties. During the same week in January, additional orders had been issued for 350 workers from

five other plantations to report for *corvée* duty. Barthélemy Guilgault, a lieutenant in the Beaufils company of the legion, claimed that he entrusted two
of his dragoons, Gilles and Cada, with delivering the work orders. Since the
orders were never delivered and therefore none of the workers showed up,
the three *légionnaires* were interrogated. Each made statements contradict-
ing those made by the other two, so that it could not be determined with
certainty which one of the three was the guilty party. An examination of their
interrogations reveals this, in all probability, to be a good case of purposeful
negligence. [91]

Of the principal insurrectionary leaders of the Platons revolt of 1792–93,
Armand and Bernard were perhaps the most diligent in carrying out their
new duties as captains in the legion and members of the French army. Given
the high rate of insubordination, indolence, and persistent resistance to his
work code among the black workers of the Plaine-du-Fond, especially on the
sequestered plantations, Polverel found it necessary to introduce additional
measures of control. At the end of March he established a team of regional
inspectors, each inspector being responsible for the surveillance of a given
number of plantations. The commissioner believed that to increase their
productivity, the workers needed only to be directed by men who knew the
nature of the land, the temperature, the climate, the effects of these upon
production, and the type of agriculture best suited to the Plaine-du-Fond.
To prevent the rhythm of production from slackening on certain plantations,
they needed supervisors who could stimulate the "lazy," who would denounce insubordination to the authorities, stir the zeal of the managers, and
reinforce the discipline demanded by the *conducteurs*. These men would be
chosen from either current or former agricultural laborers. [92]

And so, for "their zeal, talents and intelligence," Armand and Bernard
were both chosen, along with six others, as regional inspectors.[93] For the time
being, Martial and Gilles Bénech retained the positions they occupied in the
legion. Jacques Formon, the most uncompromising of the popular leaders,
had already been court-martialled and shot for perpetuating insurrectionary
activity and refusing to follow Rigaud's leadership.

What, then, can be discerned from these diverse activities? In what sense
are they an expression of the mentality, the expectations and aspirations
of the newly emancipated blacks in the face of this freedom imposed and
defined from the exterior? First of all, the demands that were placed upon
them were partly generated by the war situation in the colony and by the
necessity of a tightly regimented labor force to feed the troops and sustain
the war effort against France's enemies. The defense of Saint Domingue depended upon the black warriors, but without the arduous and constant labor
of the agricultural workers, the government, as the civil commissioners realized, "would have neither the rations with which to feed the soldier nor the

revenue with which to pay his salary."[94] However, with or without the economic pressures of the war, the regulations imposed upon the black workers were intrinsically tied to the property relations of the new economic order taking shape and replacing slavery. These, judging from the widespread and diverse acts of resistance to them, clashed head-on with the independent mentality of the ex-slaves struggling to redefine their own identity and social existence.

One colonial observer (a proponent, nonetheless, of reformed slavery) saw where Polverel could not, the futility of attempting to establish a regimen of labor that would impose upon the freed slaves a European, occidental mode of thought and of social organization, central to which are the virtues of work, in and of itself, of competitiveness, profit incentives, and ever-expanding production; in short, the virtues of the Western capitalist ethic. Freed slaves, he argued (although from a racist perspective), simply could not be induced on the one hand, by a small recompense for their labor and an amelioration of their former condition, and on the other hand by rationalized coercion and punishment, to work as assiduously as would be necessary for France to maintain the economic advantages that her colonies guaranteed under slavery: "How does one prove to a person who fulfills his needs on very little and who has not the desire for wealth that he must work without respite, as the prosperity of the colonies and the interests of national commerce do require, if just a few days work each month suffice to fill his individual needs?"[95] The difficulty, precisely, was not in obtaining work from the ex-slaves, but in obtaining work rigorous enough to maintain the wealth and superiority of France among the European nations. Reckoning that, in the tropics, only severe constraint or the violent desire for riches could push one to accomplish such painful and continuous work as crop production in the colonies requires, he saw that Polverel's system, despite freedom (or precisely because of it), went against the grain of the ex-slaves' own predispositions and habits: "Unambitious and uncompetitive, the black values his liberty only to the extent that it affords him the possibility of living according to his own philosophy."[96] Given the nature of the slaves' reaction and resistance to the system of enfranchisement that we have seen, one is inclined to ascribe a fair measure of truth to the reflections of this contemporary colonial observer who, himself, would have preferred a reorganized system of slavery that would only lead to gradual manumissions under highly restrictive conditions.

Here, then, lies the heart of the problem, for if only with a coercive system such as slavery could property owners extract enough work from the black laborer to sustain France's commercial advantage, then, for the individual black laborer, freedom was to be had at what cost and on whose terms? The blacks were no longer slaves and, for their part, generally did not expect to be required to work and (in spite of the abolition of the whip) to live as if they still were slaves, from sunrise to sunset, tied to the same plantation, often to the same owner as before, and with no opportunity to appropriate for themselves the means by which to inform this freedom with the social, material, and cultural content that would give it real meaning in their daily lives. So they often refused to work and turned fugitive. Others tried to impose their own will and exercise a small measure of control over their work conditions. To abscond from work, still others tried to slip into the ranks of the legion, and so on. But underneath all this, and far more central to it, was a fundamental claim to the land. Freedom for the ex-slaves would mean the freedom to possess and to till their own soil, to labor for themselves and their families, with no constraints other than their own self-defined needs, and to sell or dispose of the products of their labor in their own interest. Or, to put it another way, freedom would consist largely in subsistence farming based upon individual, small proprietorship of the land, in direct contradiction, at that, with the demands of a colonial economy utterly dependent upon large-scale production for external markets.

It may indeed be presumptuous to assert at this point that the popular ideological origins of the emergent Haitian peasantry lie in this immediate postemancipation period. Extensive research into peasant lifestyles, modes of social organization, the relationship of kinship ties to the land, and much more, would be needed to develop and sustain such an assertion, all of which lies far beyond the scope of the present study. It can perhaps be suggested, however, that the independent attitude toward the land and the implacable resistance to forced labor expressed in diverse ways by the black workers (whether as maroons, as in the case of the Platons rebels, or as plantation laborers, many of whom were themselves ex-Platons rebels) was at once an extension of that small measure of autonomy they had acquired under slavery with their kitchen gardens and marketing experience, and at the same time the beginning of a consciousness that later became manifest in the formation of a class of small, more or less self-sufficient, peasant producers. It was, at any rate, the very antithesis of the plantation regime and its requisite organization of labor.

The extent to which one may postulate some form of carry-over into the postslavery environment in Saint Domingue of African ways and cultural attitudes toward the land is also debatable. We do know from what studies have been done thus far on the ethnic composition of slave *ateliers* in the South that the Congolese were highly prominent, if not the most numerous of the African ethnic groups. The preponderance of the Congolese also appears to emerge after mid-century and toward the latter decades of the colonial period.[97] A letter written by Jean-Joseph Descourvières, a French missionary sent in the 1770s to the Kakongo, one of the local coastal kingdoms comprising the Ancient Congo—an area figuring prominently in the latter eighteenth-century French slave trade—reveals a singularly similar relationship to the land as that which seemed to be expressed by many a newly freed slave in this central region of the South. He writes: "Here the land belongs to its first occupant. Each one cultivates that which he [or she] deems appropriate. The division of uncultivated land is an unknown practice among these people; but when it is cultivated no one can take it away from the one who first cultivated it."[98] The writer also observed that "the land is very fertile, is easily cultivated and requires little work; it is only the women here that are engaged in tilling it."[99] In his writings on the Ancient Congo, Cuvelier also concurs on the role of women in tilling the land and producing the food, though more specifically he explains the practices governing landholding in terms of clan and kinship: "The land is possessed by clans, [and] each clan owns the lot that its ancestors left to it."[100] Within the clan, or the village, the members each possess their own personal objects which they use as they please: "The father owns the house, the mother her instruments and implements of work. The husband must provide clothing to his wife, and the wife must procure and prepare food for her husband. He cannot, however, take as he pleases the crops that belong to his wife. . . . The crops belong exclusively to the woman if they were grown by her. [But] if her husband helped to clear and untimber the land, he is entitled to his share of the yield."[101]

Small wonder that Polverel found some women in the South demanding, at least, equal pay with the men for equal work in tilling the land and in planting and harvesting the plantation crops (one-third of which was divided up in unequal values amongst the plantation workers collectively). And finally, on the distribution of wealth in society, Descourvières observed a characteristic trait among the inhabitants of the Kakongo, which was "this constant inclination to share what one has with one's neighbor. The poor and the rich have nothing in their own right, and the rich man is soon as poor as the one he helped, unless his status continually fills the holes that his generosity makes in his fortune."[102]

Certainly variations and differences existed in landholding practices, kinship ties and obligations, and cultural ways in general throughout the kingdoms making up the Ancient Congo (not to mention the rest of western Africa). The extent to which some of these may have been carried over and expressed in various ways after emancipation and later adapted to the New World environment of postindependence Haiti can, at best, only be speculative without much further and deeper research into the societies and cultures from which the African-born slaves, constituting by far the vast majority on the eve of the revolution, had originated, and in which many of them must have spent a formative part of their lives.[103]

REL. TO LAND

MORE THAN FREEDOM NOW

Whatever the case, the question of freedom as defined in one's relationship to the land (though the period under study here is admittedly too short to provide any conclusive answers) appears nonetheless to be a central factor motivating acts of resistance by ex-slaves to the new labor regime of emancipation. Also significant is the fact that these acts of resistance, numerous as they were, did not coalesce into an organized movement with designated leaders, conspirators, secret meetings, and clandestine operations, as in the more spectacular revolts and armed insurrections that punctuated the revolution. They constituted, rather, the generalized, spontaneous, and inarticulate expression of discontent in reaction to a system that had little to do with the freedom these ex-slaves had fought for, but now were not allowed to define. It was this personal attachment to the land and the active imposition of their own will upon its cultivation and utilization that would transform their past identity as slaves into that of free persons. And it was this that the new regime deprived them of.

These, then, were the troops that constituted the French republic's new army of black peasants and soldiers, and it was upon them that the government depended to sustain the war against the counterrevolutionary forces and their foreign allies, Britain and Spain, now in control of the better part of the colony. If the attitudes, expectations, and activities of these blacks ran counter to the economic exigencies of the moment, they nevertheless were the direct product of slavery itself, and the new regime of freedom, in spite of its incentives, had done little to change the conditions out of which these aspirations emerged.

8

From Freedom to Civil War

By the spring of 1794, the military situation in the colony spelled near-total ruin for France. The black troops fighting under the banner of Spain in the North now controlled the better part of the province, while at the western extremity, Môle St. Nicolas had fallen to the British. The only areas now left to France in the North were the dependencies of le Cap and Port-de-Paix, where Laveaux had established his headquarters in retreat. In the West, the British-occupied territories included a good part of that province and by the end of June would include Port-au-Prince as well, while in the South, the British remained confined to the relatively isolated regions of Jérémie and Grande-Anse.

Without the support and military allegiance of the black forces to the republican cause, the survival of Saint Domingue as a French colony was, it seemed, in serious jeopardy. Sonthonax's proclamation of emancipation in August of the previous year had done nothing to win over the mass of black troops under Jean-François and Biassou, and, with the exception of Toussaint, who remained nevertheless with the Spanish, the letters of the civil commissioners to the black leaders, filled with promises of liberty and equality, fell on deaf ears. Earlier that summer, prior to the civil commissioners' attempts to win over the black rebels to the republican side during the Galbaud affair, Toussaint had offered to join Laveaux on condition that he accord full amnesty to the black rebel forces and officially recognize the freedom of the slaves. Upon Laveaux's refusal, Toussaint remained with Spain for yet another eight months. That he espoused general emancipation (as did Sonthonax) appears to be firmly established as he had himself declared on 29 August, simultaneously with Sonthonax's proclamation of the same date, that he planned to work for the emancipation of all slaves: for the abolition of slavery. In a singular call to rally the blacks to his side, he spoke in these terms: "Brothers and friends. I am Toussaint Louverture. My name has perhaps become known to you. I have undertaken vengeance. I want Liberty and Equality to reign in Saint Domingue. I am working to bring these about. Unite with us, brothers, and fight with us for the same cause."[1]

The real question, then, is perhaps not so much why he eventually broke with Spain and turned about to fight for France in 1794, but rather, why, after Sonthonax's 29 August proclamation abolishing slavery in the North, he still decided to remain with Spain. Here, one can only surmise Toussaint's motives. In the first place, Sonthonax's 29 August proclamation followed by only a few months Laveaux's refusal to accept Toussaint's proposal for general emancipation. Had not Sonthonax himself begun his term in Saint Domingue by proclaiming, to reassure the white colonists, the inviolability of slavery? Moreover, Sonthonax's 29 August proclamation, for what it was worth, touched only the North province. Also, Toussaint's royalist leanings may have counted for something in his decision to remain with Spain.[2] Sonthonax was, after all, a mere civil commissioner, a representative of the French government vested with certain powers, but whose authority could also be revoked by the home government. When Toussaint had invited his black brothers to unite with him and fight for "the same cause," it seems evident Toussaint was referring to the cause embodied in Sonthonax's proclamation of general emancipation in the North (the legality of which he and the other black leaders denied[3]) and, by offering himself as a better alternative, was inviting the blacks to treat with mistrust and suspicion the commissioner's "cause."

But then, Toussaint's alliance with royalist Spain was hardly on solid ground itself. If, on the one hand, his personal freedom was guaranteed by the Crown, the sincerity of the Spanish government nevertheless began to wear thin as Spain was taking no visible steps toward liberating the slaves in her own colony. Whatever Toussaint's motives, in the end, he may merely have been biding his time, as he apparently did before initially joining Jean-François and Biassou in 1791. It was now obvious that he would never rise above Jean-François in command, and therefore his own goals for bringing an end to slavery would remain perpetually thwarted. As his pursuit of general emancipation eventually led him into a tenuous and increasingly conflictive rapport with Spain, who never intended abolishing slavery in the first place, he opted to join forces with France at the beginning of May 1794.[4] So by carefully—and deceitfully—disentangling himself with the Spanish government, he now became the political and military enemy of his former superiors, Jean-François and Biassou. By June, the territories he had conquered for Spain, as well as four to five thousand well-trained and loyal troops, were now under his command in the name of the republic. Though he asked of Laveaux only that he retain his rank of colonel, the latter made him a brigade general. Among Toussaint's chief officers were the intrepid Dessalines, Henri-Christophe, Paul Louverture, his brother, and Moïse, his adopted nephew; Christophe, we know, was a free black at the time of the revolution, as was Toussaint.[5]

If the blacks in the North had a prominent and central figure like Toussaint, whose leadership abilities on the battlefield were equal to those he exercised in politics, and who could provide them with disciplined direction and a clear sense of their political goals, such was not the case in the West and the South. In the West, the major administrative and military positions were held by the mulatto leaders, a significant portion of whom had already defected to the English side after general emancipation was proclaimed in the fall of 1793. Thus, Saint Marc, Arcahaye, and Mirebalais in the Artibonite valley, as well as Léogane and Grand-Goâve, in the southern section of the province, and the bay of Port-au-Prince all fell under British control. Rigaud and Bauvais remained staunchly republican, defending the interests of France and the freedom of the slaves, but they could count only upon the Legion of Equality for black support, while the mass of black warriors and insurgents in the West had organized themselves independently into separate maroon bands, each with its own chosen leader, usually African-born. In general, they distrusted the mulattoes, Bauvais and Rigaud notwithstanding.[6]

It was only with the greatest difficulty that Bauvais was able to enlist the services of a few of these maroon leaders, notably Alaou—African-born of the Nago nation, a fervent voodoo adept and chief leader of over ten thousand troops throughout the Cul-de-Sac plain.[7] They maintained their camps in the mountains near the Spanish border, whence they remained at the same time in contact with agents of the Spanish government. By doing so, they sustained a covert neutrality which enabled them to obtain from both sides the arms and ammunition they needed to defend an independent position.[8] Already Hyacinthe, perhaps the most powerful and influential of the popular black leaders in the West, was in prison on suspicion of collaboration with the British, a charge which Sonthonax personally found groundless and from which he later exonerated Hyacinthe.[9] However, his imprisonment only helped to reinforce the natural circumspection and reticence of the maroon bands toward openly and loyally embracing the French cause. [10]

During the months of January and February, Bauvais remained in close contact with Alaou, who seemed, if hesitant and cautious, nevertheless on the point of joining the republican army, and a meeting was held between him and Sonthonax in Port-au-Prince on 9 February. Because of his association with Sonthonax, spurious rumors began to spread among the mulatto troops that Sonthonax, who now openly favored the blacks, had held this secret meeting with Alaou only to entrust him with the mission of assassinating Bauvais at Croix-des-Bouquets. That there were serious misunderstandings and differences between Alaou and Bauvais is certain; that Alaou wanted to assassinate him, however, was almost certainly a fabrication, and when Alaou and his troop finally met with Bauvais toward the end of March, they were apprehensive and knew that something terrible would result. Their suspicions were confirmed when a group of armed mulattoes broke into Bau-

vais's office, killing Alaou and eight of his chief officers in cold blood.[11] Over
two hundred of his band that had accompanied him and that had remained
encamped in the town were also massacred.[12]

Scarcely two weeks later, the Intermediary Commission (established to
replace the Colonial Assembly upon the arrival of the civil commissioners in
1792) reversed Sonthonax's earlier acquittal of Hyacinthe and ordered him,
as well as Jean Guyambois, also acquitted by Sonthonax, to be deported
from the colony.[13] Colonel Malenfant, who knew Hyacinthe well, claims that
the mulattoes had then laid a trap to eliminate him by sending black emissaries to request a rendezvous with them. When Hyacinthe arrived at the
designated place, his fate was sealed. He was captured and, like Alaou,
was shot dead.[14] The death of Alaou, the subsequent reversal of Sonthonax's acquittal of Hyacinthe by the Intermediary Commission, and, finally,
his assassination left the insurgent black masses feeling bitter, confused,
and betrayed. On the one hand, the majority of the mulattoes in the West
had opposed general emancipation and allied themselves with the British to
safeguard their property and privileges, telling the blacks that their freedom
was worthless and that France had no authority to abolish slavery. Yet those
mulatto leaders who did remain loyal to the republic inspired little or no
confidence in the African masses who, as we have seen, time and again felt
betrayed. What they did understand was that only they could permanently
guarantee their own freedom, and for this they must remain armed.

By the end of May 1794, combined British and French émigré forces had
captured Camp Bizoton and marched with arms on Port-au-Prince. Entirely
defenseless, Sonthonax and Polverel saw no alternative but to capitulate. Escorted by Bauvais and a small detachment of black soldiers, they retreated
to Jacmel on 4 June. A few days later a boat arrived from France carrying
two decrees of the National Convention. The one, passed on the initiative of
two members of the Massiac Club, called for the arrest and return to France
of the civil commissioners for trial; the other, ironically, was the decree of
4 February sanctioning the abolition of slavery in the colony.

Before leaving Saint Domingue, however, the civil commissioners had
placed Rigaud in full administrative and military command of the South.
Polverel specifically instructed him to lead and coordinate the insurgent
bands of Africans who, now led by Dieudonné, a Congo, and Pompée, were
still encamped in full force and armed to defend their freedom.[15] Apparently, Sonthonax had met with Dieudonné on the Nérette plantation during
his retreat to Jacmel in June. In a purely symbolic gesture, he had placed his
commissioner's medallion around Dieudonné's neck, thus nominally delegating his powers to the African leader while, reputedly, reminding him that
"so long as you see mulattoes in your ranks, you will never be free."[16] Sonthonax had also named Dieudonné a municipal officer of Port-au-Prince.[17]

But by the end of the following year, Dieudonné and Pompée, at the head of some three to four thousand insurgent blacks, were in open armed rebellion against the authority of Rigaud and Bauvais. That Dieudonné interpreted Sonthonax's parting words and gesture to the letter may partially, but only superficially, explain Dieudonné's rebellion against Rigaud. After all, the bitter fact remained that Hyacinthe and Alaou were already dead, the latter having been cruelly assassinated by a mulatto faction.

As Dieudonné was now at the point of joining the British, who, it appears, were using him to recapture Léogane, Bauvais and Rigaud both tried unsuccessfully to persuade him to cooperate with them and to bring himself back in line with the republican cause that he had formerly embraced.[18] Finally, Rigaud summoned Toussaint to intervene and to use his influence as a black general to regain Dieudonné's loyalty. Dieudonné had explained his resentment and mistrust of the mulattoes in this way: If freedom and equality reigned in the North and in those parts of the West under Toussaint's authority, it was not so in the places where Rigaud and Bauvais commanded. He and his men were fighting them in order that equality might reign among all colors, but the mulattoes did not want the blacks to be their equals. As for him, he was a good republican and loyal to France. [19]

When this was reported to Toussaint, the black general personally dictated a letter to Dieudonné, to be carried by three black envoys and read aloud to his assembled troops. In the letter he pointed out to Dieudonné his own error in having earlier been seduced by royalist Spain. He assured him that the royalists would merely use one-half of the blacks to keep the other half in chains and begged of him, if the British had succeeded in deceiving him, to abandon them and return to the republic. Their only hope to remain free, as he saw it, was with the French republic. In this, Toussaint's arguments were well founded, and even Dieudonné seemed hesitant for a moment.[20] The acuity of his political observations, his profound confidence in the French republic, and the deep personal concern that he—a black like them—expressed in his letter had decisively influenced a significant group of Dieudonné's men, led by Laplume, to rise up against him. He was arrested and sent to Saint Louis prison, where he died of starvation shortly afterward. [21]

But Toussaint was aware that, among Dieudonné's men, there was more at stake than wavering allegiances and royalist leanings, dangerous as these were. He no doubt suspected that one of their reasons for wanting to join the British was their mistrust of the republican mulatto leaders. For Dieudonné to remain on the republican side, he would have to submit to the higher command of Bauvais and Rigaud, in spite of the authority he believed was conferred upon him by Sonthonax. He had formerly been an officer in Alaou's band, and Alaou had been shot down by a mulatto faction—in Bauvais's

presence, at that. The mulattoes, he was convinced, would never embrace
real equality for the blacks. Toussaint was certainly aware of these problems
and, to counter Dieudonné's misgivings, had taken great care to mention in
his letter that "if certain reasons prevent you from having confidence in the
brigade generals Rigaud and Bauvais, the Governor-General Laveaux, who
is a good father to all of us and in whom France has placed her confidence, at
least merits yours as well." Unfortunately, Laveaux's influence never really
extended that far outside of the North. Those of Dieudonné's men who rose
up under Laplume had opted for republican France, but instead of going
with Rigaud and Bauvais, it seems they joined Toussaint with some three
thousand men. [22]

The charges leveled by Dieudonné against Rigaud and Bauvais were most
apparent in the South province. Here, Rigaud ruled with supreme political and military powers. Before leaving the colony, Polverel had, in effect,
named Rigaud interim governor-general of the South. In this capacity, the
latter had built up a virtual military state under mulatto control, a state in
which civil and municipal functions were exercised by the military, and the
military posts occupied by the mulattoes, while the black ex-slaves in the
army rarely ever advanced beyond the rank of captain. [23]

For the plantation workers, Rigaud's system was but an intensified version
of that set up by Polverel, whose aim was to provide the smooth transition of
the blacks from slavery to freedom without jeopardizing productivity levels.
Under the pretext of repressing vagrancy, or marronage, the blacks were
irrevocably bound to the same plantation, and if found elsewhere, were arrested and thrown into jail. The administration of the plantations was all but
tyrannical, with no legal recourse for the laborers against an unfair or overly
harsh punishment. Moreover, the sequestered plantations that had been
abandoned or left vacant by the émigrés were leased almost without exception to mulatto proprietors or to those aspiring to become property holders.
Plantation personnel generally tended to become the exclusive domain of
the former *affranchis*, whose military, political, and numerical superiority
over the remaining white colonists allowed them to supplant the former as
the new ruling class in the South. [24]

In a letter to Polverel, written in October 1794, only three and a half
months after the commissioner's departure, Rigaud summed up the state of
affairs in the South: "The province . . . is tranquil and in a reasonably good
state of defense. . . . Work is going well; your proclamations on agricultural production are having the full effect that you anticipated." [25] If indeed
the black laborers were, for the time being, back on the plantations and
readjusting themselves to an orderly work routine, this state of tranquility
can, in part, be attributed to the politico-military structure of the South and
to the threat and use of force to constrain the workers. Rigaud ruled the

South with an iron hand to establish the province's prosperity, thus enabling it to maintain its army without additional external financing, to sustain its defense positions, and to recapture Tiburon and Léogane from the British forces. But the interests of military defense, which depended upon economic prosperity, also provided a built-in pretext to consolidate the subjugation of the black laborers. So at the same time as they strengthened the South economically and militarily, the mulatto rulers used and extended Polverel's work codes—which defined the basis of the new plantation economy—as an instrument of black servitude and a basis from which to build a virtual mulatto oligarchy.

One such instance of abuse involved Faubert, a mulatto division commander of the legion in the South. A favorite of his own men, "with whom he associated on amicable terms and who familiarly called him Trois Bouteilles," [26] he was not well liked by the plantation workers. He had received an ordinance from Polverel concerning worker absenteeism during the working day, but had rewritten it to make it harsher than Polverel had ever intended. By his own ordinance of 19 April, Faubert forbade the black farm workers during their specified working hours to leave their plantation, for any reason, without the express permission of the manager, under penalty of eight days detention in jail.[27] What was particularly irritating for the workers in this ordinance was that it also penalized everyone else by depriving the entire *atelier* of a worker for a whole week (and for a minor cause), therefore reducing their collective productivity and potential revenue, small as it was.

It was at this time, in April-May 1794, that the last independent insurrectionary movement of the black workers occurred, just prior to the forced departure of the civil commissioners. Under the leadership of Appollon, a lieutenant in the local militia at Petit-Goâve, the blacks on several plantations around the area had organized mass meetings to oppose the ordinance published by Faubert. Appollon knew that it had been rewritten and rendered much harsher than Polverel's original version, and he made it known to the workers that it was a false proclamation. However, his underlying purpose in organizing these gatherings was to agitate the workers, using this issue as grounds to assassinate Faubert. In his defense, Faubert claimed that the insurrectionary movement of the black workers was really instigated by the mulatto military commander of Petit-Goâve, Brunache, who, seeing his own authority threatened by Faubert, was behind the movement in order to get the ordinance annulled.[28] His only grounds for the claim, however, were that the blacks were by nature too apathetic and too void of any sense of common interest to be the responsible ones.[29] As a popular leader, however, Appollon had been actively agitating for quite some time amongst the workers he was supposed to be policing. And though Polverel did, in the end, annul Faubert's ordinance, he nonetheless said of Appollon that "his spirit of domination and insubordination, his influence over the Africans, and the misuse he has been making of that influence, the stockpiles of powder and cartridges that he had accumulated behind the backs of his superiors, prove that he had been contemplating armed rebellion for a long time."[30] In addition to Appollon, two other black workers, Atity and Tausia, were also arrested as active instigators who, knowing that the plot was to kill Faubert, approved of it and agitated amongst the other blacks to solicit their adherence.[31]

With the departure of the civil commissioners from the colony and the consequent consolidation of Rigaud's authority in the South, the indigenous protest movements of the black workers had markedly subsided. The basic explanation for this apparent absence of independent popular activity on a widespread or noticeable scale must lie in the particular conditions that distinguished the South from the rest of the colony.

Since the war with Britain, normal communication links between the North and the South had effectively been severed, thus leaving the province almost completely isolated from the centers of activity and agitation in the rest of the colony. By keeping the British forces at bay, from Tiburon at the west to Léogane at the east, Rigaud managed to preserve the greater part of the South from foreign occupation. These circumstances enabled him to assume and consolidate in the South a supreme authority that remained largely uncontested. As Garran-Coulon observed, "It is doubtful that the authority of the Governor [Laveaux], residing in the North, would have been respected, even if the opportunities of recourse to his authority were available."[32] By the same token, the blacks were left isolated from the course of events elsewhere in the colony.

While Dieudonné and his troops were in open rebellion against Rigaud and Bauvais in the West, the mulattoes in the North were plotting to overthrow Laveaux and thereby allow Villate, the mulatto commander of the Cap area, to replace him as governor-general of the colony. Villate had been in full command of le Cap since the departure of the civil commissioners in July 1794. As the war situation had kept Laveaux in retreat at Port-de-Paix, it was not until October 1795 that he moved the seat of government back to le Cap. When he arrived with Perroud, the treasurer, he put an end to the flagrant abuses the mulattoes had made of their authority and freed a considerable number of blacks from the prisons.[33] The mulattoes, already uneasy over Laveaux's close association with Toussaint and the blacks, saw these measures as a direct threat to their assumed authority, cried tyranny, and began mobilizing opposition to the governor. Things finally came to a head and exploded on 20 March 1796. A group of mulattoes arrested Laveaux and threw him into prison along with Perroud. Toussaint was informed of Laveaux's arrest through the vigilance and initiative of two black officers, Jean-Pierre Léveillé of the Cap regiment, and a brigade colonel, Pierre-Michel, both of whom the municipality of le Cap had tried to win over. [34]

Faced with the threat of some ten thousand black troops under Toussaint's command, and upon orders given by Toussaint (who was in Gonaïves) to Henri-Christophe, the municipality released Laveaux and Perroud. However, Villate refused to concede authority to the governor, while his men tried to provoke Laveaux's assassination by telling the blacks that the governor had ships in the harbor filled with chains to put them back into slavery. When Toussaint arrived in le Cap, he quickly and convincingly put an end to these lies, and Laveaux welcomed him as his liberator. It was by now clear that Toussaint and his army were the strongest force in the colony; more than that, Toussaint appeared to hold the undivided confidence of the black masses. Laveaux realized this, too, and proclaimed Toussaint lieutenant to the governor. [35]

In all likelihood, the ordinary black worker in the South had never even heard of Toussaint, or knew of him by name only, but knew little or nothing about him. Most of their own leaders were by now serving as regional agricultural inspectors or as active soldiers in the legion and, as part of the army in the South, were now devoted to Rigaud and their mulatto superiors. The legion itself was organized into four divisions of roughly twelve hundred men each and, with the single exception of Jean-Cécile, all of the division commanders were mulattoes.[36] Of the former Platons leaders, only Martial maintained an autonomous position, with his band encamped in the mountains outside les Cayes. But although independent of Rigaud, they were isolated, and, like Jacques Forman, who had also refused to take orders from the mulatto general, Martial, too, met with his court-martial, if under quite different circumstances. In this, his old enemy Jean Kina was instrumental.[37] But however harsh the inequalities of Rigaud's regime, the mulatto leader did succeed in keeping several ports open and free from foreign interference, thus permitting the South to sustain its commercial relations with the United States and other neutral countries and, at the same time, to provide a market for the crops produced by the black laborers and allocated to them as their portion of plantation revenues. Up to now, the South had remained largely unaffected by the power struggles that beset the North and relatively untouched by the treasonable activities of the mulattoes and whites, who had delivered the greater part of the West to the British.

Under these circumstances, the popular activity of the blacks had effectively subsided and did not resurface until the summer of 1796. In France, Sonthonax had been tried and triumphantly acquitted of the charges brought against him by the colonists of the Massiac Club. By October 1795, the National Convention had been dissolved and replaced by two elected Councils and the Directory, which sent as its agents to Saint Domingue a new civil commission composed of five members. Among them was Sonthonax, who carried by far the greatest authority. [38]

The main purpose of the commission was to survey the administration and application of French law in the colony, to keep Saint Domingue "both French and free," and to restore its economic prosperity based on a system of general emancipation in what had by now become, at least nominally, a multiracial, egalitarian society. The revolution had reached the stage where both mulatto rights and the abolition of slavery were accomplished facts, where the regimen of legally and racially defined "castes," of slavery and of white supremacy, had been overthrown and supplanted by the regime of equality, and where the ex-slaves now stood on a potentially equal footing with the former *affranchis*. Racial conflict and class contradictions had always been deeply embedded in the very nature of Saint Domingue's colonial social structure and slave society. But now, with the established freedom of both the mulattoes and the slaves, racial and class conflict—accompanied by the ensuing political struggles of each indigenous group for power—took on a particular, a very bitter, and in the end, devastating acuity. Each group, seeing itself as heir apparent to the new Saint Domingue, would eventually seek to consolidate power in its own hands as the question of who would govern the emerging society, in whose interests and for what ends, began, imperceptibly at first, to take on increasing political importance. The first of these power bids was the Villate affair. One of the tasks facing the new civil commission upon its arrival in Saint Domingue, then, was to check what seemed to be an alarming tendency among the mulattoes to defy national authority and to assume political autonomy to further their own interests.

Among the first measures taken by the commission upon its arrival in May 1796 was to open an official investigation of the attempted coup d'état of March; Villate, though he had fled le Cap, was immediately arrested and orders issued for his deportation. However, Sonthonax was convinced that the origins and ramifications of the coup extended equally into the South, where the mulattoes held supreme power to the exclusion of both blacks and whites. Although incontrovertible proof could not be found, Pinchinat was strongly suspected as the chief instigator of the movement to overthrow Laveaux. The civil commission therefore sent to the South three delegates, Kerverseau, Rey, and Leborgne, who was a mulatto, with a mandate to investigate any possible links there with the mulatto coup in the North. Desfourneaux, a fourth delegate, was sent as military attaché to inspect the troops and to make proposals for the reorganization of the army in the South. In addition, the delegation was given the task of surveying the administration of the South and providing for its replacement by a constitutional regime that would establish racial equality and place civil authority back in the hands of local and provincial magistrates. The delegates had also been given a specific mandate to arrest Pinchinat and send him to le Cap to account for his activities during his previous stay in that city.

In the South, the outcome of the Villate affair only served to further irritate the mulattoes and, rather than bring them back into closer conformity with French law, actually stimulated a self-defensive stance by which they sought to consolidate their authority. So before Sonthonax's delegation even arrived, they felt their political position threatened; once it did arrive their tolerance was rapidly and predictably exacerbated. Sonthonax could not have chosen four persons more politically inept to carry out such a delicate mission. Rey, for one, had been an avowed enemy of the free coloreds and of their struggle for equal rights back in 1791; Rigaud saw him as a personal enemy who, he believed, had been involved in an earlier assassination attempt against him. Leborgne was well known in some of the other islands for his avaricious pecuniary pursuits and outright swindles, while Kerverseau, though inoffensive by comparison, was nonetheless ineffective. [39]

Before arriving at les Cayes to be received by Rigaud, the delegates began agitating amongst the black workers, reminding them that they were free and yet still oppressed by their mulatto rulers. The delegates made Augustin Rigaud, the general's brother, and another of his associates disclaim rumors, in front of the blacks, that the delegates had come from British-occupied Jérémie and not from France, the implication being that the delegates aimed to reestablish slavery.[40] When they spoke to the black soldiers, they pointed out to them that they were kept in inferior ranks by the mulattoes. According to the report written by Kerverseau and Leborgne, the plantation workers showed the delegates the *cachots* that were still used as a form of punishment for recalcitrant workers,[41] and the delegates would have them demolished.[42] When the delegation destroyed one of these on a Laborde plantation, Rigaud wrote to Raimond, stating that "this prison served to punish workers who abandoned their work for a life of brigandage. . . . I am not insinuating that it was wrong for the delegates to have abolished this house of correction, but the manner in which they did it made the workers understand that there were no longer any restrictions against those whom it pleased to become idle."[43] If the workers now did not openly resist the conditions of their existence under Rigaud's regime through widespread acts or movements of protest, the letter to Raimond does suggest, however, that a fair degree of worker discontent and even desertion, or marronage, still existed in 1796. Why, otherwise, had Rigaud himself not abolished the *cachots* that were to have been abolished along with slavery?

As the delegates arrived at Camp Périn, just outside the Plaine-du-Fond, they excited the black soldiers to the point where they imprisoned their superior officer.[44] And when they arrived in les Cayes and were shown the prisoners, many of them incarcerated for several years and still awaiting trial, they found only two mulatto prisoners out of nine hundred, the rest being either black or white.[45] They immediately set out to dismantle the entire structure of the government as it stood, in addition to proposing a total reorganization of the army. As they wasted no time in carrying out the instructions given them, the abrupt manner in which they did so could only be received by the mulattoes as a direct provocation. They were bitter over the deportation of Villate and even more outraged at the orders to arrest Pinchinat, who, upon learning of them, had fled. To add to it all, the delegates unscrupulously and immorally conducted their private affairs in public. Rey, it seems, had even entertained Rigaud's fiancée in bed and unabashedly made it known to the general. [46]

Tensions and agitation continued to build among the mulattoes, who, on the one hand humiliated and provoked by the conduct of the delegation, saw, on the other, the developing threat to their political power as the delegates high-handedly executed their instructions. So, to divert attention from the measures being taken by the delegation, and in particular to avoid an open confrontation between Desfourneaux and Rigaud, the delegates ordered an expedition against the British at Grande-Anse, an expedition in which Rigaud would also be given a command. As it turned out to be a drastic failure, Desfourneaux accused Rigaud of lukewarm leadership and blamed the defeat on the *légionnaires*. Upon returning to les Cayes, he arrested Gavanon, the treasurer of the South, as well as Lefranc, military commander at Saint Louis, both mulattoes. As Lefranc was being taken to les Cayes harbor, he managed to elude his captors and join with a group of *légionnaires* along the route. Giving a call to arms, they marched on to take cover at the house of Augustin Rigaud, the general's brother. From there, they rang the alarm and were joined by the Cayes garrison and their mulatto supporters from all parts of the city, who together took over the two forts along the shore. Armed insurrection had now begun, and it was led by the chief political and military leaders of the South against French authority.

Bauvais, provisionally in command of les Cayes, intervened as negotiator and tried to achieve a temporary reconciliation between the rebels and the French delegates. The mulattoes refused to listen and said they would speak only to Rigaud, who at this time was still encamped at Tiburon. During the night, Augustin Rigaud left the fort to call to arms the blacks of the plain, who had already been alerted of some impending danger by three cannon shots discharged as a signal from one of the forts. To mobilize their support, the mulattoes and their black allies in the legion were telling the workers that the delegates were there as agents of the European-born French to suppress the mulatto caste and restore slavery. [47]

By now, the insurrection was in full force as the mulattoes, the *légion-*

naires, and three to four thousand blacks from the plantations began systematically massacring the white property owners and city dwellers, burning their property, pillaging and ransacking their stores. The whites, naturally, had welcomed the delegates as "liberators." Even those blacks known to have supported the delegation were not spared.[48] In the midst of all this, Desfourneaux and Rey fled for their lives and managed to escape safely to Spanish Saint Domingue, now under the jurisdiction of the civil commissioner, Roume. Leborgne and Kerverseau, under close protection by Bauvais, remained. Rigaud, the only person capable of restoring order, was not there. The remaining delegates were now left with no alternative but to summon Rigaud, who had secretly been informed of the events by emissaries of Lefranc. Leaving Tiburon with his division of five to six hundred soldiers, Rigaud summoned the blacks on the plantations along the way and especially those of the Plaine-des-Cayes. By the time Rigaud entered les Cayes, his combined forces were three to four thousand strong.[49] His presence, however, only seemed to intensify the killings, the pillaging, and the incendiary activities of the rebels. On the day of his arrival, sixty more persons were killed.[50] Totally incapable of reasserting their authority, the remaining delegates finally authorized Rigaud to adopt whatever measures he deemed necessary to bring an end to the chaos and destruction. With this carte blanche, he proclaimed he was taking over the reins of government in the South until further instructions from France. When all was over, close to three hundred persons, the majority of them whites who had sided with the delegation, had been killed and their property destroyed.[51]

Concerning the role of the black laborers in this revolt, a few observations may be offered. First, aside from those in the legion, the insurrection was neither organized nor was it led by the blacks. Themselves unaware of the specific political purpose of the delegates' mission, they were left vulnerable to the agitations and instigations perpetrated by both sides. While the delegates told them the mulattoes were their oppressors, the mulattoes were convincing them that the delegates had come to restore slavery. Out of this confusion, those who opted to support the mulattoes did so in what they believed to be a defense of their freedom, and thereby unknowingly served the particular interests of Rigaud and mulatto rule. In the North, Toussaint had put an end to the base intrigues of the mulatto rebels who attempted to use the "return to slavery" argument to gain black support; here in the South, there were no independent black leaders of Toussaint's stature and influence to make clear to them exactly where, the midst of this power struggle, their own interests lay. When Kerverseau and Leborgne left, Rigaud reinstated his own people in office, drastically reduced the power of the municipalities, and placed political authority back into the hands of the military apparatus.

Although Rigaud and the mulattoes of the South had been provoked and

humiliated by the actions of the delegation, he and those who led the insurrection had nonetheless committed a serious act of rebellion against French
authority. The civil commission in le Cap condemned as leaders and chief
instigators of the revolt both the Rigaud brothers, Lefranc, and Pinchinat,
as well as the municipal auditor, and another mulatto military commander.
Upon learning of the Cayes insurrection, the Directory specifically excluded
from amnesty those who had been designated by the commission as the principal leaders. The Directory did not, however, formally remove Rigaud from
office. Thus, de facto, he remained in power, and the social inequalities of
his regime were kept virtually intact for yet another four years until the civil
war between the South and the forces under Toussaint would irrevocably
seal his doom.

The events leading up to that fratricidal war involve a long and tangled
series of political and diplomatic maneuvering on all sides, and can be dealt
with here only rather reductively.

By the end of the summer of 1796, primary electoral assemblies were
formed in accordance with the Constitution of the Year 3 to elect colonial
representatives to the new legislative body in France. The outcome of those
elections, facilitated by Toussaint, secured a seat for both Laveaux and Sonthonax as deputies to the French legislature. While Laveaux left for France
in October, Sonthonax, pressured by his colleagues to remain in the colony
as civil commissioner rather than assume his duties as deputy in France,
reluctantly postponed his departure.[52] At the same time, Toussaint, having
recaptured the Mirebalais valley from the British, was rapidly proving himself a formidable force with which Sonthonax would have to contend in the
inevitable power struggles to come. As Rigaud and the mulattoes were still
strongly entrenched in the South, Sonthonax needed a counterweight against
any further threat on their part to eventually take control of the colony. To
solidify his own position and to reinforce his ties with Toussaint, Sonthonax conferred upon the black leader the title of commander-in-chief of the
army in Saint Domingue, a post left vacant since the departure of Laveaux.
But Sonthonax himself would also have to leave, not only to take his seat in
the metropolitan legislature, but because his mission to Saint Domingue, an
eighteen-month term, would eventually come to a close.

Much ambiguity surrounds the circumstances of Sonthonax's departure
from Saint Domingue, and in the end we may never quite know fully what
did, and what did not, transpire nor, exactly, why. In spite of Sonthonax's
repeated desires to leave his commission in Saint Domingue to assume his
responsibilities in France, Toussaint finally maneuvered to forcibly expel
Sonthonax only a few months before the end of his mandate, thus turning a
peaceable departure and an approaching eventuality, as Stein put it, into an
immediate necessity and a forcible expulsion.[53] Ultimately, it was perhaps

not so much Sonthonax's departure itself nor the arguments presented by Sonthonax and by Toussaint, each in his own defense, that mattered, but rather the manner in which the whole affair was handled by Toussaint. And the explanation for this lay not in Saint Domingue but with the course of events in France.

C. L. R. James has argued that Toussaint knew of the direction in which the revolution in France was going, of the growing strength of the counter-revolution, and of the steps that certain colonists were taking toward an eventual restoration of slavery. He knew, as well, of the disfavor into which Sonthonax was falling under this conservative tide. Although the Directory itself had no immediate intention of restoring slavery, it would not, on the other hand, remain forever. In the struggles that lay ahead, Toussaint probably saw in Sonthonax a cumbersome accessory, perhaps even a liability, and thus threw him to the wolves.[54] While all this is certainly plausible, Stein sheds further light on the matter by suggesting that it was not just the need for Toussaint to be rid of Sonthonax that mattered, for, on the whole, there was never any real animosity or fundamental conflict between the two men. Moreover, Sonthonax's mission would be over in a few months, anyway. Rather, Toussaint staged Sonthonax's departure in such a dramatic and humiliating (for Sonthonax) fashion for the impression it would create in France. That is, by forcibly expelling the commissioner, who was already losing his standing in the French government, and then by writing a defense of his actions and a condemnation of Sonthonax, he hoped to increase his own favor with France and thereby to consolidate on firmer ground his leadership in Saint Domingue.[55] In other words, if Sonthonax was doomed in France, then so, too, would be the cause of general emancipation. To guarantee general liberty, then, the only alternative was to place himself as its sole protector in Saint Domingue. Thus he expelled Sonthonax, denounced him to the Directory, and purposefully tried to facilitate the commissioner's discredit in order to enhance his own position with an ominously conservative government. But such a Machiavellian move was not without its risks, for if the removal of Sonthonax by Toussaint may implicitly have fallen into the interests of the metropolitan government, still, there was no reason for the French government to be any more favorable toward Toussaint, a black upstart general and former enemy of France, than it would be toward the radical Sonthonax. In fact, by his very expulsion of Sonthonax, Toussaint was becoming far too dangerous and may already have begun to overplay his cards. At any rate, with Sonthonax gone, Roume in Spanish Saint Domingue, and Leblanc and Giraud already back in France, the civil commission was now effectively reduced to one member, Raimond, who wisely deferred to Toussaint's authority. The Directory did not send its official agent until March 1798.

During this time, most of British-occupied Saint Domingue had been re-conquered by Toussaint's army in the West and by Rigaud's in the South at Jérémie. By March, Toussaint had already entered into negotiations with General Maitland, the commander of the British army in Saint Domingue, for the total evacuation of the British. Full amnesty was accorded to all French citizens in the occupied areas who had not served in the ranks of the British army, to all black troops who had been enrolled into the British army, whether by force of arms or by the force of circumstances, and to the émigrés who had abandoned the British prior to the opening of nego-tiations.[56] This was the political and military situation when the Directory's agent, General Hédouville, arrived in the colony on 28 March 1798.[57] As official representative of the French government, his mission was to promul-gate the laws of the legislative body, to entrench respect for French national authority, to prevent abuses against the freedom of the blacks, and to strictly enforce French law against the émigrés. His functions, however, were to remain purely civil. In addition, he was given the authority to arrest Rigaud —if he deemed it necessary. [58]

But it was no longer Rigaud that the French bourgeoisie feared; it was Toussaint and the blacks. In fact, Hédouville's design upon arriving in Saint Domingue was to publicly favor Rigaud and create enough dissension be-tween him and Toussaint to then be able to defeat the latter. After receiving Hédouville in le Cap, however, Toussaint immediately set off for Port-au-Prince, met with Rigaud to inform him of the agent's arrival, and the two of them, mutually agreeing to support one another against any intrigues that Hédouville might attempt, then rode back to le Cap to confer with him. Over-whelming Rigaud with high esteem and government favor to the detriment of Toussaint, Hédouville pointedly proposed that the two of them unite in their efforts to remove Toussaint from his position of supreme authority. What Rigaud did not, or could not, see was that Hédouville was merely using him to defeat Toussaint, only to turn on him afterwards. If Rigaud felt that such a coalition would favor his own political ambitions, he did not realize that it would also lead to his ruin. Hédouville carefully nurtured a series of hu-miliating insinuations, unjust accusations, political, diplomatic, and even outright personal insults against Toussaint, causing him finally to submit his resignation to the Directory. Hédouville neither formally accepted nor re-jected the resignation, but systematically began to replace black troops with white ones along the coast, sending the blacks back to the plantations, and arranged with the Directory to have Toussaint replaced by three European generals.

As for the black laborers, he issued a decree that would tie them to the same plantations for six to nine years and, for anyone caught in vagabondage without a farm contract, six months detention in jail.[59] Another ordinance imposed four years imprisonment for the simple theft of a horse or any other domestic animal, and the death penalty for armed theft.[60] These new regulations, as well as the reimposition of earlier ones which, in a few cases, even predated the abolition of slavery, provoked tensions and unrest among the farm workers to the point where, in one area, they were driven to near insurrection. In the southern region around Petit-Goâve, the black laborers began to form illegal gatherings, as they had done in May 1794 under Appollon's leadership, this time to protest Hédouville's regulations, which they saw as a practical step toward the reestablishment of slavery. As could be expected, Faubert was incapable of containing them, and Rigaud had to be called in to persuade them to return to work. [61]

Finally, when a simple quarrel broke out in the North between two soldiers of the Fifth Regiment commanded by Moïse, Hédouville played his last card and lost. He arranged to have Moïse, the idol of the black workers and Toussaint's own adopted nephew, arrested, and placed a black municipal official in command. As the official began fulfilling his mandate, Moïse staunchly resisted; the national guard opened fire, forcing Moïse to escape. As soon as Toussaint got word of what was happening, he ordered Dessalines to march on le Cap with his troops and place Hédouville under arrest, while Moïse had swiftly called to arms the black plantation workers throughout the plain. Hédouville was finished and, in spite of a few final blundering attempts at reconciliation, was forced to leave the colony, taking with him a great number of his functionaries. He now washed his hands of all responsibility for the troubles that had occurred in the colony during his commission and effectively left the blame to Toussaint. [62]

Prior to his departure, Hédouville had taken care to plant yet another seed of contention between Toussaint and Rigaud, one which would instrumentally contribute to the outbreak of civil war. In a secret letter to Rigaud, he had officially absolved Rigaud from Toussaint's authority as commander-in-chief and reinstated Léogane and Jacmel under Rigaud's jurisdiction as commander-in-chief of the South.[63] For the time being, however, and in the name of peace, Rigaud did not insist upon the integration of these areas into his jurisdiction but remained within the limits of his command as far as Miragoâne. At the same time, Toussaint strongly suspected the French government would send another agent to the colony, and this time with troops. And if such were the case, he would no longer be able to count on Rigaud, who, despite the tremendous services he had already rendered and the sincerity of his principles in favor of emancipation, would inevitably welcome a French expeditionary force to solidify his own precarious position in the colony. If control of the colony thus fell to Rigaud and the mulatto élite, even under the auspices of French authority, it would mean the end of the black revolution and all that it was still striving to achieve. In a sense, the former *affranchis* represented by Rigaud were caught between the white colonists, who no longer exercised political power of any consequence, but who were still fairly strong because of their wealth and their commercial ties with Britain and the United States, and the newly freed blacks, who were dominant in the North and a good part of the West, and who were rapidly aspiring to political power. The mass of black laborers, because of class affinities and racial identity, would, for their part, almost invariably give decisive weight to the side of the emergent black elite against the mulattoes in any conflict of significant political scope.[64] For the mulattoes, then, the only salvation would be in republican France. Hédouville had kindled these nascent tensions from the very beginning by playing one leader against the other, and had caused relations between Toussaint and Rigaud to degenerate to the point where their differences had become irreconcilable. Finally, the bitterness between the two eventually found explicit expression in racial terms.

But the race question as a cause of the civil war must be seen with a certain degree of discernment, for it played a contributory role only to the extent that the classes in Saint Domingue were so sharply identified, as much by racial as by economic characteristics. More than superficially a race war, the impending conflict for which the stage was now set was, rather, a struggle between two opposing interests or parties, between the former *affranchis*, who were massively mulatto, and the former slaves, who were massively black, as to which group would eventually determine the political and economic orientation of the new society, and in whose interests. If Rigaud's administration of the South was any indication, the blacks under mulatto rule of the colony would be doomed, the elite as well as the mass of plantation workers. Toussaint could not afford for this to occur any more than the mulattoes (perhaps not Rigaud himself, but those of his class) could accede to the sharing of power under the supreme authority of a black. In the end, as Sannon so lucidly stated the case, it was not that Toussaint detested the mulattoes any more than Rigaud hated the blacks, but to guarantee the interests they represented, "each of them needed the united force of a party, sustained by the force of commonly shared attitudes, in a society where the parties were confounded with the classes and the classes with color."[65]

Thus the historically "logical" emergence of a combined mulatto and black bourgeoisie did not occur. In fact, the black elite, of which Toussaint was the most prominent member, was itself only barely removed from the laboring masses upon whom its support ultimately reposed. It was, after all, Toussaint, and not Rigaud, who embodied for the black workers the preservation and consolidation of their freedom and the principles of general emancipation. Rigaud, for his part, cast his lot and that of his people with the French bourgeoisie, while Toussaint saw in this tendency a potentially dangerous threat (given the direction of the revolution in France) to general emancipation and equality for the blacks; to consolidate his control over the situation he would have to defeat Rigaud. Finally, then, the racial issue, in and of itself, was not the determining factor in precipitating the civil war, but to the extent that race so exclusively represented distinct and opposing class interests, it became a pretextual justification for each side. Now, mulattoes began leaving from all points of the colony to coalesce around Rigaud, and Toussaint began reorganizing and strengthening his own army in the North. It was Rigaud who made the first move by publicly declaring that he was taking over command of Léogane and Jacmel as authorized by Hédouville, even though Roume had rescinded that mandate nearly six months before. Two of Rigaud's men precipitously led an attack on Petit-Goâve and took over command by force of arms. Civil war had now begun.

But there was even more to the Saint Domingue civil war than just the racial and class interests of two contending parties. A confrontation between Toussaint and Rigaud in fact served the economic interests of the United States and Britain in their aim to maximize trade with Saint Domingue to the detriment of France. Whereas Hédouville had tried to crush Toussaint by deceitfully supporting Rigaud in order, then, to reestablish metropolitan control over the colony, Britain and the United States, for commercial reasons, among others to be discussed, secretly supported Toussaint in the war against Rigaud. From the vantage point of international politics, Saint Domingue was being manipulated as a piece on a chessboard, and the outcome of its internal struggles would be a key to the particular political and economic advantages that each of the three contending foreign powers intended to reap. Britain was still at war with France, and the United States, "under the pressures of French aggression" against American shipping, was in a state of quasi-war in which commercial relations with France and her dependencies had been suspended. The United States, however, desired a resumption of the lucrative trade activity it had enjoyed with Saint Domingue, protection from attack by French privateers in Saint Domingue waters, and a normalization of the clandestine trading that had been going on in spite of interdiction. For this, American consul Edward Stevens negotiated a treaty with Toussaint to open the ports of Saint Domingue to American trade in exchange for protection against French privateer attack. Toussaint requested, however, that the ports of the South under Rigaud's jurisdiction be formally excluded. And to avoid any potential troublesome interference by the British in light of American privileges, it was agreed that England should also enjoy the same commercial prerogatives as the United States; thus a three-way treaty between Toussaint, the United States, and Britain was negotiated and concluded by British general Maitland.

The advantages to Toussaint of such an agreement were obvious. It would enable him at once to equip and feed his own army, blockade the South, and facilitate his victory over Rigaud. But the politics behind this treaty were even more astute on the side of the Anglo-Americans who, in addition to direct commercial advantages, were also pursuing the separation of Saint Domingue from France by ensuring Toussaint's victory over Rigaud. Strategically, they desired an independent Saint Domingue under Toussaint's supremacy, precisely to prevent the spread of slave emancipation to their own territories. It was known, for one thing, that the Directory had issued orders for a French expedition under Toussaint against Jamaica and that, although Toussaint opposed the expedition in the interests of the trade treaty, Rigaud approved of it and, were he in command, would carry it out. Thus by separating the colony from France and then isolating it from the outside world by virtue of a hermetic Anglo-American trade monopoly, the cancerous threat of general emancipation and of a future black state in the New World might be contained. For Toussaint, however, the stakes were doubly high, as he had now allied himself economically with two slave powers in order, conversely, to consolidate the achievement of general emancipation. Thus profiting from the commercial advantages of the arrangement, Toussaint also greatly facilitated his struggle against Rigaud. He did not, however, fall into the trap of Anglo-American interests by declaring Saint Domingue independent. [66]

During the course of this fratricidal war, which lasted for over a year, there were significantly few signs in the South of black mass support for Rigaud. Only during the first moments of the war following the attack on Petit-Goâve by the southern army did the blacks in the region around Léogane rise up in support of Rigaud or, as Cabon put it, "perhaps more precisely, against Toussaint and the northern troops." [67] Already Rigaud had sent emissaries to penetrate the areas around Port-Républicain and the Cul-de-Sac plain in an attempt to create unrest and rebellion amongst the black workers. [68] His only weapon was to spread word that Toussaint was a traitor, that he had sold out to the British and would lead them back into slavery. Effectively, insurrections did break out in the hills around Léogane and Grand-Goâve, [69] but they never developed into any sort of organized, widespread, or coordinated movement.

At the outset, the mulatto forces were well equipped, well armed, well fed, and well paid. Their cavalry, in the opinion of Edward Stevens, was the best in the colony. [70] Fighting with tremendous vigor and optimism, they pushed onward to capture Grand-Goâve and then Jacmel, holding out at Jacmel against Dessalines' troops and a total military blockade for nearly five months before starvation forced them to evacuate across enemy lines. Bauvais, who could have made all the difference for an earlier end to this struggle had he pronounced himself decisively in favor of Toussaint, thus leaving Rigaud politically defenseless, could not bring himself to take sides. During the siege of Jacmel, he remained faithful to his own inner principles and moral standards, gave up his command, and left for France. Rigaud, for his part, remained noticeably inactive as he waited for troops from France that never came.

After the fall of Jacmel, the southern army was left in near shambles and, with no clear sense of direction or strategy, fought desperately against Dessalines's advancing troops that forced them successively into retreat. Already, the town of Saint Louis had deserted Rigaud's cause by welcoming Dessalines and his officers, offering a banquet at which officers of both armies began fraternizing. At Miragoâne, the black plantation workers refused to follow Rigaud's army into retreat.[71] When Rigaud received word of the reception accorded to the conquering troops, he suspected a plot to deliver him personally into enemy hands, rode back to les Cayes, and in a last desperate effort, rang the tocsins as a signal and call to arms of the black laborers throughout the Plaine-des-Cayes. No one came forward to answer the call.

If, in 1796, they had come forward in great numbers to help drive out the delegation sent by Sonthonax to reorganize the South, they had also been persuaded by the mulattoes that the delegates were there as a threat to their freedom. In spite of the harshness of his regime, some support could still be mobilized in his favor. Now, they had deserted him altogether. They had no reason to support a man who was leading them into disaster, causing them personally to suffer the privations of a war in which, as far as they were concerned, they had no apparent stake. The political intrigues of Hédouville, the resulting conflicts, power struggles, Anglo-American trade conventions, and, finally, civil war between Toussaint and Rigaud, did not touch them directly. The outcome of that tangled and tortuous series of events did. And when France's expeditionary army landed in the colony two years later, they were the first to rise up against it in the South, using the same methods and guerilla tactics they had used to win their freedom during the early years of 1792–93.

9

From Civil War to Independence

Toward the beginning of July 1802, roughly five months after the arrival of the French expeditionary forces, indigenous popular movements in the South had reemerged, as they did throughout the colony, this time with clear and concise objectives. In spite of official proclamations about the sanctity of general emancipation for the blacks and the inviolability of the government's intentions to defend it, the French had come to restore slavery, and when this fact became unequivocally clear in the eyes of the people, their resistance proved to be the cornerstone of the struggle that was now a war for independence. The events and issues leading up to that struggle, and to the massive, self-mobilized intervention of popular forces in its course, will need to be examined at some length.

If Toussaint's need to defeat Rigaud was largely determined by apprehensions of the emerging political situation in France, of the growing strength of reactionary elements in government circles, and of the possibility that France may at some point send armed forces to the colony, the same considerations also determined his move to bring Spanish Saint Domingue under his military and political control. Although the colony had been ceded to France by the terms of the Treaty of Bâle, the French government had not yet officially undertaken its administrative reorganization. Thus using as a pretext the fact that Spain had already resumed the slave trade and that Spanish colonists were now stealing French blacks from the bordering regions to sell them as slaves in the eastern colony, Toussaint requested permission from Roume to take formal possession of Spanish Saint Domingue in accordance with France's treaty rights. Upon Roume's refusal, the matter was temporarily set aside.

At about this same time, prior to the conclusion of the war against Rigaud, he sent to France Colonel Vincent, a white officer and close friend, to obtain government approval of his position in the civil war against Rigaud. By the time Vincent arrived in France, the Directory had fallen and was superseded by the consular regime of Napoleon Bonaparte, to whom the "bourgeois republic" now looked to strengthen its control, and to whom the former colonists now looked to restore their possessions and a prerevolutionary social regime of white supremacy in the colonies. Instead of writing directly to

Toussaint, Bonaparte made his intentions known by way of a new commission composed of Vincent, Julien Raimond, and General Michel. In addition to a confirmation of Toussaint's rank as commander-in-chief and governor, the commissioners would bring with them a proclamation signed by the consuls, informing the population that the old Constitution of Year 3 was now abolished. According to France's new Constitution of Year 8, the colonies would henceforth be governed by a set of "special laws" that would take into account the particularities of each colony. What this meant was that Saint Domingue would no longer be represented in a French legislative body, nor would she be subject to the same laws as those governing French citizens in France. And because the new constitution neither reconfirmed nor even mentioned general emancipation at all, Napoleon took the precaution of including in his proclamation a carefully worded statement to the effect that, as to their freedom, the blacks could be assured of its inviolability. The commissioners did not arrive until May 1800.

During this time, Toussaint concentrated his efforts on terminating the civil war in the South, and arranged a temporary exile for Rigaud in France. Following Rigaud's departure, Toussaint reestablished the former limits of the South at Miragoâne and divided the province into four military districts: les Cayes, Jérémie, Tiburon, and Anse-à-Veau, each to be commanded by an officer of his army.[1] He had also proclaimed a general amnesty for all who had taken sides with Rigaud to fight him, with the exception of Pétion, an outstanding mulatto officer who had deserted from the ranks of Bauvais to join Rigaud during the civil war, and three others. In spite of his amnesty and insistence upon drawing a curtain over the past, horrible acts of reprisal were committed by the lesser officers of the occupying army, for which both Christophe and Toussaint must share part of the blame.[2] Dessalines, for his part, had personally saved a good number of Rigaud's officers from an otherwise certain death.[3] Yet as chief military commander, and therefore chief agricultural inspector of the South, Dessalines's extended rule over the black laborers was notoriously cruel, and his impatience with undisciplined farm workers often led him to deal out or to order punishments that were far harsher than any the blacks had ever suffered under Rigaud.[4] So for them, as for the mulattoes, the legacy of the civil war was a bitter one, and one that would not help Toussaint's cause when the French forces did land a year and a half later.

With Rigaud defeated and the administration of the South now firmly under his authority, Toussaint moved to further consolidate his position with a military expedition into Spanish Saint Domingue, to bring it, as well, under his rule. Just prior to the commissioners' arrival in May, a mass rising of armed black workers broke out in the North. Numbering in the thousands, they marched on le Cap and forced Roume to rescind his earlier refusal to

authorize Toussaint's taking of the Spanish colony, which, for them, was
necessary to put an end to the ignominious slave trade. As Toussaint's negotiations with the Spanish had failed, and as he now had mass popular support, he ordered Moïse to march into Spanish Saint Domingue at the head
of ten thousand troops to take possession by force. By January 1801, the
Spanish governor had ceded control of the territory to Toussaint.

Not only was he the supreme authority, he was now the only authority
in the colony, and to render his achievements permanent, he called for the
formation of electoral assemblies to choose deputies to a central assembly
that would write a constitution for the whole of the island. The constitution was promulgated in July, months before Vincent had even arrived in
France with the printed copy given him by Toussaint for Bonaparte's sanction. The abolition of slavery was, of course, reconfirmed and consecrated
in law, and in recognition of his great services to the colony, Toussaint was
named governor-for-life with the power to name his own successor. All laws
would be proposed by the governor and merely executed by the assembly;
although Saint Domingue was to remain a part of France's colonial empire,
the constitution left no room whatsoever for a French representative in the
colony's administrative structure. Thus, while remaining attached to France,
the relationship of the colony to the metropolis would be almost like that of
two equal powers. [5]

The constitution was not in itself a formal declaration of independence,
but for Bonaparte, it was dangerously close to being one. His immediate reaction upon Vincent's presentation of the constitution was violent: Toussaint
was no more than a rebel slave who needed to be removed, whatever the
cost. This, after his armed entry into Spanish Saint Domingue, was the last
straw and no doubt the end factor in Bonaparte's final decision to reassert
metropolitan control by sending out an expeditionary army. But Toussaint's
moves toward independence from French authority and the progressive consolidation of power in his own hands were not, in themselves, the essential
cause of the expedition. In fact, before Vincent had even arrived with Toussaint's constitution, preparations for a military invasion of Saint Domingue
were already under way. In the interests of the former colonial aristocracy,
reactionary white émigrés, and the maritime bourgeoisie, Bonaparte's intentions were no less than the reimposition of slavery, of the Black Code, the
slave trade, and the pre-1789 colonial regime. That Toussaint had risen to
the powerful position he occupied in the colony, at the head of a people
armed and engaged in ten years of emancipation struggles, only made the
task that much more difficult, that much more complicated, delicate, and,
in the end, costly, an operation. It was, as Toussaint himself had warned the
Directory in a letter four years earlier, literally, *"to attempt the impossible."* [6]

Prior to his final decision on an armed expedition to the colony, Bonaparte had solicited support from both the United States and Britain, with whom France would imminently be concluding a peace. Since England still dominated the seas, and since ongoing United States commerce with Saint Domingue would aid Toussaint in furnishing the colony's needed goods, the concurrence of these two powers was therefore essential to France. And since it was no longer the Directory, but Napoleon Bonaparte, at the helm of France, the perceived threat of French republican emancipationism spreading through the Caribbean no longer posed a problem for the Anglo-Americans. Both countries were now opposed to an independent Saint Domingue and sympathetic toward the reassertion of French supremacy over the colony. So they left to Bonaparte the job of reestablishing slavery and, additionally, of safeguarding slavery in their own territories. [7]

It was the conclusion of peace with Britain and the rapprochement with the United States that Toussaint, in fact, feared the most at this point, for France was now free to concentrate all her military efforts on Saint Domingue, while he was now deprived of the secret aid and special commercial arrangements he had previously enjoyed with the two powers. But these were not his only difficulties. Although he had reached the pinnacle of power, internally Saint Domingue was a divided society. In the course of consolidating his position in relation to France, Toussaint had progressively weakened and all but destroyed it in relation to those he governed; for, if the Constitution of 1801 left little room for French authority on the one end, it left none at all, at the other end, for the political and economic participation of the masses in the new social order.

First, the plantation system of large holdings was maintained at all costs. Toussaint's overriding economic objective was to make the colony produce, to produce for an export market, and to produce enough to place it back on the road to economic prosperity. He believed this could be done only by retaining and reinforcing the existing latifundian system, and he therefore restricted the acquisition of land to lots no smaller than 50 *carreaux* (roughly 3.3 acres).[8] By this measure he placed the accession to personal proprietorship of land far beyond the reach of the rural masses, who were condemned to remain as "salaried" workers under a "slave-type" plantation regime. The plantations were now either back in the hands of reintegrated white émigré colonists, of the mulatto elite in the South and parts of the West, or, increasingly throughout the colony, under the administration of the newly emerged black elite, army generals and high-ranking officers of the military to whom the sequestered plantations were leased out. So the farm workers were now laboring either for their former masters or for a new segment of the ruling elite with whom they had previously shared a common status under slavery.

Within such a system, in which the vast majority of blacks had no practical access to individual landholding and, in this sense, no tangible evidence of their freedom, Toussaint knew that the only way managers could obtain the requisite labor from the workers was through coercive measures, and his rural code reflected this. It was at once an extension and a reinforcement of the earlier work codes promulgated by Sonthonax, Polverel, and Hédouville. Not only did workers no longer have the option of changing plantations at the end of their contracts, they were also forbidden to change occupations. That is, in order to stabilize the agricultural labor force, only those individuals who had held domestic positions or trades prior to emancipation were allowed to exercise these functions. In addition, the authority of the *conducteurs* in work relations was now replaced by that of district inspectors, who were themselves military officers.[9] By blocking the acquisition of land for the masses and tying the plantation system to the military apparatus, by inviting former white colonists to repossess their plantations, by having alienated, after the civil war, so important a sector of the indigenous population as the mulattoes, Toussaint was forging a society with no real foundation. It was a society of disparate and contradictory elements at the head of which he had placed himself as governor-for-life. And the one sector of Saint Domingue society in which Toussaint would have found his most logical and most natural ally, the mass of black laborers, stood in fundamental opposition to his own social and economic philosophy.

The workers resisted Toussaint's rural code just as they had resisted that of Polverel. Without harsh constraints and physical punishments, the farm workers would spend more time on their own kitchen gardens than at the plantation; they were often errant, and their work, when they did perform it, was slack and unproductive.[10] They were legally, physically, and psychologically no longer slaves, and Toussaint's system, like that of the civil commissioners before him, deprived them of any means by which to give substance and real meaning to their freedom. Freedom, rather, was being thrown at them as an abstraction, for it was always in the name of general emancipation that Toussaint, "a black like them," as he would put it, regimented their labor, deprived them of land, and deprived them by the constitution of the right to practice voodoo; in short, imposing upon them Western modes of thought and of social organization in an attempt to bring an autonomous, and economically viable Saint Domingue into the modern world.

In the North, toward the end of October 1801, the dissatisfaction and disaffection of the rural masses were channeled into an organized uprising of farm workers throughout the parishes of Dondon, Marmelade, Plaisance, Acul, Plaine du Nord, Limbé, and Port-Margot—the traditional centers of revolutionary activity. The victims were the white colonists (some three hundred were killed[11]), and the leading spokesman for the revolt was Moïse, who, as agricultural inspector for the North, let it be known that he opposed his uncle's regime for its constraints against the aspirations of the workers. He refused the use of physical violence that Dessalines had encouraged in forcing the laborers to work, and had also requested of Toussaint that he allow the parcelling and sale of state land to the lower-ranking officers, and even soldiers.[12] He would scrupulously make certain that the workers received their one-quarter share of the plantation revenue first, before the owners or managers received theirs, and he had personally relinquished the administration of his own plantation holdings to a company of *négociants*.[13] In this sense, it was Moïse, and not Toussaint, nor even Dessalines, who still bore scars of the whip and horrible memories of his own life as a slave, who embodied the aspirations and needs of the rural masses. More than that, he also believed in their economic and social legitimacy, and, if he did not ostensibly organize the insurrection, he nevertheless wholly supported it in opposition to Toussaint.

Other issues were at stake, as well. One of the means by which Toussaint aimed at increasing Saint Domingue's labor force was to "import" workers from Africa, presumably by buying them from slave traders and then freeing them in the colony. He never made clear, however, exactly how he intended to do this and, in light of his policies favoring the return of white émigré colonists, left the impression among the black workers that he was planning a return to the old regime. No doubt Moïse was among those who believed that Toussaint was in some way moving toward a restoration of slavery in Saint Domingue, and if such rumors were circulating, Toussaint, as a revolutionary leader, made the fatal error of not taking concrete and vigorous measures to dispel them. By focusing his regard on the émigrés, whose capital and technology he saw as indispensable, he proportionately removed himself from the masses, in whose name he governed and whose support he believed was implicit. He had thrown out the British, crushed Rigaud, expelled by force three civil commissioners, taken over the eastern part of Saint Domingue, elaborated and promulgated a constitution—all in the name of general emancipation, which served almost as a political leitmotiv justifying his ambitions. But if Moïse was able to rally the workers under his command so effectively on arguments (however unfounded in fact) that Toussaint wanted to reestablish slavery, one may surmise that their conditions under his regime must have lent a good deal of credibility to the claims.

As to the attitudes and aspirations of the black workers, one may see here (though the documentation, where it does exist, remains yet to be systematically analyzed) an organized and articulate expression of what we saw earlier in a more diffused, spontaneous manner among the blacks of the Plaine-des-Cayes and surrounding region in the South, as they reacted to emancipation.[14] Politically, this popular consciousness reflected a profound cleavage between the policies, the economic orientation, and general philosophy of a supreme revolutionary leader and the deep-rooted aspirations of his people. Personal attachment to the land, and popular claims to small individual holdings and to the parcelling of sequestered plantations, was a powerful current that Toussaint knew well enough, but it was not what he envisioned for Saint Domingue's future. Moïse's embodiment of these goals, his close attachment to the workers, enhanced by his authority and stature as military commander and chief agricultural inspector of the North, constituted all the reasons Toussaint needed to remove him. Toussaint charged him with inciting and propagating the revolt against his authority and had him, along with a good number of his aides and close officers, shot by a firing squad without a trial. Among these was Joseph Flaville, one of the first leaders of the 1791 conspiracy that inaugurated the black revolution.

But if Toussaint aimed at reinforcing his control over the situation by smashing the rebellion, executing Moïse and dozens of local leaders, and forcibly repressing the unfulfilled aspirations of the rural masses, he actually widened the breach and only further alienated himself from those he was leading. For by executing Moïse, he did not merely eliminate a political and ideological rival; he also eliminated the one prominent leader capable of rapidly galvanizing the plantation workers and of coordinating, on a massive scale, popular armed resistance to Leclerc's expedition (the full scope of which Toussaint was as yet unaware) at the very outset of its landing.

Moïse was executed in mid-November; in France, the preparations for the anticipated expedition had been completed. On 31 October, Bonaparte handed to General Victor-Emmanuel Leclerc, his brother-in-law, a set of special instructions outlining each stage of the expedition that he would command. The first stage was to last no more than fifteen to twenty days, during which time Leclerc would win over the black generals with assurances of his peaceful intentions and good will. Leclerc would tell them that the twenty thousand European troops—the elite of the French army—had merely come to protect the colony, preserve its peace and tranquility, and suppress any rebel elements that might emerge. This would then enable the expeditionary forces to land and take possession of all major port cities. During the second stage, they would wage an unremitting war against the black army generals, in particular Toussaint, Dessalines, and Moïse, then still believed to be alive. This was to break the morale of the blacks and leave them leaderless. By the third stage, the entire black population would be disarmed, forced back onto the plantations, and the groundwork laid for the restoration of slavery.[15] Napoleon's instructions relating to this last phase were explicit: "Do not allow any blacks having held a rank above that of captain to remain on the island."[16] The whole operation, barring any unforeseen difficulties, would take roughly three months from the first attack.

On 3 February 1802, Leclerc arrived in le Cap harbor with a squadron of over five thousand troops, a quarter of the entire expeditionary force.[17] After some hesitation, Christophe, in command of le Cap, refused to allow the troops to land without orders from Toussaint. Christophe requested a forty-eight-hour delay. Leclerc refused, sent back a letter greatly exaggerating the forces at his disposal, charging Christophe with rebellion, and holding him personally responsible for whatever happened. When Leclerc did land, le Cap was little more than a pile of ashes. The city had been evacuated, all of the main government buildings burned out, and the gunpowder factory blown up. It was not a spontaneous riot, but a strategically organized act of military resistance, and the most devastating war in the entire history of Saint Domingue had now begun.

Toussaint hastily dispatched instructions to Dessalines in the West, to Laplume and Dommage in the South, and to Paul Louverture in command at Samona, vigorously warning them that the French had come to restore slavery, that they must meet them with open resistance and burn, annihilate everything, if they were forced to retreat. All of these letters were intercepted by enemy troops.[18] Laplume, blindly loyal to France, readily succumbed to the solicitations of a number of mulatto officers and of Célestin, a black officer from Port-au-Prince sent by the French general Boudet, with a copy of Bonaparte's spurious proclamation attesting to the inviolability of their freedom and the peace-keeping aims of the expedition.

With the defection of Laplume, the other black commanders of the South followed suit. At Jérémie, Dommage was now completely isolated. He had prepared on his own authority to resist with force if possible, and if necessary by fire, but, betrayed by his European adjutant and two of his brigade leaders, he was forced to allow the French troops to enter Jérémie.[19] By mid-February, the entire province of the South had fallen to the enemy. Nearly half of Toussaint's army was now fighting under the French. His only hope was to be able to hold out long enough defensively with roughly ten thousand troops until the coming of the rainy season, several months away, when the French would invariably fall prey to sicknesses and diseases endemic to the tropical climate. While Christophe and Toussaint managed to neutralize the attacks of the French army in the North, the black resistance forces in the West, roughly fifteen hundred, were concentrated at Crête-à-Pierrot. Having taken the fort, they now faced the twelve thousand troops, European and colonial, that Leclerc had dispatched to recapture the fort, break the resistance in the West, and then proceed with his instructions, already critically behind schedule. It was here that Dessalines spoke to his troops, making it unequivocally clear that it was a war for independence that they were fighting, for without independence their freedom would always remain endangered:

> Take courage, I tell you, take courage. The whites from France cannot hold out against us here in Saint Domingue. They will fight well at first, but soon they will fall sick and die like flies. Listen well! If Dessalines surrenders to them a

hundred times, he will betray them a hundred times. I repeat it, take courage and you will see that when the French are reduced to small, small numbers, we will harass them and beat them; we will burn the harvests and then take to the hills. They will be forced to leave. Then I will make you independent. There will be no more whites amongst us. [20]

They held out against two successive attacks, after which Dessalines executed a brilliantly maneuvered evacuation through enemy lines, ten times their own number. [21]

The situation remained nonetheless critical, and Leclerc's even more so. Within the first two weeks of his arrival, two thousand European troops were already in the hospital, three-quarters of them sick and the rest wounded; within another week, five hundred more had become victims of a devastating climate, with an additional one thousand wounded.[22] He would need another six thousand troops, apart from those already promised, and a further reinforcement of two thousand per month for the next three months if he were to carry out his instructions.[23] At the end of April, three months after the first attack, when, according to the original plans, the entire expedition was to have been completed, he realized that the difficulties involved in reconquering Saint Domingue and bringing it fully under French domination were eminently more formidable than Bonaparte had ever presumed. By now, roughly one-third of his original army was incapacitated, not counting those killed in battle. It would require no fewer than twenty-five thousand fighting troops to conquer and occupy the mountains of the North and West, where the black resistance troops were concentrated, while maintaining the points he already held. [24]

Leclerc's first offer to negotiate with Toussaint had failed. He had already published orders for the arrest and capture of both Toussaint and Christophe. Each side had suffered great losses, and now Toussaint was preparing a new offensive. Before launching the attacks, however, Toussaint attempted to negotiate a settlement with Leclerc. He allowed Christophe to confer with the French general to discover Leclerc's intentions. Christophe deserted, and with him went twelve hundred soldiers and a mass of artillery and munitions. Toussaint's position no longer enabled him to sustain the blow. Leclerc now made an offer whereby Toussaint would retire with his staff to a place of his choosing in the colony. The officers of his army would retain their ranks as well as their functions. Toussaint accepted, leaving Dessalines with no choice but to follow suit. This was in May. The following month, Toussaint was lured into a conference with the French general Brunet, who had him arrested on the spot, bound as a common criminal, and placed aboard a ship ready to leave for France. There he was incarcerated and left, tragically, to die of consumption in an isolated prison cell high in the French Alps.

The reasons for Toussaint's defeat at this stage are numerous and will doubtless continue to provoke much speculation. For those who would seek to vindicate the black leader, it may appear that Toussaint had been betrayed by his own generals; or that his capitulation was merely a ruse to gain time until the rainy season; or even, that he was unaware of the actual shambles of Leclerc's army at that moment and believed that the French forces no longer permitted him to resist. Yet the few hastily dispatched letters (all of which were intercepted) advising his commanding generals at the port towns to resist the French landing at all costs had hardly prepared them for the war that would have to be fought. They did what they could under the circumstances, and were it not for these initial defeats, Christophe would never have been in the position to desert, if only as a last-resort strategy, three months later. In fact, Christophe himself was the first to forcefully resist Leclerc, and without authorization from Toussaint, by burning le Cap. One senses that, from the very beginning, Toussaint never really held control of the situation.

If, in the past, his political judgments were so remarkably astute in relation to Sonthonax, in relation to the British, to Hédouville, and to the changing direction of the French government itself and the dangers of the emergent reaction, such political perspicacity now failed him altogether. His letter to the Directory in 1797 forewarning the French government of the impossibility of reimposing slavery in Saint Domingue, should ever France attempt it, had come at a time when the formal restoration of slavery was not even an issue, yet his apprehensions were singularly well placed. And that he had, up to now, so catastrophically misjudged the motives of Bonaparte and the new French regime, and perhaps even, in the end, had seen the expedition rather as an attempt to remove him from power than to remove the freedom of half a million blacks, is difficult to understand. Such political short-sightedness on the part of so brilliant a leader as Toussaint makes little sense unless it is seen in the context of the path he followed after the writing of the letter.

He had pursued a policy of power consolidation and a political vision of social conservatism that, rather than solidifying his forces, ended up dividing and weakening them. He fought a civil war to defeat the mulattoes in their bid for power but, once defeated, estranged them and the province, generally, by exercising brutal and bitter reprisals, and by deporting rather than reconciling Rigaud. Effectively, to reanimate animosities between Toussaint and the mulattoes in the South, and to readily facilitate the fall of the province into French hands, Rigaud, Villate, Pétion, and a few other mulatto leaders were sent to accompany the Leclerc expedition. But if class and race differences had prevented Toussaint from forging a cooperative alliance with the mulattoes, nothing required him to reintegrate former white colonists as economic partners in building a new social and political order. In fact, by doing so, he contributed to the alienation of the black laborers and reinforced their alienation with a rural code that emptied their freedom of any practical substantive meaning. Even worse, he executed the one leader they trusted implicitly, in whom they saw their own aspirations represented, and upon whom Toussaint could have counted for swift, organized mass resistance. Finally, in crowning his ambitions, however justified they may have been, by unilaterally drawing up and promulgating a constitution that established himself as supreme ruler, it was almost as if he assumed Saint Domingue was already independent of France, de facto, and, because of the actions he had already taken to make it so, needed only the eventual agreement of the French government. But by attempting to forge a new society, an economically and socially viable Saint Domingue under his sole authority, he was placing the cart before the horse and, simultaneously, removing himself from those elements he would need most; for, independence was not a reality nor did Bonaparte have any intention of ever granting it. Toussaint's political awareness, so acute in the past, was now far behind the stark realities that faced him and his people. Leclerc himself had remarked that, since Toussaint was removed from events on the European front, his successes against the British in Saint Domingue had spoiled him, made him over-confident; however, if he had had a more accurate and realistic appreciation of the power France imposed throughout Europe, he would have met the challenge accordingly, and Saint Domingue would be irretrievably lost to France. [25]

In the present situation, it was obvious Toussaint could not expel Leclerc as he had forcibly expelled Sonthonax, Hédouville, and even Roume, and when he capitulated to Leclerc, it is possible he conserved the illusion that he could work out a negotiated arrangement with Bonaparte. Politically, the events had passed Toussaint by, for the stakes were now unequivocal: either total independence or a restoration of the colonial regime, of white supremacy and slavery. While progressively assuming an independent status for Saint Domingue over the past three years, Toussaint never formally proclaimed it, and by resisting such a proclamation he therefore placed himself in a situation impossible to resolve except by the force of arms, and one that could only lead to his liquidation.

All of the major black leaders were now either deported outright (as was Rigaud for whom the French no longer had any use) or incorporated into the French army, and it was the masses, against whom the black generals would now be fighting, who led the way out of this treacherous impasse.

Leclerc's next step was to proceed with the general disarmament of the blacks. Yet his own position had greatly deteriorated. One of the deadliest epidemics of yellow fever the colony had known broke out in April, at the time when Toussaint, had his strategy and objectives been clear and aggressive at this early stage, could have turned the impending fatality to his advantage, rather than attempt to negotiate a settlement and finally capitulate. These first three months of the expedition had already cost Leclerc one-third of his entire army.[26] By June, the European troops were dying in the hospitals at a rate of thirty to fifty per day; the principal cities that had been burned to the ground offered little or no resources at all. Medical supplies, clothing, and shoes for the troops were severely lacking. On 6 June, Leclerc summed up the situation: "Every day the blacks become more audacious. . . . I am not strong enough to order a general disarmament or to implement the necessary measures. . . . The government must begin to think about sending out my successor."[27] By the end of July, as French losses were dramatically accelerated by the persistent ravages of the fever, news arrived in the colony announcing that slavery had been officially restored in Guadeloupe by decree, while persons of color were now forbidden to take the title of citizen. In addition, the French government had just passed a law reopening the slave trade. Significantly, it was from these sources, and not from Toussaint Louverture, their own leader who had always justified his own acts in the name of general emancipation, that the masses learned of the true purpose of the expedition. It was a terrific blow to Leclerc, who now blamed his inability to effectively carry out the general disarmament of the blacks upon the "premature" restoration of slavery and the arrival of news in Saint Domingue confirming it at this juncture.[28] For Leclerc to take away their arms was to take away their freedom. Sonthonax had warned them of this in so many words prior to his first departure from the colony in 1794. Had there been any initial doubt as to the purpose of Leclerc's mission with its secret instructions, the restoration of slavery in Guadeloupe, combined now with his measures to disarm the black population and troops, unequivocally dispelled it and left the masses with one imperative objective: the unmitigated and permanent destruction of the French presence in Saint Domingue.

Popular resistance now began to coalesce into insurrectionary movements. While the rapid formation, or reemergence, of massive maroon bands and strong centers of aggressive, armed rebellion characterized the resistance of the blacks in the North, from the island of Tortuga across to the entire North Plain region, it was often the concerted acts of resistance, carried out by small numbers or groups of individuals, that prompted the formation of similar movements in the South and the creation of a network of resistance, whose aim it was to proselytize, to gather additional recruits and supporters, to call meetings and assemblies, and to devise plans of action. The whole burden of resistance now lay squarely upon their shoulders, and for resisting they would face firing squads, be hanged, drowned, even gassed to death.[29] The reprisals were terrible, and yet such atrocities seemed only to reinforce the determination of the blacks as they made the political situation and the single alternative to it clearer by the day. Christophe, fighting on the side of the French, told General Pamphile Lacroix candidly and lucidly, in answer to Lacroix's query as to why the insurrections were spreading, that the danger did not lie with the brigands in armed bands who had given out signals for insurrection in the North, but rather, "the danger is in the general opinion of the blacks" who know of the recent French decrees and who fear a restoration of slavery in Saint Domingue.[30] His observations went straight to the heart of the matter. For ten bloody and strife-ridden years, the blacks had fought to obtain, to preserve, and to define their freedom. The course of the struggle that they began in 1791 had transformed them; they were no longer, nor could they ever again be, slaves. And so it was not merely the diverse insurrectionary bands that punctuated the countryside and the hills that Leclerc would have to crush. These he expected to be able to subdue, one by one, since there seemed to be no real cohesion to them, and no central leader. It was, as he would come to realize, the entire black population that would have to be annihilated in order to restore slavery and complete his mission.

Who, then, were these black masses and their leaders in the South who, on their own initiative and with the meager means at their disposal for effective resistance, fought the French army by themselves, while Dessalines, Christophe, Laplume, and the other black generals were still cooperating with Leclerc, and whom Leclerc himself could not deport because he needed them to carry out the repression?

Around the beginning of July, while Leclerc claimed to have succeeded in disarming the South,[31] the first outward signs of organized armed rebellion appeared in the Corail district near Jérémie, where Dommage had attempted unsuccessfully to resist the arrival of the French expeditionary troops five months earlier. The military had discovered a coordinated conspiracy between the town and the plantation workers of Corail to promote a general insurrection on all the plantations in the district and to kill off all the whites. The chief organizer of this insurrectionary movement was an obscure black by the name of Toussaint Jean-Baptiste, familiarly known as Lapaquerie, a butcher by occupation. He had assembled his fellow conspirators and held meetings at his house to discuss the means and methods by which to execute their project. In addition to Toussaint Jean-Baptiste, the principal ringleaders included his wife, "who fully shared her husband's intentions, had often vociferously manifested her hatred toward the whites, and desired nothing more than to see them all exterminated."[32] Two others, Lazare and Malbrouk, both fishermen, were also singled out as principal accomplices. Another was Claude Chatain, a deserter from Jérémie sent as emissary to talk with the plantation workers, to find out their attitudes, and to enjoin them to revolt. As a cover, Chatain claimed he was operating under instructions from Rigaud. Unfortunately for him, Rigaud had already been deported two months earlier. Eight more were arrested with no evidence other than a letter from one resident to the local commandant stating that these eight were aware of the preparations and were prepared to participate in the execution of the plot. According to the local officer, their past acts and attitudes proved their guilt, and, especially since the arrival of the French, they had manifested "criminal intentions." It was the only evidence the authorities could come by, but it was enough to get them arrested, sent to les Cayes for interrogation, and sentenced to the chain gang.[33] In all, the group consisted of two butchers, one officer of the national guard, one carpenter, three fishermen, one domestic, one deserter, one individual listed "without occupation," two others listed by name only, and Toussaint's wife, listed as "femme Toussaint." At les Cayes, Toussaint Jean-Baptiste, his wife, Lazare, and Malbrouk were executed by a firing squad.

In addition to these individuals were six plantation workers, also arrested in connection with this projected rebellion, among them Pierrot, a worker on the Etienne plantation, who was considered to be a most dangerous menace to society since punishments only made him more rebellious. Several times, he had attempted to assassinate the *procureur* with a dagger. Pierrot had a history of "bad conduct" and under Rigaud's regime had committed numerous acts warranting severe punishment. When dragoons were sent at that time to arrest him, he had stabbed one of them in the chest, and when Laplume arrived to investigate, Pierrot was whipped with rods, became all the more enraged, and had incited the workers to revolt. The full extent of this current insurrection was discovered only a few months after the initial arrests, but there were already indications that the revolt was far from being a localized affair. Among the five other plantation workers arrested was a black named Cupidon, who had brazenly entered a house in Jérémie, sat himself down at the table beside the occupants, and demanded something to eat. When the proprietor told him to get out on the porch if he wanted to eat, Cupidon lashed back vociferously with insults and invective and said that soon all the whites would be finished off, and that in three days' time they would all know what he meant. [34]

On 6 July, all nineteen of the Corail instigators arrived in les Cayes to be sentenced, and by the tenth, a full-scale insurrectionary movement was uncovered in this city.[35] The Corail conspirators had already sent out agents to les Cayes, where they began agitating and propagandizing among the black colonial troops to rouse them against the government and incite them to rebel. Their activities had been planned to coincide precisely with the moment when measures were taken to reorganize the troops as part of Leclerc's general disarmament of the blacks. Less than a week before the arrival of the Corail group, two blacks had already attacked and beaten up the Cayes militia commander.[36] The aim, once the revolt began, was to break into the prison, liberate their companions from Jérémie, as well as others, and set fire to the city.

At the same time that this was going on, some black residents of les Cayes had organized a meeting and were preparing a plan of action that would, coincidentally, converge with the anticipated rebellion of the black troops. On the night of the ninth, roughly a hundred of them gathered at the house of Cofi where they were all engaged in heated discussion, using most "incendiary" language. Berger, the white military commander of les Cayes, had been spying on them and came back with a contingent to arrest them, whereupon they swiftly dispersed and issued a call to arms. Immediately, a general alarm spread through the city. The black colonial garrison took up arms without orders and began beating its own alarm in the troops' quarters, only to be immobilized, however, by another battalion.[37]

Whether the Cofi conspiracy and the revolt of the black troops in les Cayes had been logistically planned in combination with the original Corail movement of Toussaint Jean-Baptiste at the beginning of July, or whether the Corail agents who appeared in les Cayes had come because of the arrest of their fellow conspirators, is not entirely clear. Whichever the case, the two movements did coincide, and had they not both been foiled, the repercussions and extent of the insurrections would have been considerable.[38] In fact, by this time insurrectionary activities, far from being isolated or local affairs, had spread throughout the department from Jérémie at the west to Miragoâne and the two Goâves at the east, the rebels in the latter region having made contact with the established bands of the Léogane plain under the maroon leadership of Lamour Dérance.[39] The increasing desertion of plantation workers, the assassination of a white resident, followed by the total burning of a sugar plantation in Cavaillon, indicated growing tensions and simmering rebellion in an area that had up to now been relatively tranquil.[40]

The French were in serious trouble. The effects of the disarmament program were already becoming evident, as many soldiers had deserted with their rifles before their units could be reorganized. Desbureaux, the commander of the southern army, now found it urgently necessary, in order "to discover their hideout [and] abort the plots they are conceiving," to publish an ordinance forbidding all inhabitants of city and country to house or shelter a soldier without a duly authorized leave, as it would be assumed they were sheltering deserters and would therefore be sentenced accordingly.[41] Among the arms confiscated by the authorities during the 10 July insurrectionary movement were a good number of rifles belonging to soldiers in the Eleventh Half-brigade that had been slated for disarmament.[42]

Although the black resistance forces were temporarily defeated at les Cayes, the movement in the Grande-Anse district continued to spread. Desbureaux had gone to Jérémie following the Cayes affair and, toward the end of the month, informed General Rochambeau, commander of the expeditionary army for the West and the South: "I am relentlessly pursuing these dangerous individuals; since my arrival here, I have already broken up several gatherings of workers on two or three plantations in the area around this city."[43] The blacks continued to circulate rebellious ideas, including threats to kill off the whites, to burn the city and destroy the plains. Among the dozen or so whom Desbureaux managed to arrest, most were *conducteurs* and were believed to be the leaders and principal accomplices in this movement. Desbureaux had all the *conducteurs* shot and sent the rest to les Cayes, where they perished in the same manner. All of them were well known for the assassinations, thefts, and acts of pillage they had committed during the whole course of the revolution. [44]

But, throughout the colony, the innocent were thrown in indiscriminately with the guilty. Arrested with no proof other than the circumstantial suspicions of a military commander, they were executed by the dozen, the score, and the hundredfold, the helpless victims of French reprisals whenever the slightest signs of agitation or discontent were discovered. The day-by-day executions were often conducted on the plantations, in front of the assembled blacks, so as to set an example for the others and, through terror, to force them into complete submission. In general, however, these executions tended to produce covert solidarity and encouraged the proliferation of the underground resistance movement. The white inhabitants who had welcomed the expedition from the start now began to see gatherings, conspiracies, and plots everywhere. Desbureaux dismissed these whites as being paranoid.[45] Their fears may have grown out of the general atmosphere of insecurity and were no doubt prompted by the increasing number of executions, but they were in fact well founded.

While Desbureaux was still in Jérémie, an armed rebellion broke out at Aquin and Saint Louis. The assassination of a white Aquin resident, Casamajor, had given the signal for a renewal of agitation.[46] Taking advantage of the inadequate supply of European troops in the district, a black militia lieutenant, Charles, and a number of deserters from various other units had captured the fort during the night and taken the city of Saint Louis on 27 August.[47] This was the first time a city had successfully been captured by insurgent blacks in the South. Joussaume, the black militia captain at Aquin, was apparently given orders by Laplume to march against Saint Louis. He denied having ever received Laplume's orders and had written instead to Rochambeau in the West requesting his instructions, stating in his letter to the general that "there is a conspiracy under way here [in Aquin] that has not yet broken into the open, given the precautions I have taken with the feeble means at my disposal to thwart their projects."[48] While it is most likely that Joussaume was a covert sympathizer, or perhaps even a fellow conspirator, the evidence remains insufficient. Nevertheless, Laplume arrested him and had him sent to Port-au-Prince for execution. [49]

The Saint Louis and, earlier, the Cayes insurrections clearly indicated the increasing participation of black soldiers and lower-ranking officers. Forced to fight for the French by the desertion of their commanders from Toussaint's army, they now began using their positions and their access to arms to aid the insurgent movements of blacks in town and country. By the time Desbureaux arrived in Saint Louis on 6 September, the rebels had come under fire. Pursued and shot on sight as wild game, a dozen or so had escaped into the Anse-à-Veau region, which had been up to now relatively quiet. [50]

While both Laplume and Nérette were engaged in pursuing the fugitive insurgents in the mountainous areas around Cavaillon, Aquin, and Saint Louis, new troubles beset les Cayes.[51] The troop situation there was far from reassuring. The militia was badly organized, the national guard badly armed, and the number of troops sorely insufficient. A handful of blacks initiated an attempt at insurrection on 4 September, but were unsuccessful. It was enough, however, to create panic and to spread a general alarm throughout the city. On the eighth, only two days after Desbureaux's arrival in Saint Louis, nearly four hundred blacks, armed as best they could be, some not at all, some with rifles, had gathered near Fort Islet, located behind the house of Joseph Darmagnac, the black leader of the movement.[52] Having fought off the first patrol sent to attack them, they made their way across a nearby plantation and began attacking the post protecting the city in order to make an inroad into the Plaine-des-Cayes, and possibly to spread the revolt to the plantations.[53] Twenty-five or thirty were captured immediately, most of them wounded. That they should be executed was taken for granted, yet Berger insidiously posed the question to his superior, Desbureaux: "Should I hang them or shoot them?"[54] A week later, as the incessant pursuit of insurgent forces continued, Desbureaux informed Rochambeau: "Everything [*sic*] that is captured is hanged on the spot."[55] The authorities exploited this incident to "empty" the prisons of les Cayes. A week after the Darmagnac revolt, Lalance, a local European commander, wrote of the affair: "The insurrection at les Cayes has served to rid the colony of 310 villains. Finally, all is quiet today."[56]

The French had no qualms when they spoke of exterminating blacks who fought back, and of making countless more innocent victims pay the same price. They had even developed a terminology of extermination: to drown two or three hundred individuals at one shot was called a *coup de filet;* for a person to die on a tree cross, the French invented the sarcastic expression *monter en dignité;* when someone was to be devoured by the bulldogs that Rochambeau later introduced into the colony, the term used was *descendre dans l'arène.*[57] Such atrocities were notoriously commonplace, and they seemed to increase, not only in number, but in degree, becoming ever more garish and heinous as the position of the French army progressively deteriorated, especially after the death of Leclerc later in November, when Rochambeau would assume command of the expedition, and in spite of the influx of fresh troops from France.[58] In fact, as early as August, Leclerc had announced his intentions to take recourse in terror to put down the insurrections.[59]

But what exacerbated the French the most was that the blacks mounted the scaffolds in stoic dignity. They encouraged each other to face their executions bravely. In le Cap, three blacks who had been caught setting fire to a plantation near the town were sentenced to be burned alive in an auto-da-fé. One tried to suffocate himself while another began howling in pain. The third turned and said to his companions, "You do not know how to die! Watch me, I will show you how to die." He turned his neck around in the iron collar and, facing the post to which he was tied, sat down in the flames, and without uttering a single moan was burned to death. Mary Hassal, an American residing in le Cap at this time, referred to the incident and, insightfully, wrote that these executions by fire were blamed by everyone as "giving a bad example to the negroes, who will not fail to retaliate with the first prisoners they take."[60] Lemmonier-Delafosse, a French general in the expeditionary army, had also witnessed the spectacle with his own eyes and, dumbfounded, wrote, as did General Leclerc: "These are the men we have to fight!"[61] Leclerc wrote of them: "These men die with incredible fanaticism; they laugh at death, and the same is true of the women."[62] One woman, reportedly, had turned to her husband who seemed hesitant as they were both about to die, and said: "Do you not know how sublime it is to die for liberty?" whereupon she proudly took hold of the rope and hung herself rather than die at the hands of the hangman. Another woman embodied in her own words the existential and historical reality of this whole nightmare, for it was a return to slavery that they were fighting against. Fearing the worst, she consoled her weeping daughters, who marched with her toward the place of execution: "Rejoice that your wombs will not have to bear slave children."[63]

After the Darmagnac revolt in les Cayes, harsher measures of repression accompanied the wholesale murder of hundreds, whose only crime was to be colored. Aimed at breaking the resistance of the blacks, the measures indicated, at the same time, that the French were now not only militarily on the defensive, but were fighting a lost cause. On 12 September, Desbureaux ordered that, in the event of an alert, anyone found on the streets who was not in the military, i.e., "domestics, workers, or other individuals," would be exposed indiscriminately to military fire.[64] The following day, he published another order whereby the plantation *conducteurs* were held personally responsible should disturbances occur among the workers. Their hierarchical position and the influence over the workers which that position afforded them rendered the *conducteurs* "infinitely more guilty than the laborers, [since] it would be impossible for them to be unaware of conspiracies in the making." Therefore, by not reporting them, they automatically became criminals, were singled out as insurrectionary leaders, and hanged. [65]

The Darmagnac revolt did not succeed in this second attempt to destroy the city and spread the insurrection into the plain. Yet the popular network of resistance that had emerged was rapidly solidifying. The paradox of the whole situation was that to restore slavery in Saint Domingue the French would have to exterminate nearly the entire black population. Those blacks who seemed docile and submissive one day could, and did, after witnessing the ruthless execution of friends and family members on their own plantation or at the town square, become hardened rebels the next. Leclerc had finally come to understand this and, scarcely a month before he died, advised Bonaparte of the necessity, as the single recourse left, of extermination: "[For] if my position has turned from good to critical, it is not just because of the yellow fever, but, as well, the premature reestablishment of slavery in Guadeloupe and the newspapers and letters from France that speak of nothing but slavery. Here is my opinion on this country: We must destroy all of the blacks in the mountains—men and women—and spare only the children under 12 years of age. We must destroy half of those in the plains and must not leave a single colored person in the colony who has worn an épaulette." [66] Presumably France would then be able to start her colonial enterprise all over again with additionally imported Africans through the slave trade, blacks who could be molded into submission as in the past, who had never known what it was to be a slave, nor what it was to have broken the chains and conquered their freedom in the New World.

Freedom is a great revolutionary ideal, a watchword of the great revolutions in history, and, in the hands of prominent and influential leaders, it can often be imbued with emotionalism and used as an effective propaganda piece. On one level, Toussaint used it to define and justify most of his own actions and ambitions, all in the name of his people. But even here, toward the latter years of his regime, general emancipation had, in many ways, become little more than a political abstraction with no meaningful substance in the daily lives of the greater mass of black laborers. For these blacks, freedom had little to do with bourgeois-democratic ideals. They were now once again living and experiencing the horrible realities of this life-and-death struggle. When Desbureaux wrote after the Cayes events of September that "they will see that there is no middle ground between death and obedience to the laws of the government," he was merely confirming what the masses already knew and had accepted as the price to pay.[67] In this, he also spelled out the ultimate defeat of the French in Saint Domingue.

Toward the end of September, the Grande-Anse movement had resurfaced. It was discovered that the Corail rebel leaders who were executed in July had been collaborating, not only with agitators in les Cayes, but, at the same time, with others in the region of Plymouth to the south of Jérémie. Five of these Plymouth rebels, having already committed a number of assassinations in the area some time ago, were captured on the twenty-fifth and sent to Jérémie.[68] A general insurrection throughout the entire Grande-Anse district—the greater part of the northwestern section of the South—was indeed afoot, and had been for some time. The projected insurrection began the next night, on the twenty-sixth, during a period of superficial calm, in the Fond Rouge quarter of Jérémie. A band of maroons descended from their mountain retreat and succeeded in setting fire to five plantations, on which they slaughtered six white managers. For the most part badly armed, they were forced to flee when a military detachment arrived to capture them. It was only after subsequent investigation and interrogations were conducted that the authorities realized the full extent of the movement. Those who had escaped that night were, in fact, leaders of the recent conspiracies that had been plaguing the area. Having taken to the hills, they had organized themselves as maroons and maintained contacts with their friends on the same plantations that they burned on the twenty-sixth.[69] The principal leader of these maroon rebels was Jean Panier, whose band extended from Irois along the peninsular coast into the Hotte mountain range as far as Macaya.[70] Apparently, Panier had become a maroon as early as May,[71] and, if so, had been forming his band and actively agitating over the past four months.

While the military pursued the incendiary rebels in a rabid manhunt, Bernard, the white commander at Jérémie, went to the plantations that had been burned and, in accordance with Desbureaux's recent ordinance, arrested the *conducteurs* of these plantations, along with all workers suspected of complicity, and had them hanged on their plantations.[72] Panier was shot down while defending himself. Critically wounded, he was subjected to an immediate interrogation and revealed that the chief architect behind all these incidents was Dommage, who had been secretly working with the insurgents ever since his first unsuccessful attempt in February to resist the arrival of the expeditionary forces at Jérémie.[73] Upon further investigation of the plantation workers in the area, for whom the only choice was to tell what they knew or be hanged, Panier's statements were confirmed. Dommage had established a whole network of spies and agents who carried out his instructions to visit the plantations of the area, to convince the workers that the French had arrived to put them back into slavery, that they must rise in revolt against the French government, and that at a given time they should assemble at Fond Rouge to receive orders and munitions from Dommage.

Magdelon, a worker and the wife of the *conducteur* on the Parouty plantation in Fond Rouge (one of the five plantations burned by the maroons of Jean Panier's band, and on which the incendiaries had "friends"), declared under questioning that, around mid-July—just after the Corail conspiracy —her husband, Jean-Louis, had been visited by a *conducteur*, Izidor, of another plantation in the same quarter. (Izidor had been executed just prior to Magdelon's interrogation.) He was from the Petitgo estate, which the military authorities had qualified as "a refuge and a retreat for assassins and vagabonds,"[74] and had been sent by Dommage to engage Jean-Louis to revolt against the French government. At the time, Jean-Louis claimed, according to his wife, that "he was not accustomed to revolting and that he strove to respect and obey those persons in a position to give him good advice."[75] From another worker, Corus, on the Leroux plantation, the authorities learned that a black by the name of Jean-Jacques, from the Trippin estate, was sent out to raise the workers at Leroux to rebel by telling them that he was acting under orders from Dommage, and that "all the men should meet at Fond Rouge to await further orders and arms from commander Dommage." Thomas, another black from Trippin, was entrusted by Jean-Jacques (whom the military arrested) with "spreading the word." Finally, from two others whose names and plantations were not identified, they learned that, by way of a third party, Dommage had offered them arms to distribute to those blacks who were in agreement to encamp at Fond Rouge, where he had already arrived and was waiting for them. The two workers were also told that the French had come to put them back into slavery and that they must take up arms to keep their freedom. They identified two others, Jean-René and Pierre (both executed), as having received orders to "make the rounds" of the plantations to win over the workers.[76]

Following these investigations, Panier, Dommage, and his entire half-brigade were shipped to Port-au-Prince to meet their fate at the hands of Rochambeau.[77] And to block any possible communication between Panier and Dommage, Panier was sent on a separate ship.[78] Sixteen other prisoners, arrested on suspicion, were also sent for execution, most of them ex-officers of various companies.[79]

To read the daily reports of the French military, one would have the impression that they had the situation well in hand: constant pursuit of fugitive rebels; workers terrorized to the point where some were cooperating with the army and denouncing additional individuals; the awakening of the white inhabitants who had placed their confidence in Dommage. Yet other maroon bands, equally as numerous as Panier's, had already emerged and had been operating in this western region of the South. At the head of these bands were three ex-slave leaders of the Platons insurrections of 1792–93: Goman, Nicolas Régnier, and the veteran Gilles Bénech, or *ti malice*. Like Bénech, Goman and Régnier had been made company captains in the Third Regiment of the legion, Goman being a chronic deserter. During the purges of the southern army that followed the civil war, both Gilles and Régnier were arrested, imprisoned at Port-au-Prince, and later sent to Saint Marc, whence they escaped to the South upon the arrival of the expeditionary forces. To avoid similar imprisonment, Goman took to the woods after the civil war, later returned to the plantation of his former master, and when the French arrived, became a maroon once again. It was then that he met with Jean Panier, took over the leadership of the band upon Panier's death, and by the end of the year had joined forces with Gilles Bénech and Nicolas. [80]

To the east, concentrated maroon activity continued in the Miragoâne-Goâves area as insurgents there, working closely with the bands from Léogane and Jacmel, repeatedly attacked enemy posts and swiftly retreated into the mountains, only to reorganize their forces, by now five thousand strong, conduct expeditions on the plantations to gather additional recruits, and return to attack again with greater force. In October, when Delpech, the mulatto commander of Petit-Goâve, made his rounds in the area, he could not find even one plantation where the workers had not deserted to take up arms.[81] The same day, over a hundred black soldiers and officers that had been enlisted by the French into companies to protect Aquin, where insurrection had been brewing since August, deserted with their arms and military equipment. Now openly supporting the rebel movement, they assembled additional forces and attacked the city with a vigor that left the French incredulous. The organizer of this mass desertion was a black by the name of Jean-Louis Louiseau, called Jeudy, a former battalion leader of the Eleventh Half-brigade; it was from this half-brigade that rifles had been found among the fugitive insurgents of the first revolt in les Cayes early in July. [82]

In less than a week, another band emerged in the Torbeck plain not far from les Cayes. Here, a group of workers on the Smith and Laplace plantations had revolted and assassinated their masters after they had dealt them one blow too many. Those who led the revolt were the domestics and an experienced *conducteur*, Samedi Smith. Born a slave, Samedi had displayed qualities of leadership early in life that secured him the position of *conducteur* at the age of twenty. Samedi, along with thirty other rebel workers, armed with little more than sticks and knives, fled to safety in the woods and later (as we shall see) participated with Gilles Bénech and others in a widespread operation that marked the decisive turning point of the war in the South. The reprisals following Samedi's rebellion claimed the lives of fifteen men and three women on the two plantations. [83]

These, then, were the black masses who, alone for the past eight months, had sustained the war against the French army in the South. The most significant feature of their efforts to organize and resist Bonaparte's expeditionary forces is that there was no single leader around whom the movement united, but literally hundreds of them throughout the department, and hundreds more throughout the colony, for the most part, obscure individuals. In August, once the news that slavery had been restored in Guadeloupe and the French slave trade reopened, Leclerc remarked, and certainly did not exaggerate the case, that it was not enough to have removed Toussaint: "[For] here there are two thousand leaders that must be removed."[84]

We have seen a few of these in the South. There were the urban blacks with a trade, like Toussaint Jean-Baptiste at Corail, butchers, carpenters, fishermen, and others with no occupation at all. On the plantations, there were domestics and *conducteurs*, as well as ordinary farm workers, who acted as spies or agents. Some of these had deserted, like Samedi Smith and Jean Panier, to become active maroon leaders at the head of insurrectionary bands, whose numbers were drawn largely from the plantations on which they maintained ties with *conducteurs* and workers. There were also black officers of the French army like Dommage, who operated jointly and clandestinely with urban blacks, maroons, and plantation *conducteurs*, like Jean-Louis and Izidor, to establish points of contact in the cities and on the plantations in order to develop a network of popular resistance. Here, those like Jean-Jacques, Jean-René, Pierre, and no doubt countless other unknown individuals, operated under Dommage's instructions to make the rounds of the plantations, distribute arms, and assemble the workers to strike at Fond Rouge. The whole operation was to be carried out in concurrence with Jean Panier's maroon band. The women, like Toussaint Jean-Baptiste's wife at Corail, or Magdelon, the *conducteur* Jean-Louis's wife, were equal and active participants in these insurrectionary conspiracies. In the military, there were other officers, like Charles or Jeudy, who openly deserted the French army with an entire batallion in armed revolt and took to the hills. In addition, there were the former slave leaders of the first insurrectionary struggles against slavery at Platons in 1792–93, ex-officers of the legion like Gilles Bénech, Goman, or Nicolas, who had become hardened warriors and now active maroon chiefs.

From these diverse sources of resistance we may discern at least three sectors of the black population: the civilian, which included both urban blacks and plantation blacks, with the *conducteurs* figuring prominently; the military, the black officers and soldiers in the French army that would desert with arms; and maroons, fugitives and deserters of recent or of long standing from both the civilian and the military sectors, who organized into separate bands. At a certain point, all three sectors become entirely interrelated, interconnected, and often interchangeable as spheres of revolutionary activity. Pamphile Lacroix, a general in the French expeditionary army, observed what few people at the time seemed to fully grasp: "[It is that,] in this new insurrection of Saint Domingue, as in all insurrections that attack constituted authority, it was not the avowed leaders who gave the signal for revolt, but rather, obscure individuals, for the most part personal enemies of the colored generals."[85] The initial attempts of these individuals in the South did not always meet with much success, but their significance lies in the very nature of the war they were fighting. The blacks began by building networks of resistance, organized in clandestinity, often in marronage, and finally sustained by guerilla warfare.

While the use of the term marronage may seem somewhat inappropriate at a time when slavery had already been abolished, slavery and a return to the colonial regime were nevertheless hanging ominously over the heads of the blacks as the alternative to implacable resistance. Bonaparte himself had foreseen the resurgence of marronage and, in this vein, identified as maroons those who would sustain their resistance. He wrote in his instructions: "Toussaint, Moyse and Dessalines [in this final phase] will have been eliminated, and three or four thousand blacks, entrenched in the hills of the Spanish part of the colony will form what is known in the islands as the Maroons, whom we will with time, perseverence and a well-combined system of attack, finally destroy."[86] Not only did Bonaparte grossly underestimate their number, but he did not conceive that, far from escaping in final recourse into Spanish territory, there to form relatively isolated entities, these new fugitives would organize within the colony, under the noses of the French officers and generals, to combine, in an integrated struggle, with the wholly unanticipated phenomenon of widespread and diverse popular resistance. If marronage was no longer exactly as it was in the days of slavery and, rather, took the form of armed insurrection and insurgency, it is perhaps that the revolution itself, and now the annihilative nature of the war against the French, had imposed a set of political and military realities in which marronage, or desertion, or flight, necessarily turned into an active revolutionary force.

It was a recurrent popular strategy, and it was basically this strategy that would break the French army. Christophe realized it, too, and said so to Leclerc before he finally deserted the French and rejoined the black revolution. In fact, Dessalines had been preparing to defect with the black and mulatto generals for some time and had forged a pact with Pétion, the most prominent mulatto military leader since Rigaud's deportation. Around mid-October, Pétion and Clerveaux, an outstanding mulatto officer from Toussaint's army, opened fire on le Cap. Dessalines received word of the revolt while in the West, made a spectacular escape, and issued a general call to arms. The

Cap rebellion also brought forth another talented mulatto leader, Nicolas Geffrard, who would later play an instrumental role in the South.

It has generally been considered, almost as a detached matter of fact, that the defection of the black and mulatto generals from the French army marked the decisive turning point in this war for independence. It was a treacherous and an eminently dangerous act, and it was a tremendous blow to Leclerc who, with one or two exceptions, was now left only with European troops, and even some of these were beginning to abandon him.[87] But to see this phase of the war for independence as having been inaugurated by Dessalines and the other black and mulatto leaders, supported by the armed masses as auxiliaries in a collective military drive toward independence, is to overlook one of the most profound lessons of the revolution. For the defection of the generals could only be meaningful or militarily effective, or even possible, because the movements of popular resistance had reached not only an irreversible stage, but a level that involved nearly the entire population. It was out of individual initiatives that a network of unrelenting popular resistance and insurgency had been formed and had grown to what it was by October, when Dessalines, Clerveaux, Pétion, and the other black and mulatto "jacobins" defected. Actually, their defection was perhaps not even, in and of itself, the turning point; it became a turning point because mass resistance had reached a level that made it clear the French were fighting a lost cause. The masses had resisted the French from the very beginning, in spite of, and not because of, their leadership. They had shouldered the whole burden and paid the price of resistance all along, and it was they who had now made possible the political and military reintegration of the leaders in the collective struggle. Were it otherwise, Dessalines and the generals would have been defecting toward what? Would they, or could they even, have defected? Defection would seem, at best, suicidal under any circumstances other than those that prevailed at the moment they abandoned Leclerc. In this sense, it may be inappropriate, and almost superfluous, to establish a demarcation that fixes the decisive phase of the war for independence with the defection of the black and mulatto colonial generals.

But Dessalines was now the recognized commander-in-chief of the indigenous army, and it was a united black and mulatto army. The force of events, the assured knowledge that the French aimed at restoring slavery, the brutal acts of extermination from which mulattoes and blacks now suffered alike, even the earlier deportation of Rigaud, had buried the old rivalries that led to the civil war and the racial animosities that accompanied it. Leclerc had become one more victim of yellow fever and died during the night of 2 November. Command of the French forces thus fell to Rochambeau, in whose name and by whose orders so many atrocities and mass-murders, ghastly acts unparalleled since the days of slavery, had already been committed in the South and the West. As early as May, Leclerc had written to Bonaparte, suggesting Rochambeau as his successor: "He is a person of integrity, a good military man, and he hates the blacks."[88] Now in command, Rochambeau extended his barbaric policies throughout the entire colony. He purchased a special breed of bulldog from Cuba that had apparently been carefully trained to attack and devour humans. For entertainment in le Cap, he set up an arena into which he threw the blacks to be torn to pieces by these dogs.[89] Upon assuming command of the expedition, he wrote to the minister of the marine that he would need an additional thirty-five thousand troops to defeat the rebel forces, disarm the population, and drive the blacks back onto the plantations. In January 1803, he requested special permission to proclaim immediately the restoration of slavery in Saint Domingue.[90]

The French now held only le Cap, Môle, and Tortuga island in the North. In the West, the rebel army held Archahaye and the entire Artibonite, with the exception of Saint Marc. The South, however, was still dominated by French troops. So, to clear a passage for Geffrard into the South, Dessalines entrusted Pétion with the mission of winning over the independent blacks under the African leader Lamour Dérance and his chief lieutenant, Cangé, a mulatto, both of them former enemies of Dessalines and partisans of Rigaud during the civil war.[91] They had both joined the French side when Leclerc's forces landed in the colony with Rigaud conspicuously present. However, when Leclerc deported Rigaud, who had served his purpose, and when it had become clear that the French intended to subjugate both mulatto and black alike, Dérance abandoned the French but remained independently organized in the hills around Léogane and Jacmel. Cangé, a former free mulatto who had taken part in the early struggles of the *affranchis* for political equality, had become a captain of the legion in the West and, following the civil war, was demoted to common soldier. Once Dérance had deserted the French, Cangé then fled to the southern region to join in resistance with Dérance.[92]

In December 1802, Cangé had written a letter to Delpech, a fellow mulatto and commander for the French at Petit-Goâve, trying to make him understand that it was only a matter of time before the French would exterminate all the black and mulatto officers, that the French sought only to restore slavery and the colonial regime, that they had allowed themselves to become divided and to become the executioners of their own people, black and mulatto alike. Delpech obtusely stuck to the French; he was proud to be a Frenchman and he would die one.[93] His defection, however, would have been pivotal and certainly would have facilitated the penetration of Geffrard's forces into the South. Finally, by the end of December, it was the independent insurgent bands that infested this area, progressively increasing their numbers, munitions, and military equipment with each attack, which had cleared the way for Geffrard's first entry into the South.[94] On 16 January, his troops had captured Anse-à-Veau.[95] At this point, Geffrard opened a sealed envelope that Dessalines had given him before setting out, to be opened only when he had taken a southern port city of some importance. Dessalines had promoted him to division general and chief commander of the forces in the South. Laplume, in command at les Cayes and still fighting for the French, had immediately set out, however, to aid the French at Anse-à-Veau and force Geffrard to retreat temporarily to the West.[96]

But a massive—and decisive—popular insurrection was already under way and had broken out at Tiburon when Laplume returned to les Cayes. Unaware of Dessalines's alliance with Geffrard, independent rebels, encamped in the Hotte and Macaya mountains and led by Gilles Bénech, Nicolas Régnier, and Goman, had devised a collective plan to attack Tiburon. Plantation workers had been deserting massively to join the insurgents, and they were now two thousand strong. The three rebel leaders were secretly aided by two officers of the French army, both of them mulattoes, the one, Desravines, in charge of Tiburon, the other, Férou, in command at Cotteaux. Desravines had been covertly supplying them with munitions and "against orders, had diverted into rebel hands two ships carrying abundant food supplies."[97] Under the experienced guerilla leadership of Bénech, they had captured the city and held out until mid-February, then swiftly evacuated and made off with huge quantities of munitions as they forged their retreat.[98] For the time being, Férou dissimulated his defection and, from Cotteaux, agreed to march against them.[99]

Instead of setting out immediately for Tiburon to crush the insurrection, Berger waited at les Cayes—one day too long. While on his way to Port-Salut to join with the national guard in the expedition against the rebel forces at Tiburon, a collective insurrection of plantation workers and national guard broke out right under his nose. They had prepared successive ambushes, pelleting his troops with bullets, falling rock and debris, forcing them back to les Cayes.[100] At this point, Férou made his position unequivocally clear and led the revolt at Cotteaux. On 1 February, Berger, renowned for his cruelties in the South, wrote to Rochambeau from les Cayes, dumbfounded by what was happening: "These men who have risen today in insurrection have always conducted themselves in a manner deserving of praise for their leaders and the confidence of the government."[101] He went on to write in the same letter: "I am without forces, and I fear that this little insurrection at Port-Salut might spread." Indeed, it did. The insurgent blacks and their mulatto allies were now in armed revolt and striking at all points throughout the interior, from Tiburon to as far as Port-Salut. At the same time, Armand Bérault, the leader of the Platons slave insurrections and later a regional agricultural inspector for the Plaine-des-Cayes under Rigaud, along with

Bazile, another popular leader of these early struggles and ex-officer of the Legion, had been agitating amongst the plantation workers of the Plaine-des-Cayes, inciting them to revolt.[102] So by now, the entire plain was in a state of insurrection as the black laborers began to raze the cane fields and set the plantations ablaze.[103] In the foothills outside the plain, Samedi Smith held Camp Périn along with another black leader, Guillaume Lafleur, and one Lafredinière, a European white and ex-commander of the national guard, who deserted the French and now fought for the black revolution. [104]

This, then, was the situation at the beginning of March when Geffrard made a second entry into the South, and it was the widespread insurrection of these black masses that made his entry practicable. Self-mobilized and independently organized, this latest insurrection had effectively begun with the attack of Goman and Bénech at Tiburon. Coordinated with the local mulatto and black officers who diverted arms and munitions and finally deserted their posts in the French army, it rapidly assumed the proportions of a generalized insurrection throughout the interior, as the blacks of the Plaine-des-Cayes, under Bérault, Bazile, Samedi Smith, Lafleur, and others, simultaneously led the plantation workers to mass insurgency. On 5 March, Geffrard arrived in the Plaine-des-Cayes, where he met with Férou, urging that they support and recognize Dessalines as commander-in-chief. The two military leaders immediately combined their forces, completely encircled les Cayes, and kept the French immobilized. (See Map 3.)

At this juncture it becomes difficult to discern exactly when and where and even *if* the popular insurrectionary movement in the South had come to an end as an autonomous force. It is also at this juncture that the problematic necessity of leadership comes into play. The war was not yet over, nor was the popular army yet officially regimented and incorporated under the supreme command of Dessalines. In the North and the West, a multiplicity of competing bands had emerged in armed resistance to Leclerc immediately following Toussaint's deportation and in response to learning of the restoration of slavery in Guadeloupe, as well as the possibility of its imminence in Saint Domingue. Almost all of their leaders, like Sylla, Sans-Souci, Petit-Noël Prieur, and Macaya in the North, or Lamour Dérance in the West, were African and refused to be commanded by the creole generals, notably Dessalines and Christophe, who only the day before had been ostensibly fighting for the French and waging an unremitting and merciless war against them. They had organized and sustained the resistance against Leclerc independently from the start, and they did so in spite of, in opposition to, rather than because of, the black jacobin leadership. They practiced voodoo, organized their following on an independent basis and with goals, cultural values, and a world view that placed them outside of what has often unquestioningly been accepted as the "national interest" and "national unity." But if they

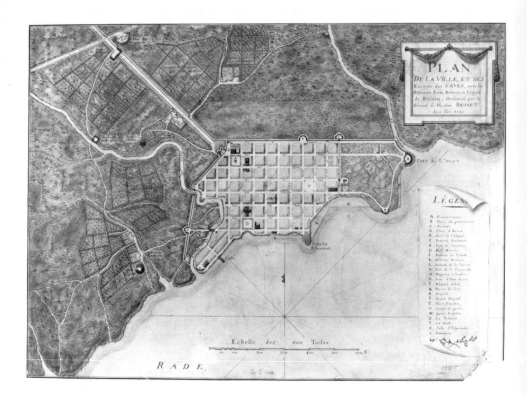

Map 3. The city and environs of les Cayes, with its forts, batteries, and
defense positions, by order of division general Brunet, year 11 (1803).
By permission of the Bibliothèque Nationale, Paris.

were fighting purely and simply for their own independence, outside of the national interest, it was because they had no real place in the Louverturian society that Toussaint had forged; they had no personal claim to land, and though their freedom from colonial slavery was real, it existed more as a rhetorical abstraction than as a practical, substantive reality that informed their daily lives. Thus, their refusal to submit to Dessalines and the black generals after their defection from the French was a logical one, but in so doing they had, in Dessalines's own words, "become obstacles to freedom" and therefore had to be liquidated. [105]

It has been insightfully argued by one historian that, in unequivocally pursuing independence, Dessalines saw so clearly what was under his nose because he, as opposed to Toussaint, could see no further.[106] It might also be argued, however, that it was because he could see no further that he resorted to a crude policy and military strategy of outright liquidation of those independent leaders refusing his authority, but yet who had initially sustained the war against Bonaparte's army and had made his own defection effectually possible and meaningful. Because Dessalines embraced political independence, because he became the military leader of independence, and because independence was indeed achieved under his military leadership, it is generally assumed, after the facts, that the violent elimination of these independent maroon and voodoo leaders was therefore a justifiable, if unfortunate, necessity in the name of national unity. But one may equally consider the possibility that, in the end, the assassination of these leaders who were closest to the masses was no more necessary than was Toussaint's execution of Moïse. One may pose the question: Were they any more of an obstacle to independence than Toussaint, himself, in his hesitation and equivocation in the face of Leclerc at the head of an invading and occupying army; or, were they any more of an obstacle than Christophe whose unauthorized defection to Leclerc in May 1802 effectively changed the situation and closed off any real alternative for organized mass resistance under the black military leadership after these first months of the expedition? Yet few would argue that Toussaint or Christophe should have been liquidated by their own officers.

In the South, the violent elimination by Dessalines's generals of uncompromising independent popular leaders did not occur as it did in the North and West. A possible explanation for this may reside in the fact that, by the time Geffrard had made his second entry into the province, the French in the rest of the colony, and in most of the South, were already fighting on losing ground. In the South, independent popular activity had practically liberated the province without the aid of Dessalines's army, but if, contrarily, much of the southern province had still been left to be retaken, independent maroon leaders like Goman no doubt would have been liquidated in the process, as well. When Dessalines did meet with the popular indigenous leaders of the South, the defeat of the French was already a foregone conclusion. So while the political justifiability of eliminating through violence the competing and resistant band leaders in the North and West may continue to be debated, it is, nevertheless, clear that their removal by Dessalines ultimately helped to prepare and consolidate his personal rise to power.

In the South, Goman, Gilles Bénech, and Régnier were still separately organized in the mountains around Tiburon and, for the time being, did not officially submit to any authority other than their own, in spite of the formalized coalition between Férou and Geffrard. By now, almost the entire black population of the province was in arms, fighting at every point along with their mulatto allies. When Rochambeau received news of the critical state of the French army in the South, he sent twelve hundred of the freshly arrived European troops to Jérémie under the command of Sarrazin, who was to take them directly to les Cayes by sea. Overly confident, he landed at Tiburon instead, expecting to wipe out the insurrectionary rebels who infested the area. Some three thousand plantation workers armed with sticks and stones for the most part, and perhaps only a hundred with rifles, vigorously attacked Sarrazin's troops every inch of the way in a torrent of falling rocks. Already, he had lost nearly three hundred of his men when the independent rebels were seconded by Bazile, sent out from the Plaine-des-Cayes by Férou and Geffrard.[107] Losing time and men, Sarrazin requested a temporary cease-fire and desperately proposed to Bazile a mutual agreement whereby the winning party would arrange to care for the wounded and dying soldiers of the losing party. Though the blacks had nothing to gain from this proposal, Bazile accepted the offer and, as Sarrazin pushed on, he and his troops began to gather the bodies that lay dying, administering treatment to the Europeans as to their own. One of them exclaimed: "By god, these blacks aren't the cannibals that we were made to believe!"[108]

Out of the horrors of this war, the blacks made a distinction between the ordinary soldiers, who were merely pawns in the hands of Bonaparte, fighting for the interests of an alien bourgeoisie with whom they had no kinship, and those who used their authority to commit countless acts of sadistic and wholesale murder against the black and mulatto population. These were treated in a manner befitting their crimes. Kerpoisson, Berger's chief executioner in the South, was one of them. While on his way back to les Cayes with armaments from Jérémie, his ship was intercepted by rebel barges awaiting him in the Anglais bay. The two captains who directed the siege, Bégon, a mulatto, and Aoua, a black, captured Kerpoisson, bound him up, and sent him to the post commander at Anglais. Here they attempted to drown him, then butchered his body, and sent the monster with scarcely a breath of life left in him, to the Quatre Chemins crossroads just outside les Cayes, there to atone for his atrocities with the inscription on his back: "There are certain crimes that the wrath of the gods never pardons."[109]

The next three months spelled out utter defeat for the French. In April, they made an all-out but futile effort to smash the rebel forces. The yellow fever, which had subsided somewhat, resurged. Famine began to take its toll in les Cayes, where the French were without money, without medical supplies, without food. When Geffrard agreed to open the doors of the city for the entry of food supplies, the black market women from the plantations swarmed the streets, clandestinely exchanged their fruits and vegetables for gunpowder, and carried it back under their dresses to the rebel camps.[110] By mid-June, General Brunet, now in charge of the French army in the South, began evacuating the sick with great difficulty. On the twenty-eighth, he wrote: "The rebels become more insolent by the day. I pursue them from time to time, but it is useless."[111]

The last French stronghold in the department was Grande-Anse, which now became the scene of a new insurrection. The black plantation laborers around Abricots and Cap Dame-Marie had risen in rebellion with a few local officers. The mass of them burned and totally devastated the region between these two towns and carried their insurrection as far as a quarter of a league from Jérémie. The worst of it all, wrote Brunet, "is that Grande-Anse affords these rebels twenty-five to thirty thousand black laborers, one quarter of whom have already waged war against Rigaud during the British occupation."[112] One of the rebel leaders, an unknown black by the name of Atlas, had, along with over a hundred others, taken over an old fortress just below Cap Dame-Marie. When Berger arrived in the area, instead of finding the scouts from Jérémie that he was supposed to meet, he was relentlessly attacked for over a day and a half by the rebels under Atlas's command.[113] Here again, it was the popular initiative of the black population in the Grande-Anse, a center of revolutionary activity since the very arrival of the French expedition in 1802, that had immobilized the French until Dessalines could enter the South, reorganize the army, and order the full-scale attack against Jérémie.

Arriving in the Plaine-des-Cayes on 5 July, Dessalines met the black and mulatto leaders of the South, some of them for the first time, and made a number of promotions. Gilles Bénech, Nicolas Régnier, and Goman, the intrepid maroon chiefs whose activities had proved decisive in the military turning point of the war in the South, were still not officially incorporated into the regular ranks. Up to now, both Régnier and Goman had considered themselves colonels, and each wore a set of corresponding epaulets. Bénech, the oldest and most experienced of the three, had none. To settle the issue, Dessalines, in his characteristically crude manner, took from Régnier and Goman one epaulet each and gave them both to Gilles with these words:

"You are [brigade] colonel, and Goman and Nicolas are battalion leaders."
Disillusioned and no doubt personally offended by the injustice he had just
received, Goman kept repeating over and over to his friends after Dessalines
left for the West: *"Negre-là dimini moin,"* meaning in English, "That black
has demoted me." Goman continued his own struggle for independence long
after the revolution. It was at the head of an armed community of blacks in
the mountains of Grande-Anse that he died in 1820, as he had always lived
—a maroon defending his own freedom against the onslaughts of established
regimes. [114]

After Dessalines's arrival in the South, the defeat of the French was a
matter of course. Jérémie was evacuated in August, and on 17 October Geffrard took possession of les Cayes. In November, when Rochambeau finally
capitulated at le Cap, the ill-fated expedition that had cost France the lives
of over fifty thousand troops came to an end. In the name of slavery, she lost
what had been the wealthiest and most flourishing colony in the Caribbean.
On 1 January 1804, Dessalines published a declaration of independence.
The French name of Saint Domingue was abolished forever and the original
Arawak name of Hayti restored to inaugurate the new nation. The proclamation was a formal acknowledgment of the self-determination of those diverse and ordinary individuals of whom the black masses were composed.
In their own way, they not only contributed to but were the very foundation
of Haiti's independence.

Conclusion

It has been said of the French Revolution that the ultimate explanation of what took place during its early years must be sought in the popular mentality, "in the profound and incurable distrust born in the soul of the people" in regard to the ruling classes of the Ancien Régime: "the people and their unknown leaders knew what they wanted," and if they momentarily followed the official leadership of the revolution, it was only to the extent that it appeared to embrace their own goals and aspirations.[1] In this, the Saint Domingue revolution, like most revolutions aiming at essential social change, was no exception. That the explanation of what took place from 1791 onward lies largely in the profound and irrevocable distrust of the slaves in regard to the white masters and in their hatred of the plantation regime, which exploited their labor and robbed them of their humanity; in short, that the primary objective of the slaves was to become socially free persons, is all too evident. But once they were free, the problems then of informing that freedom with substantive meaning for themselves, as well as the political imperative, later, of safeguarding it from armed intervention, both impelled and characterized the popular movements. These thus developed in response to the changing situations brought about by the revolution.

However, slave resistance had existed for as long as slavery itself, and during the colonial period, those slaves who chose to resist their oppression, whatever the cost, did so in many ways. We have seen that the earliest revolts occurred in the very first stages of enslavement aboard the ships, although within the colony, under the regimen and social structure of slavery, organized slave revolts were proportionately far fewer, and each was quickly circumscribed and crushed. The higher proportion of slave revolts aboard the ships, however, may partially be explained by the fact that, other than throwing oneself to sea or committing suicide in some other manner, alternative avenues of resistance were practically nonexistent. Under slavery, a diversified labor system with a corresponding set of human relationships and complexities offered more varied opportunities for resistance which, on the whole, must have appeared at least somewhat less risky to the slave than open revolt against white society. A domestic, for example, who knew his or her master well, could, for that very reason, administer the poison all the more effectively.

Perhaps the most significant and persistent of these avenues of resistance, though, was marronage. Yet it has been claimed that marronage in Saint Domingue was nothing when compared with the other islands in the Caribbean.[2] And so the question may be asked as to why a black slave revolution occurred in Saint Domingue when resistance and marronage appeared to be so much more prevalent elsewhere. It is a justifiable question only insofar as one exclusively identifies marronage in terms of collectively armed bands or large socially organized communities of fugitive slaves living independently and outside the system. Indeed, if one attempts to quantitatively register the extent of resistance in any given slave society by merely counting the number of openly organized revolts, or the number and duration of large maroon communities such as the *quilombos*, then one risks looking in the wrong direction.

One may also be looking in the wrong direction by assigning to slave resistance, *in and of itself*, a determining causal role in black colonial revolution. Saint Domingue does, indeed, stand out as a unique occurrence, not only in the political conjuncture of the French Revolution, but in all of human history, as the only slave revolt that succeeded in abolishing slavery. More than that, Saint Domingue emerged from its revolution a politically independent nation. But if it was a unique occurrence, it was no accident of history, and, while the metropolitan revolution was intrinsic to the Saint Domingue revolution, still, similar agitation and unrest in other French colonies like Martinique and Guadeloupe (where slave resistance, on a quantitative level, seemed to be more prevalent) did not develop into the violent struggles that were evidenced on all levels of society in Saint Domingue. The ideology of the French Revolution certainly had an impact upon the unfolding and development of the revolution in Saint Domingue, but even here, if ideas play a role in the emergence of revolutionary events, they cannot in themselves produce those events. Ultimately, if the material conditions and stage of development had not been what they were in Saint Domingue by the third quarter of the eighteenth century, the French revolutionary ideology may not necessarily have propelled or provoked that tremendous explosion of events. The phenomenal economic and demographic growth that Saint Domingue underwent during the eighteenth century, and that was discussed in Chapter 1, far surpassing, qualitatively and quantitatively, that of any other West Indian colony, may go a long way in explaining why a revolution occurred here and not elsewhere in the Caribbean.

By 1789 the whole social fabric of the colonial regime and the economic basis of its relationship to the metropolis were rapidly disintegrating, providing fertile ground in which revolutionary movements could take root.

Each social group involved in colonial Saint Domingue—wealthy planters, the maritime bourgeoisie, *petits blancs*, the free coloreds, the slaves—had claims of its own. Each represented particular and generally opposing interests that arose out of the contradictions of class and caste, intertwined and confounded as they were by the metropolitan and colonial politics of race. And so it is important to remember that the Saint Domingue revolution began with the breakup of its own ruling class, and not with slave rebellion. The organized slave revolt that broke out in 1791, with long-term antecedents and a continuity of its own, became inscribed in a process of revolution that had been in motion for several years.

Among these antecedents and within that continuity of slave resistance was, of course, marronage. In Saint Domingue, the "maroons" were never entirely an outside entity, as seems to have been the case in some of the other slave colonies, nor did they constitute a single, easily identifiable and circumscribed group, although there were organized bands and one large community that gained its independence by treaty. In this vein, much closer attention ought to be paid, in colonial Saint Domingue, to the day-to-day marronage of slaves as an integral part of their life experience, to those fugitives who never joined the armed bands, but who were indeed maroons and, judging from the branded stamps they bore and the mutilations of their bodies, were often incurable recidivists. There existed reciprocal relationships between the plantation slaves and the individual maroons, each of whom could, depending upon circumstances, end up in the place of the other. If plantation slaves often sheltered the maroons, they could themselves become maroon upon witnessing the abominable cruelties administered as punishments. Maroons were also sheltered by free blacks who, by doing so, risked becoming slaves themselves. There were also urban maroons, slaves who practiced a trade and passed themselves off as free blacks.

Far from constituting an exclusively escapist phenomenon, then, marronage (or at least certain aspects of it) was essentially connected with the whole system. Also, as we have seen, the greater social and economic development of Saint Domingue, as compared with the rest of the Caribbean, had given rise to a huge free class of colored persons and slave descendants, who could offer convenient avenues for marronage and who, by procuring arms, gunpowder, poisons, or by providing shelter, also facilitated the means by which to sustain it. So although these maroons had escaped the conditions of slavery, they were nonetheless part, albeit a clandestine one, of colonial slave society, with which they necessarily maintained a minimum of reciprocal contact.

What, then, can be said of marronage, or the tradition of marronage, in relation to the revolution? The first real attempt at widespread organized revolt that aimed at destroying the white ruling class, and with it, slavery, was Makandal's conspiracy of 1757–58. Here, we have seen that the significance and political genius of this maroon leader lay not so much in the fact that he was the chief leader of an intrepid band of fugitives, as it does in the regular contact he and his followers maintained over a period of many years with the slaves on the plantations. He seemed, as de Vaissière insightfully observed, "to have sensed the possibility of forging out of marronage a center of organized black resistance against the masters." And, to the extent that marronage played a role in the 1791 revolt, the question, it would seem, is not whether Jean-François, Biassou, and Boukman were leaders of maroon bands (which they were not), but rather, as was equally the case with Makandal, the relationship of their activities, and those of other slaves who were involved in the plans, to the mass of plantation slaves in the North Plain.

It has been suggested by the present writer that the 1791 revolt was organized *both* from outside and from within the system; that is, by sustained clandestine activity (often short-term or *petit* marronage) coordinated with that of the core conspirators, who, in relatively advantageous positions on the plantations, had access to the outside society or who could even themselves become short-term maroons for the purposes of organizing. It should be remembered that the organizational meeting at Morne-Rouge which preceded the revolt involved representatives from over one hundred plantations throughout the North Plain. Many had traveled considerable distances to get there during the night and, to do so, would either have had to forge themselves a Sunday pass if they did not have one from the master, or would have had to take an unauthorized leave of a day or two to get themselves to and from Morne-Rouge to attend the meeting. Moreover, these meetings, according to the civil commissioner, Roume, had been going on every Sunday night for several weeks prior to the outbreak of the revolt. Jean-François and Boukman (it is now known) also had an acquired experience of marronage on the eve of the revolution.

In this light, one would be justified in interpreting the temporary absences of these *commandeurs* and domestics from their plantations as simply another case of *petit* marronage, of that type of marronage the colonists considered more a recurrent and endemic manpower problem than actual or total desertion. Certainly the masters knew nothing of the motives for these absences and, should the *commandeur* not get back to his post on the Monday morning, would likely assume their slave had run away for mundane reasons, or to visit family or friends. Were it not that the revolt actually broke out on the night of 22–23 August, the Morne-Rouge gathering probably would have been cited as simply another of those illicit groupings of slaves, in considerable numbers, that were noticed here and there by colonists during the two or three years preceding the revolt; or as the clandestine gathering of slaves from various Cul-de-Sac plantations in July. After these latter slaves were attacked, those who managed to escape remained in marronage. And then, what does one make of the Vaudreuil slaves who deserted in the North Plain parish just a few days before the outbreak of mass violence, and whom the manager clearly described as having gone maroon? So those aspects of marronage, so habitual and relatively innocuous up to now, may have figured somewhat more significantly in the impending rebellion than has generally been conceded. In any event, given the rapidity, the efficiency, and the extent of the revolt once it broke open, it could not have been planned haphazardly or with a small and loosely formed group of ringleaders, as the colonists themselves admitted.

And who were these leaders? We know that they came from the upper strata of the slave system and were notably *commandeurs*, coachmen, and domestics, in one case a cook, as well as a few mulatto slaves. In addition were a number of slaves who held the "semifree" status of *liberté de savanne*, as well as a few free blacks, and at least one free mulatto. Among the free blacks were some who had been sentenced *in absentia* after the Ogé uprising. Toussaint Louverture, we now know, was himself a free black. Once the signal for revolt was given, then, the events that followed all occurred, on the whole, according to plan, and the field laborers, under the directives of their *commandeurs*, rose massively and swiftly at the chance to strike down their masters and the objective realities of their oppression.

If, in regard to the August 1791 conspiracy, the social identity of the leadership has been fairly well established (the vast majority of the two hundred slave delegates to the Morne-Rouge assembly we know were *commandeurs*), the social and cultural components of the religious ceremony held in Bois-Caïman after the Morne-Rouge meeting are somewhat less clear. That it was an authentic Dahomean Vodu ceremony is highly unlikely. However, African religious elements characteristic of Saint Dominguean voodoo in a broader composite sense, especially petro rites, certainly predominate: the sacrificial pig, the drinking of its blood, the militaristic atmosphere and call to arms, the vow of secrecy, and the invocation of the gods. But it is in this last point, in the opposition of the god of the whites to that of the blacks, as well as the reference to the omniscient Good Lord or Creator beyond the clouds, that much confusion arises and a suggestively creole element appears. It has been suggested by this writer in Chapter 4 (and pursued in Appendix B) that, rather, the invocation of the "Good Lord beyond the clouds who sees all that the white man does" may well be a reference to the Supreme Being that is found in nearly all African animistic religions. But if Boukman, who participated in this ceremony as one of the prominent figures and delivered the controversial speech, was himself a coachman and creole,

then perhaps we need to know much more about the degree of Christian-
ization among creole or upper-strata slaves and their apparent or assumed
antipathy toward voodoo. Prior to the revolt, the princess Amethyst, a mulatto student at the Ordre de Notre Dame du Cap and a voodoo initiate,
was heard invoking the "Eh! eh! Mbumba" chant with her friends at night.
Cécile Fatiman, another mulatto, actually participated in the Bois-Caïman
ceremony, and she, as we know, was a mambo. So unless additional complementary sources are uncovered, any analytical explanation of this event
will remain, unfortunately, speculative.

As for marronage, a marked transformation had taken place once the revolt began. The term itself was rarely used by the colonists in reference
to slaves who had taken up arms and whom they now designated as insurgents, rebels, or brigands. Desertion was no longer called marronage for the
simple reason that the slave deserters—fugitives, in reality—had entered
the revolutionary scene on an equal and armed footing with the other actors,
and were actually in the forefront of events, if not, at times, dominating
them. Through offensive action and armed struggle, they had created situations, militarily and politically, to which the colonists were forced to respond
in their defense. In a sense, then, the tables had turned. These "rebels,"
"brigands," and "insurgents" were unlike the local armed bands of colonial
maroons only in the sense that they no longer formed a clandestine, self-
defensive movement to escape their enslavement, but, rather, were now an
active part of a process to destroy slavery that required political objectives
and strategy on their part. And Makandal notwithstanding, this was simply
not materially possible prior to 1789. What is more, they now had massive
popular support; marronage had in one sense become a movement of the
masses.

Yet legally, these insurgent blacks were still slaves, and the fact that
their leaders initially had to negotiate for a few hundred enfranchisements
and nominally agree for the rest to be sent back to the plantations was proof
that slavery was still slavery, and they were fugitive slaves. They had embarked on a collective revolutionary struggle never before waged in such a
way by colonial maroons, whose activities in the past were historically and
materially limited (not necessarily "backward-looking"), though their goal
was a common one—to be free. So we can see that marronage was, with the
opening of the black revolution, something qualitatively new and different
in scope; that is, an organized black guerilla army of men and women at
various points throughout the colony, armed to be free but who were, until
1793, legally still slaves. The old colonial notion of the maroons and of marronage was part of the past because the times had changed; the mentality
of the colonists had not. In the South, the popular movements could sometimes take the form of collective marronage, as in the Platons revolt that

culminated in the formation of a vast maroon community numbering ten to twelve thousand men, women, and children, who were there because they wanted to be free. They called the territory they occupied the Kingdom of Platons, built homes for themselves, and chose their own ruler. More than that, at one point they even claimed full territorial rights for the land they had conquered.

At this point we may raise some questions as to the pertinence, in relation to the Saint Domingue revolution, of such categories as "modern" and "restorationist." As argued above, the success of the 1791 Saint Domingue slave revolt as a revolutionary movement had much to do with the prevailing stage of historical development in the colony and in Europe, and with a combination of both African and creole elements, of the modern and the presumably restorationist. African elements—one thinks here of voodoo as both an ideological and a political vehicle for revolution—played equally as important a role in the success of the modern slave revolution of 1791 as did the creole leadership, later, of a Toussaint Louverture or a Christophe. Conversely, if we look at the Makandal conspiracy of the 1750s, the first real, but groping, attempt at revolution, it may superficially appear as a restorationist-type movement with its messianic style of leadership, the clandestine use of poison as opposed to open warfare, African "superstitions," and so on. Yet the avowed goal, if historically premature and expressed as a primitive consciousness, was nevertheless independence, certainly a modern notion. It also occurred at a time, in the 1750s, when the eighteenth-century "bourgeois-democratic wave of revolution" was not yet entirely manifest.

So if models are to have meaningful historical validity, they need to be systematically tested out, almost case by case, with evidential data. In the case of Saint Domingue, the categorization of "modern," if taken in an exclusive sense, would at the same time tend to camouflage the dynamic nature and revolutionary role of cultural diversity. In fact, there are elements that may appear to be "backward-looking," and therefore contradictory from the perspective of bourgeois-democratic ideology, but they are perfectly logical when seen from the perspective of the slaves' own origins; that is, from the African context in which the vast majority had been born and in which many must have spent the formative years of their youth or even a part of their adulthood. The Platons rebellion in the South may be but one case in point, for here was a massive community of fugitive slaves that, by one model, might be seen as *grand* marronage or, by another, as a restorationist movement. The evidence has shown that it was actually a constituent and integrated part of the developing revolutionary struggle toward general emancipation.

As for voodoo, we have seen its revolutionary potential in the August

1791 revolt in the North and some of the early struggles in the West, in the utilization of religion, or a god-figure, as a force behind a popular leader to galvanize support, justify the cause, and promote the belief in the inevitability of its success. In the South, curiously, there seems to be no evidence at all of voodoo as an organizational vehicle, either in the Port-Salut conspiracy or in the Platons rebellion. But the spiritual power of voodoo on the battlefield remained, throughout the colony and throughout the revolution (and probably still does, on a certain level, in Haiti today), a tremendous inner force, a force by which to make a mockery of death in the face of Leclerc's army or Rochambeau's firing squads, one that certainly contributed to and reinforced the determination of the blacks in their armed struggles for freedom.

In the area of leadership, a constant factor throughout the revolution was the particular and pivotal role of the *commandeur*. Generally, the slaves followed his decision, or authoritative directives, to rebel. Yet if he himself refused to rebel, then those slaves fomenting the subversive activity would often take him by force or kill him as an untrustworthy element, as in the case of the Fortin-Bellantien conspiracy in July 1791, or the Port-Salut conspiracy of January 1791. In another case, however, on the Laborde plantations in the South, we saw the slaves support the decision of André, one of the *commandeurs* on the third (highly creolized) estate, who refused to join the confederate army of mulattoes and free blacks and turn his workers to rebellion. But once the popular black movement had disassociated itself from the confederates, over one hundred of Laborde's slaves from the first and largest of his three estates were among the rebels at Platons. These were chiefly African-born. But if creolization was an important factor in deterring some slaves from rebelling, it could, as in the case of the *commandeur* Armand Bérault, have been an equally important factor in determining independent slave leadership.

The importance of the *commandeur*'s relationship, one of authority and control, to the workers in his charge continued after abolition (when the term was changed to *conducteur*) and could be witnessed, for example, in the increased severity of punishments under the work codes for the misdeeds of the *conducteurs*, as opposed to those dealt out to ordinary field laborers committing the same offense. Later during the war for independence, the *conducteurs* were automatically and unconditionally singled out as culprits whenever disturbances occurred on a plantation. In general, whether in resistance to Polverel's regime of freedom or to the presence of the French expeditionary army, there existed a good deal of complicity and mutual accord between the *conducteurs* and the workers. This was particularly evident in the Grande-Anse movements during the war for independence.

Earlier, it was argued that one factor distinguishing marronage from its colonial antecedents was the need, in this revolutionary context, for the slaves to develop political objectives and strategy. The slave leaders of the Platons movement in the South had originally demanded, as did Jean-François and Biassou in the North, the freedom of three to four hundred of their chief officers and secondary leaders. They did not, at any point in these early negotiations, demand the outright abolition of slavery, for this, as they knew as well as the colonists, was not something that could be negotiated. But by demanding three free days per week for every slave (also the motive of the 1791 Port-Salut conspirators), they may have been aiming at the eventuality of general emancipation. To claim that the masters should no longer have exclusive property rights over the slaves and that they, the slaves, would have a measure of control over their social existence, was something entirely unheard of within the context of a colonial society. Such a status—half-free, half-slave—would have created a fundamentally contradictory situation that the slaves would, in time, have had to resolve in one way or another. Though the demand was never granted, it did mark an initial stage in the developing struggles and consciousness of the slaves for their freedom. It also marked a beginning in their political education.

Negotiation with the colonial and metropolitan authorities thus served as tactical strategy, as in their demand for the emancipation of a limited number of their leaders and officers. This apparent retreat and acquiescence on the part of the slave leaders has, however, led some historians to the conclusion that general emancipation was therefore never their ultimate goal, and that this demand for only a restricted number of freedoms was inspired, rather, by self-centered motives and crude political opportunism. Whatever the particular case may be (and even Toussaint himself had reduced the number they demanded from four hundred to sixty in his efforts to negotiate with the civil authorities), the overall impact of these demands created a new set of circumstances in the midst of rapidly changing political conditions, and in some measure contributed to their culmination in general emancipation. In fact, prior to the abolition of slavery, the granting of freedom in small numbers had even become an accepted practice and was used by Governor Blanchelande in the West to effect the general disarmament of the slaves who had fought with Rigaud and Bauvais. Polverel, for his part, also used this method with the Platons rebels before finally proclaiming general emancipation in the South.

To this extent, the early stages of the slave struggles throughout the colony were similar. However, differing aspects of the black struggles in the three provinces lay in the area of alliances. The rebellions in the North were led and directed entirely by the black leaders who commanded a solidly black army from the outset. Under Jean-François and Biassou, they were closely allied with counterrevolutionary French elements and with the

Spanish, fighting for freedom but in the name of monarchy and royalism. For Toussaint, this unholy alliance was one of military and political convenience, and when he fully realized that general emancipation could never be achieved under the government of his Spanish protectors, he abandoned them, left Jean-François and Biassou behind, and fought under the banner of the French republic.

In the other two provinces, the situation was initially dominated by the armed revolts of the mulattoes and free blacks for political equality, and it was from these struggles, in which the black slaves participated with motives of their own, that the autonomous black movement emerged and strove continually to realize its aspirations within the overall context of mulatto authority in the West, and virtual hegemony in the South. Theirs was thus an association of convenience and contradiction with the mulattoes. Because of the predominant authority of the mulattoes in the West, the independent black maroon leaders like Alaou and Dieudonné found it difficult to fully embrace the republican option Toussaint had chosen, since, in their case, they would be subject to the higher authority of Bauvais and Rigaud who, they felt, opposed the extension of liberty and equality to the blacks. It is perhaps not so surprising, then, that both Hyacinthe and Dieudonné were suspected of looking to the British for arms, while Alaou accepted military aid from the Spanish, as well as the French, remained highly ambivalent toward both, and, on the whole, deeply distrusted the mulatto generals.

In the South, as in the West, the slaves were originally allied with the mulattoes and free blacks in the confederate army. In some cases, the slaves may have been swept into the revolt by promises of freedom, three free days per week, or other such allurements. The Port-Salut affair of 1791 indicated, however, that their alliance with the mulattoes later that year was engaged in their own interest, and the Platons revolt of 1792–93 confirmed it. Here, they could rightly say (in words similar to those of Bauvais regarding his original alliance with the royalists): We were never really the dupes of the mulattoes, but we had to conquer our rights and needed aid. These gentlemen offered us guns and freedom, and we used their guns to win our freedom, while they believed they were using us.

The problems of maintaining an autonomous position in the face of mulatto rule after emancipation and the deportation of the civil commissioners, however, proved infinitely more difficult. Also, during the period of British occupation (1793–98), the blacks in the South were further isolated from the course of events in the rest of the colony. Whereas in the North the blacks under Toussaint had rapidly mobilized themselves to defeat Villate and his followers in their bid for mulatto control, in the South, believing their freedom was jeopardized, the blacks had come forward to support Rigaud (and consequently mulatto rule) against the intrusions and usurpations of Sonthonax's delegation.

Other sources of disparity were evidenced in the relationship of the popular masses to revolutionary leadership. During the first struggles of the slaves in all parts of the colony, the popular leaders thoroughly embodied the aspirations of their followers, as the slaves and their leaders were united around the single objective of freedom. It was during the periods of negotiation with the adversary, as occurs almost inevitably in the course of revolutionary struggles, that conflicts arose in the relations between rank-and-file and popular leaders; the masses followed their leaders so long as they continued to represent commonly shared goals. And when the slaves saw that their leaders began to diverge from those goals, they reacted violently. Such was the case in the North, when Jean-François and Biassou entered into negotiations with the civil commissioners, and in the South, at Macaya, when Armand, Martial, and Gilles Bénech accepted Polverel's offer of freedom (transmitted by Rigaud) provided they join the legion, police the countryside, and send their comrades back to their plantations; and slavery in the South had still not as yet been abolished, at that. Once it was, the black workers continued to resist, but on their own, in a generalized, inarticulate movement of protest and discontent over the constraints perpetuated by the new labor system that replaced slavery.

Only Toussaint was able to maintain the undivided confidence and support of the black masses in the North, even after he had become commander-in-chief of the Saint Domingue army. But when he began to invite the émigré colonists back to the colony and farmed out the sequestered plantations among the black generals, insisting upon the preservation of large estates, it was to Moïse that the blacks turned for leadership and a guarantee that the future provide them with the means to realize their individual aspirations. Having eroded their confidence, Toussaint also opened the way for his own downfall.

Finally, the war for independence, in itself a product of developing political conflicts and the changing nature of the Saint Domingue revolution, once again reopened the question of leadership. These developing conflicts, however, had little, if anything, to do with popular aspirations; the outcome of these events did. Until the arrival of General Hédouville, there had been no hostility between Toussaint and Rigaud. But through a careful use of deceit and political manipulation, Hédouville played one off against the other and managed to drive a wedge between the two to the point where their aims and interests finally became irreconcilable. When the French agent left, the damage had been done, and civil war became unavoidable. Toussaint's victory over Rigaud, also encouraged and sustained by his secret commercial arrangements with Britain and the United States, thus placed the black general in a position of supreme command that was then reinforced by his occupation of Spanish Saint Domingue and by his constitution. While Toussaint aimed to arrive at a new entente, based on a more independent relationship with France, the French Revolution was moving continually to the right. For Bonaparte, it was now a question of setting the stage for the restoration of slavery. The arrival of his armed expedition, followed by Toussaint's deportation, the news that slavery had been restored in Guadeloupe, and the beginning of a general disarmament of the black troops had made it unequivocally clear to the masses that the French had come to take away their freedom.

Independence thus became a political imperative, and it was the former slaves who provided the very foundation of that goal and the driving force that led to its achievement. As we have seen, there was no single or exceptional leader to direct and coordinate opposition to the French army during the early stages of that struggle. Rather, individuals serving in various capacities, both civil and military, had taken the initiative of organizing themselves clandestinely, in the face of overwhelming odds, to build a network of resistance. As the war progressed, so, too, did the regimen of repression, and with it the popular forces of opposition. Here, the merging of new or already-existing maroon leaders with subversive elements in the army under French command, along with armed defectors, even entire regiments, as well as civilian insurgents, all contributed to the creation of a full-scale popular military effort against the French expedition. What is most significant, however, is that all this took place in the South independently of, in spite of, and in opposition to, the black jacobin leadership, notwithstanding the difficult situation in which the black generals found themselves. The masses did not follow their leadership into submission or accommodation with the French occupying forces, but, in their own ways, organized and prepared their resistance because they knew the alternative was a return to slavery. Absurdly, they would now have to be fighting each other in order to fight the French.

And so, if any lessons are to be learned of the Saint Domingue revolution, they are not, ultimately, in the bravery and courage of the masses, for heroics and sentiment have little place in the material foundations of history. In the end, all peoples fighting for their freedom do so with unparalleled fortitude. Rather, it is the political impact that the self-mobilization and the independently organized resistance of these masses had upon the direction and outcome of the revolution that matters. It was, as we have seen in Chapter 9, the self-sustained activities of diverse segments of the population, of largely unknown and obscure individuals, as well as the popular leaders who had played a role in the earlier struggles, that made the defection of Dessalines,

Christophe, Clervaux, and the other colored generals both practicable and militarily meaningful.

Finally, permanent freedom from slavery had been won through independence. But the masses had not yet won the freedom to till their own soil. And this, perhaps more than anything else, sums up what the peasant masses expected out of freedom. A personal claim to the land upon which one labored and from which to derive and express one's individuality was, for the black laborers, a necessary and an essential element in their vision of freedom. For without this concrete economic and social reality, freedom for the ex-slaves was little more than a legal abstraction. To continue to be forced into laboring for others, bound by property relations that afforded few benefits and no real alternatives for themselves, meant that they were not entirely free.

The importance of an independent claim to the land was, for example, seen in the aspirations of the Platons rebels. Though their settlement was short-lived and part of a developing revolutionary process, these maroons had nevertheless demanded, at one point in their negotiations, full territorial rights to the region. When troops came to attack them, they told the soldiers the land belonged to them, not to the whites. Then, during the transitional period from the abolition of slavery to the implantation of the new labor regime, some ex-slaves, we have seen, freely engaged themselves in what appeared to be an anarchistic appropriation of plantation property for personal use. Underlying these activities, however, is a discernable aspiration toward economic (and cultural) self-determination that had little, if anything, to do with the dominant political economy.

Significantly, this individual attachment to the land and expression of opposition to the new system through diverse acts of resistance never substantially coalesced in the South, as it did in the North under Moïse, into an organized, collective movement with prominent and vigorous leaders, petitions, assemblies, political objectives, and a call to arms. It was, rather, a leaderless phenomenon, a generalized and inarticulate, but deep-rooted and persistent movement of protest against an externally imposed labor regime that clearly went against the grain of their own aspirations. Though the concrete political and economic impact of these undercurrents toward agricultural self-sufficiency was hardly felt during the course of the revolution, their persistence and survival long outdated the revolution itself. This mode of reaction to the new system of freedom suggests perhaps an early manifestation of the pattern of agricultural development, with corresponding peasant life styles and social relations, that eventually characterized Haiti's rural economy. As opposed to most other Latin American and Caribbean countries, a great number of Haiti's ex-slaves did accede to small peasant propietorship and defined their lives accordingly.

By seeing the embodiment of the Saint Domingue revolution in the figure of Toussaint Louverture, we may interpret that revolution as part of the modern age, and rightly so. But by doing so, we also risk reducing to a level of impertinence those vital social, economic, and cultural realities of the ex-slaves whose independent relationship to the land, African in outlook, formed the foundation of their own vision of freedom, while it flew in the face of the needs of the modern state that Toussaint was trying to build. It has been argued, in a somewhat reductionist vein, that after the revolution "Haiti thus slipped into a system of peasant proprietorship—wonderful euphemisms for the poverty and wretchedness of bourgeois-egalitarian swindles—and the dream of a modern black state drowned in the tragic hunger of an ex-slave population for a piece of land and a chance to live in old ways or ways perceived as old."[3] But then one must pose the question: Would the ex-slaves have been any better off under the plantation labor regime of Toussaint, a regime they hated almost as much as slavery? In the end, their agricultural egalitarianism had more to do with their own African origins and the desire to define their lives through their relationship to the land than to French bourgeois-revolutionary notions of liberty and equality. And to categorically place the blame for Haiti's poverty and post-independence isolation on small peasant proprietorship, or the "counterrevolution of peasant property," is to grossly oversimplify the insurmountable odds Haiti faced as an independent black nation in a world that was still generally hostile to slave emancipation. But if, in this vein, the goals of the peasant masses of the Haitian revolution are seen by historians as one of those unfortunate "lost causes" of history, still, one must remember that landholding in peasant societies, far beyond purely economic considerations, fundamentally embraces family and kinship ties and responsibilities, defines one's social identity, provides a sense of personal dignity, and, for the Haitian peasant, unequivocally marked the break from slavery.

A case may thus be proposed for the ideological origins of Haiti's peasantry in the postslavery period or perhaps even, pushing further back, in the period of slavery with the kitchen gardens and limited marketing experience of some slaves. However, the study of its characteristic development and proliferation socially and culturally, as well as the economic impact of that proliferation, properly belongs to Haiti's postrevolutionary history. And this, unfortunately, but for obvious reasons, lies far beyond the scope of the present study.

APPENDIX A

Interrogation of the Negress Assam

Extract of the minutes from the registry of the Tribunal of le Cap

27 September 1757

ASKED to state her name, age, status and residence.

She said her name is Assam, Negress slave of Sieur Vallet, planter at la Souffrière; does not know her age and is of the Poulard nation.

She said that her master, having lost many slaves whose bodies had become swollen[2] ([this] having ceased for about a year) and that a slave named François and a small Negress named Victoire were smitten with the same illness, which caused her master much chagrin, she, the interrogated, said to him that if he wanted to give her a pass, she would go get some remedies from a slave of Sieur Lamanay whose name she does not know, but who is still alive, and whom her master knows, because he had been brought to him a year ago by a free black, Diola, of la Souffrière, who said that this slave could tell him what it was that was making his slaves die. Her master gave her a pass for one day to go and find that slave, and while leaving her master's plantation, she met at the gate the free black Pompée, a farmer of Sieur Deseuttres [des Gentres?] and who is her friend, because his wife had named one of [Assam's] children. He said to her, "Hello my friend, where are you going like that?" She said that she was going to the Lamanaie [*sic*] plantation to find a slave who would give her some remedies to cure her master's slaves. Pompée told her that that slave had died, that it was no longer necessary for her to go to the Lamanay plantation, but that he knew of a slave named Jean on the Laplaine plantation at Limbé who was a good doctor and who would give her the drugs she needed. She replied that she did not know the way. Pompée told her he was going to show her the way, and they went together . . . , and Pompée led her as near as the guava trees in the savanna of the Laplaine plantation, and then he told her to address herself on his behalf to the guard at the gate, and to ask him to show her the quarters of the slave, Jean. She found an old slave at the gate whose name she does not know, but who is of the Bambara nation, who limps and who has big cuts on his face, and whom she saw yesterday in prison. She addressed herself to him on Pompée's behalf and asked him to show her

:an's quarters, but she did not tell him why. The slave led her into the savanna and showed her Jean's quarters from afar and then went back. She found the slave, Jean, at the door of his quarters, entered with Jean, and found three Negresses from le Cap who are merchants and who sell poultry and salted meat. She knows the three Negresses by sight, but does not know their names.

FINALLY Assam was reprimanded and told that she [could] undoubtedly name them, since she stayed with them for a few days.

She said that one was called Marie-Jeanne and the other Madeleine, that the Negress Marie-Jeanne was of the Niamba nation and the Negress Madeleine of the Nago nation; that they belong to le Cap merchants whose names she does not know. When she entered, the slave, Jean, said to her, "There is someone who sent you here"; she said to him, "You must be a sorcerer to know that I was sent here." He replied that he knew for a long time that she would be coming. She asked him how he could know that, and he told her that two or three days ago he had seen Pompée, who told him that there were two sick slaves on her plantation, and that when he would see her, he would tell her to address herself to him. She told him that it was true that Pompée had addressed himself to her to help her find some reme-dies for her master's slaves. Jean said to her that he would give her some, provided she stay four or five days in his quarters, so that he could go and find the herbs that he needed.[3] She said to him that she would stay four days since that was what he wanted, provided that he give her good remedies, which he promised. During this time, the two Negresses, Marie-Jeanne and Madeleine, remained in Jean's quarters . . . , but the Negress who she be-lieved belonged to Sieur Arnaud left the same day and she did not know that the Negress was carrying out drugs; but the Negress, Madeleine, told her that a slave of the Laplaine plantation named Coffi, who is always running away,[4] had given her some herbs to give to two of her master's slaves, a man and a woman, who were sick. But she learned since then that these two slaves died after taking this drug; [she said] that the slave, Jean, at whose quarters she arrived on Friday, went to find some herbs on Sunday,[5] and he brought the herbs into his quarters; that they were blue verbena, wild raspberry, and *pois puants* with their roots, which he piled into a wooden container in front of Assam, the interrogated; that he mixed an egg yolk into them along with boiler scrapings, and made it all into a ball as fat as his finger was black, and that he gave it to her telling her to administer it to her master's slaves. In fact, she said that this ball was about as fat as half a wrist and that he told her to administer a po[r]tion—as big as the tip of a finger—to the sick slaves . . . and that that would cure them. On the Monday morning, she left with this drug and returned to her master's plantation after dinner-time. As soon as she arrived, she gave the drug to the sick slaves, [and] it caused the slaves to have a heavy stomach and made the little Negress constipated and made her swell up; that five or six days later, while going to the butcher shop of a mulatto named Aisson, she met Pompée who carried her meat. He asked her how it went. She told him that it was not going very well; that since she had given Jean's drug to the two sick slaves, it was getting worse. Pompée told her to continue, which is what she did and, having given the little Negress, Victoire, an enema that night, and wanting to put her on the chamber pot, she became stiff, and having put her back on her [bed], she began frothing at the nose, and she suddenly died. She did not give any at all to the other slave because, at any moment, he was going to stool, having a continual heavy stomach; [she said] that he became less swollen and dehydrated, and thus he died two or three days after the little Negress. Her master did not know that she had given drugs to the slaves, because the slave, Jean, had forbidden her to say anything about it to anyone. But suspecting that she had given them something, he said he wanted to know what it was, and had her arrested; when she saw that she was going to be arrested, she threw what Jean had given her, which was wrapped up in a sack, on the other side of the fence into the coffee grove. Her master said to her that she had something in her pocket, and she said that she had thrown it away and she would show him the next day; that they looked everywhere, but did not find it, because it was dark; and the next morning, all the slaves and she, as well, looked for it and found a sack which was lodged in a coffee tree; and under the coffee tree they found the big packet dangling from its string; and against a lemon tree they found the rest of the drug which Jean had given her; and on the other side of the fence [another packet] which Jean had also given her. Her master asked her to tell the whole truth, and she told him the above-mentioned.

She said that one day while walking with Pompée to his place, he told her that all the whites of la Souffrière were scoundrels, that they inflicted cruelties on their slaves without any legal authority when they suspected them of poisoning their slaves, and that one day her master would do as much to her; that it was necessary for her to find justice. She said that she did not know justice; that on another day, about a year ago, when she went to see Pompée during the [absence] of his wife, who went to visit her mother who lives in le Cap, Pompée told her that she was a fool, that she had nursed three of her master's children and that he should grant her freedom. She told him that she got along well with her master; and Pompée told her there were black doctors who gave drugs to stupefy the minds of whites to make them grant liberty; that all the free blacks—men and women—used [this drug] to procure their liberty.[6] She told him she did not want to use those drugs.

She said that it is the free blacks who spoil the slaves and give them bad advice against the whites.

ASKED about what happened after she was arrested.

She said that two or three days later, Sieur Deseuttres had come to her plantation. Her master had her taken to his plantation and, upon arriving, she found the said Sieur Deseuttres and told him that it was Pompée who was the cause of her misfortune. . . . The next day he came to her master's plantation with Sieur Dufau, and they wrote down all that she told them. And there they read to her the declaration which is submitted in [this] trial, and she said that the declaration was authentic and that it was the same she had given to her master.

ASKED how she knew that the two slaves to whom the Negress Madeleine, Nago, had given the drug that Coffi gave her were dead.

She said that when she was arrested by her master after the death of his two slaves, her master, wanting to know if it was true that she had been to the quarters on the Laplaine plantation to obtain the drugs she had given to the slaves, sent her to the [said] plantation, accompanied by a slave named Perrot; that while passing in front of the church on the way, she met the said Negress Madeleine, Nago, who was at the market selling salted meat; that Madeleine asked her how the drug that Jean had given her was working; and she told her that it went badly and that the two slaves were dead. Madeleine, Nago, told her that the drug which Coffi had given her had caused her master's slaves to die; [she said] that she continued along her way to the quarters on the Laplaine plantation with Perrot; that they went to Jean's quarters; and that she did not tell him at first that the two slaves had died; that she asked him for other remedies; and that he gave her a small calabash and a big calabash, which are the same as those used in making syrup; that he told her to put them in hot ashes, then to extract the juice and have [them] drink it; and that she then returned with the slave Perrot; and that she did not tell the slave, Jean, that the two slaves were dead, because her master had forbidden her so as not to scare the slave Jean.

ASKED why she did not tell her master when she got back the first time from Jean's quarters that she was bringing some remedies.

She said that the slave, Jean, had forbidden her by telling her that the whites must not have knowledge of those drugs.

POINTED OUT to her that she should have thought that these were bad drugs that the slave, Jean, had given her, since he did not want them to be discovered, and that she should not have administered them without her master's knowledge.

She said that when she left Jean's quarters she felt dizzy and did not know what she was doing, and that he had assured her that they were good drugs, which made her decide to administer them.

POINTED OUT to her that she knew the bad effects of the drugs after having tested them the first time.

She said that it was Pompée's advice that convinced her to continue their usage, all the more so since the slave François—who was badly swollen before having taken them—became less swollen all of a sudden . . . ; that he could scarcely walk before, and that he began to walk afterwards.

ASKED why she told Pompée that the slaves were getting worse, since she had just said that the slave François was getting better.

She said that she told Pompée that as far as she could see, François was getting better, but that the Negress was getting worse; and that Pompée told her to continue.

ASKED why she kept continuing to give it to the little Negress since she saw that it was making her more ill.

She said that, as the little Negress was vomiting worms, she thought, finally, that it would help her.

ASKED why, when she was arrested, she threw away the packet of drugs.

She said that Jean had told her to throw the packet away when her master would have her arrested.

ASKED why the slave, Jean, had told her that her master would have her arrested.

She said that the slave, Jean, told her that her master would have her arrested.

ASKED why the slave, Jean, had told her that her master would have her arrested, since he assured her that he only gave good remedies.

She said that the slave, Jean, told her that, supposing her master had her arrested, to throw the packet away.

POINTED OUT to her that since this slave suspected or had her understand that she could be arrested, that she should have thought that he was not giving her good drugs.

She said that this slave swore and affirmed that he was giving her good drugs, and that if they did not produce a good effect, it would only be then that she could be arrested.

POINTED OUT to her that her answer is contradictory; that it is not possible that this slave could attest with such assurance to the benignancy of this drug, and at the same time forbid her to speak of it to her master.

She said that Jean had forbidden her, because he said that it was not advisable that her master have knowledge of it.

ASKED if she did not see any other slaves in Jean's quarters while she stayed there; and who were the slaves in front of whom he prepared the drugs.

She said she only saw one slave in Jean's quarters on the Laplaine plantation, whose name she does not know and who is a big, stout caretaker, whose legs pain him and who walks with a stick, and in front of whom the slave Jean prepared his drugs; and that he put all his drugs in a small box which was at the bottom of his cabin.

WAS PRESENTED to her the sack containing the four packets placed in the clerk's office, and she was asked to identify them.

She said she recognized the small sack made of fine cloth as being the same in which the three packets that Jean had given her were placed; that the largest packet, which was about five inches long and tied at both ends with the same string to which it is attached, was entirely composed in the quarters of the slave, Jean, who had around a dozen of these all made up the same way and who gave her this packet to recognize the herbs; that it spins around when one comes upon the herbs, and that the slave, Jean, showed her how this occurs, but she herself did not try it; that the second packet, which is the size of an almond, had to be placed in the same sack with the big packet; that when she would go to look for the herbs, they would indicate to her whether or not the herbs were the right ones to pick;[7] that the slave, Jean, carries these with him every time he goes to pick herbs; that, as to the third packet containing a brown powder, it is the remainder of the drug which he had given her to give to the two slaves, and which he composed in front of her with an herb that he calls sage, and which is milky and has white flowers; *pois puants*; verbena; and wheat herb; that the fourth packet which is fully as big as a finger, was made by her, under orders from her master when she was arrested; and that she told him she knew the composition of the drug which she had given to the slaves.

She said that the black powder that Jean gave her, as well as that which she made, is composed solely of the milky herb that she calls sage, mixed with an egg yolk and boiler scrapings; but that to use it, one mixes it with *pois puants,* blue verbena, and wheat herb—all boiled together. Into this concoction, one mixes the black powder, and it is taken either as a drink or an enema.

TWO HOUR RECESS

ASKED what the slave Jean told her when he caused her shoulder to bleed.

She said that he said it was for her well-being, and that she was not hurt.

ASKED if he drew a lot of blood, and what instrument he used.

She said that he used a piece of a glass bottle, that he drew a few drops of blood, and that he then rubbed her shoulder with a black powder like gunpowder, which made her bleed a little more; that he scratched the powder with his knife and placed the blood into a small piece of ram's horn the length of a finger; that he closed the end with a stopper . . . and put it in his pocket. [8]

ASKED if, upon Pompée's solicitation, or for any other reason, she did not give the drugs to her master's slaves to poison them.

She said no; that she only knew Pompée for one year and that she does not know in the least if the first slaves died by poison or not; and that she only gave drugs to the slave, François, and the small Negress, Victoire.

ASKED if she did not follow the advice of Pompée, if she did not give drugs to her master in order to induce him to grant her freedom.

She said that she never gave any drugs to her master, that it is true that a year ago Pompée told her that when the whites lived too long, the slaves who were waiting for their freedom gave them drugs to make them die sooner; that since she had nursed three of her master's children, she had to make him take some drugs, because surely he would grant her freedom; that the whites only granted it when they were ready to die; that Pompée, seeing that she did not want to consent to what he proposed, said to her: "Well! So much the worse for you since you do not want to become free"; that some time later, Pompée, seeing that she still felt the same way, told her that she must propose to her master that he sell her, and that he would lend her the money to buy her freedom; but that she did not want to consent to this proposition, because she got along well with her master.

ASKED if Pompée did not advise her to poison her master's slaves to force him to abandon his plantation at la Souffrière and to sell her.

She said no.

ASKED why she continued to see Pompée, since he gave her the bad advice of poisoning her master.

She said that for one year she no longer went to Pompée's quarters and that, having established himself at another place near Sieur Lamanay, she met Pompée at the gate when she was going to look for some remedies, and that Pompée mentioned the slave, Jean.

ASKED why she did not warn her master of the bad advice that Pompée had given her, and did not warn him that he should distrust that black.

She said that she considered what Pompée had told her to be like the ramblings of a drunk man and that, of all he told her, she did not take any of it into account.

Manuscript Prison Record
Le Cap Prison
Extract of the minutes from the registry of the Tribunal of le Cap[9]

9 November 1757

We, Sébastien Jacques Courtin, Counsellor of the King, seneschal, civil and criminal judge of the Tribunal of le Cap, accompanied by the crown prosecutor, seconded by the court clerk . . . , arrived at the prison of this city to effect an inspection and report on the state of said prison. . . . The first *cachot* being opened for us, we found it approximately six feet wide along the entire length of the room, which is roughly twenty feet long, having no other opening than a grating above the door of around three feet large, one foot deep and two feet high. And in the said *cachot* we found one *Jean-Venus*, accused of having made an attempt on the life of Sieur Desjoncheur [de Juchereau?] during the night; one *Pompée*, a free black accused of having induced the Negress of Sieur Vallet, called *Assam*, to poison her master and the slaves of the plantation and for having identified for her a slave who would provide her with the poison; one *Laurent*, slave of M. Dubuisson, accused of poison; one *Jolycoeur*, a free black of Sieur Brossard, accused of having made an attempt on the life of his [former?] master; one *Gar*, slave of Sieur La Robinière, accused of poison; one *Francillon*, called Pajon, a free black accused of distributing poison; one *René*, slave of M. de Gallifet; one *Horou* [Haurou], slave of Sieur de la Coursière, both accused of distributing poison; one *Armand*, a free black sentenced by decree of the counsel to the galleys for horse thievery; and one *Roux*, sentenced to the same punishment for counterfeiting, both of whom were ready to leave and be put aboard to serve their sentences; and, as well, three English prisoners of war.

The first gate being opened for us, we came upon the gallery which faces the yard, to the west, and upon crossing the yard we found on the left-hand side a room of around twenty feet square and which serves to lodge and sleep seventy slaves, as many arrested for marronage as for other various crimes. . . . Beside this room is an old shed, roughly ten feet wide by twenty feet long, made into the criminal chamber, and which opens onto rue Dermattre, the lock of which seemed to us very weak. And at the end of the gallery was a small cabinet made from boards, in which we found one *D'Armand,* a free Negress accused of having wanted to poison her son in prison; one *Rozette,* called Lizette,[10] accused of having poisoned the son of her mistress; one *Marie-Jeanne,*[11] a free Negress of Sieur and Dame Chiron, accused of having had her master poisoned by the slave, *Nanon;* and the said *Nanon,* accused of having administered poison to her master, the late Sieur Chiron; the slave *Assam,* accused of having poisoned the slaves of her master, Sieur Vallet, and of having twice administered poison to him. And having reminded Sieur Macé that it was absolutely necessary to separate all the Negresses accused of the same crime and especially the Negresses Marie-Jeanne and Nanon, accomplices to the same crime, he told us that these two Negresses were brought in very late . . . , and not knowing of what they were accused, he had placed them together; that he had made remonstrance over this with the crown prosecutor and that he did not know how he could separate the two, since there was no other room where he could place them, having already placed in the two military *cachots* on the coast one Coffy,[12] slave of Sieur Laplaine, and one *Jean,* or Paul, slave of the same master,[13] both accused of distributing poison.

[In another room] we found *Jacques Joseph Francillon* and *Louis Francillon,* his brother, both free blacks accused of composing poisons; the slaves *Hyppolite, Cupidon, Darius, Titus* and *Thélémaque,* all black slaves of Sieur Cousard and accused of animal thievery; *Léveillé,* slave of Sieur Laplaine; *Ja[ss]emin,* slave of Sieur Leroux; and *Tony,* slave of Sieur [Cannay?], all accused of poison; and *Jacques,* slave of Sieur Gaillard, judged at counsel and destined to become an executioner at Port-de-Paix;[14] *Joseph,* slave of Sieur Ribaud de Lisle, accused of having poisoned several slaves of his *atelier;* and *Léveillé,* slave of Sieur Dumas, accused of homicides; *Jean-François,* creole slave from Martinique, giving himself out as a free black and arrested by order of the Governor.

We found, as well, in a small cabinet made out of the north gallery, eight Negress slaves, as many arrested for marronage as for other crimes, one of whom was with her child.

Signed: Macé
    Dumesnil
    Courtin
    Bordier, court clerk

APPENDIX B

Bois-Caïman and the August Revolt[1]

The following is an extract of an address of the Colonial Assembly of Saint Domingue, dated 3 November 1791, signed by its commissioners, to the National Assembly in France:

> The General Assembly of Saint Domingue, after having established itself at Léogane, had designated the city of le Cap to hold its sessions. The deputies made their way there to fulfill their mission.
>
> Some of them arrived on the sixteenth in the district of Limbé, six leagues from le Cap. There they witnessed a fire that broke out in the *case à bagasse* on the Chabaud plantation.[2] The arsonist was a *commandeur* from the Desgrieux plantation. The slave, armed with a saber, fled. M. Chabaud opened pursuit and reached him. A combat ensued between them, and the slave was wounded. He was captured and put in irons.
>
> Interrogated . . . , he stated that all the *commandeurs*, coachmen, domestics, and other slaves of the neighboring plantations in whom was placed the utmost confidence, have formed a conspiracy to set fire to the plantations and to slaughter all the whites. He designated as leaders certain slaves from his master's plantation [Desgrieux], four from the Flaville plantation located in Acul, three leagues from le Cap, and the slave, Paul, *commandeur* of the Blin plantation at Limbé.
>
> Some members of the municipal government of Limbé went to M. Chaubaud's place. The same questions were put to the slave who set the fire, and the same answers were given. The municipal officials drew up a written statement, sent it to the Provincial Assembly of the North, warned the planters of the district, and gave the manager of the Flaville plantation the names of the slave conspirators who were at his place, suggesting that he apprehend them and send them to le Cap prison.
>
> The manager, a sensitive and mild-mannered person, more confident than suspicious, assembled the slaves under his authority, conveyed to them the information received from the municipality, told them that he could not believe such an atrocious conspiracy to be possible, and offered them his own head if they so desired it. All the slaves replied that the statement made by the Desgrieux *commandeur* was false and swore an inviolable loyalty to him. He had the weakness, [however], of believing them. This excess of confidence has ruined us.
>
> The municipal government of Limbé requested that M. Planteau, manager of the Blin plantation, present his slave *commandeur* for questioning. Under

interrogation, [Paul] replied that the accusation brought against him was false and slanderous, that, filled with gratitude for the goodness of his master, who extended him renewed acts of kindness every day, one would never see him involved in plots hatched against the existence of whites and their property.

Under cover of this perfidious declaration and upon the assurance M. Planteau gave that this slave merited confidence, he was released.

Things remained in this state until the twenty-first, when the public authorities of Limbé, upon the request of the municipality, went to the Desgrieux plantation to arrest the cook, who was denounced as one of the principal leaders.

The slave fled, went off to find Paul from the Blin plantation, and, in agreement with the other conspirators, they prepared the iron and the torch destined for the execution of their horrible projects. [3]

In his *Rapport sur les troubles de Saint-Domingue*, Garran-Coulon quotes the declaration made before the municipality of Limbé by François, a slave from the Chapotin plantation, who was among those setting fire to part of the Chabaud plantation, and who was arrested on the night of the twentieth. In his declaration, François states:

On Sunday, 14 August, on the Lenormand [de Mézy] plantation at Morne-Rouge, a large assembly of slaves was held, comprised of two delegates from all of the plantations of Port-Margot, Limbé, Acul, Petite-Anse, Limonade, Plaine du Nord, Quartier-Morin, Morne-Rouge, etc., etc. The purpose of this assembly was to fix the date for the insurrection that had been planned for a long time. They nearly agreed that the conspiracy should take place that very night; but the slaves went back on this decision, because, upon reflecting, they reasoned that a project conceived in one evening would be difficult to execute that very night.

Garran-Coulon states, as well, that in the declaration

François adds that public papers were read to the assembled slaves by a mulatto or quarteroon who was unknown to him and who announced that the King and the National Assembly had accorded them three days of freedom per week; that the white planters were opposed to this and that they must await the arrival of troops who would come to enforce the execution of this decree; that this was the opinion of the majority, but that the slaves from some of the plantations in Acul and Limbé wanted, at any cost, to begin the war against the whites before the arrival of the troops. [4]

Garran-Coulon also refers to memoirs written by colonists at this time which indicate that the number of slave delegates to the assembly was two hundred, all of them *commandeurs*. [5]

It seems clear that this incident constituted the beginning of the insurrection, planned for the following week. Moreover, the slave, François, mentions in his declaration cited by Garran-Coulon, that some of the slaves from Limbé and Acul wanted to begin the war immediately. Fire was set to the Chabaud plantation two nights later. The French historian Gabriel Debien

raises some doubt, however, as to whether the Bois Caïman conspiracy organized on the night of 14–15 August was in fact that which was denounced
by the slaves captured in the Chabaud incident. He erroneously situates the
Chabaud affair on the night of the eleventh (as does Garran-Coulon who,
in this particular case, does not document the date with any reference to a
primary source) and confuses the sequence of events:

> The affair on the Chabaud plantation revealed a conspiracy. To be sure! But
> there had been talk here and there of a conspiracy since 1789. This time again,
> no one believed in the danger.
>
> However, during the night of 14–15 August on the Le Normand plantation
> at Morne-Rouge, the *commandeurs* of the plantations formed an assembly. Who
> were they? How many were they? Was this assembly one of those denounced by
> the Chabaud slaves, or was it organized as a reprisal against the descent of the
> Cap *maréchaussée* on the Chabaud estate? One does not know what to answer.
> There is no evidence permitting one to believe that it was a very big conspiracy. [6]

All of these are legitimate questions *if* one accepts 11 August as the date
of the Chabaud incident. However, at least three archival sources refer to
the occurrence of this incident during the week prior to the outbreak of the
insurrection of 22–23 August. One document begins by stating that

> It was in Limbé, on the Chabaud plantation, that the first signal for the incendi-
> ary revolt was given on the night of 17–18 August. A slave *commandeur* from the
> Desgrieux plantation, a mulatto slave of M. Chapotin, and one other had set fire
> to the *case à bagasse*, which was soon reduced to ashes. But the *commandeur* of
> the Desgrieux plantation was immediately arrested, and his declarations warned
> numerous planters of the district of horrible plots ready to be executed, saving
> them from betrayal and death. [7]

A letter written from le Cap and dated 27 September 1791 also refers to
a prelude to the insurrection during the one week prior to the 22–23 August
outbreak:

> It was on 23 August, at midnight, that the carnage began. We had already un-
> mistakably seen the prelude of this bloody scene eight days earlier with the
> burning of a sugar plantation at Port-Margot; we had even learned, through the
> statements made by the guilty ones, that a massive attack was being prepared. [8]

Probably, the fire to which the author refers at Port-Margot was in fact the one
which broke out at the Chabaud plantation, given the proximity of Limbé to
Port-Margot and the date—eight days prior to the night of the twenty-third,
or 15 August.

The report of the civil commissioner, Roume, also refers to this incident
and places its occurrence on the night of 16–17 August on the Chabaud
plantation in Limbé. When the arsonists were brought before the municipal
government, they confessed to a conspiracy that was to be executed on the

night of 24–25 August. Roume also states that for several weeks, slave delegations had assembled on Sundays to work out together the plans for this destructive project. [9]

In addition to these documents, numerous accounts published after the revolution corroborate the date, as well as the identity, of the participants.[10] Pamphile Lacroix states that a fire broke out at the Chabaud plantation in mid-August; around that time, the slaves of the Lagoscette plantation in a neighboring district attempted to kill the manager.[11] Léon Deschamps states that the incident occurred on the sixteenth, and named Paul Blin, as well as the Desgrieux cook, as the leaders denounced by the slave captured on the Chabaud plantation. Pauléus Sannon cites the 3 November address of the Colonial Assembly, situating the event on the sixteenth.

In light of the information provided in these documents, Debien's questions can be answered and the sequence of events clearly established. The plans for the insurrection had been under way several weeks before the actual outbreak, as mentioned in Roume's report. The final plans were confirmed at the mass assembly of 14–15 August on the Lenormand plantation, and the date was fixed, at the earliest, for 22–23 August. The agreement reached was sanctified by the famous and awesomely impressive voodoo ceremony in Bois-Caïman. Those who set fire to a part of the Chabaud plantation either misunderstood the instructions or insisted upon executing their part of the plans for the revolt at the first possible moment. In either case, the event occurred sometime between the fifteenth, at the earliest, and the seventeenth, at the latest, only a few days *subsequent* to the 14 August assembly where the plans were set.

Nor was this the only incident to occur prematurely. A letter written from le Cap by M. Testard to M. Cormier in le Havre contains extracts from two letters that he had received from le Havre. The author of the first letter quoted by M. Testard refers to correspondence from le Cap all prior to 25 August, the day on which the insurrection broke out in the Plaine du Nord parish. This correspondence reveals an incident occurring on the Vaudreuil plantation in the parish:

> The *commandeur* . . . was taken by surprise by the manager while setting fire to part of the cane fields; the other slaves, upon seeing the manager struggling with the *commandeur*, caught the latter, who confessed having been influenced by a free mulatto. [12]

The second letter contained in that written by M. Testard reveals that twenty-eight slaves had deserted the Vaudreuil plantation and had taken to marronage. Three of them were captured and had revealed the conspiracy.[13] The information contained in the second letter deserves special attention insofar as it helps shed some light on the dynamics of marronage in association with the August 1791 conspiracy and revolt.

Finally, concerning the role of voodoo, some doubt has been raised as to whether or not the Bois-Caïman gathering was actually a voodoo ceremony, since Boukman's speech seemed, rather, to embrace the notion of a black, antiwhite, but still Christian, god put forward in opposition to the Catholic god of the whites. Some have argued that this substitution of the *Bon Dié* (Good Lord) of the blacks for that of the whites was merely an example of the syncretism between voodoo and Catholicism, and that the ceremony was still a voodoo affair. Others, arguing that the influence of Catholicism upon the slave culture was relatively insignificant before the nineteenth century, have claimed that this speech invoking the Good Lord could not, therefore, have been contemporary with the Bois-Caïman event.[14] However, equally as plausible may be the hypothesis that the *Bon Dié* appearing in the speech may in some way correspond to the concept of the *Grand Maître* in Vodu, a supreme, all-powerful, but distant being, the Creator and animator of nature, upon which "all that comes to pass on this globe" ultimately depends. In this sense, the *Bon Dié* of the blacks would characterize the notion of a Supreme Being that is generally central to nearly all African cult religions. But at the same time, in the opinion of Liliane Dévieux (researcher and specialist of oral traditions in Haiti), it presents the attributes of a vengeful god that could just as well be that of Genesis as of some warlike divinity of an African or Haitian cult.[15] In support of the hypothesis that the *Bon Dié* may broadly refer to the Supreme Being central to most West African religions, one finds in the religion of the Bakongo the supreme intangible force that is called Nzambi, creator of all life and of all things, who sees all and knows all, and is master over life and death. The word—and the concept—of Nzambi existed before the arrival of the Portuguese missionaries early in the sixteenth century, and it was also used to designate the god of Christianity.[16]

The earliest published citation of Boukman's Bois-Caïman exhortation to war was not, as is often assumed, in Pauléus Sannon's *Histoire de Toussaint Louverture* (1:89) in 1920. Sannon either quoted the material from Schoelcher (*Colonies étrangères et Haïti*, 2 vols. [Paris: 1843; Pointe-à-Pitre: Emile Desormeaux, 1973], 99) or directly from the early nineteenth-century Haitian writer, Hérard Dumesle, who was Schoelcher's source dating from 1824 (*Voyage dans le Nord d'Haïti* [les Cayes: Imp. du Gouvernement], 88). One can still argue against its authenticity, however, by supposing that Dumesle obtained the material from the oral tradition and may have taken a fair degree of license in the version he rendered. But then this argument does not entirely hold up, since there also exists a compiled text (translated and quoted below) with contemporaneous reference to the voodoo cult, citing the "Eh! eh! Mbumba" chant and, in the same text further on, to Zamba Boukman at the center of the insurgents who had come to lay siege to le Cap in the early days of the revolt at some point around the end of August, but prior to November when Boukman was killed. Boukman, in the words of the writer, reminded them that the whites were damned by God because they mercilessly oppressed the blacks, and then finished each refrain with the last words of the Bois-Caïman exhortation: "*Couté la liberté li palé coeur nous tous*" (Listen to the voice of liberty which speaks in the hearts of all of us). [17]

If the above testimony is historically valid, we may presume that the substantive content of this oration was actually delivered by Boukman, although certainly not in the pure literary form in which it is presented by Dumesle. This, then, poses the problem of the relationship between history and legend, on the one hand, and the oral and written traditions, on the other. It is a problem that will be central to the projected joint study of this enigmatic and almost quixotic exhortation to war.

As to voodoo, we know, as well, that one of the participants in the ceremony, Cécile Fatiman, was a mambo, a voodoo priestess, even though she was herself mulatto, the daughter of an African woman and a Corsican prince.[18] Here, then, two points may be offered as conclusions. First, the Bois-Caïman ceremony following the 14 August Morne-Rouge assembly did indeed take place, and, secondly, it was a voodoo affair; that is, within the parameters of the larger interpretation of the term, which, as generally used in the present study, embraces the multiplicity of African cults alongside the specifically Dahomean cult of Vodu. The ceremony actually contained discernible elements of both rada (Dahomean) and petro rites. If the blood pact was characteristically Dahomean, the insistence upon vengeance, the militaristic atmosphere and incitation to war, as well as the depiction of the whites as belonging to malevolent spirits, and the ritualistic sacrifice of a black pig (rather than a goat or fowl) all strongly suggest the predominance of petro rites.

Parallel to these indications, the above-mentioned contemporaneous passage (translated and quoted below) refers, on the eve of the slave insurrection, to the "Eh! eh! Mbumba" chant, which is, as we know, a sacramental voodoo hymn. So we have, in the same account, a reference to the voodoo hymn being witnessed just prior to August 1791 and a reference to Boukman, with his Bois-Caïman exhortation, at the end of August, in anticipation of their attack on le Cap.[19] The passage is drawn from the *Lettre annuelle de l'Ordre de Notre Dame*.[20] It goes as follows:

A former pupil [of the Order of the Daughters of Notre Dame of Cap Français],[21] one of the brightest and belonging to the class of mulattoes, who later became the head of a company of Amazons and known in history by the name of the princess Amethyst, was initiated into the cult of *Ghioux*, or Voodoo [*Vaudoux*], a sort of religious and dancing masonry introduced into Saint Domingue by Arada Negroes. She drew a good number of her companions into the sect. The schoolmistresses clearly noticed a certain agitation that increased especially after the round that they had adopted to the exclusion of all others:

'Eh! eh! Bomba eh! eh!	[Eh! eh! Rainbow spirit, eh! eh!
Canga bafio té	Tie up the BaFioti
Canga mousse [sic] délé	Tie up the whites
Canga do ki la	Tie up the witches
Canga li'	Tie them [22]]

We have no idea whether this is Senegalese or Yolof, Arada or Congolese; what we do know is that it is African and that these words form the sacramental hymn of Voodoo. One evening, the Negresses left the institution accompanied by a large number of their companions and dashed out into the darkness, outside the city, to the chant of these words that are incomprehensible to whites. The attention of the sisters had been aroused, however, since for some time these women had adopted an almost uniform type of dress, wrapping sashes of a predominantly red color around the body and wearing sandals on their feet. . . . During the nights we heard these words, incomprehensible to whites, chanted alternately by one or several voices. The king of the cult of Voodoo had just declared war on the colonists. His brow girded with a diadem and accompanied by the queen of the cult, wearing a red sash and shaking a box [rattle] garnished with bells and containing a snake, they marched to the assault on the cities of the colony. . . . They came to lay siege to Cap Français. By the glimmer of the great smoldering fires, punctuated by the silhouette of the spectacular rounds, the sisters perceived from the windows of their Monastery, overlooking the countryside and the city, barebreasted Negresses belonging to the sect, dancing to the mournful sound of the long, narrow tambourines and conch shells, and alternating with the moaning of the sacrificed creatures. In the midst of the rebels was Zamba Boukman, urging them on to the assault on the barracks and the convent, which held a good number of young girls and other colonists. He reminded them in his poetic improvisations that the whites were damned by God because they were the oppressors of the blacks, whom they crushed without pity, and he ended each refrain with these words: '*Couté la liberté li palé coeur nous tous.*'

APPENDIX C

Declarations of the Slave Antoine and Sieur Fabvre [1]

*Extract of the minutes from the register
of the Provincial Assembly of the South*

25 January 1791

On this day, a special session of the municipal government was convened to discuss a declaration made by Sieur Fabvre, planter of the district of Marche-à-Terre, before Sieur Dumont, district attorney of the said municipality of Port-Salut, at whose office he arrived at 7:00 A.M., where an official statement was prepared. This statement will remain in the archives.

At 11:00 A.M., a slave named Antoine, belonging to M. Masson Duhard, was brought forward. The said slave, creole, was caught on the road vis-à-vis the gate of Sieur Alabré, senior, by Joseph Alabré, one of his legitimate children.

Interrogated on the purpose of the slave gathering mentioned in Sieur Fabvre's declaration, the said slave answered in conformity with what he declared before M. Montier, M. Richard, and M. Alabré. Hereafter, we have copied his declaration verbatim.

Declaration made by the said Antoine, belonging to M. Masson Duhard, arrested on the said road by the children of M. Alabré.

DISTRICT LEADERS

On the plantation of:

M. Masson Duhard	Dominique
M. Fabvre	Zamore
M. Lafosse	Félix
Mme. Merlet	la Saint-Jean
M. Balix (from les Ravines)	Paris; Jean-Louis
M. Fournier	Jean-Philippe; Jean-François

In the name of the slaves on the plantations of each district, the said leaders were to demand of their masters three free days per week. This demand was to be made at some point this week. He could not give the precise date and stated that, during last night's assembly, the slaves were to fix the date, the hour, and the moment, and that each district was to do likewise. The declarant stated that Jean-Claude Lateste is supposed to have said on Sunday at M. Masson Duhard's place that the king had granted the slaves three free days per week, and that the said Jean-Claude is supposed to have said that the mulattoes were saying that the whites were the only obstacle preventing the application of this decree. The declarant stated, as well, that the slaves of the Plaine-du-Fond were armed with rifles and pistols in the region of Savanettes. He also declared that the ringleaders were on the plantations of M. Lafosse and the widow, Mme. Merlet.

Declaration certified in conformity with the statement of the said slave Antoine in the presence of the undersigned witnesses.

Signed upon presentation: Alabré; Richard; Montier; Dumont, district attorney.

25 January 1791

The said slave Antoine, while making his declaration, had one of the members of the municipality called to the bar, and declared before him that, prior to reaching their camp, the mulattoes had assured the blacks that they were going to fight the whites to obtain three free days per week; that the blacks of the Plaine-du-Fond had offered to join their camp; and that they had refused this offer for fear that some harm might befall them.

He also declared that when the mulattoes had abandoned their camp, they had told the blacks that if the whites accorded them three free days per week, they would also accord three free days per week to the blacks; but that it was their concern to act on their own behalf; and he declared that the black slaves of each particular plantation had thereafter resolved to present their demand on one day this week, and that if the whites refused to grant their demand, they would attack and slaughter them.

Signed upon presentation: Dumont, district attorney; Delamotte Flammant, secretary.

Signed: Collet, interim president
         Berrel, mayor
         Reffuveuille, district attorney
         Beaudequien, notary

On this day, 25 January 1791, at 7:00 A.M., Sieur Fabvre appeared before the district attorney of the municipality of Port-Salut. He declared in the presence of M. Buisson, planter of this district, that a considerable number of slaves not belonging to him came to his place last night around 2:00 A.M.; that he estimated the number of slaves to be two hundred; that they encircled the quarters of the *commandeur* and carried him off by force, along with three other slaves; that they wanted to take the rest of the slaves with them, but these slaves escaped into the brush, where they hid.

The *commandeur* and the three other slaves carried off by force had the good fortune to escape and arrived back at the plantation all out of breath: the above-mentioned band of slaves proposed going to round up the slaves on the plantations of the widow, Mme. Merlet, M. Lafosse, M. Duhard, etc., and were armed with machetes, sticks, lances, and, a few of them, with pistols.

The slaves of the said declarant, Sieur Fabvre, recognized in this band of insurgents several slaves whose names were as follows:

Dominique, Jean-Philippe, Hiacinte, Quiouquiou, Samedy; all belonging to Sieur Masson Duhard, residing in France and who, upon his departure, named Sieurs Comneau and D'Arboust, uncle, as his agents, and Sieur Jadouin as his manager-overseer.

Jupiter and *Etienne*, belonging to Sieur Fournier, resident planter at the place called les Ravines.

Jean-Louis and *Charles*, belonging to Sieur Michel Balix, residing in France.

La Bonté, belonging to M. Lafosse.

The case appearing to be very serious and clearly suggesting an insurrection, we have considered it appropriate to call for public assistance and to send out well-armed troops.

Signed upon presentation: Fabvre; Buisson; Dumont, district attorney.

Verified in conformity with presentation. Signed: Dumont, district attorney; Delmotte Flammant, secretary.

Signed: Collet, interim president
       Berrel, mayor
       Reffuveuille, district attorney
       Beaudequien, notary

APPENDIX D

Grande-Anse Movement Documents [1]

Declaration of citizeness Magdelon

2 October 1802

Citizeness Magdelon, a plantation worker on the Parouty plantation in the Fond Rouge quarter, wife of the said Jean-Louis, *conducteur* on the same plantation, declares that the said Izidor, *conducteur* on the Petit Gas [*sic*] plantation[2] in the same quarter and who has already been executed, came to the Parouty plantation to tell her husband [*son homme*], Jean-Louis, that commander Dommage had sent him to engage him to revolt against the French government. At the time, Jean-Louis replied that he was not accustomed to revolting and that he strove to respect and obey those persons in a position to give him good advice; this occurred around mid-July 1802.

Written in the presence of the undersigned: Parouty; Callard; Jn. Thevenard; Fourrault; Montégu; Sarrebource; Bernard, commander.

Certified true signatures.

Bernard, commander at Jérémie.

Declaration of Corus

2 October 1802

The said Corus declared that at the time of the current insurrection, the said Jean-Jacques, of the Trippin plantation, [was] sent to the Leroux plantation to raise the workers to rebellion by telling them that commander Dommage had entrusted him with this; that all the men should meet at Fond Rouge to await orders and arms from the latter. Citizen Thomas, of the Trippin plantation, was charged by the said Jean-Jacques with spreading the word; upon this denunciation, we went to the Trippin plantation and arrested the said Jean-Jacques.

Signed: Bantes, squadron leader; Poussinon, fils; Praderes.

1 October 1802

Following our investigation, we questioned the last two persons arrested. They told us that commander Dommage had arms offered to them by a third party to distribute to the blacks who would be willing to encamp at Fond Rouge, where he had already arrived and was awaiting them; that the French had arrived to put them back into slavery; and that they absolutely had to fight to maintain their freedom. They also declared that the said Jean-René and Pierre, who had already been executed, had received an order to make the rounds of the plantations to win over the workers.

Signed: Lammot; Bantes, squadron leader; Praderes, fils; Duhulque; Larue; Praderes.

1 October 1802

Nominative list of prisoners put on board ship for Port-Républicain in conformity with the orders of Division General Rochambeau.

Hugo — arrested by order of General Darbois for having taken the liberty of expressing observations detrimental to the public order.

Captain Allard — *gendarme* sent from Tiburon.

François Beauvert — sent from Abricots.

Cholet — *gendarme* sent from Corail.

Lajeunesse — deserter from the former Twelfth (half-brigade).

Ciprien — former officer sent from Abricots.

Savary — secretary to Dommage.

Michel — former justice of the peace.

Azor — captain of the 2nd battalion of the Ninetieth Half-brigade.

Jean-François — deserter from the former Twelfth (half-brigade).

Michel-Jérôme — former reformed captain of the Fourth Half-brigade.

Casimir — reformed soldier of the Fourth Half-brigade.

Augustin Parouty — reformed officer of the national guard.

Gillot Berquier — reformed officer of the national guard.

Lamadieu — dismissed officer of the Fourth Half-brigade.

Signed: Bernard, commander at Jérémie.

Abbreviations

AHR	*American Historical Review*
AN	Archives Nationales (Paris)
ANSOM	Archives Nationales—Section Outre-Mer (Aix-en-Provence)
Arch. Col.	Archives Coloniales (at AN, Paris)
BPL	Boston Public Library
CIDIHCA	Centre International de Documentation et d'Information Haïtienne, Caraïbéenne et Afro-Canadienne (Montréal)
HCA	High Court of Admiralty (at PRO, London)
IFAN (*Bull.*)	(*Bulletin* de l') Institut français de l'Afrique noire
ISL	Institut Saint-Louis de Gonzague (Port-au-Prince)
NYPL	New York Public Library
PRO	Public Record Office (London)
PUF	Presses universitaires de France
RHAF	*Revue d'histoire de l'Amérique française*
RSHH(G)(G)	*Revue de la Société haïtienne d'histoire (de géographie) (et de géologie)*
SHHG (*Bull.*)	(*Bulletin* de la) Société haïtienne d' histoire et de géographie
UFL	University of Florida Libraries (Gainesville)

Notes

Introduction

1. C. L. R. James, *The Black Jacobins* ([1938]; 3d ed., London: Allison and Busby, 1980), 25.

2. See Colonel Malenfant, *Des colonies et particulièrement de celle de Saint-Domingue* (1814); Pamphile Lacroix, *Mémoire pour servir à l'histoire de la révolution de Saint-Domingue* (1820); Antoine Dalmas, *Histoire de la révolution de Saint-Domingue* ([1793?]1814); M. E. Descourtiltz, *Voyage d'un naturaliste en Haïti, 1799–1803* (1809); or, a bit later, M. Lemonnier-Delafosse, *Seconde campagne de Saint-Domingue* (1846).

3. James, *Black Jacobins*, 383.

4. T. G. Steward, *The Haitian Revolution, 1791–1804* (New York: T. Crowell, 1914), v.

5. T. Lothrop Stoddard, *The French Revolution in San Domingo* (New York: Houghton-Mifflin, 1914; reprint, Westport, Conn.: Negro Universities Press, 1970), viii.

6. James, *Black Jacobins*, 283. Stoddard made it a fundamental question in support of white supremacy. On the other hand, James's insistence upon the importance of the race question, albeit as a derivative of the class question, prompted another historian of the revolution, Thomas O. Ott, in *The Haitian Revolution* (Knoxville: University of Tennessee Press, 1973), to erroneously cast James as a black racist unable to reconcile his Marxism with his "black racist" West Indian nationalism (199). Where Stoddard made race fundamental, Ott treated it as incidental to the overriding power struggles of vying factions and leaders. Not too much better in this particular respect is David Nicholls's *From Dessalines to Duvalier: Race, Colour and Independence in Haiti* (Cambridge: Cambridge University Press, 1979) in which race, in addition to constituting the basis for the Haitian claim to independence, was also one of the most important factors explaining why Haiti has failed to maintain an effective independence. On James and the race question, however, Nicholls justly criticizes Ott's flagrant and abusive distortion of James's views (263–64, n.91). The most balanced rendering of James's position in relation to politics and race is Cedric Robinson's recent article "C. L. R. James and the Black Radical Tradition," *Review* 6 (Winter 1983):321–91. One of the best works to date on class and race ideology in Haiti is Micheline Labelle's *Idéologie de couleur et classes sociales en Haïti* ([1979]; 2nd ed., Montréal: Editions CIDIHCA, 1987).

7. See James, *Black Jacobins*, 243; 276, esp. n. 6; 338, esp. n. 39.

8. David P. Geggus, *Slavery, War and Revolution: The British Occupation of Saint Domingue, 1793–1798* (Oxford: Clarendon, 1982), 2.

9. Gwendolyn Midlo Hall, *Social Control in Slave Plantation Societies: A Comparison of Saint Domingue and Cuba* (Baltimore: Johns Hopkins, 1971), 52, 62.

10. The French word *marronage*, denoting desertion, is derived from the adjective *marron* (also used as a noun) used in reference to a runaway or fugitive slave. The actual origin of this word remains disputed. However, the most widely accepted explanation is that it is derived from the Spanish *cimarron*, which means savage (and by extension denotes a primitive state)

and is itself derived from the name of an Indian tribe of Panama, *los Symarons*, that revolted against Spanish domination. Equally plausible is the explanation claiming the derivation of the word from the Spanish *marro*, meaning flight or escape, or from the French verb *marroner*, to desert or maroon. (The 1977 reprint edition of *Harrap's New Standard French and English Dictionary* gives an interesting translation of the French verb *marroner:* "to carry on a trade or profession without legal qualifications," coincidentally describing the activities of the urban maroons but perhaps reflecting the influence of sociohistorical phenomena on contemporary language.) For a fuller discussion of other hypotheses printed in *Les affiches américaines* in 1786, see Jean Fouchard, *Les marrons de la liberté* (Paris: Ecole, 1972), 381–82. See also Yvan Debbasch, "Le marronage: essai sur la désertion de l'esclave antillais," *Année sociologique* 3 (1961):1; and Gabriel Debien, *Les esclaves aux Antilles françaises: dix-septième au dix-huitième siècle* (Basse Terre: Société d'histoire de la Guadeloupe, 1974), 411. For the purposes of this study the word *maroon*, as the nearest English equivalent, will be used in reference to *les marrons*. For the act or state of desertion, the French *marronage* will be retained.

11. Debbasch, "Le marronage," 1–112 passim.

12. François Girod, *La vie quotidienne de la société créole: Saint-Domingue au XVIIIè siècle* (Paris: Hachette, 1972), 168–69.

13. He is more discerning, however, in his monumental work *Les esclaves aux Antilles françaises*, where a third type of marronage is described as a prolonged, but still individual, act that may actually be a stage toward "big" marronage (424).

14. Fouchard, *Marrons de la liberté*, 38.

15. In this vein see also Edner Brutus, *Révolution dans Saint-Domingue*, 2 vols. (Brussels?: Panthéon, 1973?).

16. "The Relationship Between Marronage and Slave Revolts and Revolution in Saint-Domingue/Haiti," in *Comparative Perspectives on Slavery in New World Plantation Societies*, eds. Vera Rubin and Arthur Tuden, *Annals of the New York Academy of Sciences* 292 (1977), 420–38.

17. Ibid., 426–27.

18. Ibid., 432–36. On the question of marronage and class struggle the author observes that "marronage is history and, as such, part of the general process that led Saint Domingue to a revolution in which class struggle took the form of race struggle; . . . it seems unlikely in principle that in a country where the end product of the historical process has been revolution, that marronage, opposing masters and slaves, would have occurred outside the context of class and race struggles." (431).

19. Orlando Patterson, "Slavery and Slave Revolts: A Socio-historical Analysis of the First Maroon War, 1665–1740," in *Maroon Societies: Rebel Slave Communities in the Americas*, ed. Richard Price (Garden City, New York: Anchor Press, 1973), 279.

20. Manigat, "Relationship," 433. Contemporary documentation relating to these revolts is presented in Fouchard, *Marrons de la liberté*, 463–79.

21. Makandal was the chief architect of the wave of mass poisonings ravaging the North Plain during the 1750s. The ultimate aim was to annihilate the whites and take possession of the island. See Ch. 2 below.

22. See the discussion of the point in Ch. 6.

23. E. P. Thompson, *The Making of the English Working Class* (New York: Penguin, 1979), 13.

24. This human contradiction inherent in slavery and the slave personality has been given particular attention and treated in all its complexity in the various works of Eugene Genovese, David Brion Davis, Sidney Mintz, Orlando Patterson, and others.

25. This is not to minimize, however, the social, cultural, and even political input resulting from the slaves' day-to-day accommodation to the realities of slavery. Resistance and
accommodation often worked hand-in-hand quite effectively. As was sometimes the case, the
most loyal and trusted, and therefore the least-suspected, slaves were the ones behind plots to
kill the master or the leaders of insurrectionary movements. In a similar vein, the relationship
of the slave (or after abolition, of the black laborer) to the land was one that evolved under the
conditions of slavery but later became a revolutionary aspiration of personal "proprietorship"
of the land that one cultivated.

26. These letters were "discovered," so to speak, by French historian Bernard Foubert,
who was the first to examine them in the mid-1970s and whose archival classification of them
has enabled subsequent researchers to utilize this valuable source of historical material,
which otherwise would have gone unnoticed.

Chapter One

1. Although the *flibuste* did involve other nationalities, the French appeared predominant,
thus leading one historian, Pierre Chaunu, to characterize it as "an international crime organization of French origin." Cited in Charles Frostin, *Les révoltes blanches à Saint-Domingue
au XVIIe et XVIIIe siècles* (Paris: Ecole, 1975), 46. The term *boucanier* is derived from the
French *boucaner* (to smoke) or, perhaps more precisely, from the word *boucan*, "a kind of
wattle formed of intercrossing branches tied together with liana and supported by stakes on
which they roasted the meat, while the salted hides dried in the sun." Ibid., 50.

2. One of the few studies (and by far the best) of these early French immigrants to Saint
Domingue is Gabriel Debien's *Les engagés pour les Antilles: 1634–1715* ([Paris: Société de
l'histoire des colonies françaises, 1952], in *Revue d'histoire des colonies* 38 [1951]). The work
treats over six thousand contracts from the single commercial port of La Rochelle, the first
dating back to 1620. Geographic and occupational origins, types of engagement, and causes
of departure are analyzed and followed by a study of the conditions and integration of the
engagés into colonial society.

3. Frostin, *Révoltes blanches*, 48–49; 53–57. See also Debien, *Engagés*, 256–58.

4. While Pierre de Vaissière, an early twentieth-century historian (in *Saint-Domingue,
1629–1789: la société et la vie créoles sous l'Ancien Régime* [Paris: Perrin, 1909]), claims
a preponderant role for the lesser French nobility in the settlement and development of
Saint Domingue, Debien has found this assertion to be lacking in evidence. Those who were
genuinely of the nobility generally occupied ranks in the royal bureaucracy; others, of the
bourgeoisie, may for all intents and purposes have merely usurped noble status and a noble
life style. *Engagés*, 138–40. See also Etienne Charlier, *Aperçu sur la formation historique
de la nation haïtienne* (Port-au-Prince: Les Presses Libres, 1954), 11–15. French historian
Gaston-Martin also tends to minimize the role of the aristocracy in the settlement of Saint
Domingue and criticizes de Vaissière's overly indulgent treatment of this element. *Nantes
au XVIIIe siècle: l'ère des négriers, 1714–1774* (Paris: Alcan, 1931), 365–66.

5. De Vaissière, *La Société*, 298–301.

6. Michel Descourtiltz, *Histoire des désastres de Saint-Domingue* (Paris: Garney, 1795),
76–78.

7. Though attempts had been made by the Crown to regulate relations between master and
slave, the treatment of the latter, in reality, was the sole prerogative of the former. The Edict
of 1685, known as the Black Code, attempted to provide minimal protection for the slave
against unwarranted barbarism on the part of a master, manager, or overseer, and although

some provision was made for slaves to bring such cases to the attention of the authorities (Art. 26), a slave's word could not, in any event, be received as legal testimony (Art. 30). Rarely, moreover, did the local government intervene in such matters, leaving master-slave relations to the discretion of the owners. The church, the only other institution potentially capable of exercising a civilizing influence in the treatment of slaves was, in the opinion of historian C. L. R. James, equally as corrupt and irresponsible as the courts. *Black Jacobins*, 32. The church itself was among the largest of the slave-owning landholders in the colony. M. Placide-Justin, *Histoire politique et statistique de l'île d'Hayti* (Paris: Brière, 1826), 132–33. Also Shelby McCloy, *The Negro in the French West Indies* ([1966]; reprint, Westport, Conn.: Negro Universities Press, 1974), 24.

8. De Vaissière, *La société*, 214–16.

9. M. L. E. Moreau de Saint-Méry, *Description topographique, physique, civile, politique et historique de la partie française de l'île de Saint-Domingue*, 3 vols. (Philadelphia: 1797; reprint, Paris: Société de l'histoire des colonies françaises, 1959), 1:33.

10. Ibid. Also Frostin, *Révoltes blanches*, 319.

11. Ibid. James, *Black Jacobins*, 33.

12. Lieutenant Thomas Phipps Howard, *The Haitian Journal of Lieutenant Howard: York Hussars, 1796–1798*, ed. Roger N. Buckley (Knoxville: University of Tennessee Press, 1985), 103. The *Journal* was written by Howard during the period of British occupation in Saint Domingue (1793–98), and although slavery was abolished in Saint Domingue by French law in 1794, the institution remained intact, as did racial attitudes, in those areas occupied by the invading British forces.

13. Henri Castonnet des Fosses, *La perte d'une colonie: la révolution de Saint-Domingue* (Paris: Faivre, 1893), 10.

14. Given the wide degree of variance from one source to another, it is extremely difficult to arrive at statistically precise population figures for Saint Domingue prior to the revolution. While the most conservative figures place the white population at 30,000, other sources cite the number of whites at 40–42,000. Similarly, population figures for the *affranchis* vary from the lowest estimate of 24,000 to 37,800, giving a range of variance of well over 10,000. For the black slave population, discrepancies between sources are even wider, ranging anywhere from 452,000 at the lowest end to 700,000 at the highest. M. Placide-Justin, in his *Histoire politique et statistique de l'île d'Hayti*, was inclined to consider the figures for 1789 of the French writer Ducoeurjoly as the most accurate: 30,826 whites, 27,548 *affranchis*, and 465,429 slaves (144). Challenging official government figures, a contemporary writer and resident in the colony brings the total for the white population up to around 35,000 by taking account of those *petits blancs* (artisans, fishermen, small merchants) who would not have appeared on the census. Similarly he adjusts official figures for the *affranchis* to roughly 30,000, thus accounting for those whose enfranchisement may not yet have been ratified, and places the number of slaves at 480,000. *Précis historique des annales de la colonie française de Saint-Domingue*, 2 vols. (1:1–2.) [Typewritten copy of original unpublished manuscript deposited by Gabriel Debien at University of Florida Libraries, Rare Books Collection.] With regard to the black slave population, most figures, taken from official census reports, average between 450,000 and 500,000. Those historians whose estimates of the slave population significantly surpass 500,000 have most likely taken into account a general practice, dating back to the very beginning of the eighteenth century, among planters who, for the purposes of tax evasion, never declared the exact number of slaves in their possession, thus rendering official figures far below their actual numbers. See Castonnet des Fosses, *La perte*, 8; Descourtiltz, *Histoire des désastres*, 52; and Moreau de Saint-Méry, *Loix et constitutions des colonies françaises de l'Amérique sous le vent*, 6 vols. (Paris: By the Author, 1784), 2:433.

15. Descourtiltz, *Histoire des désastres*, 78. The *affranchis*, or free persons of color, were also referred to in French as *gens de couleur libres;* the terms "free mulattoes and free blacks" or, for convenience, "mulattoes and free blacks," are equivalent to *affranchis* in French. This does not suppose that mulatto slaves did not exist in Saint Domingue. The mulattoes, however, were few in comparison with the vast mass of black slaves, the majority of whom, by 1789, were in fact African-born. The French word *nègre*, in the colonial context, was usually used synonymously with "slave," while *mulâtre* was eventually used to designate anyone who was neither white nor *nègre*. Moreau de Saint-Méry, *Description*, 1:102–3. The mulattoes, moreover, constituted a mere 2.6 percent of the slave population. Cited in Micheline Labelle, *Idéologie*, 45.

16. Frostin, *Révoltes blanches*, 126–27; 214.

17. Ibid., 324–25. Also, Debien, *Engagés*, 258.

18. Frostin, *Révoltes blanches*, 70–71; 320–21.

19. Ibid., 69, 339, 366.

20. The figures are those cited by Frostin from the official census records for Saint Domingue. *Révoltes blanches*, 304.

21. The Saint Dominguean free colored were, in fact, three times more numerous than the *affranchis* throughout all of the remaining islands of the French Antilles. For population figures covering the islands of the French West Indies see Antoine Gisler, *L'esclavage aux Antilles françaises: XVIIe–XIXe siècle*, 2d ed. (Paris: Karthala, 1981), 35. Tables showing overall population growth (white, *affranchi*, and slave) for the one hundred–year period from the 1680s to the 1780s in the economically significant French and British West Indian islands are presented in Frostin, *Révoltes blanches*, 28–30.

22. Cited in de Vaissière, *La société*, 222–23.

23. Ibid., 223.

24. In Labelle, *Idéologie*, 46–47. Also, Léon Deschamps, *Les colonies pendant la Révolution* (Paris: Perrin, 1898), 18. Castonnet des fosses, *La perte*, 11.

25. Frostin, *Révoltes blanches*, 305.

26. In Beauvais Lespinasse, *Histoire des affranchis de Saint-Domingue*, 2 vols. (Paris: Kugelman, 1882) 1:229.

27. See James's discussion of the origins and resulting contradictions, as well as the political explosiveness of this whole state of affairs. *Black Jacobins*, 36–44.

28. Cited in Auguste Lebeau, *De la condition des gens de couleur libres sous l'Ancien Régime* (Poitiers: Masson, 1903), 4.

29. Robert L. Stein, *Léger Félicité Sonthonax: The Lost Sentinel of the Republic* (London and Toronto: Associated University Presses, 1985), 30.

30. The restriction of the *affranchis* in the case of practicing medicine or pharmacy arose from the white colonists' fears—at times reaching hysterical proportions—of poisoning, a common practice among slaves anxious to exact vengeance on their masters. Equally forbidden for women of color was the practice of midwifery, given the alarming incidence of infant mortality due to "mysterious" causes when childbirth was undertaken by a slave midwife.

31. McCloy, *Negro in the French West Indies*, 61–62. Frostin, *Révoltes blanches*, 304. For whites, militia service was voluntary. See also Ott, *Haitian Revolution*, 13.

32. In the words of Governor de Fayet, as early as 1733: "only the mulattoes can destroy the Maroons." Cited in Frostin, *Révoltes blanches*, 304. Similar views were expressed by the Chamber of Agriculture some forty-odd years later. AN, C9 B 29. Extrait d'un mémoire sur la création d'un corps de gens de couleur levé à Saint-Domingue en mars 1779.

33. Lebeau, *De la condition*, 74–78.

34. Moreau de Saint-Méry, *Loix et constitutions*, 5:855–56.

35. James, *Black Jacobins*, 41.

36. The Black Code of 1685 stipulated that "the *Affranchis* must display a singular re-spect toward their former masters, toward their widows and their children; and that the injury they will have caused to them be punished more severely than if it were caused to any other person." Moreau de Saint-Méry, *Loix et constitutions* 1:423.

37. Ott, *Haitian Revolution*, 12.

38. Moreau de Saint-Méry, *Loix et constitutions* 5:817; 6:373, 492, 295, respectively.

39. See Gabriel Debien, *Les colons de Saint-Domingue et la révolution* (Paris: Armand Colin, 1953), 50. Castonnet des Fosses, *La perte*, 8. See also Jean Jaurès, *Histoire socialiste de la Révolution française*, ed. Albert Soboul, 7 vols. (Paris: Editions sociales, 1968), 1:126. According to Castonnet des Fosses, the total property value of Saint Domingue surpassed 1.6 billion livres. *La perte*, 8.

40. Frostin, *Révoltes blanches*, 138–45.

41. See the description of the sugar production process in this chapter, below.

42. Robert L. Stein, *The French Slave Trade in the Eighteenth Century: An Old Regime Business* (Madison: University of Wisconsin Press, 1979), 7–8; 22–24. During the initial "take-off" period, roughly from 1690 to 1720, the number of slaves increased from a little over 3,000 to well over 47,000—a fourteenfold increase in thirty years. From 1730 to 1754, the slave population more than doubled, increasing from approximately 80,000 to just over 172,000, and, from the end of the Seven Years' War to the eve of the revolution (1764 to 1789), once again more than doubled from 206,000 to the officially recorded number of 465,429. The exact figures, taken from government sources, are recorded in Frostin, *Révoltes blanches*, 28. Given the notoriously low birth rate (characteristically inferior to the mortality rate) in the slave population of Saint Domingue, these increases may safely be attributed, for the greater part, to the importation of slaves by the colonial planters. In addition to the ever-expanding demand for labor generated by the rise in sugar production, the abolition of government monopolies and the opening of the trade to private traders after 1715 provided an additional, and a much-needed, stimulus. Stein, *French Slave Trade*, 13–16.

43. Ibid., 11. Up to 1666, 108 French ships had been engaged in trading off the Guinea coast, carrying a total of over 37,000 Africans; by the eve of the revolution the annual average would equal this figure. Jaurès, *Histoire socialiste* 1:141. Pierre Pluchon, *La route des esclaves: négriers et bois d'ébène au XVIIIe siècle* (Paris: Hachette, 1980), 19–20. Stein, *French Slave Trade*, 38. For 1787 alone, nineteenth-century historian Léon Deschamps cites these figures: 92 ships carrying 30,889 Africans, producing nearly 42 million livres in profits from a total investment of only 17 million. *Les colonies*, 19–20.

44. Pluchon, *La route*, 19–20. Stein, *French Slave Trade*, 32, 38.

45. See Stein, *French Slave Trade*, 116–18. Also Debien, *Les colons*, 50; Deschamps, *Les colonies*, 5; Jaurès, *Histoire socialiste*, 1:127.

46. Stein, *French Slave Trade*, 135–36.

47. Ibid., 137.

48. Ibid., 131–35.

49. Jaurès, *Histoire socialiste*, 1:127.

50. Stein, *French Slave Trade*, 134. Jaurès, *Histoire socialiste*, 1:128–30.

51. Ibid., 141.

52. Stein, *French Slave Trade*, 147.

53. Cited in Gaston-Martin, *Nantes*, 375.

54. Stein, *French Slave Trade*, 147–49.

55. Cited in Deschamps, *Les colonies*, 21.

56. Gaston-Martin, *Nantes*, 370. Stein, *French Slave Trade*, 115–16. Also Deschamps, *Les colonies*, 25.

57. Moreau de Saint-Méry, *Description*, 1:44.

58. Sidney Mintz, *Caribbean Transformations* (Chicago: Aldine, 1974), 60.

59. Jean Fouchard, "La traite des Nègres et le peuplement de Saint-Domingue," *La traite négrière du XVe au XIXe siècle* (Paris: UNESCO, 1979), 281. See also Pierre Pluchon's interesting work on the eighteenth-century French slave trade, *La route des esclaves*. One of the most detailed demographic studies available to date of the ethnic origins of the French Antillean slave population for the second half of the eighteenth century is still the collective work by Gabriel Debien, J. Houdaille, R. Massio, and R. Richard, "Les origines des esclaves des Antilles," Bull. de l'IFAN 23–29, sér. B (1961–67). The vast majority of the more than sixty plantation lists studied and presented here are for Saint Domingue and cover the period from 1756 to 1797. The study constituted only a first phase of the research, and the findings are therefore incomplete and more suggestive than conclusive. Nevertheless, a synthesis of the data treated has led Debien to put forward these observations for Saint Domingue: that it was the Congolese and the Aradas that constituted the dominant ethnic groups, though their numerical importance alternated at various times throughout the century, with the Aradas losing relative ground little by little toward the end. (29 [1967]:557). These findings have been somewhat expanded and further refined in his *Esclaves aux Antilles*, 52–68. Still, he generally concludes that the ethnic composition of Saint Domingue's slave population at the end of the eighteenth century was derived largely from the Congo groupings, from the diverse nations of the Slave Coast, and, to a much lesser degree, the Senegal region (68). A more recent and exhaustive study of the French slave trade is the late Jean Mettas's *Répertoire des expéditions négrières françaises au XVIIIe siècle*, ed. Serge Daget, 2 vols. (Paris: Société française d'histoire d'Outre-Mer, 1978 and 1984). While this source may be used profitably to gain additional insights into the French slave trade, e.g., its extent numerically and geographically, mortality rates during the voyages, conditions aboard the ships, ports of trade and departure from Africa, it cannot, unfortunately, be relied upon exclusively to establish the ethnic origins of the eighteenth-century Saint Dominguean slave population, as ship captains simply never bothered to indicate (even if they knew) the nationalities of the captives, but only the port or place at which they were traded. It can at best be used as a complementary source in conjunction with notarial papers, parish records, colonial newspapers, and plantation lists in departmental and in family archives—all of which would require unlimited research time and funding to arrive at conclusions that may, in the end, be less impressive than what initial expectations may have led one to assume.

60. On the cultural, religious, and linguistic implications of voodoo for Saint Dominguean slaves, see the discussions in the present chapter and in Ch. 2.

61. D'Auberteuil, *Considérations*, 2:63.

62. Ibid., 2:62.

63. Debien, *Esclaves aux Antilles*, 83–84; 343–47.

64. Cited in Fouchard, "La traite," 279.

65. See Korngold, *Citizen Toussaint*, 34. Testimony presented before the Select Committee of the House of Commons in 1791 revealed that some British planters found it more profitable to exhaust a slave's physical capacities within seven years, maximize their profits, and then reinvest in more slaves.

66. Debien, *Esclaves aux Antilles*, 342–43.

67. Orlando Patterson, *Slavery and Social Death: A Comparative Study* (Cambridge: Harvard University Press, 1982), 5–6. The notion of social death as a fundamental characteristic of slavery is also discussed by Gisler, *L'esclavage*, 27–33.

68. The mortality rate of newly purchased slaves on the coffee plantations was somewhat lower, it seems, than on the sugar plantations, where half generally died off in the first few years. Debien, *Esclaves aux Antilles*, 344.

69. Girod-Chantrans, *Voyage d'un Suisse en différentes colonies* (Neufchatel, 1785), 137.

70. Hall, *Social Control*, 17. For a detailed description of the stages involved in sugar production, see also Stein, *French Slave Trade*, 7–8; S. Mintz, *Sweetness and Power: The Place of Sugar in Modern History* (New York: Viking, 1985), 47–52.

71. Hall, *Social Control*, 17.

72. Ibid. Also, Debien, *Esclaves aux Antilles*, 96, 150.

73. On night work for women on the sugar plantations, see the recent work by French demographic historian, Arlette Gautier, *Les soeurs de Solitude: la condition féminine dans l'esclavage aux Antilles du XVIIe au XIXe siècle* (Paris: Editions Caraïbéennes, 1985), 200–2.

74. Debien, *Esclaves aux Antilles*, 97. Also, M. Frossard, *La cause des esclaves nègres*, 2 vols. (Lyons: Aimé de la Roche, 1789), 1:322–23.

75. Debien, *Esclaves aux Antilles*, 96–97.

76. Ibid., 145.

77. Ibid., 130.

78. Ibid., 130–31.

79. Ibid., 119.

80. Ibid., 131–32, and Fouchard, *Marrons de la liberté*, 406.

81. See especially their role in the wave of poisonings during the 1750s in Ch. 2.

82. Debien, *Esclaves aux Antilles*, 93.

83. In Gautier, *Solitude*, 89.

84. Generally, a woman worked in the fields until the sixth month of her pregnancy, after which she was allowed to perform somewhat lighter tasks. Shortly after childbirth, she returned to the fields and resumed her work as before, albeit at an interrupted pace for the eighteen-month nursing period. See Albert Savine, *Saint-Domingue à la veille de la révolution: souvenirs du Baron de Wimpffen*, ed. Louis Michaud (Paris: 1911), 95. The impact of the sexual division of labor upon the status of women under slavery in the French West Indies, a status characterized by social inequality created precisely by the sexual division of labor, is treated in the study by Gautier, *Solitude*.

85. See Debien, *Esclaves aux Antilles*, 205–9. Also in this vein, see the discussion of this notion as reinterpreted by the slaves in terms of their own vision of emancipation in Ch. 7.

86. Savine, *Saint-Domingue à la veille*, 94, n. 1. De Wimpffen's only comment was that this was the extent of their intelligence.

87. Debien, *Esclaves aux Antilles*, 156.

88. Moreau de Saint-Méry, *Loix et constitutions*, 6:657.

89. De Vaissière, *La société*, 172.

90. Cabon, *Histoire d'Haïti*, 2:537.

91. Ibid., 1:176.

92. Frossard, *La cause*, 1:341.

93. Cited in Savine, *Saint-Domingue à la veille*, 30.

94. Ibid., 30, n. 1.

95. Moreau de Saint-Méry, *Loix et constitutions*, 6:655–67.

96. Savine, *Saint-Domingue à la veille*, 63–64.

97. Cited in de Vaissière, *La société*, 183, n.2. The French used a more precise term for whipping—*tailler*, which means to cut, to hew, or to cut to pieces: "and, effectively, the whip gashed open (*entaillait*) the skin." De Vaissière, *La société*, 190. Gisler, *Esclavage*, 42.

98. De Vaissière, *La société*, 182–86. See particularly Moreau de Saint-Méry, *Loix et constitutions*, 1:421; 3:93; 6:659, 918–28.

99. See Gisler, *L'esclavage*, 42–43.

100. Moreau de Saint-Méry, *Loix et constitutions*, 2:337. Moreau comments that the ex-

cessive cruelty of the masters sometimes even necessitated decrees like the one of 1714 that absolved from all punishment a slave who, after having witnessed such cruelty, had fled and was caught in marronage. Ibid., 2:423.

101. All of the above examples are cited and amply documented in de Vaissière, *La société*, 190–94. Frossard, *La cause*, 1:335–42. Cabon, *Histoire d'Haïti*, 2:534–36. They are objectively presented, critiqued, and widely documented in Gisler, *L'esclavage*, 41–53, and are also cited and discussed in James, *Black Jacobins*, 12–14.

102. Moreau de Saint-Méry, *Loix et constitutions*, 1:421, 422. On slave marriages, see Debien, *Esclaves aux Antilles*, 260–63.

103. AN C9 A 115. Copie d'une lettre écrite de Saint-Domingue à M. le Cte de Langeron en date du 7 juin 1763.

104. In this vein, O. Patterson speaks of the slave ahistorically as a genealogical isolate and a "socially dead" person. *Slavery and Social Death*, 5ff. passim. On the question of the slave as property, however, see 21ff. The contradictions and complexities posed by the physical reality of the slave as a human being, on the one hand, and the property object of the master, on the other, are also exposed in Gisler, *L'esclavage*, 27–33.

105. The *Instructions* cover the last two decades preceding the revolution and date from the 1770s, excerpts of which are included in Debien, *Plantations et esclaves à Saint-Domingue* no. 3 (Dakar: Université de Dakar, Section d'Histoire, 1962), 117–31. The *Instructions* also provide clear and abundant insights into the various aspects of plantation organization as well as the particular role and relationship of the *commandeurs* to the mass of slaves.

106. Ibid., 119.

107. The full account of the Le Jeune case is presented in de Vaissière, *La société*, 186–88. It is also presented and its legal implications and contradictions critically treated in the context of Saint Domingue slave society by Gisler, *L'esclavage*, 117–27.

108. Moreau de Saint-Méry, *Loix et constitutions*, 6:655–67; 918–28. It does not appear that the ordinances of 1784 and 1785, though far-reaching in attempting to improve slaves' conditions, brought any changes to Article 30 of the 1685 Black Code, which disallowed a slave's testimony as legal evidence in court (ibid., 1:419–20). A 1738 decree did, however, accept the legality of a slave's testimony for lack of white witnesses if the slave was an essential witness, but the slave could not testify against his or her own master (ibid., 3:511–12). The rationale for denying the legality of a slave's testimony was that slaves were always as if in a state of war against the master and that, were their testimony received, masters could be brought to trial at will by the slaves and so become victims of false accusations. In Gisler, *L'esclavage*, 123.

109. Cited in Gisler, *L'esclavage*, 119–20.

110. De Vaissière, *La société*, 189.

111. Moreau de Saint-Méry, *Loix et constitutions*, 6:622. Moreau commented that slaves often preferred the death penalty than to become Executioners of High Justice as the price to pay to live. Ibid., 2:117–18. See also n. 14 in Appendix A.

112. See G. W. F. Hegel, *The Phenomenology of Mind*, trans. J. B. Baille (New York: Harper and Row, 1967), 237. For the full discussion of "lordship and bondage," the dialectics of which are far more complex than summarily and somewhat crudely suggested here, see ibid. 228–40.

113. On this issue, see the arguments raised by S. Mintz, *Caribbean Transformations*, 76–79.

114. Savine, *Saint-Domingue à la veille*, 147.

115. See J. Fouchard, *Les marrons du syllabaire* (Port-au-Prince: Imp. Henri Deschamps, 1953), 15–18.

116. In James, *Black Jacobins*, 18. See also G. Debien, "Gens de couleur libres et colons devant la Constituante," *RHAF* 4 (sept. 1950):228, n.50. For the decree suppressing publication of the work, see Moreau de Saint-Méry, *Loix et constitutions*, 6:805–6.

117. Many hypotheses exist as to the origins and formation of creole languages. The most plausible and generally accepted one, debunking the theory of pidgin origins, is that of a substratum. In the case of Haitian creole, the existence at a fairly early stage in Saint Domingue's development of a particular ethno-linguistic substratum, e.g., the Fon grouping, provided the basic structure for the formation of the language. Through the process of relexification it acquired its distinctive linguistic characteristics. It is this broad hypothesis that has served as a working model for a vast ongoing research project on the ethno-linguistic and historical origins of Haitian creole, conducted by Professor Claire Lefebvre, Département de Linguistique, Université du Québec à Montréal. See also the article by C. Lefebvre, "The Role of Relexification in Creole Genesis Revisited: The Case of Haitian Creole," (Proceedings of the Conference on Creole Genesis, Amsterdam, April 1985).

118. De Vaissière, *La société*, 178. See n. 120 below.

119. Moreau de Saint-Méry, *De la danse* (Philadelphia, 1796), 36. The integral text of this pamphlet, which is an extract from Moreau's "Répertoire des notions coloniales," written in 1789, is reproduced in J. Fouchard, *La méringue* (Montréal: Leméac, 1973), 161–98.

120. In the French Windward islands, principally Martinique and Guadeloupe, the *chica* was known simply as *calenda* (Moreau de Saint-Méry, *Description*, 1:64), whereas the dance specifically described by Moreau as the *calenda* in Saint Domingue (ibid., 63) perhaps more closely resembles a dance known as *bel-air* in the northern part of Martinique. For descriptions of the Martiniquean *calenda* (in all respects the same as the *chica* in Saint Domingue), as well as the *bel-air*, see Monique Desroches, "Les pratiques musicales," in *Historial Antillais*, ed. Jean-Luc Bonniol (Fort-de-France: Société Dajani, 1980), 492, 494.

121. Moreau de Saint-Méry, *De la danse*, 43–44.

122. Moreau de Saint-Méry, *Description*, 1:64.

123. On these points see M. Desroches, "La musique traditionnelle de la Martinique." Rapport de recherche (Montréal: Centre de Recherches Caraïbes, Université de Montréal, 1985), 98.

124. M. E. Descourtiltz, *Voyage d'un naturaliste en Haïti, 1799–1803* ([1809]; Paris: Plon, 1935), 125. See also Cabon, *Histoire d'Haïti*, 2:538.

125. Descourtiltz, *Voyage*, 126.

126. For a more detailed description of voodoo as religion, see the section that follows in this chapter.

127. Cited in Hénock Trouillot, *Introduction à une histoire du Vaudou* (Port-au-Prince: Imp. des Antilles, 1970), 84.

128. Although voodoo, strictly speaking, is a Dahomean religion [Vodu], the term as used throughout the present text, unless otherwise specified, will be understood to embrace the generality of the rites and religious practices of the diverse African cultures, the fundamental elements of which are essentially the same as in Dahomean Vodu: their animistic nature, the relationship between the gods and the land, the belief in the various divinities, or *loa*, as well as their personification, the existence of an all-powerful external Creator, the phenomenon of possession, animal sacrifices and communion, as well as the sacred qualities attributed to drums and dance. So whether one is actually dealing with rada, petro, congo, or other rites, the overall term of "voodoo," embracing the whole of these practices, will generally be used. In this vein, the anglicized spelling of "voodoo" will be used to distinguish these practices generally from the particularity of the Dahomean Vodu religion. For further clarification of the syncretism between Dahomean Vodu and other African cults in Saint Domingue see the section devoted to this phenomenon (esp. n. 63) in Ch. 2.

129. Also referred to as Don Pedro, Don Petro, or even Dompète. It is sometimes thought that the origins of petro rites in Haitian voodoo had their source here, thus providing a possible example of syncretism between the Dahomean cult and the later ones. On this point see Alfred Métraux, *Voodoo in Haiti*, trans. Hugo Chartiris (New York: Schocken Books, 1972), 39. Of particular interest in this respect is the discussion by anthropologist John M. Janzen of petro rites in Haitian voodoo and of the many possibilities of Old World Congo-Bantu religious carryovers, especially in the secretly celebrated Lemba-Petro rites of the Cul-de-Sac valley, as described by Jean Price-Mars in the 1930s. *Lemba, 1650–1930: A Drum of Affliction in Africa and the New World* (New York and London: Garland, 1982), 273–92.

130. Hénock Trouillot, *Introduction*, 46.

131. In addition to gunpowder mixed with clairin (raw or unrefined white rum), petro rites in Haiti are characterized by an iron bar or staff burning upright in charcoal. Katherine Dunham, *Island Possessed* (Garden City, N.Y.: Doubleday, 1969), 126. The symbolic significance of iron in Haitian petro rites is also noted by Serge Larose, "The Meaning of Africa in Haitian Vodu," in *Symbols and Sentiments*, ed. I.M. Lewiss (London: Academic Press, 1977), 111–12.

132. This blood pact was possibly of Dahomean origin. As practiced in ancient Dahomey, the Danhomênou would never confide secrets, provide mutual assistance, engage in important commercial affairs or covert plots, would never sacrifice themselves for another "unless they had first sworn their trust, discretion, sincerity, loyalty and devotion in contracting the blood pact." Moreover, this pact obligated those who partook to subordinate the interests of family and friends to those of the circle of "blood friends." Finally, far from producing the mysterious effect generally attributed to various potions, the blood pact created, rather, a spirit of unshakable solidarity, unlimited trust, and utmost discretion regarding agreements made in the name of the pact. Paul Hazoumé, *Le pact du sang au Dahomey* (Paris, Institut d'Ethnologie, 1937), Ch. 1. The blood pact also appears as a basic feature of the apparently Dahomean Vodu ceremony described and interpreted by Moreau de Saint-Méry in colonial Saint Domingue. *Description*, 1:66; cited in Ch. 2 below.

133. Voodoo, generally referred to as the worship of these deities, is a word of Dahomean origin [Vodu] meaning "spirit" or "god." Alfred Métraux, *Haiti: Black Peasants and Their Religion*, trans. Peter Lengyel (London: Harrap and Co., 1960), 59. Moreau de Saint-Méry also bears this out: "According to the Aradas [Dahomeans, generally] who are the true followers of *Vaudoux* in the colony and who maintain its principles and rules, *Vaudoux* signifies an all-powerful and supernatural being upon whom depends all of the events that come to pass on this globe." *Description*, 1:64.

134. Métraux, *Black Peasants and Their Religion*, 67. Katherine Dunham, who had begun her career in anthropology as a doctoral student under Melville Herskovits in the 1930s, and who subsequently devoted her life to professional dance, had become initiated into the Vodu cult in Haiti, as well as the animistic religions of Cuba and Brazil. Never having rejected her personal commitment to voodoo as an initiated adept—in spite of the overriding imperative of scientific objectivity as a researcher—she spoke of the influence and impact of these gods in her own life as "the driving forces of the will to seek one day after the next, [as the reason] why we go on when at times it seems unreasonable." *Island Possessed*, 111.

135. Métraux, *Black Peasants and Their Religion*, 67. As a contemporary observer, Moreau de Saint-Méry remarked that many of the requests made of the *Vaudoux* were centered around love triangles, money, good health, or a long life, but that "most of the participants asked for the ability to control the mind of their masters." *Description*, 1:66.

136. Métraux, *Black Peasants and Their Religion*, 82.

137. Ibid., 84.

138. Ibid., 89.

139. Ibid.

140. Even the Christian notion of a Supreme Being parallels the voodoo belief in the "Great Master" or "Good Lord," creator of the universe, whose force reigns above any and all of the *loa*. In voodoo, however, he is seen as a distant godhead, a vague kind of impersonal force to which humans and gods alike must yield. This "idea" of God more precisely corresponds to what is commonly referred to as fate, nature, or destiny. Ibid., 60.

141. Laënnec Hurbon, *Dieu dans le vaudou haïtien* (Paris: Payot, 1972), 77. In voodoo today, the Catholic saints rub shoulders quite freely with the *loa*, who are both subordinate to the voodoo godhead and members of the Catholic church. In the words of a Haitian peasant, related by Métraux, "one must be a Catholic to serve the *loa*." *Black Peasants and Their Religion*, 59.

142. Gabriel Debien, "Les cimetières à Saint-Domingue au XVIIIe siècle," *Conjonction* 105 (oct. 1967):31–33.

143. Cited in ibid., 32.

144. Cited in ibid., 33.

145. Ibid. Though the funeral celebrations were undeniably African, Moreau de Saint-Méry's descriptions, unfortunately, do not shed any light on the particular rites that may have determined their distinctive character. Evidence does show, at least, that slaves made no distinction between the baptized and the nonbaptized in burying their dead (34).

Chapter Two

1. Moreau de Saint-Méry, *Description*, 1:51. In fact, slaves never expressed the loss of a comrade through death by saying that the person died, but rather, *"ly allé,"* meaning that person has gone or left. Savine, *Saint-Domingue à la veille*, 94.

2. D'Auberteuil, *Considérations*, 1:141.

3. Cited in Mettas, *Répertoire*, 2:752.

4. Milscent, *Du régime colonial* (Paris: Imp. du Cercle Social, 1792), 26–27, 39. The above-cited passage was kindly forwarded to the author by J. Fouchard in personal correspondence.

5. Cited in Stein, *French Slave Trade*, 94.

6. Frossard, *La cause*, 1:263. For a description of conditions aboard the slave ships, see ibid., 261–306. See also Lucien Peytraud, *L'esclavage aux Antilles françaises avant 1789* (Paris: Hachette, 1897), 95–121, as well as Gaston-Martin, *Histoire de l'esclavage dans les colonies françaises* (Paris: PUF, 1948), 50–80, and, more recently, the exhaustive work of Jean Mettas on the eighteenth-century French slave trade, cited in Ch. 1, n. 59. Additionally, Stein's *French Slave Trade* provides a description of daily life aboard the ships, where the purely economic interests of the slaver to minimize loss of profit and to keep the greatest number of captives alive for the greatest length of time before arriving in the islands would guarantee, at least, minimum standards of health, hygiene, cleanliness, physical exercise, and psychological distraction from sheer boredom (101–3).

7. Frossard, *La cause*, 1:274–75. The inducement to death resulting from a refusal to eat, one of the symptoms of "fixed melancholy," was probably as much somatic as it was psychological. A recent study of Caribbean slavery from a biological and nutritional perspective has shown the interrelatedness between the slave's psychological and depressive "will to die" and outright nutritional starvation, which itself produces signs of personality derangement, including a refusal to eat. In fact, the reputation of Ibos as being the most prone to suicide among Africans may be related to their reputation of also being the most poorly nourished of

the West African groupings. Kenneth F. Kiple, *The Caribbean Slave: A Biological History* (Cambridge: Cambridge University Press, 1984), 63.

8. Savine, *Saint-Domingue à la veille*, 94.

9. Cited in de Vaissière, *La société*, 230.

10. AN, Arch. Col., C9 A 5. Lettre de M. de Gallifet . . . du 24 septembre 1701. Cited in de Vaissière, *La société*, 230.

11. D'Auberteuil, *Considérations*, 2:66, 70.

12. Descourtiltz, *Histoire des désastres*, 185. Also cited in de Vaissière, *La société*, 252, n. 3, and in Savine, *Saint-Domingue à la veille*, 91. One of the methods used was to insert a needle into a certain part of the baby's brain, thus causing severe jaw impediments and finally total incapacity. Unable to eat, the slave infant inevitably died in a matter of days. De Vaissière, *La société*, 252. The practice had apparently become serious enough for the Upper Council of le Cap to pass an ordinance in 1757 forbidding all women of color to practice midwifery. Lebeau, *De la condition*, 109.

13. De Vaissière claimed that infant mortality resulting from *mal de mâchoire* amounted roughly to one in three of all newborn slave children. *La société*, 252.

14. In Mettas, *Répertoire*, 2:223.

15. Stein, *French Slave Trade*, 103. In this vein, the actual number of slave revolts (like the actual frequency of other types of resistance) reported by ship captains in Mettas's *Répertoire* may well be far below reality. In roughly 3.5 to 5 percent of the more than 3,300 voyages inventoried by Mettas, some act or combination of diverse acts of resistance (e.g., revolt, marronage, suicide, etc.) occurred, but then this calculation, in all likelihood, is much too low. As Stein himself observed: "For each detailed description of a slave rebellion, there were several references to other revolts; for each uprising mentioned in passing, there were undoubtedly numerous forgotten challenges to white authority." *French Slave Trade*, 103. Moreover, even a brief analysis of Mettas's *Répertoire* reveals that over half of the combined total reports of resistance (of all types) were reports of slave revolts.

16. A narrative account of this revolt is cited in Fouchard, *Marrons de la liberté*, 467–69. In his book, Fouchard has provided an exhaustive chronological synopsis of slave resistance in Saint Domingue from 1499 to 1793 (445–557) based on primary, as well as secondary, source materials, passages from which are often quoted in full.

17. Presumably these would be considered "restorationist" movements in purely Genovesean terms since they were pre-eighteenth/nineteenth-century. See Introduction. But the fact that they did not succeed in destroying slavery and white slave society has more to do with the historical and material limitations of the period—as opposed to conditions in 1791— than with some intrinsically "restorationist" outlook.

18. An account of the Makandal conspiracy and a discussion of its implications follow in this chapter.

19. See n. 142 below and the discussion of marronage in the context of the August 1791 revolt in Ch. 4. Also, on the relationship of marronage to the revolutionary participation of the slaves in the West province, see Ch. 3.

20. See Debien, *Esclaves aux Antilles*, 465.

21. AN, Arch. Col., C9 A 131.

22. AN, Arch. Col., F3 94.

23. Cited in Fouchard, *Marrons de la liberté*, 482.

24. If the majority of the colonial maroons were African as opposed to creole, however, it should also be remembered that the vast majority of the total slave population in Saint Domingue was African-born.

25. Fouchard, *Marrons de la liberté*, 288–89. A breakdown of the maroon population

derived from archival and newspaper sources, and which considers such factors as age, sex, status, origins, occupations, and types and sizes of plantations from which slaves fled, is presented in ibid., 283–89; 373–78; 433–41.

26. De Vaissière, *La société*, 234–35.

27. Fouchard, *Marrons de la liberté*, 390.

28. By 1519, only twenty-seven years after Columbus's arrival, the Indian population of the island known to the Arawaks as Hayti, numbering roughly one million in 1492, had been ruthlessly reduced to a mere one hundred thousand. Ibid., 470. The history and struggles of the indigenous Indian population of Hispaniola is sympathetically rendered by Bartolomé de las Casas in his *History of the Indies* (ed. and trans. Andrée Collard, Torchbook Library [New York: Harper & Row, 1971]). The late nineteenth-century Haitian writer Emile Nau has written a fascinating two-volume study of these struggles, centering upon the confrontation of the *caciques*, or recognized rulers among the Arawak, with the conquering Spaniards. *Histoire des caciques d'Haïti*, 2 vols. (1894; reprint, Port-au-Prince: Editions Panorama, 1963).

29. Fouchard, *Marrons de la liberté*, 424.

30. AN, Arch. Col., C9 B 35. See n. 47 below.

31. In Moreau de Saint-Méry, *Loix et constitutions*, 2:25.

32. In fact, the first official report dealing with the problem of marronage among black slaves as a threat to the colony appeared in 1503, under the Spanish governor, Ovando, merely a decade after the arrival of Columbus. Fouchard, *Marrons de la liberté*, 464.

33. Moreau de Saint-Méry, *Loix et constitutions*, 2:36–37; 3:159–60.

34. Ibid., 2:27; 6:253, 528, 718.

35. Ibid., 3:728–29.

36. Cabon, *Histoire d'Haïti*, 1:206. Although it is impossible to ascertain the exact number of maroons in Saint Domingue at any given time, figures running into the thousands, including French slaves having fled into Spanish territory, do not seem entirely unrealistic. See, however, the brief discussion of the problem in D. Geggus, "Slave Resistance Studies and the Saint Domingue Revolt: Some Preliminary Considerations," Occasional Papers Series, no. 4 (Miami: Latin American and Caribbean Center, Florida International University, 1983), 6–7.

37. Moreau de Saint-Méry, *Loix et constitutions*, 5:142.

38. AN, Arch. Col., C9 B 15. The same year, M. Borthon, a former conselor to the king, went even further by proposing that all persons of color above twelve years of age be required to wear the identifying medallion. Those found without it would be condemned to prison for three months and fined twenty-five piastres. Those who lent their medallion to another slave would suffer whipping and be branded, in addition to a fifty-piastre fine. Men who repeated the offense would be sent to the galleys for life; women would lose their status as a free person. Arch. Col., C9 A 120.

39. Ibid. Diverse decrees forbidding slaves to be in possession of a horse date back to the 1690s, shortly after the armed revolt at Port-de-Paix in 1691, and recur throughout the eighteenth century. Moreau de Saint-Méry, *Loix et constitutions*, 1:622–23; 2:11, 660–61.

40. The practice had evidently become significantly widespread for colonial authorities to pass an ordinance forbidding the inscription of the title "*libre*" [free] on the baptismal certificates of children of the *affranchis* without due proof of the mother's freedom. Ibid., 5:802–3; 807–8.

41. AN, Arch. Col., C9 B 15.

42. AN, Arch. Col., C9 A 120.

43. The above-cited memoir of M. Borthon indicates: "One slave woman, maroon for two years and calling herself free, was recognized by chance and arrested. A *griffe* from Don-

don, maroon for three years, has just been recognized and arrested. One slave, a mason by trade and working publicly for fifteen years as a free black, has just been recognized as a slave. A cook, maroon for four to five years, has also recently been discovered, and a host of other examples like these which suffice to prove the abusive practice." Ibid. (In colonial terminology, a *griffe* was the offspring of a mulatto and a black.)

44. See the collection of articles in *Maroon Societies*, ed. Richard Price. On the Jamaican maroons see, in addition, Carey Robinson, *The Fighting Maroons of Jamaica* (Kingston?: William Collins and Sangster Ltd., 1974); Milton C. McFarlane, *Cudjoe of Jamaica: Pioneer for Black Freedom in the New World* (Short Hills, N.J.: Ridley Enslow Pub., 1977); R. C. Dallas, *The History of the Maroons*, 2 vols. (London: 1803; reprint, London: Frank Cass and Co., 1968); also, the article by Barbara Kopytoff, "The Early Political Development of Jamaican Maroon Societies," *William and Mary Quarterly* 35, ser. 3 (April 1978):287–307. On the maroons of Dutch Guyana, see also Morton C. Kahn, *Djuka: The Bush Negroes of Dutch Guiana* (New York: Viking, 1931).

45. See the articles by Aquiles Escalante, "Palenques in Columbia"; David M. Davidson, "Negro Slave Control and Resistance in Colonial Mexico, 1519–1650"; R. K. Kent, "Palmares: An African State in Brazil"; Stuart B. Schwartz, "The Mocambo: Slave Resistance in Colonial Bahia"; Roger Bastide, "The Other Quilombos"; Orlando Patterson, "Slavery and Slave Revolts: A Socio-historical Analysis of the First Maroon War: 1665–1740"; Johannes King, "Guerilla Warfare: A Bush Negro View"; and Capt. J. G. Stedman, "Guerilla Warfare: A European Soldier's View," in *Maroon Societies*, ed. R. Price.

46. This, in particular, is the opinion of Roger Bastide in his article cited above. One ought, however, to be wary of overgeneralizing the case, as does Genovese in his at-times cavalier analysis of marronage and slave revolt in *From Rebellion to Revolution*.

47. AN, Arch. Col., C9 B 36. Concernant les nègres marrons et leur refus de profiter de l'amnistie qui leur a été accordée, Port-au-Prince, 6 fév. 1786. Their adamant refusal is also related in: AN, Arch. Col., C9 A 160. Décret du roi d'Espagne concernant les nègres fugitifs de la Partie française de Saint-Domingue adressée à l'archevêque de cette isle, 23 mai 1787.

48. Moreau de Saint-Méry, *Loix et constitutions*, 2:25.

49. Ibid., 2:209–10.

50. Ibid., 2:568–69.

51. Ibid., 2:36–37.

52. While the 1705 ordinance designates the free blacks specifically in this respect, both the initial 1685 Code and a subsequent decree of 1726 use the term *affranchis*, presumably implying a potential loss of liberty to enfranchised mulattoes, as well. Ibid., 1:421; 3:159.

53. In fact, an ordinance of 1758 ordered slaves to be punished by whipping, and masters by a fine of three hundred livres, the former for having participated in, and the latter for having tolerated this slave dance. Trouillot, *Introduction*, 84. Needless to say, these laws were to no avail.

54. Ibid., 42, 48. See also by the same author "La guerre de l'indépendance d'Haïti: les grands prêtres du Vodou contre l'armée française," *Sobretiro de Revista de América* 72 (julio-dic., 1971):261–327. Along these lines, see the recent work by Pierre Pluchon, *Vaudou, sorciers, empoisonneurs: de Saint-Domingue à Haïti* (Paris: Karthala, 1987), where the author explores the diverse relationships between certain maroon leaders (notably Makandal), voodoo, and sorcery, generally, within the context of slave poisonings in eighteenth-century Saint Domingue society.

55. Trouillot, *Introduction*, 10–17. See esp. Fouchard, *Marrons de la liberté*, 188–89.

56. Ibid., 189.

57. Cited in Moreau de Saint-Méry, *Description*, 1:67; also cited in Mgr. J. Cuvelier,

L'ancien royaume de Congo (Brussels: Desclée de Brouwer, 1946), 290. The chant is also quoted from a contemporaneous passage and cited in "Notice historique sur la Communauté des religieuses filles de Notre-Dame du Cap Français (Saint-Domingue) fondée en 1733," *Lettre annuelle de l'Ordre de Notre Dame* (Bordeaux: Imp. B. Coussan et F. Constalet, 1889), 203. Excerpts from the "Notice historique" containing the chant are also quoted by Fouchard in *Marrons du syllabaire*, 39–40. See Ch. 4, n.64 below. The sometimes-cited translation (from Drouin de Bercy in the French) of "We swear to destroy the whites and all that they possess; let us die rather than fail to keep this vow," is highly inconsistent, literally speaking, with the original African words, and thus quite inaccurate. On this point, see Pluchon, *Vaudou*, 112, 114.

58. The author is most deeply grateful to anthropologist John M. Janzen for this translation (personal correspondence). Professor Janzen's knowledge of Kikongo was acquired over the many years he spent studying Congo coastal societies. It is the language used in the region where, from the beginning of the slave trade that caused such major disruptions in coastal African society, there developed an important, socially therapeutic and integrative "cult of healing, trade and marriage relations," known as Lemba, which sought to "calm" or mediate the tensions and conflicts brought about in this region by three centuries of slave trading. Janzen has studied, in great depth and with much perspicacity, the development and role of this cult (in its bio-social, political, economic, cultural, and humanistic dimensions) in response to these disruptive forces in his challenging and fascinating book, *Lemba, 1650–1930: A Drum of Affliction in Africa and the New World*. There are also many similarities between Lemba and the Haitian petro rites to which Janzen has devoted an entire chapter. See Ch. 1, n. 129 above.

59. Janzen, Personal Correspondence. Also, *Lemba*, 53. On the significance of "tying up" the elements composing a talisman, see also n. 88 below.

60. Janzen, Personal Correspondence. The present writer assumes responsibility, however, for any linguistic oversights or interpretive errors in judgment in attempting to explain the cultural significance and potentially "revolutionary" implications of this invocation in colonial Saint Domingue slave society. (While the word *mundele*, or "whiteman," is indeed derived from *mu* + *nlele*, or "person of cloth" [Janzen, personal correspondence], it should not be assumed [cf. Geggus, "Slave Resistance Studies," 16] that the colonial priests or the churches should have been objects of the slaves' vengeance at the outbreak of the revolt in 1791. The very first "whitemen" to come into contact with the African coastal peoples of the Kongo, it should be remembered, were Portuguese missionaries—Europeans, whites, and outsiders—and it was the "whiteman," the *mundele*, who transported them into bondage in the New World. In the context of the "Eh! Mbumba!" chant, *mundele* clearly refers to the white European masters, be they planters or traders.)

61. See the definition of *ndoki* as "sorcerer" or *kindoki* as "witchcraft" in Cuvelier, *Ancien royaume de Congo*, 88–89.

62. See Ch. 1, n. 133 above. Also, Moreau de Saint-Méry, *Description*, 1:64, 68. On the significance and predominance of "Guinée," as opposed to other rites in Haitian voodoo today, see S. Larose, "The Meaning of Africa." Also, Métraux, *Voodoo in Haiti*, 29.

63. Here, then, one distinguishes in voodoo both a horizontal and a vertical syncretism; that is, a syncretism between Dahomean Vodu and other African cults, as well as between voodoo (comprising the diverse whole of these cults) and Catholicism. (For this clarification, author acknowledges Serge Larose.) The reader is also referred to the discussion of this point in Fouchard, *Marrons de la liberté*, 187–89. In support of his arguments pointing to a multiplicity of African sources in Saint Dominguean voodoo, Fouchard cites the conclusions of a thesis by Lilas Desquiron de Heusch, "Evolution historique d'une religion africaine: le

Vodou" (Mémoire, Université libre de Bruxelles, 1967–68): "The heart of voodoo embraces and unifies in one and the same structure the whole wealth of the various cultures which maintained it. . . . The Dahomeans gave to voodoo its general framework, its structure; moreover, the Bantous [comprising several cultural groups] of central Africa . . . took this basic stimulus, enriched it and transformed it; in short, [they] provided the most significant input into Dahomean Vodu. Again, in the voodoo songs which evoke the gods of Africa, whether they be of the *rada* or *petro* rites, these gods are all part of a single invocation without the least concern for establishing the predominance of either Guinean or Bantou groupings."

64. See especially Fouchard, *Marrons de la liberté*, 187; Debien et al., "Origines," IFAN (*Bull.*) 29 (3–4):549–58; *Esclaves aux Antilles*, 466–67; Moreau de Saint-Méry, *Description*, 1:53.

65. Fouchard, *Marrons de la liberté*, 187.

66. See n. 54 above.

67. Moreau de Saint-Méry, *Description*, 1:66–67.

68. Ibid., 1:68–69.

69. M. de C., "Makandal, histoire véritable: extrait du *Mercure de France* 15 septembre 1787," RSHHGG 20 (janv. 1949):21–22. Also Madiou, *Histoire d'Haïti*, 1:35; Trouillot, *Introduction*, 46.

70. It is nearly impossible to know precisely to which nation Makandal belonged, since nearly the entire west coast of Africa was loosely referred to at that time as "Guinea." There is, however, the place name of Ma Kanda, or Makanda, the chief village of the Loango kingdom, a part of the ancient Congo. (See Mgr. J. Cuvelier, *Documents sur une mission française au Kakongo, 1766–1776*, Institut Royal Colonial Belge. Mémoires, vol. 1, 96–97 and map.) Although it would be tempting to try to link the origins of the Saint Dominguean maroon leader with this place, or at any rate with the surrounding region, such a linkage would still be little more than pure conjecture. Curiously, though, one finds other place names, such as that of the adjacent kingdom of Iomba, a dependency of Loango (incorrectly spelled Maïomba, or Maïombe, and then Mayombe by eighteenth-century geographers, when in fact Maïomba meant "king of Iomba"). The kingdom called Mayombe also appears among the pantheon of nations in a voodoo chant (Fouchard, *Marrons de la liberté*, 189); we know, as well, that one of Makandal's two chief associates was called Mayombé (n. 121 below), but then this was not necessarily an uncommon slave name. Without solid evidence, all of this remains speculative, nevertheless one might hazard a suggestion that, rather than "Guinea," which usually referred to the middle to upper west coast of Africa, Makandal, this messianic-type leader of slaves, may actually have come from the Congo-Angola region. Also, according to an early fifteenth-century Portuguese writer: "*Le pays du Congo, c'est en Guinée.*" Cuvelier, *Ancien royaume de Congo*, 44. Moreau de Saint-Méry observed, moreover, that among the Congolese catholicized by the Portuguese were some who also retained ideas of "Mohametanism" and "idolatry." *Description*, 1:53.

71. Cited in Fouchard, *Marrons de la liberté*, 492.

72. M. de C., "Histoire véritable," 22–23.

73. AN, Arch. Col., C9^B 29. Extrait d'un mémoire sur la création d'un corps de gens de couleur levé à Saint-Domingue, mars 1779.

74. Ibid.

75. M. de C., "Histoire véritable," 24.

76. Ibid.

77. AN, Arch. Col. C9^B 29. Extrait d'un mémoire. ISL, Relation d'une conspiration tramée par les nègres dans l'isle de Saint-Domingue, n.d. [1758?]. Moreau de Saint-Méry, *Description*, 2:629–31. Also, AN, Arch. Col. F^3 136. Moreau de Saint-Méry, "Notes his-

toriques," 198, cited in Fouchard, *Marrons de la liberté*, 495–97. M. de C., "Histoire véritable."

78. AN, Arch. Col. C9 B 29. Extrait d'un mémoire.

79. M. de C., "Histoire véritable," 24–25

80. In his discussion of marronage and the Saint Domingue revolution, Genovese does not actually state this, but circumvents his own typologies by saying simply that, in the case of Saint Domingue, restorationism gave way to the modern or revolutionary phase of slave resistance, with no analysis of the transformation (*Rebellion to Revolution*, 85). Was Makandal, then, a restorationist or a revolutionary? Surely, in the 1750s, he predated the latter eighteenth-century Age of Revolution. He was African-born and possibly, but not incontrovertibly, of the Moslem faith, and surely a practitioner of animistic African cult beliefs. Yet his ultimate aim, though historically premature and expressed as a primitive consciousness, was, like Toussaint's in his time, the creation of an independent black state. It is somewhat of a pity that Genovese felt, in discussing the historical turning point in hemispheric slave rebellion, that the Saint Domingue revolution need concern us "only in its bare outlines." For by conflating Makandal (a Muslim), then Boukman (a Vodûn priest), with the other leaders of the "modern" Saint Domingue revolution who came from the privileged slave strata (as if Makandal and Boukman did not), Genovese confounds his own typologies and is hardly immune from the dangers of sweeping historical assumptions. If anything, the sheer complexity of the Saint Domingue revolution should remind us that schematic historical interpretation, no matter how justifiable, cannot simply replace the evidential material of history, for the latter may, in the end, force us to reconsider and reformulate the former.

81. No doubt there were among these the "occasional" or "small" maroons who left their quarters at night or for a few days, but with the motive of procuring certain quantities of poison or of maintaining contacts on other plantations. Whether they were consciously aware of it or not, they may well have been participants in the general scheme conceived and propagated by Makandal (see, in this light, Appendix A, n. 3 and n. 4 below). This would render somewhat invidious the distinction that is often made between *grand* marronage and *petit* marronage, as well as the excessive need to compartmentalize in strictly defined categories such a resilient, variable, and interrelating phenomenon.

82. De Vaissière, *La société*, 237.

83. AN, Arch. Col., F3 136. Moreau de Saint-Méry, "Notes historiques," 198, cited in de Vaissière, *La société*, 237, and in Fouchard, *Marrons de la liberté*, 495.

84. AN, Arch. Col. C9 B 29. Extrait d'un mémoire.

85. Ibid.

86. He was denounced by a slave (or by several slaves) while attending a calenda on the Dufresne plantation in Limbé. While Madiou claims he was discovered by means of a trap set by some slaves whose women Makandal had stolen (1:36; also, M. de C., "Histoire véritable," 27–28), Moreau de Saint-Méry simply states that "a young male slave, perhaps taken by the impression of this colossal presence," warned the surveyor and the owner's father-in-law, M. Trévan, who thereupon gave out plenty of tafia to everyone and then captured Makandal (2:630). A third version, in a letter dated June 1758 (ISL, Relation.), claims that it was a female slave (Assam, see present chapter, below, and Appendix A) who "provided the means by which to capture Makandal who was their leader."

87. Having convinced his followers that he was immortal, Makandal had once declared that if ever the whites captured him, it would be impossible for them to kill him, for upon breathing his final breath, he would escape in the form of a mosquito, only to return one day more terrifying than ever. AN, Arch, Col., C9 B 29. Extrait d'un mémoire.

88. Trouillot, *Introduction*, 45. Pluchon has provided a detailed contemporary descrip-

tion of the preparation and utilization of "makandals" as talismen by the slaves at the time of Makandal (*Vaudou*, 211 ff.). Effectively, the preparation of a makandal involves the tying up of various symbolic elements into a small packet, thereby tying up, or containing within the packet, the evil against which one intends to be protected. This "tying up" of a makandal is much the same as the tying up of a *nkisi*, as suggested in the translation (cited in present chapter above) of the voodoo chant: "*Eh! eh! Mbumba. Canga* [tie up] *bafio té. Canga* [tie up] *moune dé lé. Canga* [tie up] *do ki la. Canga li* [tie them up]." Thus the more literal and frequently-cited translation of the word *canga* to mean merely stop, or even exterminate: *arrête* or *arrêtez* (in Pluchon, *Voudou*, 89n, and in Cuvelier, *Ancien royaume*, 290) would render only a partial and protracted meaning.

89. ISL, Relation. It should be noted that, alongside the *commandeurs*, domestic slaves also played an organizing role in the August 1791 uprising. See Ch. 4 and Appendix B.

90. The remainder consisted of seventy-eight more, as many arrested as maroons as for other diverse crimes; one slave from Martinique for passing as a free black; two accused of attempting to murder a white master—one a slave, one a free black; one slave accused of homicides; one free black accused of stealing a horse; five slaves accused of stealing farm animals, and a handful of English prisoners of war. AN, Arch. Col., C9 A 102. See Appendix A.

91. D'Auberteuil, *Considérations*, 1:137–38, n. 2. D'Auberteuil, however, discounts a conspiracy against the whites as a motive for the distribution and uses of poison by blacks and reduces the whole explanation to a question of personal vengence on the part of the perpetrators.

92. Translated and edited by author in Appendix A.

93. This act may have been a version of any of a number of typical blood pacts (or friendship pacts) practiced throughout Africa, the purpose of which was to sanctify friendship and solidarity. The ram's horn, obviously, served as a talisman.

94. Antoine Gisler describes typical torture methods used on slaves being put to "the question" in *Esclavage*, 43. See also the description of methods used in interrogating slaves in the section on torture and punishment in Ch. 1.

95. ISL, Relation. See n. 86 above.

96. See Appendix A.

97. On the attitudes and activities of the Jesuits in Saint Domingue, at times resembling a form of passive resistance, and especially on the question of marronage, see Debien, *Esclaves aux Antilles*, 282–87, 295; Gisler, *Esclavage*, 176–79, 189; Fouchard, *Marrons de la liberté*, 500–3; also Fouchard, *Marrons du syllabaire*, 89–93.

98. Gisler, *Esclavage*, 177–78; Debien, *Esclaves aux Antilles*, 284–86.

99. In Fouchard, *Marrons de la liberté*, 505.

100. Excerpts of these sermons (in AN, Arch. Col., F3 90, Règlement de discipline pour les nègres adressé aux curés dans les isles françaises de l'Amérique, n.p., n.d. [1776?]) are printed in Fouchard, *Marrons du syllabaire*, 45–46. See also by the same author *Marrons de la liberté*, 503, and Gisler, *Esclavage*, 187.

101. See de Vaissière, *La société*, 240–42. In order to determine whether the substances found in the possession of slaves arrested for poisoning were actually lethal, authorities "tested" them out on other imprisoned slaves whom they used as guinea pigs. AN, Arch. Col., C9 A 101. 27 February 1758.

102. Debien, *Esclaves aux Antilles*, 402.

103. AN, Arch. Col., C9 A 102. 6 April 1758.

104. ISL, Relation.

105. Ibid.

106. AN, Arch. Col., C9 A 101. 30 June 1758.

107. On the potential for the division of slave families in inheritance cases prompting motives for poisoning, see the points raised concerning violence and property rights in Ch. 1.

108. AN, Arch. Col., C9 A 115. 7 June 1763.

109. See de Vaissière, *La société*, 245.

110. AN, Arch. Col., C9 A 102.

111. Appendix A.

112. AN, Arch. Col., C9 A 102.

113. AN, Arch. Col., C9 A 100. 12 December 1757.

114. ISL, Relation. An extract of this letter is included in its editor's postscript.

115. Ibid.

116. De Vaissière, *La société*, 249.

117. Ibid.

118. Ibid., 250–51. In this sense, poison could be used both as an offensive and as a defensive weapon.

119. In reference to these slaves, James wrote in 1938: "An uninstructed mass feeling its way to revolution usually begins by terrorism, and Mackandal aimed at delivering his people by means of poison." *Black Jacobins*, 21.

120. AN, Arch. Col., C9 A, 100.

121. One letter dated 30 June 1758 from Port-au-Prince cites four leaders in all, but does not mention their names (AN, Arch. Col., C9 A, 101), while another, written on 6 April 1758 from Port-de-Paix, states that there were two leaders, old Negroes who had been maroons for many years and whose names were Makandal and Tassereau (AN, Arch. Col., C9 A 102). Trouillot states that Makandal's closest and best-known accomplices were Teysselo and Mayombé (*Introduction*, 47; from M. de C., "Histoire véritable," 24). Makandal's first associate could also have been the slave Jean, belonging to Tesseriau, known to be "an even greater poisoner than Makandal, who, after a falling out between the two, retired with his family to the mountains behind le Cap, where he was captured (deposition of the seneschal Courtin, cited in Pluchon, *Vaudou*, 217). Moreau de Saint-Méry, in accordance with the first letter cited above, states that there were four leaders, Makandal and three principal accomplices (*Description*, 2:631), but whether or not Médor may have been the fourth principal leader is not clear. However, having pursued the research on the Makandal phenomenon much further, Pluchon seems to have confirmed direct ties between Makandal and Médor and certainly considers Médor a "*macandaliste*" (*Vaudou*, 165–223 passim). He has also uncovered court interrogations, government reports, and procès verbaux, which, in addition to Médor, concern other principal slaves, whose identity is certain and are either mentioned in Assam's interrogation or imprisoned along with her and Pompée and listed in the 9 November 1757 le Cap prison record (Appendix A): Marie-Jeanne and Nanon, belonging to Sieur Chiron; René, belonging to Gallifet; Horou [Haurou], belonging to de la Coursière; Lisette, denounced by Sieurs Vallet, Deseuttres [des Gentres?], and Dufaut.

122. Cited in de Vaissière, *La société*, 247. On the participation of free blacks, see le Cap prison report in Appendix A.

123. AN, Arch. Col., C9 B 15. Mémoire sur les poisons qui règnent à Saint-Domingue. D'Auberteuil, *Considérations*, 1:137, n. 1. Lespinasse, *Histoire des affranchis*, 271–72. See also de Vaissière, *La société*, 246–47. Pluchon also argues against an interpretation that would ascribe to Makandal motives of eventual collective liberation, or even independence, and sees such an interpretation as the result of the hysterical imagination of certain contemporary observers. However, he dismisses such motives "for the simple reason that no insurrection ever occured before that of 1791" (*Vaudou*, 182). Yet, revolutionary change, as

is so often the case, may well be preceded by decades of structural stability in which visionaries are rarely taken seriously, if they are not taken for complete fools, by the established order.

124. In fact, Makandal had been arrested and sentenced on charges relating neither to his marronage nor to a general conspiracy against the whites, but rather "for having mixed holy artifacts with the use of reputedly magic packets to cast evil spells and, in addition, for having composed, sold, and distributed poisons of all kinds." Lespinasse, *Histoire des affranchis*, 272.

125. Ibid. Also, Cabon, *Histoire d'Haïti*, 1:228.

126. Lespinasse, *Histoire des affranchis*, 272.

127. See de Vaissière, *La société*, 238–39.

128. Cabon, *Histoire d'Haïti*, 1:251–52.

129. AN, Arch. Col., C9 B 15. Extrait des registres du Conseil Supérieur de Port-au-Prince. Saint-Domingue, 1764.

130. Moreau de Saint-Méry, *Loix et constitutions*, 5:805; 6:257–58, 429.

131. Ibid., 6:75–78.

132. De Vaissière, *La société*, 186, n. 2. In 1783, two of Le Jeune's slaves also assassinated his nephew. Moreau de Saint-Méry *Loix et constitutions*, 6:370.

133. Ibid., 5:741, 744, 906; 6:623–25, 640.

134. Ibid., 5:551.

135. Ibid.

136. Ibid., 5:800. Also Geggus, "Slave Resistance Studies," 7.

137. Fouchard, *Marrons de la liberté*, 406–7. In answer to historians who disclaim an increase in marronage, Fouchard has pointed out that what decreased was not necessarily marronage, but simply the number of reports of fugitive slaves in newspapers and journals. The entire discussion of this problem is dealt with at some length in ibid. (257–69), but is also critically treated by Geggus in "Slave Resistance Studies," 6–7.

138. Cited in de Vaissière, *La société*, 230.

139. Moreau de Saint-Méry, *Description*, 1:275–76. See also the observations of a colonist from Marmelade cited in Fouchard, *Marrons de la liberté*, 522–23. Curiously, the use of iron objects is also an essential symbolic element in the petro rites of voodoo. See Ch. 1, n. 131 above. In 1782, a *commandeur* also accused of holding nightly assemblies and spreading "superstition" was arrested and sentenced. Moreau de Saint-Méry, *Loix et constitutions*, 6:252.

140. Cabon, *Histoire d'Haïti*, 2:452.

141. Ibid., 2:453.

142. Geggus, "Slave Resistance Studies," 10. See also Fouchard, *Marrons de la liberté*, 526–27. Where Geggus agrees that "a connection can be established between the revolutionary leadership and an experience of marronage," especially in reference to Boukman and Jean-François, he nevertheless expresses doubt that marronage was directly related to the outbreak of the 1791 revolt by asserting that the two leaders were not associated with already established, separately constituted bands: "It very much seems that [the revolution] was organized from within the system and not from outside it" (10). Although these are only preliminary considerations, one does find here again the fixed notion that the only maroons worthy of the definition were those who formed independent bands. It seems rather an oversimplification to assume that fugitive slaves (and Geggus offers some evidence that Boukman and Jean-François were apparently often fugitive) were not true maroons simply because they did not belong to a maroon band; or that maroons did not return to the plantations and become slaves again (were they ever anything else?); or that on subsequent occasions they would not once

again take flight. These short periods of marronage (possibly for motives manifestly different from those which habitually characterized *petit* marronage in the colonial period) may in the long run have proved more effective an organizational tool for preparing a revolt than the existence of external autonomous bands. The evidence permitting, it seems equally plausible that the 1791 revolt was organized *both* from within *and* from outside the system. In fact, Makandal, who nevertheless *was* an independent maroon with a band of followers, always worked in close connection with slaves inside the plantation system, many of whom were often occasional maroons. This was his mainstay as well as his distinguishing feature as a maroon leader (see n. 81 above, and especially the testimony of the slave Harou, a distributor of poison, and the association that Pluchon himself derives from the evidence between poisoning and occasional marronage [*Vaudou*, 191, 193]; also Appendix A, n. 11).

143. Cited in Fouchard, *Marrons de la liberté*, 524.

144. In Begouën-Demeaux, *Mémorial d'une famille du Havre: 1743–1831*, 4 vols. (Le Havre: M. Etaix, 1957), 2:137.

Chapter Three

1. Blanche Maurel, *Cahiers de doléances de la colonie de Saint-Domingue pour les Etats-Généraux de 1789* (Paris: E. Leroux, 1933), 101.

2. Cited in Deschamps, *Les colonies*, 69. This entire debate is graphically presented in P. Boissonade, *Saint-Domingue à la veille de la révolution et la question de la représentation coloniale aux Etats-Généraux* (Paris: Paul Geuthner, 1906), 233–73.

3. Ruth Necheles, *The Abbé Grégoire, 1787–1831: The Odyssey of an Egalitarian* (Westport, Conn.: Greenwood, 1971), 59.

4. Although staunchly opposed to the representation of colonial interests in France, the fundamental goals of the Massiac Club were no different from those of the Saint Domingue colonists, i.e., the preservation of a slave-based economy and system of production, the stabilization of their landholdings, and the continued growth of profits. So, with common economic interests the two groups remained politically divided on the problem of strategy. Blanche Maurel, *Saint-Domingue et la Révolution française: les représentants des colons en France de 1789 à 1795* (Paris: PUF, 1943), 2. Debien, *Les colons*, 151.

5. Debien, "Gens de couleur libres," *RHAF* 4 (déc. 1950): 419.

6. Pauléus Sannon, *Histoire de Toussaint L'Ouverture*, 3 vols. (Port-au-Prince: A⌠ Héraux, 1920), 1:40. Deschamps, *Les colonies*, 83. Lespinasse, *Histoire des affranchis*, 1:305.

7. Necheles, *Abbé Grégoire*, 63–64.

8. Deschamps, *Les colonies*, 80.

9. Debien, *Les colons*, 192. Deschamps, *Les colonies*, 91–92. Debien, "Gens de couleur libre," *RHAF* 4 (mars 1951): 540.

10. Deschamps, *Les colonies*, 95, 176.

11. Gabriel Debien, *Esprit colon et esprit d'autonomie à Saint-Domingue au XVIIIe siècle*, 2d ed. (Paris: Larose, 1954), 46.

12. Maurel, *Saint-Domingue et la Révolution française*, 3.

13. Sannon, *Histoire de Toussaint*, 1:64.

14. Pamphile de Lacroix, *Mémoire pour servir à l'histoire de la révolution de Saint-Domingue*, 2d ed., 2 vols. (Paris: Pillet aîné, 1820), 1:32.

15. In Sannon, *Histoire de Toussaint*, 1:46.

16. Ibid., 66–67.

17. Cited in Maurel, *Cahiers de doléances*, 113. Also cited in Debien, *Les colons*, 194.

18. Maximilien Robespierre, *Oeuvres de Maximilien Robespierre*, eds. M. Bouloiseau, G. Lefebvre, A. Soboul, 10 vols. (Paris: PUF, 1930–1967), 7:362–63. A full discussion of Robespierre's famous "perish the colonies" speech, as well as a presentation of the numerous deformations it underwent at the hands of his opponents, both contemporary and subsequent, is found in the appendix to Léon Deschamp's *Les colonies*. Although a champion of mulatto rights, Robespierre was no abolitionist. See George Rudé's *Robespierre: Portrait of a Revolutionary Democrat* (New York: Viking, 1975), 140, 210; and James's *Black Jacobins*, 76–77, 141.

19. Félix Carteau, *Soirées bermudiennes* (Bordeaux: 1802), 77. See also the recent dissertation by Julius S. Scott, *The Common Wind: Currents of Afro-American Communication in the Era of the Haitian Revolution* (Ann Arbor, Mich.: University Microfilms, 1989).

20. In 1788, the marquis de Najac wrote to La Luzerne, minister of the marine and former governor of Saint Domingue (1786–1787), concerning the state of marronage in the colony: "During your administration, over four thousand slaves fled into Spanish territory; since your departure, the Spanish hardly returned any of them, and I am convinced that there are now six thousand in the Spanish colony." AN, Arch. Col., C9 B 39. See also Ch. 2, n. 137 above.

21. In Begouën-Demeaux, *Mémorial*, 2:135, 137.

22. AN, DXXV 46, 432. Copies de différentes lettres sur les événements de Saint-Domingue extraites de la gazette anglaise et transmises à Paris, Kingston. Extrait d'une lettre du Port-au-Prince en date du 20 août 1791. The above account is based on information contained in this letter. Garran-Coulon also presents an account of this incident in his *Rapport sur les troubles de Saint-Domingue*, Commission des Colonies, 4 vols. (Paris: Imp. nationale, 1797–99), 2:215.

Chapter Four

1. Documents and discussion of the events up to and surrounding 22 August 1791 are presented in Appendix B. Diverse elements in the present chapter are taken from the documents contained in Appendix B and in C. Fick, "The Black Masses in the San Domingo Revolution" (Ph.D. diss., Concordia University, 1979).

2. Beaubrun Ardouin, *Etudes sur l'histoire d'Haïti*, 11 vols., ed. F. Dalencourt (Port-au-Prince, 1958), 1:51; also, Sannon, *Histoire de Toussaint*, 1:88.

3. Jean Fouchard, Gabriel Debien, and M.-A. Menier, "Toussaint Louverture avant 1789," *Conjonction* 134 (juin 1977):65–80.

4. On the links between royalists and the slave insurrection, see Gérard Laurent, *Quand les chaînes volent en éclats* (Port-au-Prince: Imp. Deschamps, 1979), 42–46.

5. In "Notice historique," 204. Hypothetically, the word *Zamba* as cited in the "Notice historique" may be a phonetic transcription of the Congolese word *Samba* meaning, among other things, praetor; leader; commander; or, as a verb, to pray (to); to worship; adore. J. Van Wing and C. Penders, trans. and ed. *Le plus ancien dictionnaire bantu* (Louvain: Imp. Kuyl-Otto, 1928), 23. *Samba* also means "to cross over" or "transcend." Janzen, *Lemba*, 196. The writer of the "Notice historique" offers as a translation of *Zamba*: "professional poet" or "strolling musician" (*ménétrier*), 204.

6. The term *voodoo* is used here to reflect the overall composite realities of African religious cult practices in Saint Dominguean slave culture, as described in Ch. 1, n. 128, and in Ch. 2. Further discussion of the role of voodoo in the Bois-Caïman ceremony and of the preparations for the revolt is pursued in Appendix B.

7. Sannon, *Histoire de Toussaint*, 1:89.

8. Translated by author from Sannon's French translation of the creole in ibid. The very first citing of this speech at the Bois-Caïman assembly is found in Hérard Dumesle's *Voyage dans le Nord d'Haïti* (Les Cayes: Imp. du Gouvernement, 1824, 88), which was the source for its reproduction by Victor Schoelcher in *Colonies étrangères et Haïti* (2 vols. [Pointe-à-Pitre: Desormeaux, 1973], 2:99), written in 1843. The "Good Lord" or, in creole, *Bon Dlé*, invoked by Boukman may well characterize the notion of a distant supreme being "hidden in the clouds" that is generally central to nearly all African cult religions. But see the further discussion of the questions and problems raised by this speech in Appendix B.

9. In "Notice historique," 204–5.

10. Of the various accounts of the meeting and the ceremony, see Geggus's discussion in "Slave Resistance Studies," 18. Antoine Dalmas (*Histoire de la révolution de Saint-Domingue*, 2 vols. [Paris: Mame frères, 1814]), the first, if not the only, directly contemporary historian to mention the Bois-Caïman ceremony (presumably writing in 1793), does not make reference to a priestess or to Boukman, as Geggus rightly points out; Dalmas does, however, mention the ritual killing of a sacrificial black pig (1:117), a symbol of discretion in Métraux's opinion, since he proves himself not inquisitive by seldom looking to the sky. *Voodoo in Haiti*, 42–43. The black pig is usually associated with petro rites.

11. In Fouchard, *Marrons de la liberté*, 528. First cited by Etienne Charlier in *Aperçu*, 49.

12. See the description of petro rites in Ch. 1, and their relation to the Bois-Caïman ceremony in Appendix B.

13. In Geggus, "Slave Resistance Studies," 10.

14. AN, DXXV 3, 31. Précis historique de la révolution de Saint-Domingue, 9. Cited in Appendix B.

15. On the significance of *petit* marronage, see Ch. 2, n. 142.

16. AN, DXXV 66, 667. L'Assemblée Coloniale de la partie française de Saint-Domingue à l'Assemblée Nationale, 3 nov. 1791. (See n. 19 below.)

17. In Dalmas, *Histoire de la révolution*, 1:116. On the role of these, see also n. 111 below. The slave Ignace probably held the semifree status known in the French colonies as *liberté de savanne*.

18. "St. Domingo Disturbances," *Philadelphia Aurora*, 11 Oct. 1791. From a journal kept there; entry for 4 Sept. 1791. (The first part of the journal, ending with the entry for 31 Aug. 1791, is also published in Boston, *Independent Chronicle and Universal Advertiser*, 20 Oct. 1791.) On the role of Jean-Baptiste Cap, see the documents presented further in the present chapter relating to the projected attack on le Cap for 25 August.

19. AN, DXXV 56, 550. Discours fait à l'Assemblée Nationale le 30 novembre 1791 par MM. les commissaires de l'Assemblée Générale de la partie française de Saint-Domingue. (Concerning the various references to this document see Appendix B, n. 3.) In the original manuscript draft, the slave's name is clearly written throughout the document as Paul Blin, although in its printed form, the name is written first as Blin and later, in reference to the incident regarding the Baillon family (see p. 108 below), as Belin. He is also sometimes referred to as the slave Paul à Belin, presumably belonging to the Belin estate in Limbé. Extract of a letter from Cape Français of 2 November received by the brig James, Capt. Row . . . , Boston, *Independent Chronicle and Universal Advertiser*, 8 Dec. 1791. Also AN, DXXV 78, 772. Liste des sucreries incendiées à Saint-Domingue dont on a eu connaissance jusqu'au 30 septembre 1791, n.d. (oct. 1791?). The correct spelling of the name might be the latter of the two.

20. One must remember that the usual procedure for interrogating a slave "caught in the act," so to speak, or even suspected of having committed a serious crime, was a trial by torture. It is likely that the case of François, as of the Desgrieux *commandeur*, was no different. The rapidity of the attack, however, the coordination of their activities, and the methodical

movement of the slaves from plantation to plantation is proof in itself of the secrecy and loyalty of the slaves who organized and carried out the insurrection in its first days.

21. Gabriel Debien has stated in his book *Les esclaves aux Antilles françaises* that no study has yet been made of the origins, the chronology, or the geographic development of the August 1791 insurrection (468). The above presentation, as well as Appendix B, is a modest and, given the limited number of testimonies and eyewitness accounts, unfortunately only a partial, attempt at reconstructing and providing a schematic record of what actually happened and how. The map illustration (Map 2) attempts to visually represent the overall strategy of the rebel slaves, but obviously, many pieces to the puzzle are still missing. See also C. Fick, "The Black Masses in the San Domingo Revolution."

22. AN, DXXV 78, 772. AA 148. La partie du Nord, paroisse de l'Acul. DXXV 78, 772. AA 183. Deposition dated le Cap, 27 Sept. 1791. DXXV 56, 550. Discours.

23. AN, DXXV 46, 432. Copies. M. Tausias à M. Camuzat, le Cap, 1 sept. 1791.

24. The Caignet and Busson plantations. AN, DXXV 78, 772. AA 183. Deposition, le Cap, 27 Sept. 1791. DXXV 78, 772. AA 148. Partie du Nord. DXXV 78, 772. KK 175. La paroisse de l'Acul, signed M. Caignet. Caignet's plantation was burned, in any event, at some point before the end of the following month. DXXV 78, 772. Liste des sucreries incendiées, n.d. (oct. 1791?). The *ateliers* leading the revolt in Acul were those of the Molines, Flaville, Plaigne, Sacanville, and Pillat plantations. DXXV 78, 772. KK 175. La paroisse de l'Acul.

25. "St. Domingo Disturbances," Boston, *Independent Chronicle and Universal Advertiser*, 20 Oct. 1791. Entry for 23 Aug. 1791.

26. AN, DXXV 78, 772. KK 178. Renseignements sur la position actuelle du Limbé, le Cap, 7 oct. 1791.

27. "A letter from James Perkins, Esq., resident at Cape François, 9 Sept. 1791," Boston, *Independent Chronicle and Universal Advertiser*, 20 Oct. 1791.

28. Ibid.

29. AN, DXXV 78, 772. KK 179. Paroisse de Port-Margot, signed by Traynier and Palmis, n.d. (Sept.–Oct. 1791?).

30. Ibid.

31. AN, DXXV 78, 772. KK 161. Plaisance, signed Manan, fils, Ch. Escot, A. Touvaudais, le Cap, 27 Sept. 1791.

32. Ibid. Also, DXXV 47, 443. M. de Blanchelande à M. le président du Congrès de l'Amérique, le Cap, 24 août 1791.

33. "St. Domingo Disturbances," Boston, *Independent Chronicle and Universal Advertiser*, 20 Oct. 1791. Also, "Letter from James Perkins, Esq., resident at Cape François," in ibid.; DXXV 46, 432. Copies. M. de Blanchelande à M. Bertrand, Ministre de la Marine, le Cap, 2 sept. 1791. MM. Foäche, Pierre Morange, et Hardivilliers du Cap en date du 25 sept. 1791 à MM. Foäche, frères, du Havre. Lettre de M. Nicoleau, habitant de Saint-Domingue, le Cap, 3 sept. 1791. M. Tausias, négociant du Cap et habitant de la plaine du Nord à Mme. Camuzat, 1 sept. 1791.

34. Dalmas, *Histoire de la révolution*, 1:116–21. AN, DXXV 56, 550. Discours. See also, Geggus, "Les esclaves de la plaine du Nord à la veille de la Révolution française," RSHH 144 (sept. 1984):25, 36. While Dalmas places the date of the incident on the twentieth, Geggus fixes it on the twenty-first.

35. See Geggus, "Les esclaves de la plaine," RSHH 144:24–36.

36. Ibid., 32.

37. AN, DXXV 56, 550. Discours. Geggus, "Les esclaves de la plaine," RSHH 144:36. Dalmas, on the other hand, erroneously attributes Odeluc's assassination to another slave, Mathurin, "the fiercest of them all." *Histoire de la révolution*, 1:123.

38. Sannon, *Histoire de Toussaint*, 1:91.

39. "Insurrection of the Negroes in the West Indies," Boston, *Independent Chronicle and Universal Advertiser*, 22 Sept. 1791.

40. Dalmas, *Histoire de la révolution*, 1:123–24.

41. "St. Domingo Disturbances," *Philadelphia Aurora*, 10–11 Oct. 1791. Entry for 24 Aug. 1791.

42. Ibid. Entry for 25 Aug. 1791.

43. Ibid. Entry for 6 Sept. 1791.

44. AN, DXXV 78, 772. Déclaration que fait M. Robillard habitant à la Plaine du Nord des désastres arrivés sur son habitation . . . , le Cap, 29 sept. 1791. The details were related to Robillard by two mulattoes who later attacked the camp, killing four of Robillard's slaves and, to prevent the plantation from being used again as a camp, burned the slaves' quarters.

45. AN, DXXV 46, 432. Copies. Tausias à Camuzat, le Cap, 1 sept. 1791. DXXV 78, 772. AA 183. Deposition, le Cap, 27 Sept. 1791.

46. AN, DXXV 46, 432. Copies. Blanchelande à Bertrand, le Cap, 2 sept. 1791. M. de Rouvray claimed that Blanchelande had been warned of the plot as early as the nineteenth, but was too inept to crush it in its beginnings. M. E. McIntosh and B. C. Weber, eds., *Une correspondance familiale au temps des troubles de Saint-Domingue* (Paris: Larose, 1957), 41. M. de Rouvray to C [tesse] de Lostanges, 6, 7 Dec. 1791.

47. AN, DXXV 46, 432. Copies. Blanchelande à Bertrand, le Cap, 2 sept. 1791.

48. Ibid. DXXV 78, 772. AA 183. Deposition, le Cap, 27 Sept. 1791.

49. AN, DXXV 46, 432. Copies. Blanchelande à Bertrand, le Cap, 2 sept. 1791.

50. *Une correspondance familiale*, 29. Mme. de Rouvray to C [te] de Lostanges, le Cap, 8 Sept. 1791.

51. AN, DXXV 46, 432. Copies. Lettre de M. Nicoleau, le Cap, 3 sept. 1791.

52. AN, DXXV 46, 432. Copies. Rapport de M. Bagnet. Extrait de la gazette anglaise transmise à Paris, Kingstown, Ile Jamaïque, 2 sept. 1791.

53. "Letter from James Perkins," Boston, *Independent Chronicle and Universal Advertiser*, 20 Oct. 1791.

54. "St. Domingo Disturbances," *Philadelphia Aurora*, 10 Oct. 1791. Entry for 26 Aug. 1791.

55. Ibid., 10–11 Oct. 1791. Entries for 31 Aug.–1 Sept. 1791.

56. Ibid. Entry for 31 Aug. 1791.

57. AN, DXXV 46, 432. Copies. Tausias à Camuzat, le Cap, 1 sept. 1791.

58. "St. Domingo Disturbances," *Philadelphia Aurora*, 11 Oct. 1791. Entry for 5 Sept. 1791. Other evidence of this practice is revealed in various accounts of the subsequent engagements, in which blacks were taken prisoner: "The day before yesterday . . . we took the camp of Limbé . . . (and took the King Jean-Louis and the Queen alive"; "The 16th October we captured one of their head men who calls himself King"; "We have in prison a priest who was taken at the capture of Gallifet, also the Queen of that quarter." Extract of a letter from Cape Français, 3 Nov. 1791, *Philadelphia Aurora*, 15 Dec. 1791; Extract of a letter from a gentleman in Cape Français, 1 Nov. 1791, Boston, *Independent Chronicle and Universal Advertiser*, 15 Dec. 1791, respectively. Boukman, of course, was also known and respected as a chief king. See also the reference to the titular head chosen by the insurgents in the South province as King of Platons, in Ch. 6.

59. "St. Domingo Disturbances," *Philadelphia Aurora*, 11 Oct. 1791. Entry for 1 Sept. 1791. For his loyalty to the whites in denouncing Jean-Baptiste Cap, the slave Jean, *commandeur* of the Chaperon de la Taste plantation, situated behind the Pères de l'Hôpital of the city, was granted freedom and a life pension of 300 livres per year. The owner received an indemnity for his slave from the colonial government. AN, DXXV 60, 595. Extrait des registres de l'Assemblée Générale de la partie française de Saint-Domingue, 2 sept. 1791.

60. "St. Domingo Disturbances," *Philadelphia Aurora*, 11 Oct. 1791. Entry for 2 Sept. 1791.

61. Ibid.

62. A second attempt was made during September and a third at some point before early October. Boston, *Independent Chronicle and Universal Advertiser*, 13 Oct. 1791. Extract from the schooner Peggy, Capt. White, 6 Oct. 1791.

63. AN, DXXV 46, 432. Pemerle to his brother, les Cayes, 31 Aug. 1791. Here the writer states that "the 15,000 insurgent slaves had taken the route toward le Cap." Another letter, dated 22 October, relates news that had arrived in France from a boat leaving the colony on 1 September: "There is a revolt of 15,000 slaves in Saint Domingue; they appeared at the city of le Cap. The planters armed themselves and attacked. They killed some and dispersed the others." DXXV 46, 432. Extrait d'une lettre de Bordeaux datée du 22 octobre, envoyée à M. de Lartigue.

64. The account is contained within a history of the Communauté, and although compiled at a later date, is based nonetheless on the original correspondence of the nuns, as well as on information related by contemporary historians. So while some details may have somewhat gratuitously been attributed to the nuns by the reporter, the information is still based on contemporary sources. See Cabon, "Une maison d'éducation à Saint-Domingue: les religieuses du Cap," RHAF 3 (déc. 1949):417–19. Relevant passages of the text are presented in Appendix B.

65. Upon the initiative of a nun, later to be known as Mère de Combolas, whose wish was granted when le Cap was spared destruction from a British fleet threatening to attack in 1744, classes were opened for instruction to young black girls in the colony. Cabon, "Une maison," RHAF 3 (juin, 1949):77–78. That a good number of these ended up in the voodoo cult toward the eve of the revolution reflects perhaps as much on the laxity of European mores in late eighteenth-century colonial society as the tenacity of African traditions and beliefs.

66. See the translation and interpretation of this chant in Ch. 2.

67. Cabon, "Une maison," RHAF 3 (déc. 1949):418–19.

68. See the text and discussion of the Bois-Caïman speech in the present chapter above, as well as in Appendix B.

69. AN, DXXV 78, 772. AA 183. Deposition, le Cap, 27 Sept. 1791.

70. AN, DXXV 56, 550. Discours.

71. Boston, *Independent Chronicle and Universal Advertiser*, 20 Oct. 1791. *Philadelphia Aurora*, 10–11 Oct. 1791. AN, DXXV 46, 432. Copies. Blanchelande à Bertrand, le Cap, 2 sept. 1791.

72. Debien, *Les colons*, 334. AN, DXXV 46, 432. Copies. Extrait d'une lettre du Cap Français en date du 25 sept. 1791. Also, DXXV 80, 787. Liste des habitations sucreries incendiées (dans l'espace de quinze jours) dont les noms sont parvenus jusqu'à ce jour, le Cap, 30 sept. This list indicates 165 sugar plantations of the seven parishes hit during the first few days: Port-Margot, Limbé, Acul, Plaine du Nord, Petite-Anse, Quartier-Morin, and Limonade, and estimates the loss in productive value at 39,800,000 livres. (It is a recapitulation of the same list as that cited in n. 19 above.) Another list, including the parishes of Dondon, Marmelade, Grande-Rivière, and Ste. Suzanne, and therefore drawn up somewhat later, lists 172 sugar, 1,185 coffee, and 34 indigo, plantations burned during the first month or two of the revolt, making a total of 1,391 plantations. DXXV 63, 635. Liste des habitations incendiées, dépendance du Nord, n.d. (oct. 1791?). Obviously, figures vary from one source to another, making it nearly impossible to arrive at an exact count. Generally, however, colonists spoke of close to 200 sugar plantations burned during the first week, and over 200 by at least mid-September.

73. See n. 72 above.

74. AN, DXXV 46, 432. Copies. M. l'Ambassadeur à MM. les colons de l'Hôtel Massiac, 4 nov. 1791. Letter from Kingston, 17 Sept. 1791. Lettre de M. Nicoleau, le Cap, 3 sept. 1791. The four remaining districts, not including le Cap, were Ouinaminthe, Fort-Dauphin (including Terrier-Rouge), le Trou, and Dondon.

75. AN, DXXV 46, 432. Copies. Tausias à Camuzat, le Cap, 1 sept. 1791. See also Rapport de M. Bagnet, in ibid; "St. Domingo Disturbances," *Philadelphia Aurora*, 10 Oct. 1791. Entry for 23 Aug. 1791.

76. AN, DXXV 78, 772. AA 183. Partie du Nord. DXXV 56, 550. Discours.

77. "St. Domingo Disturbances," *Philadelphia Aurora*, 10 Oct. 1791. Entry for 27 Aug. 1791.

78. AN, DXXV 78, 772. AA 183. Deposition, le Cap, 27 Sept. 1791. The facility with which the slaves were able to recruit additional forces was also noted by Mr. Henry, a merchant captain, in a letter to his brother from le Cap, 27 Sept. 1791. DXXV 78, 772.

79. AN, DXXV 46, 432. Copies. Extrait d'une lettre de M. William Collann[?] à M. Thomas Collann[?] du Havre, en date du 28 octobre datée de Londres. Lettre de M. Guilhem de Bordeaux, propriétaire au Cap, 28 oct. 1791 (?). Lettre au Général Melville d'un officier d'artillerie en garnison à la Jamaïque, le Cap, 24 sept. 1791. Extrait d'une lettre du Cap Français en date du 25 sept. 1791. See also Garran-Coulon, *Rapport*, 2:215. Boston, *Independent Chronicle and Universal Advertiser*, 22 Sept., 13 Oct., 24 Nov. 1791. *Philadelphia Aurora*, 12 Oct., 14 Nov. 1791.

80. Gautier, *Solitude*, 239.

81. Patterson, "Slavery and Slave Revolts," 279. See the discussion of the debate surrounding this point in the Introduction.

82. Geggus, "Les esclaves de la plaine," RSHH 136:12.

83. AN, DXXV 46, 432. Lettre écrite par M. Testard à M. Cormier, contenant l'extrait de deux lettres qu'il a reçues du Havre, le Cap, 26 oct. 1791, cited in C. Fick, "The Black Masses in the San Domingo Revolution." Geggus also cites the second of the two letters: AN Arch. Col., CC9A. Extrait d'une lettre anonyme, 20 août 1791, in "Les esclaves de la plaine," RSHH 136:12. Also see Appendix B, n. 13.

84. It is not this writer's intention to repeat the arguments of James and of other historians on this point. James stated the case quite forcefully when he wrote that the crimes committed in the name of "property and privilege are always more ferocious than the revenges of poverty and oppression." *Black Jacobins*, 88–89. Eugene Genovese has also gone to great lengths to defend this point in *From Rebellion to Revolution*, 104–10.

85. Even today as the Haitian masses are engaged in another struggle for liberation and for the basic principles of democracy and human dignity, indeed for the bare essentials of human survival, the initial massacre (and even the occasional decapitation) of a few hundred tonton macoutes with stones, machetes, or makeshift weapons (as the civilian population has no arms), and the expiation of repressed frustrations, hatred, and suffering that accompanied the 7 February 1986 fall of Jean-Claude Duvalier's government, were selective and relatively short-lived, compared with nearly thirty years of Duvalierist repression.

86. AN, DXXV 56, 550. Discours. On his role in the organization of the 22 August outbreak, see the chronology of events presented earlier in the present chapter. On his execution on false accusations of treason, see below in the present chapter.

87. *History Civil and Commercial of the British West Indies*, 5th ed., 5 vols. (New York: ADIC Press, 1966), 3:80–81. Edwards affirms that the details of the incidents were communicated by Mme. Baillon herself to a friend of his who was with him in Saint Domingue at the time.

88. See also the remarks of M. Odeluc's coachman and assassin in the present chapter above.

89. Abundant examples of slave loyalty and humanity toward the whites (and also of the intervention of women in the insurgent bands to temper undiscerning vengeance and avoid unnecessary killing) are related in Samuel Perkins, *Reminiscences of the Insurrection in St. Domingo* (Cambridge, Mass.: John Wilson and Son, 1886), 21–70 passim. The younger brother of le Cap merchant James Perkins, he resided in Saint Domingue from 1785 until after the burning of le Cap in 1793, and returned again in 1794. Although providing many interesting details of events, the book, written as recollections of the author some fifty years later, contains more than one factual and interpretive inaccuracy, thus severely limiting its reliability as a primary manuscript source.

90. While some estimates by colonists and other residents situate the number of insurgents killed at somewhere between three to four thousand in the first few months, others claim that in one of the attacks on le Cap alone, they had suffered two thousand killed and fifteen hundred taken prisoner, of which every tenth man was decapitated; another states that in Port-Margot alone, from twelve to fifteen hundred were slain. The figures given out by the whites for these single encounters, if they are not grossly inflated, would, in contradiction, largely surpass the generally cited overall figure of three to four thousand. One report of 13 September claims that, though upwards of three thousand blacks had been killed, it would still require another one thousand to twelve hundred more killed before the slaves could be subdued. If, indeed, close to two thousand blacks were killed by white units at one single engagement, the reporter, then, would have been naïvely optimistic, for, by another's report, although "above 3,000 insurgents have been killed, they are still strong and have fortified themselves in two or three different parts of the country." Extracts from the schooners Hardy, Peggy, 6 Oct. 1791; "Letter from James Perkins," le Cap, 9 Sept. 1791, Boston, *Independent Chronicle and Universal Advertiser*, 13, 20 Oct. 1791. "St. Domingo Disturbances," *Philadelphia Aurora*, 11 Oct. (entry for 13 Sept.); 14 Nov. 1791. AN, DXXV 46, 432. Copies. Lettre écrite au Général Melville, le Cap, 24 sept. 1791.

91. "Saint Domingue Disturbances," *Philadelphia Aurora*, 14 Nov. 1791.

92. Ibid.

93. Ibid.

94. AN, DXXV 46, 431. M. de Blanchelande à M. Bertrand, Ministre de la Marine, au Cap, 29 sept. 1791.

95. "Letter from James Perkins," Boston, *Independent Chronicle and Universal Advertiser*, 20 Oct. 1791.

96. AN, DXXV 46, 431. Blanchelande à Bertrand, le Cap, 29 sept. 1791. "Saint Domingue Disturbances," *Philadelphia Aurora*, 14 Nov. 1791.

97. In G. Laurent, *Chaînes*, 28. For a vivid example of maroon organization and fighting tactics during the Jamaican maroon wars, see the descriptions in McFarlane, *Cudjoe of Jamaica*.

98. Laurent, *Chaînes*, 29–31. Also, "Saint Domingue Disturbances," *Philadelphia Aurora*, 14 Nov. 1791.

99. Ibid. "Letter from James Perkins," Boston, *Independent Chronicle and Universal Advertiser*, 20 Oct. 1791.

100. Boston, *Independent Chronicle and Universal Advertiser*, 29 Sept. 1791.

101. In Althéa de Peuch Parham, trans. and ed., *My Odyssey: Experiences of a Young Refugee from Two Revolutions, By a Creole of Saint-Domingue* (Baton Rouge: Louisiana State University Press, 1959), 32–34.

102. AN, DXXV 56, 550. Discours.

103. AN, DXXV 46, 432. Copie d'une lettre de M. de Blanchelande au Ministre de la Marine, du Cap le 22 oct. 1791.

104. AN, DXXV 20, 198. Mémoire fait par un habitant d'Ouinaminthe sur . . . les événe-

ments arrivés à cette paroisse jusqu'au 15 janvier 1792, certifié par Alexandre la Fosse, le Cap, 22 sept. 1792. DXXV 65, 662. Faits et événements relatifs à M. Wanderlinden, capitaine du régiment du Cap, lorsqu'il est venu au Fort Dauphin . . . , oct.–nov. 1791.

105. AN, DXXV 20, 198. Mémoire fait par un habitant d'Ouinaminthe. In addition to the command posts held at Ouinaminthe by Cézar and Jean-Baptiste Marc were those held by Noël, a black slave, and Jean-Simon, a free black. Their nominal general was Sieur Gérard.

106. Ibid.

107. Ibid. Also DXXV 65, 662. Faits et événements relatifs à M. Wanderlinden; and Parham, *My Odyssey*, 69–71.

108. Frequent references to the presence amongst the rebels of whites who were "not of the common or lower class, but artful fellows who appeared to have system to their designs," are made in the various accounts of residents and participants in the attacks. Extract from the schooner Hardy, 6 Oct. 1791, Boston, *Independent Chronicle and Universal Advertiser*, 13 Oct. 1791. On relations between the slave rebels and royalist factions, see also G. Laurent, *Chaînes*, 42–46. Also, mention is frequently made of priests who were captured among the rebels. One of them was the curate of Limbé: "found among the blacks in that quarter —proved to be a great rascal; brought to town; and yesterday we had the pleasure to see Mr. Abbe pendant before the church." Extract of a letter from James Perkins, 7 Nov. 1791, Boston, *Independent Chronicle and Universal Advisor*, 15 Dec. 1791.

109. Population figures for the North province in 1791 were, roughly: 16,000 whites; 9,000 *affranchis*; and 170,000 slaves. Gautier, *Solitude*, 239.

110. AN, DXXV 46, 431. Blanchelande au Ministre de la Marine, le Cap, 29 sept. 1791. The vast majority of the higher command posts in the Grande-Rivière area in fact went to the free blacks. DXXV 60, 600. Extrait des registres. Suite de la déposition du Sieur Laroque, 21 janv. 1791. The only prominent mulatto leader was Candy, fierce and courageous in battle, with little sympathy for the white prisoners. By November, he was closely associated with Jean-François and Biassou, but by January 1792, after the negotiations with the civil commissioners had failed, left to join the whites. On his defection to the whites see also Parham, *My Odyssey*, 70–73.

111. AN, DXXV 63, 635. Déclarations des prisonniers remis par Jean-François, 24 déc. 1791. Déclaration de MM. René Cossait et al. A certain segment of the mulattoes in the rebel camps had been victims of the August revolt. Their property destroyed, the only choice they had was either to join the white colonial forces against the blacks or to join—by consent or by force—the rebels, where they were closely watched. Among the mulattoes who joined the revolution voluntarily were also those condemned *in absentia* during the Ogé affair (see Ch. 3 above; see also n. 17 above). DXXV 60, 600. Extrait des registres. Suite de la déposition du Sieur Laroque. Laroque lists the names of some of these mulattoes, as well as a few of the free blacks, also condemned, whom he saw at the Grand-Cormier camp. See also Sannon, *Histoire de Toussaint*, 1:69, nn. 1–3.

112. On the death of Boukman, see the letter of M. de Cambefort recounting the incident, cited in full in Fouchard, *Marrons de la liberté*, 530–32. Also, Boston, *Independent Chronical and Universal Advertiser*, 15 Dec. 1791; Sannon, *Histoire de Toussaint*, 1:92–93; Dalmas, *Histoire de la révolution*, 1:132.

113. BPL, Gros, *Isle de St. Domingue, Province du Nord. Précis historique* . . . (Paris, 1793), 17, 26.

114. Madiou, *Histoire d'Haïti*, 1:105.

115. AN, DXXV 63, 635. Déclarations. Déclaration de M. Guillaume Moulinet. BPL, Gros, *Précis*, 25–26. See also Lacroix, *Mémoires*, 1:153–54.

116. AN, DXXV 1, 2. Adresse à l'Assemblée Générale . . . par MM. les citoyens de couleur de la Grande-Rivière, Sainte-Suzanne et autres quartiers . . . , n.d. (nov. 1791 ?).

117. BPL, Gros, *Précis*, 8–9.

118. See n. 86 above. Lacroix, *Mémoires*, 1:112–13. See also Dalmas, *Histoire*, 1:216–17. Extract of a letter from Cape Français of 2 Nov., Boston, *Independent Chronicle and Universal Advertiser*, 8 Dec. 1791.

119. Sannon, *Histoire de Toussaint*, 1:93.

120. BPL, Gros, *Précis*, 14. Madiou even states that Boukman was mourned by his companions for several months. *Histoire d'Haïti*, 1:106.

121. BPL, Gros, *Précis*, 14.

122. AN, DXXV 46, 439. Journal rédigé par M. Gros. Entry for 17 Nov., 1791.

123. BPL, Gros, *Précis*, 17. It appears evident here that Gros took a good deal of liberty to embellish Jean-François's words and feelings.

124. Ibid.

125. One wonders exactly what, if anything, Toussaint would have done in Jean-François's shoes. By doing nothing, by remaining in the background, Toussaint at least had enough political wisdom to save himself from the opprobrium cast upon Jean-François as negotiator in November–December 1791. Later events, however, did prove Jean-François incapable of pursuing to the end the fundamental cause of their collective struggle against slavery; in this, he may be seen as an opportunist and, in the final analysis, one who shamelessly betrayed the cause of his people.

126. AN, DXXV 65, 659. Extrait des archives du comté du Fort-Dauphin, 8 nov. 1791. Déclaration du Sieur Jacobet. For the whites, the tables had dramatically turned since the days of Ogé. On the Ogé rebellion, see Ch. 3 above.

127. AN, DXXV 46, 439. Journal rédigé par M. Gros. Entry for 11 Nov. 1791. BPL, Gros, *Précis*, 14.

128. Ibid., 21.

129. Ibid. AN, DXXV 46, 439. Journal rédigé par M. Gros. Entries for 17 Nov., 5 Dec. 1791. DXXV 46, 439. No. 300. M. de Rouvray to M. de Blanchelande, 8 Jan. 1792.

130. BPL, Gros, *Précis*, 21.

131. Ibid. In his observations, Gros made a distinction, however, between the slaves of the mountainous regions (where the somewhat less labor-intensive coffee estates predominated) and those of the plains (where sugar production was concentrated); the former were far less ferocious than the latter, in Gros's opinion, and even seemed grieved over the fate of their masters.

132. AN, DXXV 60, 600. Extrait des registres. Suite de la déposition du Sieur Laroque.

133. BPL, Gros, *Précis*, 22.

134. AN, DXXV 79, 779. Extrait d'une lettre par M. Abbé de la Porte à M. l'Archevesque Thibaut, Vallière, 25 mars 1792.

135. The three free days per week had become a generalized demand throughout this early period; one exaggerated version of it even claimed that the slaves would be paid an average salary of three livres per day for the other three days. AN, DXXV 78, 772. Mr. Henry, capitaine du navire *la Charlotte* à son frère, le Cap, 27 sept. 1791.

136. AN, DXXV 63, 635. Déclarations. Déclaration de M. René Guillemeton. Déclaration de MM. René Cossait et al.

137. BPL, Gros, *Précis*, 27.

138. Ibid.

139. Sannon, *Histoire de Toussaint*, 3:18.

140. BPL, Gros, *Précis*, 28.

Chapter Five

1. On this point see Stein, *Sonthonax*, 64–65.

2. Ibid., 33–37. See also *Précis historique des annales*, 1:54.

3. Born in Saint Marc in 1743, he was brought up in Toulouse, where he received a finished education. Sannon, *Histoire de Toussaint*, 1:79, n. 1.

4. Garran-Coulon, *Rapport*, 2:131–33. Also, Sannon, *Histoire de Toussaint*, 1:79.

5. Cited in full in Garran-Coulon, *Rapport*, 2:135–36.

6. Ibid., 136–38. *Précis historique des annales*, 1:53.

7. Sannon, *Histoire de Toussaint*, 1:80. In many works on the Saint Domingue revolution written by non-Haitian scholars, the mulatto leader's name is francized to read Beauvais. In his own correspondence, however, he signs his name as Bauvais.

8. Particularly indicative of his impartiality was his decision to leave the colony during the fratricidal civil war in 1799–1800. See Ch. 8 below.

9. Stein, *Sonthonax*, 36. Ott, *Haitian Revolution*, 61, n. 27. Sannon, *Histoire de Toussaint*, 1:142. James, *Black Jacobins*, 96.

10. On the Fortin-Bellantien rebels and their marronage in July 1791, see Ch. 3 above. Pamphile Lacroix, *Mémoires*, 1:119. Lacroix cites as his source *Débats dans l'affaire des colonies* (Paris: 1799), 3:185; 7:207. Fouchard places the number of *Suisses* at exactly 243: 220 black and 23 mulatto slaves. *Marrons de la liberté*, 526.

11. Madiou, *Histoire d'Haïti*, 1:112. Sannon, *Histoire de Toussaint*, 1:82. See n. 12 below.

12. It was apparently following this attack, at Nérette on 31 August, that those slaves armed by their masters deserted to join the *Suisses*. (See ibid.) Perhaps the presence of the Cul-de-Sac maroons and other former slaves already in the confederate ranks proved a decisive factor in their desertion.

13. Garran-Coulon, *Rapport*, 2:143. Lacroix, *Mémoires*, 1:116.

14. *Précis historique des annales*, 1:53–54. Sannon, *Histoire de Toussaint*, 1:81. Lacroix, *Mémoires*, 1:117. Garran-Coulon, *Rapport*, 2:143–44.

15. PRO, HCA 30, 381. Insurrection dans la partie du Port-au-Prince commencée le 27 août 1791.

16. In Garran-Coulon, *Rapport*, 2:144–45. *Précis historique des annales*, 1:54.

17. Ibid., 54, 57.

18. Garran-Coulon, *Rapport*, 2:150–51.

19. AN, DXXV 61, 615. Extrait des pièces déposées aux archives de l'Assemblée Coloniale. Précis des faits qui se sont passés dans la paroisse de Jacmel et sa dépendance depuis le commencement de septembre 1791 jusqu'à ce jour . . . , Jacmel, 11 mars 1792.

20. *Précis historique des annales*, 1:54.

21. PRO, HCA 30, 381. Insurrection.

22. Ibid.

23. Ibid.

24. NYPL, A. Schomburg Negro Collection. Concordat, ou traité de paix entre les citoyens blancs et les citoyens de couleur des quatorze paroisses de la province de l'Ouest de la partie française de Saint-Domingue, 23 oct. 1791. Also, *Précis historique des annales*, 1:57–58.

25. Garran-Coulon, *Rapport*, 3:65.

26. AN, DXXV 62, 626. Les commissaires de correspondance de l'Assemblée Générale . . . aux commissaires de ladite assemblée auprès de l'Assemblée Nationale et du Roi, les Cayes, 12 nov. 1791.

27. Sannon, *Histoire de Toussaint*, 1:85–86.

28. Cited in Garran-Coulon, *Rapport*, 3:66.

29. Ibid., 67–68. Another account, differing slightly in detail, is presented in *Précis historique des annales*, 1:60.

30. AN, DXXV 46, 439. No. 216. Les sieurs Maigret, Boisrond, prés. de Saint-Louis, Depas, Medring, sec. *ad hoc*, hommes de couleur et blancs coalisés avec eux à Aquin au sieur Pinchinat, chef du rassemblement de la Croix-des-Bouquets, 9 sept. 1791.

31. *Précis historique des annales*, 1:59–60.

32. AN, DXXV 1, 4. Histoire de la conspiration du Port-au-Prince contre les citoyens de couleur, Croix-des-Bouquets, 28 nov. 1791.

33. *Précis historique des annales*, 1:60–61.

34. Ibid.

35. AN, DXXV 1, 4. Histoire de la conspiration.

36. Ibid. *Précis historique des annales*, 1:61.

37. Boston, *Independent Chronicle and Universal Advertiser*, 5, 12 Jan. 1791. Extract of a letter from Port-au-Prince, *Philadelphia Aurora*, 28 Dec. 1791. AN, DXXV 1, 4. Histoire de la conspiration. *Précis historique des annales*, 1:62. Since the mulatto and free black forces had already left in retreat for Croix-des-Bouquets, their responsibility for setting the fires that destroyed the town is highly circumstantial, even if plausible. (See ibid.; also, Boston, *Independent Chronicle and Universal Advertiser*, 5 Jan. 1791.) Equally plausible is that they were set by patriot agitators to discredit the mulattoes.

38. AN, DXXV 1, 4. Histoire de la conspiration.

39. Boston, *Independent Chronicle and Universal Advertiser*, 12 Jan. 1791. *Philadelphia Aurora*, 28 Dec. 1791; 4, 6, 20 Jan. 1792. AN, DXXV 1, 4. Histoire de la conspiration.

40. The full text of this declaration is cited in Sannon, *Histoire de Toussaint*, 1:97; also, *Précis historique des annales*, 1:62.

41. In most of the contemporary literature, he is simply identified as a Spanish *griffe* or, in a few instances, as a *nègre espagnol*. However, in the declaration of Marie-Jeanne Harang, widow of Vissière, the captain-general of the mulatto and free black forces at Jacmel, he is clearly identified as a free black. The author of the *Précis historique des annales* also identifies him as an *homme de couleur*, of Spanish origin, and a property owner at Trou Coffy (1:63). AN, DXXV 61, 611. Rapport de Blöuet, curé de Jacmel, fait à l'Assemblée Coloniale, Jacmel, 14 fév. 1792. DXXV 61, 615. Précis des faits qui se sont passés dans la paroisse de Jacmel. DXXV 2, 14. Extrait du registre des déclarations faites à la municipalité de Jacmel. Declaration of free black, Mathurin Dubreuil, 28 March 1792. DXXV 2, 14. Extrait du registre des déclarations. Declaration of Marie-Jeanne Harang, 30 March 1792.

42. Declaration of Marie-Jeanne Harang.

43. Larose, "Africa," 111.

44. AN, DXXV 62, 618. Extrait des pièces déposées aux archives de l'Assemblée Coloniale de la partie française de Saint-Domingue. Supplément au détail des faits relatifs aux troubles . . . dans la dépendance de Jacmel depuis le onze mars 1792.

45. AN, DXXV 61, 611. Rapport de Blöuet. Two sources affirm, however, that Romaine could neither read nor write. Ibid. and DXXV 3, 26. Delagroix to Saint-Léger[?], Léogane, 4 Feb. 1792. On the other hand, Fouchard affirms the contrary and cites the existence of letters written and signed by Romaine. *Marrons de la liberté*, 539.

46. AN, DXXV 2, 24. Compte rendu à l'Assemblée Nationale, par M. Saint-Léger, commissaire civil pour l'isle de Saint-Domingue (Paris: Imp. Nationale, 1792), 27.

47. AN, DXXV 61, 615. Précis des faits qui se sont passés dans la paroisse de Jacmel. Although estimates of the actual size of his following are not given in the correspondence relating to the events at the end of 1791 (most of the correspondence covering this period

was in fact written months afterward), the civil commissioner, Saint-Léger, estimated that by March 1792, Romaine's troops had increased to over four thousand, nearly all of them slaves. AN, DXXV 2, 19. Report of Saint-Léger to National Assembly, n.p., n.d. Sent to Colonial Committee on 2 June 1792.

48. Extract of a letter from les Cayes, 11 Feb. 1792, *Philadelphia Aurora*, 16 March 1792.

49. AN, DXXV 3, 26. Delagroix to Saint-Léger[?], Léogane, 4 Feb. 1792. See also DXXV 61, 615. Précis des faits qui se sont passés dans la paroisse de Jacmel.

50. AN, DXXV 3, 26. Delagroix to Saint-Léger[?], Léogane, 4 Feb. 1792.

51. AN, DXXV 2, 19. Report of Saint-Léger to National Assembly. DXXV 1, 11. Copie de la lettre à nous écrite par M. Saint-Léger du Port-au-Prince le 23 février 1792.

52. AN, DXXV 3, 26. Delagroix to Saint-Léger [?], Léogane, 4 Feb. 1792. See also Garron-Coulon, *Rapport*, 2:493.

53. AN, DXXV 61, 614. Extrait des pièces déposées aux archives de l'Assemblée Coloniale de la partie française de Saint-Domingue, signé Fatin et al., le Cap, 5 fév. 1792.

54. Garran-Coulon, *Rapport*, 2:531–32.

55. AN, DXXV 61, 614. Extrait des pièces, signé Fatin et al., le Cap, 5 fév. 1792.

56. The full text of this proclamation is cited in Lacroix, *Mémoires*, 1:194. Also cited in Sannon, *Histoire de Toussaint*, 1:97–98. See also *Précis historique des annales*, 1:62.

57. Stein, *Sonthonax*, 64–65.

58. AN, DXXV 61, 615. Précis des faits qui se sont passés dans la paroisse de Jacmel. DXXV 62, 618. Supplément. DXXV 19, 191. Extrait des registres des délibérations de la municipalité du Port-au-Prince. Declaration of the Negress Marie, 28 Jan. 1792. DXXV 2, 14. Extrait du registre des déclarations. Declaration of Sieur Busquet, 20 March 1792.

59. The author is deeply grateful to M. Bernard Foubert who so kindly provided these details in personal correspondence.

60. Other factors, such as the greater degree of creolization on the second and third Laborde estates or, on the third estate, the general acceptance by the slaves of their plantation manager, may also have played a role in determining the participation or nonparticipation of these slaves in the insurrection that was increasingly sweeping the South. See, in any event, the highly informative article by M. Foubert, "Le marronage sur les habitations Laborde." Typewritten, 29 pp., tables. Forthcoming. (On the participation in rebellion of the slaves from the first, and least creolized, of Laborde's three plantations, however, see Ch. 6 below.) A full-length monograph by M. Foubert on the three Laborde plantations is forthcoming and will no doubt contribute to developing methods that may help point the way in eventually piecing together a more precise pattern of involvement of the slaves of this area of the South. Perhaps through individual plantation studies of this sort we may, in the long run, be able to analyze with greater accuracy and discernment the elusive reasons motivating some slaves and not others to strike out at a given moment against their masters and the existing order.

61. AN, DXXV 63, 638. Extrait des pièces déposées aux archives de l'Assemblée Coloniale. Exposition que font MM. les commissaires nommés et envoyés par l'Assemblée provinciale du Sud . . . auprès de MM. les Commissaires nationaux civils, le Cap, 5 fév. 1792. The authors of this piece erroneously cite the *commandeur* as belonging to the second Laborde estate.

62. Quoted in personal correspondence from M. Foubert to author.

63. AN, DXXV 63, 638. Extrait des pièces. . . . Exposition que font MM. les commissaires . . . , le Cap, 5 fév. 1792.

64. Garran-Coulon, *Rapport*, 2:536–37.

65. See *Précis historique des annales*, 1:64. Instances of deliberate killings of mulattoes

by the whites and of similar retaliatory acts by mulattoes are also reported in Boston, *Independent Chronicle and Universal Advertiser*, 15 March 1792. Extract of a letter from a gentleman at Aux Cayes to a merchant in Alexandria (Va.) dated Jan. 17, 1792. Also in *Philadelphia Aurora*, 5–6 March 1792.

66. AN, DXXV 94, Ds. 11. Débats entre les accusés et les accusateurs dans l'affaire des colonies, 13–15.

67. AN, DXXV 78, 772. E. Guerard to MM. P. Guerard, Rialle et cie., négociants au Havre, les Cayes, 12 July 1791.

68. AN, DXXV 61, 637. Adresse de l'Assemblée Provinciale et provisoirement administrative du Sud, les Cayes, 23 fév. 1792. DXXV 62, 626. L'Assemblée Provinciale du Sud à l'Assemblée Coloniale, les Cayes, 5 janv. 1792. DXXV 61, 612. La municipalité des Cayemittes à l'Assemblée Générale, signé, Ollivier Mareil, maire et al., Cayemittes, n.d. Sannon, *Histoire de Toussaint*, 1:102.

69. AN, DXXV 61, 613. La municipalité des Cayemittes à l'Assemblée Générale, signé Ollivier Mareil, maire et al., Cayemittes, 20 déc. 1791. DXXV 61, 613. La municipalité des Cayemittes à l'Assemblée Générale, signé, Ollivier Mareil, maire et al., 30 déc. 1791. DXXV 61, 613. Extrait des pièces déposées aux archives de l'Assemblée Coloniale. La Municipalité de Torbeck à MM. de l'Assemblée Coloniale, signé, Saint-Martin, maire et al., Torbeck, 15 janv. 1792. DXXV 61, 613. Conseil Général de la commune de Tiburon et de Dame-Marie réunies à l'Assemblée Coloniale, signé, Gachet et al., Tiburon, 29 janv. 1792. DXXV 62, 626. L'Assemblée Provinciale du Sud à l'Assemblée Coloniale, les Cayes, 5 janv. 1792. DXXV 61, 613. Assemblée Provinciale du Sud à l'Assemblée Coloniale, les Cayes, 26 janv. 1792. DXXV 63, 638. Adresse de l'Assemblée provisoirement administrative de la partie du Sud à l'Assemblée Nationale de France, signé, Billard, prés., les Cayes, n.d. DXXV 63, 637. Adresse de l'Assemblée Provinciale et provisoirement administrative du Sud à l'Assemblée Nationale de France, les Cayes, 23 fév. 1792. DXXV 61, 613. Extrait des minutes du greffe de la municipalité de Jérémie, 16 janv. 1792.

Chapter Six

1. Documents relating to these events are presented in Appendix C.

2. AN, DXXV 46, 439, No. 262. L'Assemblée Coloniale à ses commissaires en France, le Cap, 28 janv. 1792. DXXV 63, 637. Adresse de l'Assemblée Provinciale et provisoirement administrative du Sud à l'Assemblée Nationale, les Cayes, 23 fév. 1792. DXXV 61, 614. Extrait des pièces, signé, Fatin et al., le Cap, 5 fév. 1792.

3. Garran-Coulon, *Rapport*, 2:491, 498.

4. Lacroix, *Mémoires*, 1:180–81. Colonel Malenfant, *Des colonies et particulièrement de celle de Saint-Domingue* (Paris, 1814), 18–19. Garran-Coulon, *Rapport*, 2:512–13.

5. Lacroix, *Mémoires*, 1:181, 191.

6. Sannon, *Histoire de Toussaint*, 1:109. Lacroix, *Mémoires*, 1:193.

7. Garran-Coulon, *Rapport*, 2:573.

8. Selected material and passages from the remainder of this chapter and sections of the following one have been published in an article by the author: "Black Peasants and Soldiers in the Saint Domingue Revolution: Initial Reactions to Freedom in the South Province (1793–94)," in *History from Below: Studies in Popular Protest and Popular Ideology*, ed. Frederick Krantz (Oxford and New York: Basil Blackwell, 1988), 247–70. (The book issued from a Festschrift, published in 1985 at Concordia University in Montreal, in honor of George Rudé, pioneer historian of eighteen- and nineteenth-century popular protest movements in Europe

and Britain.) Permission to reprint material from the article was kindly extended by Basil Blackwell and by Frederick Krantz.

9. PRO, HCA 30 395, 259. Dubourg to Caussé, les Cayes, 23 Dec. 1792.

10. PRO, HCA 30 401, pt. 1, cote E. Interrogatoire de M. Thiballier, 14, 15 et 16 janv. 1793. AN, DXXV 63, 638. Journal exact et fidèle de ce qui s'est passé aux Cayes depuis la trop fatale époque du 23 juillet 1792, certifié par Delaval, le Cap, 1 sept. 1792.

11. Ibid.

12. PRO, HCA 30 392, 60. Bérault to Corbun, les Cayes, 17 Jan. 1793. Also, Bérault to Bérault, jeune, les Cayes, 17 Jan. 1793.

13. PRO, HCA 30 401, pt. 2, cote H. Lettre du citoyen André Rigaud au citoyen Thiballier, n.p. (Camp Gérard?), 26 juin 1792.

14. AN, DXXV 63, 638. Journal exact. Garran-Coulon, *Rapport*, 2:570.

15. See also ibid., 570–71.

16. The word *platons* was generally used in the colony to refer to mountain gorges. Because of the multiplicity of gorges and precipices in this part of the South, the word was thus applied to designate it as a distinct region. Ibid., 582–83.

17. ISL, Mémoire de l'Assemblée Provinciale et de ses municipalités réunies du Sud à l'Assemblée Coloniale en réponse à la lettre de M. Blanchelande en date du 16 août, adressée à l'Assemblée Coloniale, les Cayes, 16 sept. 1792. AN, DXXV 63, 638. Journal exact. PRO, HCA 30 401, pt. 1, cote E. Interrogatoire de M. Thiballier.

18. While it is possible that this Félix (as well as Dominique Duhard: Appendix C below) was among the district leaders of the Port-Salut conspiracy in 1791, it has not been possible to determine through available sources the plantation to which Félix, of the Platons revolt, belonged. Thus, the probability that he is the same individual as the Félix of 1791 remains speculative. However, both Dominique and Félix did become company captains in the Legion of Equality later in 1793. The captains were chosen from among those slaves demonstrating distinct qualities of leadership. Very little is known about Bernard except that, in October, he signed a communiqué with Armand, Martial, and Jacques to Montesquieu-Fezensac, commander-general of the South. That this Bernard was the same as the one who, in 1794, was made a regional inspector, along with Armand, is highly probable, but again, speculative, as his owner's name is not given. PRO, HCA 30 392, 214. *La Gazette des Cayes*, No. 82, 18 Oct. 1792, p. 339.

19. PRO, HCA 30 395, 226. Duval to Coquillon, les Cayes, 17 Jan. 1793. HCA 30 394, 15. Billard, fils to Mmes. Billard, Moreau et A[r]mand Billard, les Cayes, 16 Jan. 1793. HCA 30 393, 118. Garat to Perrigny, père, Torbeck, 10 Jan. 1793.

20. AN, DXXV 66, 671. La municipalité des Cayes à M. Delaval, député de la paroisse des Cayes à l'Assemblée Coloniale et secrétaire de sa députation, les Cayes, 27 juillet 1792.

21. PRO, HCA 30 401, pt. 1, cote E. Interrogatoire de M. Thiballier.

22. Ibid. Also, AN, DXXV 94, Ds. 11. Débats entre les accusés et les accusateurs, 16–17. DXXV 62, 628. Les commissaires de l'Assemblée Coloniale aux commissaires de ladite assemblée auprès de l'Assemblée Nationale et du Roi, le Cap, 20 août 1792. ISL, Mémoire.

23. PRO, HCA 30 401, pt. 1, cote B. Déclaration du citoyen Gaujon, les Cayes, 3 janv. 1793.

24. AN, DXXV 62, 619. Extrait des pièces déposées aux archives de l'Assemblée Coloniale. L'Assemblée Provinciale et provisoirement administrative du Sud à l'Assemblée Coloniale, les Cayes, 19 juillet 1792.

25. Ibid.

26. ISL, Mémoire.

27. See Appendix C.

28. PRO, HCA 30 392, 214. *La Gazette des Cayes*, No. 87, 4 Nov. 1792, pp. 361–62. ISL, Mémoire.

29. AN, DXXV 66, 667. Extrait des pièces déposées aux archives de l'Assemblée Coloniale. Blanchelande à l'Assemblée Coloniale, les Cayes, 28 juillet 1792. DXXV 66, 671. La municipalité des Cayes à M. Delaval, député de la paroisse des Cayes à l'Assemblée Coloniale et secrétaire de la députation, les Cayes, 27 juillet 1792.

30. Ibid. Also, PRO, HCA 30 392, 60. Bérault to Bérault, jeune, les Cayes, 17 Jan. 1793. AN, DXXV 63, 638. Journal exact.

31. AN, DXXV 62, 621. La municipalité des Cayes à MM. les membres de l'Assemblée Coloniale, les Cayes, 1 août 1792.

32. AN, DXXV 62, 621. Extrait des pièces déposées aux archives de l'Assemblée Coloniale. Copie d'une lettre écrite à Mme. Blanchelande datée des Cayes, 1 août 1792. DXXV 63, 638. Journal exact. DXXV 62, 621. Extrait des pièces déposées aux archives de l'Assemblée Coloniale. Lettre de M. de Blanchelande à l'Assemblée Coloniale, en mer, 16 août 1792.

33. PRO, HCA 30 392, 60. Bérault to Bérault, jeune, les Cayes, 17 janv. 1792.

34. Ibid. Also, AN, DXXV 62, 621. Extrait des pièces. Copie d'une lettre écrite à Mme. Blanchelande. Garran-Coulon, *Rapport*, 2:581.

35. AN, DXXV 62, 621. Extrait des pièces. Lettre de M. de Blanchelande à l'Assemblée Coloniale.

36. AN, DXXV 62, 621. La municipalité des Cayes à MM. les membres de l'Assemblée Coloniale, les Cayes, 1 août 1792. DXXV 63, 638. Journal exact. PRO, HCA 30 392, 214. *La Gazette des Cayes*, Nos. 80, 81; 11, 14 Oct. 1792, pp. 329, 333.

37. AN, DXXV 62, 621. Extrait des pièces déposées aux archives de l'Assemblée Coloniale. DeFleury, commandant à M. le Général Blanchelande, Port-Salut, 4 août 1792. DXXV 62, 621. Extrait des pièces déposées aux archives de l'Assemblée Coloniale. Dartiguier, commandant de la garde nationale à M. le Général Blanchelande, Camp Labbaye, 15 août 1792. DXXV 62, 621. Copie de la lettre de M. de Saint-Léger, commandant du Camp Labbaye à MM. de la municipalité de Tiburon, Camp Labbaye, 7 août 1792.

38. AN, DXXV 62, 621. Lettre de M. Blanchelande à l'Assemblée Coloniale. See also *Précis historique des annales*, 1:84.

39. AN, DXXV 62, 621. Lettre de Blanchelande à l'Assemblée Coloniale. ISL, Mémoire. PRO, HCA 30 392, 214. *Gazette des Cayes*, No. 85, 28 Oct. 1792, p. 352.

40. AN, DXXV 62, 628. L'Assemblée Coloniale aux commissaires de ladite assemblée auprès de l'Assemblée Nationale à Paris, le Cap, 8 sept. 1792. DXXV 63, 638. Journal exact. ISL, Mémoire. *Précis historique des annales*, 1:84.

41. PRO, HCA 30 395, 241. M. Moullin to Mlle. des Vergers, les Cayes, 15 Jan. 1793.

42. AN, DXXV 2, 23. André Rigaud à M. Roume, commissaire nationale civil, les Cayes, 16 sept. 1792.

43. AN, DXXV 63, 638. Journal exact.

44. Ibid. Also, AN, DXXV 62, 628. L'Assemblée Coloniale aux commissaires de ladite assemblée auprès de l'Assemblée Nationale à Paris, signé, Delaval, le Cap, 8 sept. 1792.

45. PRO, HCA 30 393. Demoncour to Meunier, les Cayes, 22 Dec. 1792.

46. Ibid. Also, HCA 30 393, 238. M. Bergeaud to M. Faucher, Cayes Saint Louis, 16 Jan. 1793. HCA 30 393, 248. Ferrand to Salenave, aîné, les Cayes, 30 Nov. 1792.

47. Ibid.

48. See Appendix C.

49. PRO, HCA 30 392, 214. *La Gazette des Cayes*, No. 88, 8 Nov. 1792, pp. 365–66. Procès-verbal de la sortie faite par un détachement de la paroisse de Cavillon à la réquisition

de celle du Petit-Trou, signé, F. deKrusec, lieutenant du 4e régiment, Cavaillon, 21 sept. 1792.

50. AN, DXXV 62, 628. L'Assemblée Coloniale aux commissaires de ladite assemblée auprès de l'Assemblée Nationale à Paris, signé, Delaval, le Cap, 8 sept. 1792.

51. PRO, HCA 30 395, 241. M. Moullin to Mlle. des Vergers, les Cayes, 15 Jan. 1793.

52. PRO, HCA 30 395, 248. Ferrand to Salenave, aîné, les Cayes, 30 Nov. 1792. HCA 30 395, 152. Ferrand to Salenave, aîné, les Cayes, 3 Jan. 1793.

53. PRO, HCA 30 394, 202. Thibaut to Munier, les Cayes, 30 Dec. 1792, HCA 30 395, 141. Sainet to Belbezo, jeune, les Cayes, 12 Jan. 1792, respectively.

54. See Ch. 5, n. 60 above. PRO, HCA 30 381. Papiers saisis sur François Lavignolle, procureur de la première habitation du banquier Laborde, Plaine-des-Cayes, oct. 1792 au 10 mars 1793.

55. Author is grateful to M. Bernard Foubert, who kindly forwarded the quoted passages in personal correspondence.

56. PRO, HCA 30 392, 115. Deville to Van Duffel, les Cayes, 7 Dec. 1792. HCA 30 381. Papiers saisis sur François Lavignolle.

57. PRO, HCA 30 392, 73. Lez to Muzard, les Cayes, 18 Jan. 1793.

58. PRO, HCA 30 393, 189. Pierre Gensterbloem to Mlle. Félicité Beaudrau, camp général, 20 Dec. 1792.

59. Ibid. (My translation.)

60. Ibid.

61. PRO, HCA 30 395, 254. Saint-Martin to Duplessy, les Cayes, 16 Jan. 1793.

62. PRO, HCA 30 394, 202. Thibaut to Munier, les Cayes, 30 Dec. 1792.

63. PRO, HCA 30 392, 73. Lez to Muzard, les Cayes, 18 Jan. 1793.

64. PRO, HCA 30 393, 157. Derrecard to Muzard, les Cayes, 4 Nov. 1792.

65. PRO, HCA 39 392, 232. Demaleval, Champel et Bouffart to M. Laconfourque, les Cayes, 31 Dec. 1792.

66. PRO, HCA 39 395, 115. Caudron Beauzamy et cie. to MM. Lallemand Beauzamy et cie., les Cayes, 4 Dec. 1792.

67. PRO, HCA 30 394, 2. De Coulanges to Sallonnyer de Nion, les Cayes, 16 Jan. 1793.

68. PRO, HCA 30, 392, 156. Clarac, fils to Clarac, père, Cayes Saint Louis, 10 Jan. 1793.

69. PRO, HCA 39 395, 13. Letter to MM. Gamba and Archdeacon, les Cayes, 20 Dec. 1792. HCA 30 392, 1. Montbrun to Desmirail, Cayes Saint-Louis, 24 Jan. 1793. The Plaine-du-Fond was also referred to as Plaine-des-Cayes, and the designations are used interchangeably.

70. PRO, HCA 30 395, 264. Vernet to Corbun, les Cayes, 15 Jan. 1793. HCA 30 394, 36. Chavanet to Portier, Cayes Saint-Louis, 13 Jan. 1793.

71. PRO, HCA 30 392, 140. Letter to M. Farthonat, les Cayes, 15 Nov. 1792.

72. PRO, HCA 30 392, 1. Montbrun to Desmirail, Cayes Saint-Louis, 24 Jan. 1793.

73. Lacroix, *Mémoires*, 1:223. Also, PRO, HCA 30 392, 1. Montbrun to Desmirail, Cayes Saint-Louis, 24 Jan. 1793. HCA 30 395, 7. A. Clée to J. Clée, Camp Laplace, 20 Dec. 1792.

74. PRO, HCA 30 394, 136. Provot to his parents, les Cayes, 1 Dec. 1792. Cited in Bernard Foubert, "Les volontaires nationaux de la Seine-Inférieure à Saint-Domingue (octobre 1792–janvier 1793)," *Bulletin de la Société d'histoire de la Guadeloupe* 51 (1er trim. 1982):17.

75. PRO, HCA 30 393, 40. Gensterbloem to his wife, les Cayes, 1 Dec. 1792. Cited by Foubert in ibid., 29.

76. PRO, HCA 30 393, 78. Bricaud to M. Bernard, les Cayes, 12 Dec. 1792. Cited in ibid.

77. PRO, HCA 30 395, 9. Solon de Bénech to Mlle. Gauthier, les Cayes, Fond de l'Isle-à-Vache, n.d. (Dec. 1792?).

78. Céligny Ardouin, *Essais sur l'histoire d'Haïti* (Port-au-Prince: B. Ardouin, 1865), 103. PRO, HCA 30 401, pt. 1. Attaque des Platons, signé, Harty, commandant en chef provisoire de la province du Sud, 13 janv. 1793. HCA 30 394, 8. Dubreil to LeJeune, commissaire de la Marine à l'Orient, Cayes Saint-Louis, 19 Jan. 1793.

79. Estimates of the number of slaves composing the community at Platons vary considerably, ranging from eight to sixteen thousand. The most frequently cited estimates, however, place the number of slaves at ten to twelve thousand. PRO, HCA 30 393, 8. Mazarquil, fils to Mazarquil, père, Cayes Saint-Louis, 11 Jan. 1793. HCA 30 394, 202. Thibaut to Munier, les Cayes, 30 Dec. 1792. HCA 30 393, 234. Merlin to Simon, les Cayes, 6 Dec. 1792. HCA 30 392, 100. J. B. Rocton to Cherbonnier, Cayes Saint-Louis, 1 Dec. 1792. HCA 30 393, 189. Gensterbloem to Mlle. Félicité Beaudrau, camp général, les Cayes, 20 Dec. 1792. HCA 30 392, 127. Reffuveuille to Mme. Ridon, Camp Labiche, Cavaillon, 10 Jan. 1793. HCA 30 392, 34. H. Duvau to M. Duvau, les Cayes, 17 Jan. 1793. HCA 30 394, 184. DeJoye to Perdigon, jeune, les Cayes, 1 Jan. 1793.

80. PRO, HCA 30 394, 8. Dubreil to LeJeune, Cayes Saint-Louis, 19 Jan. 1973.

81. PRO, HCA 30 394, 15. Billard, fils to Mmes. Billard, Moreau et A[r]mand Billard, les Cayes, 16 Jan. 1793.

82. Ibid. Also, HCA 30 395, 143. Dubreil to citoyenne Piquot, les Cayes, 17 Jan. 1793. HCA 30 394, 8. Dubreil to LeJeune, Cayes Saint-Louis, 19 Jan. 1793. HCA 30 392, 146. R. Bouard to Dervillé, les Cayes, 14 Jan. 1793.

83. PRO, HCA 30 394, 8. Dubreil to LeJeune, Cayes Saint-Louis, 19 Jan. 1793. See also Ch. 4, n. 58 above.

84. See the previous discussion of their demands in the present chapter.

85. In this respect, see the attitude and activities of Vendôme and Grégoire in the present chapter, above, and of Jacques Formon in Ch. 7 below.

86. On suspicions of Perrigny's involvement with the rebels, see *Précis historique des annales*, 1:95, 122.

87. PRO, HCA 30 394, 57. Saint-Martin to LeBourg, les Cayes, 23 Dec. 1792. HCA 30 395, 63. Gasteau to Chaillon, les Cayes, 25 Dec. 1792. HCA 30 393, 118. Garat to Perrigny, père, Torbeck, 10 Jan. 1793. HCA 30 392. Perrigny, fils to Perrigny, père, les Cayes, 8 Dec. 1792. HCA 30 392, 32. Léon de Perrigny to M. le Commissaire National Civil, la prison des Cayes, 21 Dec. 1792. HCA 30 393, 233. Caudron Beauzamy et cie. to M. J.-B. Lafosse, les Cayes, 4 Dec. 1792. HCA 30 393, 231. Philibert to Mme. Derouaudier, les Cayes, 13 Jan. 1793.

88. PRO, HCA 30 395, 108. Letter to Dr. Smith from his student, la sucrerie paternelle . . . , 1 Dec. 1792. HCA 30 394, 201. Lezognac to Mlle. Sophie Ladurautie, les Cayes, 17 Jan. 1793. HCA 30 395, 233. Caudron Beauzamy et cie. to J.-B. Lafosse, les Cayes, 4 Dec. 1792. HCA 30 393, 262. Belloc to Mme. Azard, les Cayes, 10 Jan 1793. HCA 30 392, 115. Deville to Van Duffel, les Cayes, 7 Dec. 1792. HCA 30 393, 248. Ferrand to Salenave, aîné, les Cayes, 30 Nov. 1792.

89. This observation is made by Debien and, based on the existing plantation lists studied thus far, appears to be representative. *Esclaves aux Antilles*, 56–61.

90. On this recurrent question of class and color in Saint Domingue, see the discussion in Labelle, *Idéologie*, 44–51.

91. PRO, HCA 30 392, 115. Deville to Van Duffel, les Cayes, 7 Nov. 1792.

92. Ibid. HCA 30 393, 233. Caudron Beauzamy to M. J.-B. Lafosse, les Cayes, 4 Dec. 1792.

93. PRO, HCA 30 393, 213. Gayes to Pelletan, Saint-Louis, 17 Nov. 1792.

94 PRO, HCA 30 395, 13. Letter to MM. Gamba and Archdeacon, les Cayes, 20 Dec. 1792.

95. PRO, HCA 30 393, 227. Prudent Boisgerard to Mlle. Tasset, les Cayes, 6 Jan. 1793.

96. PRO, HCA 30 392, 196. Toirac, jeune to Duveau, frères, les Cayes, 12 Jan. 1793. HCA 30 392, 34. H. Duvau to M. Duvau, les Cayes, 17 Jan 1793.

97. PRO, HCA 30 401, pt. 1. Attaque des Platons. As early as April 1792 Jean Kina had been freed by his master and armed by the white planters of Tiburon, who, upon his solicitation, provided him with four hundred of their slaves to fight the mulattoes and free blacks, along with their slave allies. ANSOM, RC 2, 175. *La Gazette des Cayes*, No. 33, 22 avril 1792, p. 133. AN, DXXV 94, Ds. 11. Débats entre les accusés et les accusateurs, 16–23. Lacroix, *Mémoires*, 1:198. After the attack on Platons, he offered to destroy the remaining slave forces that had fled to Macaya (see below in the present chapter) if the planters furnished him with an army of one thousand slaves. PRO, HCA 30 395, 244. Letter to Mme. Leplicher, les Cayes, 23 Jan. 1793. Adventurer, opportunist, mercenary, Jean Kina left Saint Domingue to fight for England and received the rank of colonel in the British army. Yet on the other hand, in 1800, he was discovered fomenting a revolt of free blacks in Martinique. Fouchard, *Les marrons de la liberté*, 462. See also the interesting and highly informative article on Jean Kina by David Geggus, "Slave, Soldier, Rebel: The Strange Career of Jean Kina," *Jamaican Historical Review* (1980):33–51.

98. PRO, HCA 30 393, 61. Demaleval, Champel et Bouffart to Mme. Leplicher, Cayes Saint-Louis, 12 Jan. 1793. HCA 30 395, 59. Caudron Beauzamy et cie. to J.-B. Lafosse, les Cayes, 14 Jan. 1793. HCA 30 394, 15. Billard, fils to Mmes. Billard, Moreau et A[r]mand Billard, les Cayes, 16 Jan. 1793.

99. Ibid. Also, HCA 30 394, 8. Dubreil to LeJeune, commissaire de la Marine à l'Orient, Cayes Saint-Louis, 19 Jan. 1793. HCA 39 395, 156. Gabriel Filleux to Filleux, père et mère, les Cayes, 10 Jan 1793. HCA 30 392, 196. Toirac, jeune to MM. Duvau, frères, les Cayes, 12 Jan. 1793. HCA 30 392, 171. Demaleval to Champel, les Cayes, 19 Jan. 1793.

100. PRO, HCA 30 392, 34. H. Duvau to M. Duvau, les Cayes, 17 Jan 1793. HCA 30 392, 129. Sainet to Mme. veuve Sainet, les Cayes, 19 Jan. 1793. HCA 30 395, 254. Saint-Martin to Duplessy, les Cayes, 16 Jan. 1793.

101. It is almost impossible to arrive at an accurate estimate of those who did return. One colonist stated that these slaves were very few in number, while another estimated that some three thousand had returned. PRO, HCA 30 393, 5. F. Peche to Mme. Peche, Fond de l'Isle-à-Vache, 17 Jan. 1793 and HCA 30 392, 55. Martin to M. Party, n.p. (Jan. 1793?).

102. PRO, HCA 30 395, 142. Guénin to Mme. Guénin, les Cayes, 24 Jan. 1793. HCA 30 394, 2. DeCoulanges to Salonnyer de Nion, les Cayes, 16 Jan. 1793. HCA 30 392, 2. Deville to B. Deville, les Cayes, 27 Dec. 1792. HCA 30 392, 128. Deville to B. Deville, les Cayes, 19 Jan. 1793.

103. PRO, HCA 30 393, 266. C. Vigarous, frère to Mlle. Marianne Vigarous, Cayes Saint-Louis, 23 Jan. 1793.

104. PRO, HCA 30 393, 189. Gensterbloem to his mother, les Cayes, 16 Jan. 1793.

Chapter Seven

1. AN, DXXV 12, 113. Le citoyen Polverel, commissaire national civil au citoyen Sonthonax, son collègue, les Cayes, 15 janv. 1793. DXXV 20, 206. Harty, commandant en chef
de la province du Sud au citoyen commissaire civil, les Platons, 13 janv. 1793.

2. AN, DXXV 11, 106. Le citoyen Polverel, commissaire national civil . . . à la Convention Nationale, les Cayes, 22 janv. 1793. DXXV 39, 399. Registre d'ordres et décisions,
Polverel, les Cayes, 27 janv. 1793. Garran-Coulon, *Rapport*, 3:277.

3. The civil commission was composed of three members: Sonthonax, commissioner for
the North; Polverel for the West; and Ailhaud for the South. One month after his arrival,
Ailhaud abandoned his post and returned to France, leaving the administration of both the
West and the South to Polverel. Desparbès was sent as interim governor-general to replace
Blanchelande, and generals Lasalle (West), Hinisdal (North), and Montesquieu-Fezensac
(South) were sent to take over command of the army in the various provinces. They were
accompanied by six thousand French troops to enforce the 4 April decree and put down the
black slave insurrections throughout the colony. Within two months, over half of these troops
were killed off by the deleterious effects of the climate.

4. See Garran-Coulon, *Rapport*, 3:264–65.

5. *Précis historique des annales*, 1:100.

6. Garran-Coulon, *Rapport*, 3:295–303. Sannon, *Histoire de Toussaint*, 1:115–16. Malenfant, *Des colonies*, 32–39. Lacroix, *Mémoires*, 1:235–37. Cabon, *Histoire d'Haïti*, 3:128–29.
Dalmas, *Histoire*, 2:119–20. This whole episode is also recounted in the *Précis historique des
annales*, 1:97–100.

7. Garran-Coulon, *Rapport*, 3:258–59.

8. The irregularity in his nomination stemmed from the fact that he had recently inherited
some property in Saint Domingue and, as a colonial property owner, was legally ineligible to
hold an administrative post. But, as Robert Stein has argued, this technicality served as a
pretext for the civil commissioners to further consolidate their own position since they, on the
one hand, and Galbaud, on the other, stood in mutual competition for supreme authority in
the colony. As it was Galbaud's intention to return to France to denounce the civil commissioners before the National Convention, the commissioners had humiliated him by staging
his departure on grounds of insubordination and lack of patriotism so as to discredit him
even before his arrival in France. *Sonthonax*, 70–73. See also, *Précis historique des annales*,
1:106–8.

9. AN, DXXV 41, 406. Sonthonax et Polverel à la Convention Nationale, le Cap, 10 juillet
1793. Lacroix, *Mémoires*, 1:243–44. Malenfant, *Des colonies*, 50–54. Dalmas, *Histoire*,
2:190–96. Sannon, *Histoire de Toussaint*, 1:121–23. Garran-Coulon, *Rapport*, 3:440–46.

10. AN, DXXV 41, 406. Sonthonax et Polverel à la Convention Nationale, le Cap, 10
juillet 1793. Garran-Coulon, *Rapport*, 3:448, 476. Lacroix, *Mémoires*, 1:244–45.

11. AN, DXXV 40, 400. Registre servant à la transcription des proclamations, ordon-
nances et autres actes de la commission civile, imprimés depuis le 13 juin [1793] jusqu'au
13 mai 1794, Haut de Cap, 21 juin 1793.

12. Lacroix, *Mémoires*, 1:251. Malenfant, *Des colonies*, 57.

13. AN, DXXV 61, 609. Extrait des pièces déposées aux archives de l'Assemblée Coloniale. Extrait du journal du Camp des Mornets . . . , commencé le 23 août 1791, signé,
Salet, Dessources et Larroque, officiers. Entry for 5 Sept. 1791.

14. Garran-Coulon, *Rapport*, 4:44.

15. Ibid., 50. AN, DXXV 42, 413. Correspondance avec tous les officiers militaires de
terre et de mer, en date du 12 juin 1793 jusqu'au 6 nov. 1793. Les commissaires civils à

Dubisson, commandant au Haut du Cap, le Cap, 6 juillet 1793. Les commissaires civils à Dubisson, commandant des postes extérieurs de la ville du Cap, le Cap, 7 juillet 1793. DXXV 43, 415. Registre de la correspondance des commissaires civils en date du 12 juin 1793 jusqu'au 26 juillet 1793, Les commissaires civils à Dubisson, le Cap, 13 juillet 1793. DXXV 42, 412. Les commissaires civils au commandant Pierrot, le Cap, 13 juillet 1793. DXXV 23, 231, CQ69-CQ75, Nos. 53–59. Various letters written by Pierrot, some of them to the civil commissioners, all of them reiterating his allegiance to the republic. Also in the DXXV 23, 231 dossier are letters written by Macaya, Barthélemy, Benjamin, Michaud, and Thomas, all popular maroon leaders, expressing an unflinching loyalty to Jean-François, their *Grand Amiral*, and a deep distrust of the French and their commissioners.

16. AN, DXXV 43, 418. Correspondance des commissaires civils avec divers particuliers, en date du 13 juin 1793 jusqu'au 20 mai 1794. Les commissaires civils à Biassou, le Cap, 22 juin 1793.

17. AN, DXXV 12, 118. Letter from Jean-François and Biassou, gouvernement de la Mine, 28 June 1793.

18. This letter is cited in Garran-Coulon, *Rapport*, 4:48. Also cited in Lacroix, *Mémoires*, 1:252.

19. See Stein, *Sonthonax*, 82–83.

20. The full text of Toussaint's letter is quoted in Sannon, *Histoire de Toussaint*, 1:165, and in Victor Schoelcher, *La vie de Toussaint Louverture* (Paris: Ollendorf, 1899), 98–100. On the various interpretations concerning Toussaint's turnabout to join the French republican forces a year later, see the points raised in D. Geggus, "From His Most Catholic Majesty to the godless République: the 'volte-face' of Toussaint Louverture and the ending of slavery in Saint Domingue," *Revue française d'histoire d'Outre-Mer* 65 (1978):481–99.

21. AN, DXXV 40, 399. Registre d'ordres et décisions, en date du 4 mai 1793 jusqu'au 19 juin 1793, suite. Proclamations from 15 May to 3 June 1793.

22. Stein, *Sonthonax*, 85–87. Garran-Coulon, *Rapport*, 4:53.

23. AN, DXXV 44, 419. Polverel, commissaire national civil à Sonthonax, son collègue, Port-au-Prince, 26 août 1793. DXXV 44, 419. Polverel, commissaire national civil à Delpech, 31 août 1793. DXXV 12, 118. Copie littérale d'une lettre de Jean-François, grand amiral, adressée à Guyambois, commandant pour le roi en chef de l'Artibonite, en date du 10 août 1793 et trouvée à la barrière du Camp Prumer le 15 sept. 1793.

24. Malenfant, *Des colonies*, 59–60. Lacroix, *Mémoires*, 1:260.

25. Stein, *Sonthonax*, 88–89. *Précis historique des annales*, 1:111.

26. *Sonthonax*, 79. For Stein's discussion of general emancipation and of Sonthonax's role in its realization, see ibid., 75–95 passim. Also, C. Fick, review of *Léger Félicité Sonthonax: the lost sentinel of the Republic*, by Robert L. Stein, *Nieuwe West-Indische Gids/New West-Indian Guide* 62, nos. 3–4 (1988): 207–8.

27. AN, DXXV 97, 849, Ds. 18. Proclamation de Polverel et Sonthonax du 25 juillet 1793, le Cap, 25 juillet 1793.

28. AN, DXXV 21, 212. André Rigaud aux citoyens Polverel et Sonthonax, commissaires civils, les Cayes, 1 août 1793.

29. Armand, Martial, Bernard, Jacques Formon, and Gilles Bénech were all made company captains in the Legion. AN, DXXV 27, 281. Prison records for les Cayes, Sept. 1793 to Jan. 1794.

30. AN, DXXV 21, 212. Le colonel Rigaud, commandant provisoire de la province du Sud au citoyen Polverel, commissaire civil de la république, les Cayes, 22 août 1793.

31. Ibid.

32. The Cayes prison record (August 1792 to 6 October 1793, the date of Polverel's ar-

rival in the South), from which this evidence is derived, lists the number of *nègres épaves*, or fugitive slaves that were captured but neither reported nor claimed by their masters, who presumably had fled the colony, been killed off, or were otherwise uninterested in claiming their slaves; these slaves were destined to be sold at public auction. In July 1793, there were ten. In August, there were twenty-seven more, followed by an additional fifty-two in September. During the first week of October, from the second to the sixth, a mere five-day period, twenty-five others had been jailed. If the trend continued, there would have been a one-month increase for October of over a hundred. AN, DXXV 27, 281. Etat de ce qui est dû au citoyen l'Abbé, concierge, pour nourriture et frais de géolle des nègres ci-après nommés, lesquels ont été élargis de prison en vertu de la proclamation du citoyen Polverel . . . , le 7 octobre 1793, les Cayes, 10 oct. 1793.

33. AN, DXXV 21, 212. Le colonel Rigaud, commandant provisoire de la province du Sud au citoyen Polverel, commissaire civil de la république, les Cayes, 22 août 1793.

34. AN, DXXV 21, 215. Le colonel A. Rigaud, commandant provisoire du Sud au citoyen Polverel, commissaire civil de la république, les Cayes, 12 sept. 1793.

35. AN, DXXV 42, 413. Correspondance avec tous les officiers militaires de terre et de mer, en date du 6 nov. 1793 jusqu'au 24 mai 1794, de la commission nationale civile. Sonthonax à Bauvais, commandant à la Croix-des-Bouquets, Port-Républicain, 17 mars 1794.

36. Ibid. AN, DXXV 12, 116. E. Polverel à Sonthonax, les Cayes, 30 nov. 1793.

37. AN, DXXV 22, 223. Petit, commandant du Camp Périn à Polverel, commissaire civil, Camp Périn, 7 déc. 1793. DXXV 22, 224. Petit, commandant au Camp Périn à Polverel, commissaire civil, Camp Périn, 16 déc. 1793. The Mocos, or Mokos, were generally considered to be taciturn and easily given to sickness because of the swampy marshlands throughout their country, situated at the southern end of the Gold Coast. For this reason, very few were brought into the colony by the slave traders, and if they were, were usually passed off as Ibos, a reputedly melancholy people prone to suicide. Moreau de Saint-Méry, *Description*, 1:51–52.

38. AN, DXXV 22, 225. Petit, commandant au Camp Périn à Polverel, commissaire civil de la république, Camp Périn, 1 janv. 1794.

39. He was ordered to select a certain number of armed slaves for service in the legion, but instead sent them into the enemy camp. AN, DXXV 21, 212. André Rigaud aux citoyens Polverel et Sonthonax, commissaires civils de la république, les Cayes, 1 août 1793. DXXV 21, 211. Sévré, adjudant de Tiburon au citoyen André Rigaud, commandant en chef de l'armée de la république, Tiburon, 2 août 1793.

40. In Foubert, "Volontaires nationaux," 37.

41. AN, DXXV 21, 212. André Rigaud, colonel, commandant provisoire de la province du Sud, les Cayes, 14 août 1793.

42. The insurgents from Platons and Macaya did not descend until August. Remaining in the Plaine-du-Fond in their various camps, their official enrollment into the diverse companies did not take place before September. By October, within one month, they were being arrested day by day, in numbers varying from one or two, to twenty or more at a time. During the three-month period, from October to December 1793, the prison records for les Cayes indicate over three hundred entries for arrests of black soldiers from the various companies of the legion, many of them chronic absconders. AN, DXXV 27, 281; 282. Also, AN, DXXV 22, 220. Elie Bourg, commandant militaire de Torbeck au citoyen Polverel, commissaire civil, Torbeck, 1 nov. 1793.

43. AN, DXXV 12, 219. Polverel, commissaire civil de la république à Sonthonax, son collègue au Cap, Port-au-Prince, 3 sept. 1793.

44. Garran-Coulon, *Rapport*, 4:97.

45. Ibid., 88. On Polverel's progression toward general emancipation in the West and the South (as opposed to that of Sonthonax in the North) and his own vision of freedom for the slaves within the parameters of property rights and obligations, see also Stein's discussion of the issues in *Sonthonax*, 90–94.

46. Letter from Delpech to his colleagues. Cited in Garran-Coulon, *Rapport*, 4:94–96. Also Stein, *Sonthonax*, 92.

47. Cited in Stein, *Sonthonax*, 93.

48. Cited in Garran-Coulon, *Rapport*, 4:88.

49. Stein, *Sonthonax*, 93.

50. *Précis historique des annales*, 1:116.

51. Stein, *Sonthonax*, 93–94. See Polverel's reiteration of the owner's property rights in present chapter below.

52. AN, DXXV 41, 404. Procès-verbal de la célébration de la fête de la république française au Port-au-Prince, E. Polverel, Port-au-Prince, 21 sept. 1793. Also, Proclamation of 27 August 1793, printed in Garran-Coulon, *Rapport*, 4:81–85.

53. Unless otherwise indicated, the following section will be based on the statements and observations made by Polverel in his 7 February proclamation. AN, DXXV 28, 286. Règlement sur les proportions du travail et de la récompense, sur le partage des produits de la culture entre le propriétaire et les cultivateurs, petite habitation O'Sheill, Plaine-du-Fond de l'Isle-à-Vache, 7 fév. 1794, signé, E. Polverel. Various prison lists and other related documents for this period, indicating a high incidence of arrested black workers, as well as soldiers in the legion, are found in AN, DXXV 27, 281 and 282; DXXV 37, 373 and 374; DXXV 41, 404; DXXV 44, 421 and are cited throughout the chapter in reference to diverse incidents involving the ex-slaves.

54. AN, DXXV 41, 404. Registre d'ordres et décisions, petite habitation O'Sheill, Plaine-du-Fond de l'Isle-à-Vache, 25 mars 1794.

55. *Précis historique des annales*, 1:127, 133.

56. Ibid. Stein, *Sonthonax*, 94.

57. AN, DXXV 28, 286. Règlement sur les proportions.

58. Ibid.

59. AN, DXXV 41, 404. Registre d'ordres et décisions, petite habitation O'Sheill, 18 oct. 1793.

60. DXXV 14, 137. Declaration of Polverel, habitation Vernet, 10 Oct. 1793. Declarations of Vernet workers, habitation Vernet, 30 Oct. 1793.

61. Ibid.

62. AN, DXXV 28, 286. Procès-verbaux de la commune de Cavaillon sur la lecture faite aux cultivateurs du règlement du 7 février 1794, Cavaillon, 21–28 fév.; 3–5 mars 1794. Of the twenty-three plantations interviewed, the final decisions of twenty are recorded. Thirteen opted to work six days per week, and seven chose five days per week.

63. AN, DXXV 44, 421. Sonthonax à Blanchet, petite habitation O'Sheill, 22 mars 1794. DXXV 37, 374. Blanchet, commandant militaire à Aquin à Polverel, commissaire civil, Aquin, 28 mars 1794.

64. A majority consisted of one half of the plantation workers, plus one.

65. AN, DXXV 28, 287. Règlement de police sur la culture et les cultivateurs, E. Polverel, commissaire civil de la république, petite habitation O'Sheill, 28 fév. 1794. Of the hundreds of workers arrested on the plantations in the Plaine-du-Fond, roughly from the end of February, when the penal code was published, to the beginning of April 1794, the cause of arrest is not always indicated. However, in most cases, the black workers were condemned

to "public works without pay until further orders," a sentence that could apply to almost any of the offenses specified in Polverel's 28 February police proclamation. AN, DXXV 27, 281, 282; DXXV 37, 373, 374; DXXV 41, 404; DXXV 44, 421.

66. AN, DXXV 41, 404. Registre d'ordres et décisions, petite habitation O'Sheill, 19 fév.; 10 mars; 4, 8 avril 1794. DXXV 37, 373. Dalesme, gérant sequestre de l'habitation Formon au citoyen commissaire, au Vieux Bourg, 17 mars 1794. DXXV 37, 374. Petit, commandant au Camp Périn à Polverel, commissaire civil, Camp Périn, 25 mars 1794. DXXV 37, 373. Salomon, commandant militaire à Polverel, commissaire civil, les Cayes, 19 mars 1794. DXXV 44, 421. Sonthonax à Lachapelle, petite habitation O'Sheill, 24 fév. 1794.

67. AN, DXXV 41, 404. Registre d'ordres et décisions, petite habitation O'Sheill, 16, 24 fév.; 12, 17, 20, 21, 27 mars 1794. DXXV 44, 421. Sonthonax à Lachapelle, petite habitation O'Sheill, 24 fév. 1794. Sonthonax à Boury, petite habitation O'Sheill, 9 mars 1794. Sonthonax à Baulos, petite habitation O'Sheill, 11 mars 1794. DXXV 22, 226. Beauregard, commandant militaire à Etienne Polverel, commissaire civil, Cavaillon, 2 avril 1794. DXXV 37, 373. Thiveruy, gérant de l'habitation Labiche et Dunezac au commissaire civil, au Fond, 20 mars 1794. DXXV 37, 374. Attestations of concierge, les Cayes prison, les Cayes, 28 March 1794. Petit, commandant militaire à Polverel, commissaire civil, Camp Périn, 25 mars 1794. Salomon, commandant militaire à Polverel, commissaire civil, les Cayes, 30 mars 1794. Poulain, économe-gérant de la deuxième habitation Laborde à E. Polverel, deuxième habitation Laborde, 23 mars 1794.

68. AN, DXXV 44, 421. Sonthonax à Salomon, petite habitation O'Sheill, 2 avril 1794.

69. AN, DXXV 41, 404. Registre d'ordres et décisions, petite habitation O'Sheill, 15, 28 mars 1794. DXXV 44, 421. Sonthonax à Petit, petite habitation O'Sheill, 9, 13, 15 mars 1794. Sonthonax à Salomon, petite habitation O'Sheill, 2 avril 1794. DXXV 37, 373. Petit, commandant militaire à Polverel, commissaire civil, Camp Périn, 15 mars 1794. Lacolle, gérant de l'habitation Coderc au commissaire civil, habitation Coderc, 20 mars 1794. DXXV 37, 374. Salomon, commandant militaire à Polverel, commissaire civil, les Cayes, 30 mars 1794. DXXV 22, 226. Beauregard, commandant militaire à Etienne Polverel, commissaire civil, Cavaillon, 2 avril 1794. Also, DXXV 27, 281. Etat de ce qui est dû.

70. AN, DXXV 37, 373. Petit, commandant au Camp Périn à Polverel, commissaire civil, Camp Périn, 15 mars 1794.

71. AN, DXXV 37, 374. Petit, commandant au Camp Périn à Polverel, commissaire civil, Camp Périn, 27 mars 1794.

72. AN, DXXV 37, 374. Petit, commandant au Camp Périn à Polverel, commissaire civil, Camp Périn, 25 mars 1794.

73. AN, DXXV 41, 404. Registre d'ordres et décisions, petite habitation O'Sheill, 2, 19 mars. DXXV 44, 421. Sonthonax à Marin, procureur de la commune de Torbeck, petite habitation O'Sheill, 16 mars 1794.

74. AN, DXXV 41, 404. Registre d'ordres et décisions, petite habitation O'Sheill, 20, 31 mars; 3 avril 1794. DXXV 44, 421. Sonthonax à Salomon, petite habitation O'Sheill, 20 mars 1794. DXXV 37, 373. François Médor au citoyen commissaire civil, au Fond, 20 mars 1794. Elie Boury, commandant militaire de Torbeck à Daniel Gellée, secrétaire à la commission civile, Torbeck, 13 mars 1794.

75. AN, DXXV 37, 373. Lacolle, gérant de l'habitation Coderc au commissaire civil, habitation Coderc, 20 mars 1794. DXXV 41, 404. Registre d'ordres et décisions, petite habitation O'Sheill, 20 mars 1794.

76. AN, DXXV 37, 373. Marelot, gérant au commandant militaire des Cayes, troisième habitation Laborde, 19 mars 1794. Salomon, commandant militaire à Polverel, commissaire civil, les Cayes, 19 mars 1794.

77. On their attitudes toward the mulattoes and free blacks seeking to recruit them in their armed struggle for political equality, and their reluctance to participate in the Platons insurrection, see Chs. 5 and 6 above. The third Laborde estate was the most highly creolized of the three, and the *procureur*, Emmanuel Delolocque, also seems, "through the influence of his personality and ascendancy over the workers, to have maintained the fidelity of a large part of this *atelier* until the very end [1802]." Foubert, "Marronage sur les habitations Laborde," 3, 28.

78. AN, DXXV 37, 374. Etienne Rostand au commissaire civil, habitation Gallais, 29 mars 1794. Salomon, commandant militaire à Daniel Gellée, secrétaire *ad hoc* de la commission civile, les Cayes, 29 mars 1794. Salomon, commandant militaire à Polverel, commissaire civil, les Cayes, 30 mars 1794.

79. AN, DXXV 41, 404. Registre d'ordres et décisions, petite habitation O'Sheill, 10 mars 1794. DXXV 44, 421. Sonthonax à Salomon, petite habitation O'Sheill, 20, 24 mars 1794. Sonthonax à André Piqueret, gérant de l'habitation Regnier, petite habitation O'Sheill, 28 fév. 1794. DXXV 37, 373. Beauregard, commandant militaire à Etienne Polverel, commissaire civil, Cavaillon, 20 mars 1794. DXXV 37, 374. Salomon, commandant militaire à Polverel, commissaire civil, les Cayes, 30 mars 1794.

80. AN, DXXV 28, 286. Règlement sur les proportions.

81. AN, DXXV 37, 373. [Bazille?] Poulain au citoyen commissaire, n.p., 20 mars 1794.

82. AN, DXXV 41, 404. Registre d'ordres et décisions, petite habitation O'Sheill, 31 mars 1794. DXXV 37, 373. Lachapelle, capitaine à l'adjudant général au citoyen Polverel, commissaire civil, les Cayes, 20 mars 1794. DXXV 37, 374. Salomon à Duboisgéheneul, secrétaire *ad hoc* de la commission civile, les Cayes, 21 mars 1794.

83. AN, DXXV 37, 374. Lacolle, gérant de l'habitation Coderc au commissaire civil, habitation Coderc, 30 mars 1794.

84. AN, DXXV 37, 374. François Poulain à Salomon, commandant militaire, au Fond, 30 mars 1794.

85. AN, DXXV 28, 286. Règlement sur les proportions.

86. AN, DXXV 37, 373. Dalesme, gérant séquestre de l'habitation Formon, au Vieux Bourg, 17 mars 1794. DXXV 37, 374. Salomon, commandant militaire au commissaire civil, les Cayes, 26 mars 1794. Attestations of concierge, les Cayes prison, les Cayes, 29 March 1794. Petit, commandant au Camp Périn à Polverel, commissaire civil, Camp Périn, 25 mars 1794. DXXV 41, 404. Registre d'ordres et décisions, petite habitation O'Sheill, 25, 29 mars; 6, 8 avril 1794.

87. AN, DXXV 37, 373. Lachapelle, capitaine à l'adjudant général au citoyen Polverel, commissaire civil, les Cayes, 20 mars 1794. Salomon, commandant militaire provisoire aux Cayes à Duboisguéheneul, secrétaire *ad hoc* de la commission civile, 21 mars 1794.

88. AN, DXXV 22, 226. Beauregard, commandant militaire à Etienne Polverel, commissaire civil, Cavaillon, 2 avril 1794. DXXV 41, 404. Registre d'ordres et décisions, petite habitation O'Sheill, 3 avril 1794.

89. AN, DXXV 41, 404. Registre d'ordres et décisions, petite habitation O'Sheill, 6, 8 avril 1794.

90. AN, DXXV 38, 387. Etat des africains cultivateurs commandés pour les travaux des fossés et fortifications, qui ne se sont point rendus cette semaine aux dits travaux, les Cayes, 24 janv. 1794, signé, Morancy.

91. AN, DXXV 38, 387. Interrogation of citizen Barthélemy Guilgault, habitation O'Sheill, 2 Feb. 1794, signed, Barthélemy Guilgault, E. Polverel and Duboisguéheneul, sec. *ad hoc*. Interrogation of citizen Pierre Gilles, habitation O'Sheill, 1 Feb. 1794, signed, E. Polverel and Duboisguéheneul. Interrogation of citizen Cada, habitation O'Sheill, 2 Feb.

1794, signed, Barthélemy Guilgault, E. Polverel and Duboisguéheneul. Barthélemy Guilgault to Polverel, les Cayes, 1 Feb. 1794. Bazille Poulain, gérant sur l'habitation au citoyen commissaire civil, habitation Mercy, 1 fév. 1794. Letter to Augustin Rigaud, n.p., n.d.

92. AN, DXXV 28, 288. Proclamation of 31 March 1794, signed, Polverel, petite habitation O'Sheill, Plaine-du-Fond de l'Isle-à-Vache.

93. AN, DXXV 41, 404. Registre d'ordres et décisions, petite habitation O'Sheill, 31 mars 1794. The other six were; Bartholo, Baptiste, Jacquet, Jean Créole, Thomas, and Amant. DXXV 28, 288. Tableau des habitations séquestrées dans la Plaine-du-Fond . . . distribuées en sections par ordre du commissaire civil, petite habitation O'Sheill, 31 mars 1794.

94. AN, DXXV 44, 421. Les commissaires civils à Simonet, préposé de l'administration à Jacmel, Port-Républicain, 6 mai 1794.

95. *Précis historique des annales*, 1:128.

96. Ibid., 125.

97. See Debien, *Esclaves aux Antilles*, 56–61.

98. Cuvelier, Mgr. J. B., ed., *Documents sur une mission française au Kakongo, 1766–1776*, Mémoires, Vol. 1 (Brussels: Institut Royal Colonial Belge, 1953), 50.

99. Ibid.

100. Cuvelier, Mgr., *Ancien royaume de Congo*, 194.

101. Ibid., 192.

102. Cuvelier, ed., *Documents*, 54.

103. The points raised in this respect are merely to suggest an area of research that may, in the end, reveal a far richer cultural input into slave society, if not into Haitian rural society, from the eighteenth-century Congo than has generally been assumed.

Chapter Eight

1. Cited in Sannon, *Histoire de Toussaint*, 1:139, and in Schoelcher, *La vie de Toussaint*, 94.

2. On the generalized preference of the blacks for a king, see Stein, *Sonthonax*, 98.

3. Ibid.

4. This early date seems to be confirmed and is set, though not conclusively, on the sixth by D. Geggus in his critical discussion of Toussaint's political and military turnabout. "Volte-Face," 485.

5. In his book *Christophe: King of Haiti* (London: Eyre and Spottiswoode, 1967), Hubert Cole, a British historian, strongly suggests that Christophe was actually born a free black and bases his arguments upon information concerning Christophe's origins in Vergniaud Leconte, *Henri-Christophe dans l'histoire d'Haïti* (Paris: Editions Berger-Sevrault, 1931), 1. However, another version, that of the Haitian historian Pauléus Sannon, states that Christophe was indeed a free black before the revolution, but that he had purchased his own freedom while working at the Hôtel de la Couronne in le Cap. *La guerre de l'indépendance* (Port-au-Prince: Chéraquit, 1925), 89.

6. Sonthonax's intention was to win over these maroons to the French side and, partly as a counterweight to the legion, now thoroughly devoted to the mulattoes, to bring them under the banner of France as a separate corps of national volunteers. Officially, however, they would still be under the command of Bauvais.

7. AN, DXXV 20, 196 and 197. Letters from Bauvais to Sonthonax, Croix-des-Bouquets, Jan. 1794 to 24 March 1794. *Précis historique des annales*, 1:147.

8. AN, DXXV 20, 197. Bauvais, commandant militaire de la Croix-des-Bouquets au commissaire civil de la république, Croix-des-Bouquets, 28 fév. 1794. Madiou, *Histoire d'Haïti*, 1:264–65.

9. AN, DXXV 42, 413. Sonthonax to Bauvais, Port-Republicain, 11 March 1794. DXXV 40, 403. Registre d'ordres et décisions. Decision of 8 March 1794. Thus, brought to trial on 13 August 1793, he was acquitted by Sonthonax on 8 March 1794.

10. AN, DXXV 20, 197. Bauvais, lieutenant-colonel de la Légion de l'Egalité et commandant militaire à la Croix-des-Bouquets au commissaire civil de la république, Croix-des-Bouquets, 1 fév. 1794.

11. AN, DXXV 20, 197. Declaration of Bauvais, Croix-des-Bouquets, 27 March 1794, countersigned by officers of the Croix-des-Bouquets garrison. *Précis historique des annales*, 1:148. According to the author of the *Précis* it was Montbrun and Pinchinat who gave the orders to Marc Borno, commander of a post at Léogane, to eliminate Alaou and his band.

12. Ibid.

13. AN, DXXV 40, 403. Registre d'ordres et décisions. Decision of Intermediary Commission of 9 April 1794.

14. Malenfant, *Des colonies*, 75. Madiou, on the other hand, places the blame for Hyacinthe's assassination upon rival black leader Dieudonné (see below in the present chapter). *Histoire d'Haïti*, 1:282.

15. Letter from Polverel to Rigaud, Jacmel, 11 June 1794. Cited in full in Sannon, *Histoire de Toussaint*, 1:155–57. Sannon also states that Dieudonné was a lieutenant in Alaou's army and held his camp at Nérette (ibid., 182), one of the several places specifically mentioned by Polverel in his letter to Rigaud, cited above. Also *Précis historique des annales*, 1:206.

16. Related in Madiou, *Histoire d'Haïti*, 1:275.

17. *Précis historique des annales*, 1:150.

18. AN, DXXV 50, 481. Copie de la lettre datée de Léogane le 8 nivôse An 4, écrite par Rigaud et Bauvais, généraux de brigade commandant les départements du Sud et de l'Ouest à Etienne Laveaux, général et Gouverneur de Saint-Domingue. Extrait d'une lettre du général de brigade Bauvais au général et Gouverneur Laveaux, Jacmel, 21 nivôse An 4. Extrait d'une lettre écrite par le général et Gouverneur Laveaux en date du 20 pluviôse An 4 à Pierre Dieudonné, commandant en chef au poste et camp Néret.

19. AN, DXXV 50, 481. Extrait d'une lettre du général de brigade Toussaint Louverture au général et Gouverneur Laveaux en date du 17 pluviôse An 4. Etienne Laveaux, général de division et Gouverneur de Saint-Domingue au Ministre de la Marine et des Colonies, le Cap, 20 pluviôse An. 4. See also, Madiou, *Histoire d'Haïti*, 1:338–39.

20. The full text of Toussaint's letter is cited in Schoelcher, *La vie de Toussaint*, 135–39, and in Sannon, *Histoire de Toussaint*, 1:182–84.

21. *Précis historique des annales*, 1:206.

22. James, *Black Jacobins*, 150.

23. Garran-Coulon, *Rapport*, 4:247–48. Lacroix, *Mémoires*, 1:319–20. Schoelcher, *La vie de Toussaint*, 203–4.

24. *Précis historique des annales*, 1:226–27. Cabon, *Histoire d'Haïti*, 3:322; 4:84–86. See esp., Antoine Michel, *La mission du général Hédouville* (Port-au-Prince: Imp. La Presse, 1929), 42ff. Also Paul Moral, *Le paysan haïtien: étude sur la vie rurale en Haïti* (Paris: Maisonneuve et Larose, 1961), 13–15.

25. Cited in Cabon, *Histoire d'Haïti*, 3:294.

26. Alibée-Féry, *Essais littéraires* (Port-au-Prince: Imp. E. Robin, 1876), 246.

27. *Précis historique des annales*, 1:152.

28. Ibid., 153.

29. Ibid.

30. AN, DXXV 43, 418. Les commissaires civils à Figuière, faisant fonction de commissaire instructeur à St. Louis, Port-Républicain, 20 mai 1794.

31. Ibid.

32. Garran-Coulon, *Rapport*, 4:248.

33. Schoelcher, *La vie de Toussaint*, 156, 160–61. Sannon, *Histoire de Toussaint*, 1:188–89.

34. AN, DXXV 45, 422. La municipalité de la ville et banlieue du Cap en séance le 30 ventôse An 4 au citoyen Pierre-Michel, chef de brigade commandant au Haut-du-Cap. Pierre-Michel aux citoyens maire et officiers municipaux, Haut-du-Cap, 30 ventôse An 4. La municipalité du Cap en séance le 1 germinal An 4 aux citoyens Jean-Pierrot, commandant général au Port-François, Barthélemy et Thomas, commandants militaires au Limbé, Pierre-Michel, commandant au Haut-du-Cap, Joseph Flaville, commandant militaire et autres chefs de l'extérieur. Also, Extrait des registres de la municipalité de la ville et banlieue du Cap, séance du conseil général de la commune du 1 germinal An 4. Pierre-Michel was among the few black insurgent leaders that Sonthonax, in June 1793, succeeded in winning over to the republican side in exchange for freedom. See Ch. 7 above.

35. Stein, *Sonthonax*, 126–27. Michel, *Mission*, 35. Sannon, *Histoire de Toussaint*, 1:193. See also James, *Black Jacobins*, 171–72.

36. Madiou, *Histoire d'Haïti*, 1:478.

37. See *Précis historique des annales*, 1:298.

38. The other four were Roume, who was placed in charge of Spanish Saint Domingue; Raimond, the mulatto spokesman for the *affranchis* in Paris at the very beginning of the revolution; Giraud and Leblanc, both whites.

39. *Précis historique des annales*, 1:226.

40. Ibid., 227.

41. Schoelcher, *La vie de Toussaint*, 204.

42. *Précis historique des annales*, 1:227.

43. Lettre confidentielle du Général Rigaud au citoyen Julien Raimond, commissaire du gouvernement français, les Cayes, 29 messidor An 4. Cited in full in Edmond Bonnet, *Souvenirs historiques de Guy-Joseph Bonnet* (Paris: A. Durand, 1864), 449–51. The extract from the letter that is presented in Schoelcher (205) is incorrect and misleading.

44. Sannon, *Histoire de Toussaint*, 2:10.

45. *Précis historique des annales*, 1:227. Also, report of Kerverseau and Leborgne to the civil commission, in Schoelcher, *La vie de Toussaint*, 204.

46. James, *Black Jacobins*, 183.

47. Report of the civil commission to the Directory, in Michel, *Mission*, 63.

48. *Précis historique des annales*, 1:231.

49. AN, DXXV 45, 427. Joint declaration of citizens Sental, captain of *La Soutien*, and Garigou[?], Santo-Domingo, 6 vendémiaire An 5.

50. Ibid. *Précis historique des annales*, 1:231. Also Sannon, *Histoire de Toussaint*, 2:13.

51. See Michel, *Mission*, 59.

52. Stein, *Sonthonax*, 163–64.

53. Ibid., 168–69.

54. See *Black Jacobins*, 188–93.

55. *Sonthonax*, 169–70. Another interpretation of Sonthonax's expulsion is argued by E. Charlier, who sees in it an underlying expression of embedded class and caste antagonisms in Saint Domingue (*Aperçu*, 98–100). Drawing from Cabon's *Histoire d'Haïti*, Charlier argues that the conflict between Sonthonax and Toussaint over the question of the émigrés

was a serious one; therefore Toussaint, who favored a return of the émigrés, would have to get rid of Sonthonax, whom the mulattoes, in an effort to keep the émigrés from Saint Domingue, would support against Toussaint. In this simple issue, seeds of the future struggle as to which race would eventually assume the direction of Saint Domingue were already present. The argument, however, loses some of its plausibility by prematurely introducing irreconcilable race and class interests. There is no reason why the mulattoes, even over the question of the émigrés, should rally to Sonthonax any more than he to them. The "republicanism" of the mulattoes, especially after the Villate affair and the Cayes rebellion, was hardly exemplary.

56. Michel, *Mission*, 179–80.

57. Having gone first to confer with Roume in Spanish Saint Domingue, Hédouville did not arrive in le Cap until some time in April.

58. Michel, *Mission*, 79.

59. Sannon, *Histoire de Toussaint*, 2:114. *Précis historique des annales*, 2:11–12.

60. Ibid., 10.

61. Sannon, *Histoire de Toussaint*, 2:114–15.

62. *Précis historique des annales*, 2:32–33.

63. Ibid., 39–40. Sannon, *Histoire de Toussaint*, 2:127.

64. See Charlier, *Aperçu*, 122–24.

65. *Histoire de Toussaint*, 2:141.

66. On the politico-economic interests of the United States and Britain in the Saint Domingue civil war and the deliberate policy pursued by the two nations to ensure Toussaint's victory, and even encourage independence, the discussion of the issues raised by E. Charlier is particularly pertinent. *Aperçu*, 126–48. Even more revealing are the "Letters of Toussaint Louverture and of Edward Stevens," in AHR 16 (Oct. 1910):64–101. See, as well, the work by Alexander de Conde, *The Quasi-War: The Politics and Diplomacy of the Undeclared War with France, 1797–1801* (New York: Charles Scribner's Sons, 1966), 124–38; also, *Précis historique des annales*, 2:58–62, 109, 139–40.

67. Cabon, *Histoire d'Haïti*, 4:51.

68. For a short period, Port-au-Prince had been renamed Port-Républicain.

69. Ibid.

70. "Letters," 76.

71. Cabon, *Histoire d' Haïti*, 4:56. Madiou, *Histoire d'Haïti*, 2:38.

Chapter Nine

1. The commanding officers were, respectively, Laplume, Dommage, Desravines, and Mamzelle, the former independent maroon leader of Bahoruco.

2. Popular rumor had it that some ten thousand mulattoes were assassinated in this manner. Lacroix, *Mémoires*, 1:394. Cabon, *Histoire d'Haïti*, 4:60. Beaubrun Ardouin, *Etudes*, 4:liv. 5, p. 58. The figure was a gross exaggeration. On this point see Sannon, *Histoire de Toussaint*, 2:203.

3. Sannon, *Histoire de Toussaint*, 2:203. Madiou, *Histoire d'Haïti*, 2:47.

4. *Précis historique des annales*, 2:198–201.

5. The integral text of this constitution is reproduced in Colonel A. Nemours, *Histoire militaire de la guerre d'indépendance de Saint-Domingue*, ed. Berger-Levrault, 2 vols. (Paris: 1925), 1:98–112.

6. Cited in full in James, *Black Jacobins*, 195–97.

7. Charlier, *Aperçu*, 179–84. De Conde, *Quasi-War*, 322–24. The one factor, however, that mitigated American support of Bonaparte's expedition was France's recent acquisition of

Louisiana from Spain. In this light, a French victory in Saint Domingue would allow France to supply and exploit the territory, consolidate her empire in the New World, and solidly penetrate the North American continent. So while initially favorable to the French expedition, once France was actually engaged militarily, United States aid to the French army was singularly absent.

8. Moral, *Le paysan haïtien*, 13. Kenneth Lacerte, "The Evolution of Land and Labor in the Haitian Revolution: 1791–1820," *Américas* 34 (April 1978):453–54. A *carreau* equalled one hundred paces of 3 ½ feet square, or 3.3 acres. See Lacroix, *Mémoires*, 1:vi.

9. *Précis historique des annales*, 2:174–76, 192–93, 205.

10. Ibid., 178–80, 204. Roger Dorsainville, *Toussaint Louverture: ou la vocation de la liberté* [1965]; 2d ed. (Montréal: Editions CIDIHCA, 1987), 201–2.

11. *Précis historique des annales*, 2:222.

12. Dorsainville, *Toussaint*, 209.

13. Ibid., 211.

14. Since Moïse and his closest officers were all summarily executed without a trial, much of the data that would otherwise shed light on the organization of the insurrection may not exist. Who were the local ringleaders? To which plantations did they belong? What were their occupations or status, and their relation to the military officers under Moïse? How was the popular will in regard to landholding politically channeled into a mass insurrectionary movement? Was there continuity in popular leadership among individuals between 1791 and 1801? All are questions that the apparent absence of sufficient data leaves unexamined.

15. V.-E. Leclerc, *Lettres du général Leclerc, commandant en chef de l'armée de Saint-Domingue en 1802* (Paris: Leroux, 1937), Appendice I, 265–74. Notes pour servir aux instructions à donner au capitaine-général Leclerc, Paris, 9 brumaire An 10, signé, le Premier Consul: Buonaparte.

16. Ibid., 272.

17. On the numbers, composition, outfitting, and organization of the expedition, see the material presented in Claude B. and Marcel B. Auguste, *L'expédition Leclerc, 1801–1803* (Port-au-Prince: Deschamps, 1985), 21–55. On the landing of the forces see ibid., 92–118.

18. Lacroix, *Mémoires*, 2:136–40. Sannon, *Histoire de Toussaint*, 3:55, 57–60. See also Leclerc, *Lettres*, 115:no. 38 (5 mars 1802).

19. Ardouin, *Etudes*, 5:liv. 6, p. 18.

20. Cited in M. E. Descourtiltz, *Voyage*, 212. Descourtiltz was a prisoner in the Crête-à-Pierrot fort during the siege.

21. Lacroix, *Mémoires*, 149ff. Descourtiltz, *Voyage*, 211ff. Nemours, *Histoire militaire*, 1:228 ff.

22. Leclerc, *Lettres*, 102, 109: nos. 34, 35 (19 fév.; 27 fév. 1802).

23. Ibid., 109–10: no. 35 (27 fév. 1802).

24. Ibid., 131: no. 47 (21 avril 1802).

25. Ibid., 118: no. 40 (1 avril 1802).

26. Charlier, *Aperçu*, 254, 258.

27. Leclerc, *Lettres*, 157: no. 65 (6 juin 1802).

28. Ibid., 200: no. 108 (6 août 1802); also, in the same vein, ibid., 229, 243, 256: nos. 129, 135, 145 (16, 26 sept.; 7 oct. 1802).

29. A not uncommon practice was to burn sulfur in the holds of the ships in which black and mulatto prisoners alike were incarcerated. Dead from asphyxiation, the bodies would be dumped into the sea the next morning to make room for more prisoners. Madiou, *Histoire d'Haïti*, 2:301. Antoine Métral, *Histoire de l'expédition des Français à Saint-Domingue* (Paris: Fanjat aîne, 1825), 176.

30. Lacroix, *Mémoires*, 2:226–27.

31. Leclerc, *Lettres*, 190: no. 99 (6 juillet 1802).

32. UFL, Rochambeau Papers, No. 624, pièce no. 1. Rapport pour servir d'instructions relative aux accusations portées contre les nommés . . . , les Cayes, 23 messidor An 10, signé, B. Madier, capitaine.

33. Ibid.

34. UFL, Rochambeau Papers, No. 624, pièce no. 2. Rapport pour servir d'instructions relative aux plaintes portées contre les nommés . . . , les Cayes, 26 messidor An 10, signé, B. Madier, capitaine.

35. UFL, Rochambeau Papers, No. 653. Desbureaux, général de division au général Rochambeau, commandant les divisions de l'Ouest et du Sud, quartier général des Cayes, 28 messidor An 10.

36. UFL, Rochambeau Papers, No. 572. Desbureaux, général de division au général de division Rochambeau, commandant les départements de l'Ouest et du Sud, quartier général des Cayes, 13 messidor An 10.

37. UFL, Rochambeau Papers, No. 624, pièce no. 3. Copie du rapport fait par le chef de brigade Berger, commandant de la place des Cayes par (*sic*) le mouvement du 22 messidor An 10.

38. On the involvement of the Corail leaders in the broader Grande-Anse insurrectionary movement that resurfaced in September 1802, see below in the present chapter.

39. UFL, Rochambeau Papers, No. 582. Delpech, commandant l'arrondissement au général Rochambeau, commandant les départements du Sud et de l'Ouest, Petit-Goâve, 16 messidor An 10. On the role of Dérance in the war in the South, see below in present chapter.

40. UFL, Rochambeau Papers, No. 559. Delpech, chef de bataillon, commandant l'arrondissement au général de division Rochambeau, commandant les départements de l'Ouest et du Sud, Petit-Goâve, 8 messidor An 10. No. 572. Desbureaux, général de division au général de division Rochambeau, commandant les départements de l'Ouest et du Sud, quartier général des Cayes, 13 messidor An 10. No. 617. Desbureaux, général de division au général Rochambeau, quartier général des Cayes, 23 messidor An 10.

41. UFL, Rochambeau Papers, No. 652. Desbureaux, général de division au général Rochambeau, commandant en chef les divisions du Sud et de l'Ouest, quartier général des Cayes, 28 messidor An 10.

42. UFL, Rochambeau Papers, No. 624, pièce no. 3.

43. UFL, Rochambeau Papers, No. 710. Desbureaux, général de division au général Rochambeau, commandant les départements de l'Ouest et du Sud, quartier général de Jérémie, 8 thermidor An 10.

44. Ibid.

45. UFL, Rochambeau Papers, No. 887. Desbureaux, général de division au général Rochambeau, Jérémie, 9 fructidor An 10.

46. Ibid.

47. UFL, Rochambeau Papers, No. 983. Desbureaux, général de division au général de division Rochambeau, commandant les départements de l'Ouest et du Sud, quartier général de Saint Louis, 21 fructidor An 10.

48. UFL, Rochambeau Papers, No. 897. Joussaume, capitaine de la gendarmerie, commandant provisoire de la place au citoyen Rochambeau, général de division, commandant en chef les départements du Sud et de l'Ouest, place d'Aquin, 10 fructidor An 10. No. 1069. Joussaume, ex-capitaine de gendarmerie d'Aquin au général Rochambeau, commandant en chef les départements du Sud et de l'Ouest, à bord la frégate *la Guérier*, 2e jour complémentaire An 10. Encl. of 1069. Statements of character reference made by various planters of the district in praise of Joussaume, 3 Jan. 1802.

49. UFL, Rochambeau Papers, No. 1039. Lalance to Rochambeau, Aquin, 14 Sept. 1802.

50. UFL, Rochambeau Papers, No. 983. Desbureaux to Rochambeau, 7 Sept. 1802. No. 1039. Lalance to Rochambeau, 14 Sept. 1802.

51. UFL, Rochambeau Papers, Nos. 978, 979. Pellissier to Rochambeau, les Cayes, 6 Sept. 1802.

52. UFL, Rochambeau Papers, No. 997, pièce no. 5. Copie d'une lettre adressée au général de division Desbureaux à son quartier général de Saint-Louis, par le chef de brigade Berger, commandant la place des Cayes, 23 fructidor An 10.

53. Ibid.

54. UFL, Rochambeau Papers, No. 997, pièce no. 5.

55. UFL, Rochambeau Papers, No. 1043. Desbureaux, général de division au général Rochambeau, commandant les départements de l'Ouest et du Sud, quartier général des Cayes, 29 fructidor An 10.

56. UFL, Rochambeau Papers, No. 1039. Lalance to Rochambeau, 14 Sept. 1802.

57. Métral, *Histoire de l'expédition*, 184. See n. 89 below.

58. Every history of the Saint Domingue revolution will confirm this assertion.

59. Leclerc, *Lettres*, 200: no. 108 (6 août 1802).

60. *Secret History, written by a Lady at Cape Français to Colonel Burr*, (Freeport, N.Y.: Books for Libraries Press, 1971), 99–100.

61. *Seconde campagne de Saint-Domingue* (Le Havre: Imp. Brindeau, 1846), 70–71.

62. Leclerc, *Lettres*, 202, 206: nos. 109, 112. (6, 9 août 1802).

63. Métral, *Histoire de l'expédition*, 180–81.

64. UFL, Rochambeau Papers, Encl. of 1011. Au quartier général des Cayes, Ordre du jour, 26 fructidor An 10, signé, le général de division Desbureaux.

65. UFL, Rochambeau Papers, Encl. of 1011. Au quartier général des Cayes, Ordre du jour, 27 fructidor An 10, signé, Desbureaux. The same ordinance was rendered at Aquin on 8 September, the day of the Darmagnac revolt at les Cayes. Encl. of 1043. Au quartier général d'Aquin, Ordre du jour, 22 fructidor An 10, signé, Desbureaux.

66. Leclerc, *Lettres*, 256: no. 145 (7 oct. 1802).

67. UFL, Rochambeau Papers, No. 1118. Desbureaux, général de division au général Rochambeau, quartier général des Cayes, 7 vendémiaire An 11.

68. UFL, Rochambeau Papers, No. 1104. Le commandant de la place et de la paroisse au général de division Rochambeau, commandant les divisions de l'Ouest et du Sud, Jérémie, 5 vendémiaire An 11, signé, Bernard.

69. UFL, Rochambeau Papers, No. 1112. Le chef de brigade, Bernard, commandant de la place au général divisionnaire Rochambeau, commandant les divisions de l'Ouest et du Sud, Jérémie, 6 vendémiaire An 11. The five plantations were: Carin, Parouty, Farouilh, Tauzias, and Lafresnay. Ibid.

70. C. Ardouin, *Essais*, 107.

71. B. Ardouin, *Etudes*, 5:liv. 6, p. 36.

72. UFL, Rochambeau Papers, No. 1112. Bernard to Rochambeau, 27 Sept. 1802. No. 1117. Le commandant de la place et de l'arrondissement au général de division Rochambeau, commandant les départements de l'Ouest et du Sud, Jérémie, 7 vendémiaire An 11.

73. UFL, Rochambeau Papers, No. 1123. Le commandant de la place et de l'arrondissement au général Rochambeau, commandant les départements de l'Ouest et du Sud, signé, Bernard, Jérémie, 8 vendémiaire An 11.

74. UFL, Rochambeau Papers, No. 1124. Le chef de brigade, commandant de la place [et de] l'arrondissement par interim au général divisionnaire Rochambeau, commandant les départements de l'Ouest et du Sud, Jérémie, 8 vendémiaire An 11.

75. Assam, the slave woman accused of poisoning in the Makandal affair of 1757–58 also claimed, under the torture tactics of interrogation procedures, that she only listened to persons giving "good advice." See Appendix A. In the case here, it may not be inappropriate to surmise that Magdelon was lying to cover for her husband, a *conducteur*, who was sure to be shot or hanged.

76. The report of these investigations is presented in Appendix D.

77. UFL, Rochambeau Papers, No. 1142. Desbureaux, général de division au chef de brigade Dommage à Jérémie, quartier général des Cayes, 11 vendémiaire An 11. No. 1147. Le commandant de la place et de l'arrondissement au général de division Rochambeau, Jérémie, 12 vendémiaire An 11.

78. Ibid.; No. 1123. Bernard to Rochambeau, 29 Sept. 1802.

79. UFL, Rochambeau Papers, No. 1134. Le commandant de la place et de l'arrondissement par interim au général de division Rochambeau, commandant les départements de l'Ouest et du Sud, Jérémie, 10 vendémiaire An 11. A list of the sixteen, giving their names and positions, is provided in Appendix D.

80. See C. Ardouin, *Essais*, 101ff.

81. UFL, Rochambeau Papers, Nos. 1191, 1210. Delpech, chef de bataillon, commandant l'arrondissement du Petit-Goâve, Grand-Goâve et Miragoâne au général de division Rochambeau, commandant les départements de l'Ouest et du Sud, Petit-Goâve, 25, 28 vendémiaire An 11. Leclerc, *Lettres*, 255: no. 145 (7 oct. 1802).

82. UFL, Rochambeau Papers, No. 1236. Berger, chef de brigade, commandant de la place au général divisionnaire Rochambeau, commandant les départements de l'Artibonite et du Sud, les Cayes, 2 brumaire An 11. No. 1278. Desbureaux, général de division au général Rochambeau, commandant les divisions de l'Ouest et du Sud, quartier général des Cayes, 10 brumaire An 11.

83. UFL, Rochambeau Papers, No. 1276. Berger, chef de brigade et commandant de la place au général de division Rochambeau, les Cayes, 10 brumaire An 11. No. 1278. Desbureaux to Rochambeau, 31 Oct. 1802. No. 1344. Berger, chef de brigade, commandant de la place au général Rochambeau, commandant en chef de l'armée de Saint-Domingue, les Cayes, 29 brumaire An 11.

84. Leclerc, *Lettres*, 217: no. 120 (25 août 1802).

85. Lacroix, *Mémoires*, 2:225.

86. Leclerc, *Lettres*, Appendice I, 268–69. Notes pour servir.

87. See Charlier, *Aperçu*, 282ff.

88. Leclerc, *Lettres*, 148: no. 56 (7 mai 1802).

89. Usually the dogs did not attack and had to be goaded into fury by slitting open the body of the victim so that the smell of blood would incite them to attack, after which they began to howl strangely. A shipment of these dogs was sent to Petit-Goâve. When the French soldiers landed, they were attacked by rebel forces. During the fighting, the dogs were let loose and, according to Ardouin, then began attacking the French. *Etudes*, 5:liv. 6, pp. 84–86.

90. Reports from Rochambeau to the minister of the marine, cited in Sannon, *Histoire de Toussaint*, 3:133.

91. See *Précis historique des annales*, 2:233–35.

92. Sannon, *La vie de Toussaint*, 3:138n. In this light, Genovese's observation that "[the maroons] greeted Napoleon's army, which came to restore slavery, as allies and later gave some support to their old archenemies, the mulattoes, against the blacks," would not have suffered from such distortion if a closer and more careful scrutiny of the facts, rather than the bare outlines, had been made. *From Rebellion to Revolution*, 55.

93. UFL, Rochambeau Papers, No. 1345. Cangé, général de brigade commandant provisoire les arrondissements de Léogane et Petit-Goâve au citoyen Delpech, commandant l'arrondissement du Petit-Goâve, n.d. (brumaire An 11?). No. 1345. Delpech, chef de bataillon, commandant l'arrondissement du Petit-Goâve, Grand-Goâve et Miragoâne au général de brigade Cangé, 29 brumaire An 11. Also, No. 1330. Cangé, général de brigade, commandant en chef les forces armées en activité dans les arrondissements de Léogane et Petit-Goâve contre les ennemis de la liberté aux citoyens composant la garnison de la ville de Léogane, sans distinction de grades ni de couleurs, Léogane, 22 brumaire An 11.

94. UFL, Rochambeau Papers, Nos. 1228, 1243, 1269, 1306, 1413. Letters from Delpech to Rochambeau, Petit-Goâve, 21, 24, 30 Oct.; 5 Nov.; 5 Dec. 1802. No. 1406. Pageot, général de brigade au général en chef Rochambeau, capitaine-général de la colonie, quartier général de Jacmel, 13 frimaire An 11.

95. UFL, Rochambeau Papers, No. 1554. Berger, chef de brigade, commandant de la place et du quartier au général Rochambeau, les Cayes, 2 pluviôse An 11.

96. Charlier, *Aperçu*, 294.

97. UFL, Rochambeau Papers, No. 1525. Lecharpentier, adjudant à l'état major . . . au général en chef Rochambeau, capitaine-général, les Cayes, 27 nivôse An 11.

98. UFL, Rochambeau Papers, No. 1577. Berger, chef de brigade, commandant du quartier au général en chef Rochambeau, les Cayes, 11 pluviôse An 11. B. Ardouin, *Etudes*, 5:liv. 6, p. 83.

99. UFL, Rochambeau Papers, No. 1486. Berger, chef de brigade, commandant de la place et du quartier au capitaine-général Rochambeau, les Cayes, 12 nivôse An 11.

100. UFL, Rochambeau Papers, No. 1578. Berger, chef de brigade, commandant de quartier au capitaine-général Rochambeau, les Cayes, 12 pluviôse An 11.

101. Ibid.

102. B. Ardouin, *Etudes*, 5:liv. 6, p. 83. Madiou, *Histoire d'Haïti*, 2:404. Sannon, *Histoire de Toussaint*, 3:145. Sannon incorrectly includes Jacques Formon among these leaders in the Plaine-des-Cayes. Formon was, as we know, court-martialed and shot on Polverel's orders in November 1793 for refusing to submit to Rigaud's authority. See Ch. 7 above.

103. UFL, Rochambeau Papers, No. 1665. Berger, chef de brigade, commandant du quartier au capitaine-général Rochambeau, les Cayes, 10 ventôse An 11.

104. B. Ardouin, *Etudes*, 5:liv. 6, p. 83. Madiou, *Histoire d'Haïti*, 2:406. Sannon, *Histoire de Toussaint*, 3:145. C. Ardouin, *Essais*, 101–2.

105. In Dorsainville, *Toussaint*, 234.

106. James, *Black Jacobins*, 288.

107. UFL, Rochambeau Papers, No. 1835. Berger, chef de brigade, commandant de la place au général en chef Rochambeau, les Cayes, 11 florial An 11. Madiou, *Histoire d'Haïti*, 3:11ff.

108. Ibid., 11–12 and B. Ardouin, *Etudes*, 5:liv. 6, p. 83.

109. Sannon, *La guerre de l'indépendance*, 39.

110. Madiou, *Histoire d'Haïti*, 3:18.

111. UFL, Rochambeau Papers, No. 1959. Le général Brunet au général en chef Rochambeau, les Cayes, 9 messidor An 11.

112. Ibid.

113. UFL, Rochambeau Papers, No. 1954. Rapport de la mission exécutée d'après des ordres du général de brigade Sarrazin, commandant l'arrondissement de Jérémie en date du 2 messidor An 11, certifié par Berger, 7 messidor An 11.

114. C. Ardouin, *Essais*, 108–9.

Conclusion

1. Georges Lefebvre, *Les Cours de Sorbonne*, 6 vols. Centre de Documentation Universitaire (Paris: Tournier et Constans, 1946–47). The full passage is cited and translated in James, *Black Jacobins*, 338, n. 39.

2. G. Debien, "Marronage in the French Caribbean," in *Maroon Societies*, 110. On the minimization of slave resistance in Saint Domingue, see also D. Geggus, *Slavery, War and Revolution*, 2, 26ff.

3. Genovese, *From Rebellion to Revolution*, 89.

Appendix A

1. AN, Arch. Col. C9ᴬ 102. (Edited and translated by author.)

2. A state resembling dropsy, perhaps.

3. By having extended her absence to three days beyond the one-day pass her master gave her, one wonders whether this may not exemplify "trivial" and innocuous instances of *petit* marronage, practiced, however, precisely for the purposes of obtaining and distributing poisonous substances. Admittedly she was on an errand with her master's permission, but had her absence lasted seven or eight or nine days, her master by this time surely would have considered her maroon. See Ch. 2, nn. 81 and 142. On the relationship between *petit* marronage and the distribution of poison, see especially the interrogation of the slave Haurou, an accused distributor imprisoned (le Cap prison record, 9 November 1757, below) at the same time as Assam, in Pluchon, *Vaudou*, 191–92, 193.

4. The same question may be posed here, as well.

5. Sundays, of course, were the slaves' only free days.

6. This, in essence, was also the revelation of Médor just before he killed himself to escape the justice of the colonial authorities. See Médor's statement in Ch. 2.

7. This packet, and especially the larger one composed and tied at both ends by Jean, and which would indicate to her whether the herbs were the right ones to pick for the purpose intended, were most certainly makandals. See the descriptions of the preparation, the uses, and the powers believed by the slaves to be contained in the makandals, in the report of Sébastien Courtin, interim seneschal of le Cap, in Pluchon, *Vaudou*, 209–19.

8. Perhaps a blood pact committing each party to secrecy? In any event, it is obvious the slave, Jean, had made a fetish, or talisman.

9. Edited by author.

10. Lizette was arrested upon declarations made by Sieurs Vallet, Deseutres [des Gentres?] and Dufau, who are mentioned in Assam's interrogation (above). Lizette and her accusers are specifically named in this connection in a letter relating the alarming incidence of poisoning in the Fort-Dauphin-le Cap region, of which Médor was one of the known perpetrators. AN Arch. Col., C9ᴬ 100. Letter from M. de Lalanne, Port-au-Prince, 12 Dec. 1757. See Ch. 2, n. 121 above. Lisette was condemned and burned at the stake. Pluchon, *Vaudou*, 166.

11. Possibly the Marie-Jeanne in Assam's declaration. Marie-Jeanne's interrogation, as well as that of Nanon, to whom she gave the poison to kill Seiur Chiron, Nanon's master, is in Pluchon, *Vaudou* (188–92), as is that of the distributor, Horou [Haurou], also listed above.

12. Also mentioned in Assam's declaration.

13. This Jean was undoubtedly the one to whom Assam was referred on the Laplaine plantation.

14. Sometimes a slave having received the death penalty would, in commutation, be required to serve as executioner of other slaves. In the face of such an alternative, slaves often preferred to die than to ransom their lives at this cost. See Ch. 1, n. 111, above.

Appendix B

1. The primary documents herein have been edited and translated by the author.

2. Bagasse is the remaining straw of the sugarcane after it has been processed through the mill. This straw was commonly used for fuel. Debien, *Les colons*, 332, n 3. The *case à bagasse* is therefore the cabin or shed in which the straw of the sugarcane was stored.

3. A rough draft of the beginning of this address, with corrections and marginal insertions, is found in AN DXXV 66, 666. The completed address, in proper handwritten form, is in DXXV 66, 667. It was delivered to the National Assembly in France on 30 November 1791 and exists in printed form in DXXV 56, 550. All future references to this document will use the latter archival reference.

4. Garran-Coulon, *Rapport*, 2:211–12.

5. Ibid., 212.

6. Debien, *Les colons*, 333.

7. AN DXXV 78, 772, KK 178. Renseignements sur la position actuelle du Limbé depuis le commencement de la révolte, le Cap, 1 oct. 1791.

8. AN DXXV 78, 772. Letter from le Cap, 27 September 1791.

9. AN DXXV 3, 31. Précis historique de la révolution de Saint-Domingue, 3 brumaire, 3e année française, 9.

10. Lacroix, *Mémoires*, 1:89. Deschamps, *Les colonies*, 247. Sannon, *Histoire de Toussaint*, 1:89–90.

11. The smallest of the three Gallifet estates in Petite-Anse. See Ch. 4 above.

12. Perhaps the one who allegedly read the false gazette at the 14 August Morne-Rouge assembly.

13. AN, DXXV 46, 432. Lettre écrite par M. Testard à M. Cormier, contenant l'extrait de deux lettres qu'il a reçues du Havre, le Cap, 26 oct. 1791. The reference which the slave makes to a free mulatto in the first letter quoted by M. Testard, as well as the reference to a mulatto or quarteroon in the declaration of the slave François should not be construed to assume that the blacks had been organized or were being politically directed by the free mulattoes. The temporary coalition that was formed later between themselves and the blacks under Jean-François was one of mutual convenience only.

14. See D. Geggus's discussion of the issue in "Slave Resistance Studies," 16, 18.

15. This tentative hypothesis has served as a rough starting point for an in-depth and systematic analysis, in collaboration with author, of the religious, linguistic, and literary, as well as historical components of the text.

16. Vincent Mulago, "Le dieu des Bantous," *Présence* (12–19 Nov. 1987): 10. See also, R. P. J. van Wing, *Etudes Bakongo*, 2 vols. (Brussels: Institut Royal Colonial Belge, 1938), 2:23–36.

17. "Notice historique," 204–5; also see Ch. 4, n. 64 above.

18. In Fouchard, *Marrons de la liberté*, 528, n.3.

19. On this point, however, see the remarks of Adolphe Cabon in "Une maison," RHAF 3 (déc. 1949):418–19.

20. See note 17 above.

21. See Ch. 4, n. 65 above.

22. On the translation of this chant, see Ch. 2, n. 58 above.

Appendix C

1. AN, DXXV 63, 638. (Translated by author.)

Appendix D

1. UFL, Rochambeau Papers, Encls. of 1147, 1134. (Translated by author.)

2. Citizen Petitgo was arrested and sent to Rochambeau as a person detrimental to the public interest by virtue of his conduct and the laxity of surveillance on his plantation. UFL, Rochambeau Papers, No. 1124. Le chef de brigade, commandant de la place [et de] l'arrondissement par interim au général divisionnaire Rochambeau, commandant les départements de l'Ouest et du Sud, Jérémie, 8 vendémiaire An 11.

Bibliography

Archival Manuscript Sources

Paris, Archives Nationales
  Series C9 A–B—(Archives Coloniales, Correspondance Générale)
  Series DXXV—(Colonies: A comprehensive collection of documents relating to Saint Domingue, including official reports and correspondence to and from various government ministries, to the Constituent Assembly, the National Convention, and the Directory; private correspondence; prison records; court interrogations; correspondence and proclamations of the civil commissioners; memoirs, pamphlets, eyewitness accounts; official reports and correspondence of the colonial administrative bodies; correspondence of maroon leaders. 114 cartons consulted.)
  Series F 3—(Fonds Moreau de Saint-Méry)
London, Public Record Office
  Series HCA 30—(High Court of Admiralty Papers: Chiefly private correspondence; a few plantation records; some administrative documents; a few issues of the *Gazette des Cayes*. Cartons 380–81; 385–86; 390–95; 401, pts. I–II consulted.)
Port-au-Prince, Institut Saint Louis de Gonzague
  (Mémoire de l'Assemblée Provinciale et de ses municipalités réunies du Sud à l'Assemblée Coloniale en réponse à la lettre de M. Blanchelande en date du 16 août, adressée à l'Assemblée Coloniale, les Cayes, 16 sept. 1792.)
  (Relation d'une conspiration tramée par les Nègres, dans l'isle de Saint Domingue; défense que fait le jésuite confesseur aux Nègres qu'on supplicie de révéler leurs fauteurs et complices, n.p. [1758?].)
New York, New York Public Library: A. Schomburg Negro Collection
  Series F—(Fisher Collection)
Gainesville, Florida, University of Florida Libraries
  (Précis historique des annales de la colonie française de Saint-Domingue depuis 1789. . . . 2 vols. [A typewritten copy of the original unpublished manuscript])
  Rochambeau Papers (Military correspondence; government proclamations and reports [primarily 1802–4].)

Printed Contemporary Sources

Begouën-Demeaux, M. *Mémorial d'une famille du Havre (1743–1831)*, 4 vols. Le Havre: Imp. Etaix, 1957, vol. 2.
Bonnet, Edmond, ed. *Souvenirs historiques de Guy-Joseph Bonnet*. Paris: A. Durand, 1864.
[Carteau, Félix]. *Soirées bermudiennes*. Bordeaux: Pellier-Lawalle, 1802.

Casas, Bartolomé de las. *History of the Indies.* Translated and edited by Andrée Collard. New York: Harper & Row (Tochbock), 1971.

Castonnet des Fosses, Henri. *La perte d'une colonie: la révolution de Saint-Domingue.* Paris: A. Faivre, 1893

Cuvelier, Mgr. J. B., ed. *Documents sur une mission au Kakongo, 1766–1776.* Mémoires, Vol. 1. Brussels: Institut Royal Colonial Belge, 1953.

Dalmas, Antoine. *Histoire de la révolution de Saint-Domingue.* 2 vols. [1793?] Paris: Mame frères, 1814.

Descourtiltz, M. E. *Histoire des désastres de Saint-Domingue.* Paris: Garney, 1795.

————. *Voyage d'un naturiste en Haïti (1799–1803).* [1809] Paris: Plon, 1935.

Dumesle, Hérard. *Voyage dans le Nord d'Haïti.* Les Cayes: Imp. du Gouvernement, 1824.

Edwards, Bryan. *History Civil and Commercial of the British West Indies.* 5th ed. 5 vols. New York: ADIC Press, 1966. Vol. 3.

Frossard, M. *La cause des esclaves nègres.* 2 vols. Lyon: Aimé de la Roche, 1789.

Garran-Coulon, J. Ph. *Rapport sur les troubles de Saint-Domingue.* 4 vols. Commission des Colonies. Paris: Imp. nationale, 1797–99.

[Girod-Chantrans, Justin]. *Voyage d'un Suisse dans différentes colonies.* Neufchatel: Imp. de la Société typographique, 1785.

Gros. *Isle de Saint Domingue, Province du Nord. Précis historique.* Paris: Imp. L. Poitier de Lille, 1793.

Hassal, Mary. *Secret History, Written by a Lady at Cape François to Colonel Burr.* Freeport, N.Y.: Books for Libraries Press, 1971.

Hilliard d'Auberteuil, Michel René. *Considérations sur l'état présent de la colonie française de Saint-Domingue.* 2 vols. Paris: Grangé, 1776.

Howard, Lt. Thomas Phipps. *The Haitian Journal of Lieutenant Howard: York Hussars, 1796–1798.* Edited by Roger N. Buckley. Knoxville: University of Tennessee Press, 1985.

Labat, R. P. Jean Baptiste. *The Memoirs of Père Labat, 1693–1705.* Translated and abridged by John Eaden. London: Frank Cass & Co., 1970.

————. *Nouveau Voyage aux isles de l'Amérique.* 2 vols. La Haye, 1724. Vol. 1.

Lacroix, Pamphile de. *Mémoires pour servir à l'histoire de la révolution de Saint-Domingue.* 2d ed. 2 vols. Paris: Pillet aîné, 1820.

Laujon, A. *Précis historique de la dernière expédition de Saint-Domingue.* 2 vols. Paris: Schwartz et Gagnot, 1835.

Leclerc, V.-E. *Lettres du Général Leclerc, commandant en chef de l'armée de Saint-Domingue en 1802.* Edited by Paul Roussier. Paris: Ernest Leroux, 1937.

Lemonnier-Delafosse, M. *Seconde campagne de Saint-Domingue.* Le Havre: Imp. Brindeau, 1846.

M. de C. "Makandal, histoire véritable: extrait du Mercure de France, 15 septembre 1787." In RSHHGG 20 (janv. 1949):21–28.

Malenfant, Colonel. *Des colonies et particulièrement de celle de Saint-Domingue.* Paris, 1814.

Mettas, Jean. *Répertoire des expéditions négrières françaises au XVIIIe siècle.* 2 vols. Edited by Serge Daget. Paris: Société française d'histoire d'Outre-Mer, 1978 and 1984.

Milscent. *Du régime colonial.* Paris: Imp. du Cercle Social, 1792.

Moreau de Saint-Méry, M. E. L. *De la danse.* Philadelphia: 1796.

————. *Description topographique, physique, civil, politique et historique de la partie française de l'isle de Saint-Domingue.* 3 vols. Philadelphia: 1797; reprint ed., Paris: Société de l'histoire des colonies françaises, 1959.

————. *Loix et constitutions des colonies françaises de l'Amérique sous le vent.* 6 vols. Paris: By the Author, 1784.

My Odyssey: Experiences of a Young Refugee from Two Revolutions. Edited and translated by Althéa de Peuch Parham. Baton Rouge: Louisiana State University Press, 1959.

"Notice historique sur la Communauté des religieuses filles de Notre-Dame du Cap Français (Saint-Domingue) fondée en 1733." *Lettre annuelle de l'Ordre de Notre Dame.* Bordeaux: Imp. B. Coussan et F. Constalet, 1889.

Perkins, Samuel. *Reminiscences of the Insurrection in St. Domingo.* Cambridge, Mass.: John Wilson & Son, 1886.

Robespierre, Maximilien. *Oeuvres de Maximilien Robespierre.* 10 vols. Edited by M. Bouloiseau, G. Lefebvre, and A. Soboul. Paris: PUF, 1930–67. Vol. 7.

Rouvray, M. et Mme. de *Une correspondance familiale au temps des troubles de Saint-Domingue.* Edited by M. E. McIntosh and B. C. Weber. Paris: Société de l'histoire des colonies françaises, 1959.

Savine, Albert, ed. *Saint-Domingue à la veille de la révolution: souvenirs du Baron de Wimpffen.* Paris: Louis Michaud, 1911.

Stevens, Edward, and Toussaint Louverture. "Letters of Toussaint Louverture and of Edward Stevens, 1798–1800." In AHR 16 (Oct. 1910):64–101.

Wing, R. P. J. van, and C. Penders, S. J., eds. and trans. *Le plus ancien dictionnaire Bantu.* Louvain: Imp. Kuyl-Otto, 1928.

Contemporary Newspapers

Aix-en-Provence, Archives Nationales—Section Outre-Mer
    Series RC-2, 175:
    Aviseur du Sud
    Bulletin Officiel de Saint-Domingue
    Gazette des Cayes (nos. 1–84, 86–87)
    Observateur Colonial
London, Public Record Office
    Series HCA 30, 392: *Gazette des Cayes* (nos. 85, 88–93.)
United States, University libraries (microfilm holdings)
    Boston Gazette (1789–1802)
    Boston Independent Chronicle (1789–1804)
    Boston Price Current (1795–1798)
    Charleston Times (1800–1804)
    New York Evening Post (1801–1804)
    Philadelphia Aurora (1790–1804)
    State Gazette of South Carolina (1789–1793)

Private Collections

Port-au-Prince

    Collection Edmond Mangonès (The Mangonès Collection was partially microfilmed in 1974 by Yale University, Antillean Studies Program. There are also a number of reels at the University of Florida Libraries.)
    Collection Jean Price-Mars
    Collection Jean Fouchard

Secondary Sources

BOOKS

Alibée-Féry. *Essais littéraires.* Port-au-Prince: Imp. E. Robin, 1876.

Ardouin, Beaubrun. *Etudes sur l'histoire d'Haïti.* 11 vols. Edited by François Dalencourt. Port-au-Prince, 1958.

Ardouin, Céligny. *Essais sur l'histoire d'Haïti.* Port-au-Prince: B. Ardouin, 1865.

Auguste, Claude B., and Marcel B. Auguste. *L'expédition Leclerc, 1801–1803.* Port-au-Prince: Imp. Deschamps, 1985.

Barskett, Sir James. *History of the Island of St. Domingo.* 2d ed. London: Frank Cass and Co., 1972.

Boissonade, P. *Saint-Domingue à la veille de la révolution et la question de la représentation coloniale aux Etats-Généraux.* Paris: Paul Geuthner, 1906.

Brown, Johnathan. *The History and Present Condition of St. Domingo.* 2d ed. London: Frank Cass and Co., 1971.

Brutus, Edner. *Révolution dans Saint-Domingue.* 2 vols. [Brussels?]: Panthéon, [1973?].

Cabon, R. P. Adolphe. *Histoire d'Haïti.* 4 vols. [1895–1919] Port-au-Prince: Editions de la Petite Revue, 192?–1940.

Césaire, Aimé. *Toussaint Louverture.* [1961] revised ed. Paris: Présence africaine, 1962.

Charlier, Etienne. *Aperçu sur la formation historique de la nation haïtienne.* Port-au-Prince: Les Presses Libres, 1954.

Cole, Hubert. *Christophe: King of Haiti.* London: Eyre & Spottiswoode, 1967.

Conde, Alexander de. *The Quasi-War: The Politics and Diplomacy of the Undeclared War with France, 1797–1801.* New York: Charles Scribner's Sons, 1966.

Crouse, Nellis M. *French Pioneers in the West Indies, 1624–1664.* New York: Columbia University Press, 1940.

Cuvelier, Mgr. J. B. *L'ancien royaume de Congo.* Brussels: Desclée de Brouwer, 1946.

Dallas, R. C. *The History of the Maroons.* 2 vols. 2d ed. London: Frank Cass and Co., 1968.

Davis, David Brion. *The Problem of Slavery in the Age of Revolution.* Ithaca: Cornell University Press, 1975.

Debien, Gabriel. *Les colons de Saint-Domingue et la révolution: essai sur le Club Massiac.* Paris: Armand Colin, 1953.

————. *Les engagés pour les Antilles (1634–1715).* [In *Revue d'histoire des colonies* 38 (1951).] Paris: Société de l'histoire des colonies françaises, 1952.

————. *Les esclaves aux Antilles françaises: XVIIe–XVIIIe siècles.* Basse-Terre: Société d'histoire de la Guadeloupe, 1974.

————. *Esprit colon et esprit d'autonomie à Saint-Domingue au XVIIIe siècle.* 2d ed. Paris: Larose, 1954.

————. *Etudes antillaises, XVIIIe siècle.* Cahiers des Annales, no. 11. Paris: Armand Colin, 1956.

————. *Plantations et esclaves à Saint-Domingue.* Dakar: Université de Dakar. Section d'histoire, no. 3, 1962.

Deschamps, Léon. *Les colonies pendant la Révolution: La Constituante et les colonies.* Paris: Perrin, 1898.

Dorsainville, Roger. *Toussaint Louverture, ou la vocation de la liberté* [1965] 2d ed. Montréal: Editions CIDIHCA, 1987.

Dunham, Katherine. *Island Possessed.* Garden City, New York: Doubleday, 1969.

Fouchard, Jean. *Les marrons de la liberté.* Paris: Ecole, 1972.

————. *Les marrons du syllabaire.* Port-au-Prince: Imp. Deschamps, 1953.

————. *La méringue.* Montréal: Leméac, 1973.

Franklin, James. *The Present State of Hayti*. 2d ed. London: Frank Cass and Co., 1971.

Frostin, Charles. *Les révoltes blanches à Saint-Domingue au XVIIe et XVIIIe siècles*. Paris: Ecole, 1975.

Gaston-Martin. *Histoire de l'esclavage dans les colonies françaises*. Etudes coloniales, no. 1. Paris: PUF, 1948.

——— . *Nantes au XVIIIe siècle: l'ère des négriers (1714–1774)*. Paris: Félix Alcan, 1931.

Gautier, Arlette. *Les soeurs de Solitude: la condition féminine dans l'esclavage aux Antilles du XVIIe au XIXe siècle*. Paris: Editions Caraïbéennes, 1985.

Geggus, David P. *Slavery, War and Revolution: The British Occupation of Saint Domingue, 1793–1798*. Oxford: Clarendon Press, 1982.

Genovese, Eugene. *From Rebellion to Revolution: Afro-American Slave Revolts in the Modern World*. Baton Rouge: Louisiana State University Press, 1979.

Girod, François. *La vie quotidienne de la société créole: Saint Domingue au XVIIIe siècle*. Paris: Hachette, 1972.

Gisler, Antoine. *L'esclavage aux Antilles françaises*. 2d ed. Paris: Karthala, 1981.

Hall, Gwendolyn Midlo, *Social Control in Slave Plantation Societies: A Comparison of Saint Domingue and Cuba*. Baltimore: Johns Hopkins University Press, 1971.

Hazoumé, Paul. *Le pact de sang au Dahomey*. Paris: Institut d'Ethnologie, 1937.

Hegel, G. W. F. *The Phenomenology of Mind*. Translated by J. B. Baille. New York: Harper & Row, 1967.

Herskovitz, Melville J. *Life in a Haitian Valley*. New York: Octagon Books, 1964.

Hurbon, Laënnec. *Dieu dans le Vaudou haïtien*. Paris: Payot, 1972.

James, C. L. R. *The Black Jacobins: Toussaint Louverture and the San Domingo Revolution*. [1938] 3d ed. London: Allison & Busby, 1980.

Janzen, John M. *Lemba, 1650–1930: A Drum of Affliction in Africa and the New World*. New York and London: Garland, 1982.

Jaurès, Jean. *Histoire socialiste de la Révolution française*. 7 vols. Edited by Albert Soboul. Paris: Editions sociales, 1968. Vol. 1.

Kahn, Morton. *Djuka, the Bush Negroes of Dutch Guiana*. New York: Viking, 1931.

Kiple, Kenneth. *The Caribbean Slave: A Biological History*. Cambridge: Cambridge University Press, 1984.

Korngold, Ralph. *Citizen Toussaint*. 2d ed. New York: Hill & Wang, 1965.

Labelle, Micheline. *Idéologie de couleur et classes sociales en Haïti*. [1979] 2d ed. Montréal: Editions CIDIHCA, 1987.

Laurent, Gerard. *Le commissaire Sonthonax à Saint-Domingue*. 4 vols. Port-au-Prince: La Phalange, 1965–74.

——— . *Pages d'histoire d'Haïti*. Port-au-Prince: La Phalange, 1960.

——— . *Quand les chaînes volent en éclats*. Port-au-Prince: Imp. Deschamps, 1979.

Laurent, Mentor. *Erreurs et vérités dans l'histoire d'Haïti*. 2 vols. Port-au-Prince, 1945. Vol. 1.

Lebeau, Auguste. *De la condition des gens de couleur libres sous l'Ancien Régime*. Poitiers: Masson, 1903.

Lespinasse, Beauvais. *Histoire des affranchis de Saint-Domingue*. 2 vols. Paris: Imp. Kugelman, 1882.

McCloy, Shelby T. *The Negro in the French West Indies*. [1966] reprint ed. Westport, Conn.: Negro Universities Press, 1974.

McFarlane, Milton. *Cudjoe of Jamaica: Pioneer for Black Freedom in the New World*. Short Hills, N.J.: Ridley Enslow Publ., 1977.

Madiou, Thomas. *Histoire d'Haïti*. 3 vols. 2d ed. Edited by Département de l'Instruction Public. Port-au-Prince: Edmond Chenet, 1922.

Maurel, Blanche. *Cahiers de doléances de la colonie de Saint-Domingue pour les Etats-Généraux de 1789.* Paris: Leroux, 1933.

──── . *Saint-Domingue et la Révolution française: les représentants des colons en France de 1789 à 1795.* Paris: PUF, 1943.

──── . *Le vent du large.* Paris: Editions la Nef de Paris, 1952.

Métral, Antoine. *Histoire de l'expédition des Français à Saint-Domingue.* Paris: Fanjat aîné, 1825.

Métraux, Alfred. *Black Peasants and Their Religion.* Translated by Peter Lengyel. London: George Harrap & Co., 1960.

──── . *Voodoo in Haiti.* Translated by Hugo Chartiris. New York: Schocken Books, 1972.

Michel, Antoine. *La mission du général Hédouville à Saint-Domingue.* Port-au-Prince: Imp. La Presse, 1929.

Mintz, Sidney. *Caribbean Transformations.* Chicago: Aldine, 1974.

──── . *Sweetness and Power: The Place of Sugar in Modern History.* New York: Viking, 1985.

Moral, Paul. *Le paysan haïtien: étude sur la vie rurale en Haïti.* Paris: Maisonneuve et Larose, 1961.

Nau, Emile. *Histoire des caciques d'Haïti.* 2 vols. [1894] reprint ed. Port-au-Prince: Panorama, 1963.

Necheles, Ruth. *The Abbé Grégoire (1787–1831): The Odyssey of an Egalitarian.* Westport, Conn.: Greenwood Publ. Corp., 1971.

Nemours, Col. Auguste. *Histoire militaire de la guerre d'indépendance de Saint-Domingue.* 2 vols. Paris: Berger-Levrault, 1925.

Nicholls, David. *From Dessalines to Duvalier: Race, Colour and Independence in Haiti.* Cambridge: Cambridge University Press, 1979.

Ortiz, Fernando. *La musica afrocubana.* Madrid: Jucar, 1974.

Ott, Thomas O. *The Haitian Revolution, 1789–1804.* Knoxville: University of Tennessee Press, 1972.

Pachonski, Jan, and Reuel Wilson. *Poland's Caribbean Tragedy: A Study of Polish Legions in the Haitian War of Independence, 1802–1803.* Boulder: East European Monographs, 1986.

Parkinson, Wenda. *'This Gilded African', Toussaint L'Ouverture.* London: Quartet Books, 1978.

Patterson, Orlando. *Slavery and Social Death: A Comparative Study.* Cambridge, Mass.: Harvard University Press, 1982.

Peytraud, Lucien. *L'esclavage aux Antilles françaises avant 1789.* Paris: Hachette, 1879.

Placide-Justin, M. *Histoire politique et statistique d'Hayti, Saint-Domingue.* Paris: Brière, 1826.

Pluchon, Pierre. *La route des esclaves: négriers et bois d'ébène au XVIIIe siècle.* Paris: Hachette, 1980.

──── . *Toussaint Louverture, de l'esclavage au pouvoir.* Paris: Ecole, 1979.

──── . *Vaudou, sorciers, empoisonneurs: de Saint-Domingue à Haïti.* Paris: Karthala, 1987.

Price, Richard, ed. *Maroon Societies: Rebel Slave Communities in the Americas.* New York: Anchor Press, 1973.

Price-Mars, Jean. *La république d'Haïti et la république dominicaine.* 2 vols. Port-au-Prince, 1953. Vol. 1.

Robinson, Carey. *The Fighting Maroons of Jamaica.* [Kingston?]: William Collins & Sangster, 1974.

Rubin, Vera, and Arthur Tuden, eds. *Comparative Perspectives on Slavery in New World Plantation Societies.* Annals of the New York Academy of Sciences 292 (1977).

Rudé, George. *Robespierre: Portrait of a Revolutionary Democrat.* New York: Viking, 1975.

St. John, Sir Spencer. *Hayti, or the Black Republic.* London: Smith, Elder and Co., 1884.

Saint-Rémy. *Pétion et Haïti.* 2d ed. Paris: Berger-Levrault, 1956.

Saintoyant, J. *La colonisation française pendant la Révolution française.* 2 vols. Paris: la Renaissance du Livre, 1930.

Sannon, Pauléus. *La guerre de l'indépendance.* Etudes historiques. Edited by Chéraquit. Port-au-Prince, 1925.

———. *Histoire de Toussaint Louverture.* 3 vols. Port-au-Prince: Imp. Héraux, 1920–33.

Schoelcher, Victor. *Colonies étrangères et Haïti.* 2 vols. Paris: 1843; reprint ed., Pointe-à-Pitre: Desormeaux, 1973.

———. *La vie de Toussaint Louverture.* Paris: Ollendorf, 1889.

Stein, Robert L. *The French Slave Trade in the Eighteenth Century: An Old Regime Business.* Madison: University of Wisconsin Press, 1979.

———. *Léger Félicité Sonthonax: The Lost Sentinel of the Republic.* Rutherford: Fairleigh Dickinson University Press; London & Toronto: Associated University Presses, 1985.

Steward, T. G. *The Haitian Revolution, 1791 to 1804.* New York: Thomas Crowell, 1914.

Stoddard, T. Lothrop. *The French Revolution in San Domingo.* New York: Houghton Mifflin, 1914; reprint ed., Westport, Conn.: Negro Universities Press, 1970.

Thompson, E. P. *The Making of the English Working Class.* New York: Penguin, 1979.

Trouillot, D. *Esquisse ethnographique: le Vaudou, aperçu historique et évolutions.* Port-au-Prince: Imp. R. Ethéart, 1885.

Trouillot, Hénock. *Introduction à une histoire du Vaudou.* Port-au-Prince: Imp. des Antilles, 1970.

Tyson, George F., Jr., ed. *Toussaint Louverture.* Englewood Cliffs, N.J.: Prentice-Hall, 1973.

Vaissière, Pierre de. *Saint-Domingue: la société et la vie créoles sous l'Ancien Régime (1629–1789).* Paris: Perrin, 1909.

Wing, R. P. J. van. *Etudes Bakongo.* 2 vols. Brussells: Institut Royal Colonial Belge, 1938.

ARTICLES, THESES, CONTRIBUTIONS TO BOOKS
OR SERIES AND LECTURES

Cabon, R. P. Adolphe. "Une maison d'éducation à Saint-Domingue: 'Les religieuses' du Cap." RHAF 2 (mars 1949):557–75; 3 (juin 1949):75–80; 3 (déc. 1949):402–22.

Debbasch, Yvan. "Le marronage: essai sur la désertion de l'esclave antillais." *Année sociologique* 3 (1961):1–112.

Debien, Gabriel. "Les cimetières à Saint-Domingue au XVIIIe siècle." *Conjonction* 105 (oct. 1967):27–40.

———. "L'esprit d'indépendance chez les colons de Saint-Domingue au XVIIe siècle et l'appel aux Anglais en 1793." RSHHG 17 (oct. 1946):1–46.

———. "Gens de couleur libres et colons de Saint-Domingue devant la Constituante." RHAF 4 (sept., déc. 1950):211–32, 398–426; (mars 1951):530–49.

———. "Notes bibliographiques sur le soulèvement des esclaves (août–sept. 1791)." RSHHG 17 (juillet 1946):41–57.

———, J. Houdaille, R. Massio, and R. Richard. "Les origines des esclaves des Antilles." Bull. de l'IFAN 23–29, sér. B (1961–67).

Desroches, Monique. "La musique traditionnelle de la Martinique." Rapport de recherche. Montréal: Centre de Recherches Caraïbes, Université de Montréal, 1985.

———. "Les pratiques musicales." In *Historial Antillais*, 491–500. Edited by Jean-Luc Bonniol. Fort-de-France: Société Dajani, 1980.

Fick, Carolyn E. The Black Masses in the San Domingo Revolution, 1791–1803. Ph.D. diss., Concordia University, Montreal, 1979.

———. "Black Peasants and Soldiers in the Saint Domingue Revolution: Initial Reactions to Freedom in the South Province (1793–94)." In *History From Below*, 247–70. Edited by Frederick Krantz. Oxford & New York: Basil Blackwell, 1988.

———. Review of *Léger Félicité Sonthonax: the lost sentinel of the Republic*, by Robert L. Stein. *Nieuwe West-Indische Gid/New West-Indian Guide* 62, nos. 3–4 (1988):206–9.

Foubert, Bernard. "Colons et esclaves du Sud de Saint-Domingue au début de la révolution." *Revue française d'histoire d'Outre-Mer* 61 (1974):199–217.

———. "Le marronage sur les plantations Laborde." Typewritten, 29 pp.; tables. Forthcoming.

———. "Les volontaires nationaux de l'Aube et de la Seine-Inférieure à Saint-Domingue (oct. 1792–janv. 1793)." *Bulletin de la Société d'histoire de la Guadeloupe* 51 (1er trim. 1982):3–56.

Fouchard, Jean. "La traite des Nègres et le peuplement de Saint-Domingue." In *La traite négrière du XVe au XIXe siècle*, pp. 278–85. Paris: UNESCO, 1979.

Geggus, David P. "Les esclaves de la plaine du Nord à la veille de la révolution." RSHH 135–36; 144 (juin, sept. 1982; sept. 1984):85–107; 5–31; 15–35. Revised and expanded. Latin American Collection, University of Florida Libraries.

———. "From His Most Catholic Majesty to the godless République: The 'volte-face' of Toussaint Louverture and the ending of slavery in Saint-Domingue," *Revue française d'histoire d'Outre-Mer* 65 (1978): 481–99.

———. "On the Eve of the Haitian Revolution: Slave Runaways in Saint Domingue in the year 1790." *Slavery Abolition: A Journal of Comparative Studies* 6 (December 1985):112–128.

———. "Slave Resistance Studies and the Saint Domingue Revolution: Some Preliminary Considerations." Occasional Papers Series, no. 4. Latin American and Caribbean Center, Florida International University, 1983.

———. "Yellow Fever in the 1790s: The British Army in Occupied Saint-Domingue." *Medical History* 23 (Jan. 1979):38–58.

Kopytoff, Barbara. "The Early Development of Jamaican Maroon Societies." *William and Mary Quarterly* 34 (April 1978):287–307.

Lacerte, Kenneth. "The Evolution of Land and Labor in the Haitian Revolution, 1791–1820." *Américas* 34 (April 1978):449–59.

Larose, Serge. "The Meaning of Africa in Haitian Vodu." In *Symbols and Sentiments*, 85–116. Edited by I. M. Lewiss. London: Academic Press, 1977.

Lefebvre, Claire. "The Role of Relexification in Creole Genesis Revisited: The Case of Haitian Creole." In the proceedings of the Conference on Creole Genesis (Amsterdam, April 1985).

Lefebvre, Georges. Les cours de Sorbonne. 6 vols. Centre de documentation universitaire. Paris: Tournier et Constans, 1946–47.

Marcelin, Jocelyn. "La guerre de l'indépendance dans le Sud." RSHHG 6 (avril 1933):1–70.

Mulago, Vincent. "Le dieu des Bantous." *Présence* (12–19 Nov. 1987):10.

Price-Mars, Jean. "Le sentiment et le phénomène religieux chez les nègres de Saint-Domingue." Bull. de la SHHG 1 (mai 1925):35–55.

Robinson, Cedric. "C. L. R. James and the Black Radical Tradition." *Review* 6 (Winter 1983):321–91.

Scott, Julius Sherrard, III. *The Common Wind: Currents of Afro-American Communication in the Era of the Haitian Revolution*. Ann Arbor, Mich.: University Microfilms, 1989.

Trouillot, Hénock. "La guerre de l'indépendance d'Haïti: les grands prêtres du Vaudou contre l'armée française." *Sobretiro de Revista de Historici de América* 72 (julio–dic. 1971):261–327.

Index

absenteeism: of planters, 16, 18
affranchis
—armed struggles for civil rights: *in absentia* sentences, 95, 241, 304n.111; Ogé rebellion, 82–84; royalist alliance, 121, 127, 128, 130, 139, 246; and slaves, 86, 118, 121–25, 127–34, 137–38, 140–41, 146, 246, 268, 307n.41, 320n.77; in South, 118, 122, 127, 129–34, 138, 246, 268; in West, 118–29 passim, 246
—and August 1791 rebellion, 95, 105, 109, 111–12, 263, 304nn.10–11, 331n.13
—and colonial representation, 78–82, 84–85
—defection to British, 161, 185–86
—economic growth of, 19–20, 239
—and *maréchaussée*, 20–21, 52, 72, 279n.32
—and maroons, 53, 74, 87, 289n.52
—and *petits blancs*, 18–19, 79, 87
—and poison, 63, 173, 279n.30
—population figures, 17, 19, 278n.14, 279n.21, 304n.109
—social definition used, 279n.15
—social restrictions, 20–21, 72, 279n.30, 280n.36
—and white supremacy, 17–21
—*see also* free blacks; French Revolution; manumission; mulattoes
Ailhaud, Jean Antoine, 315n.3
Alaou: assassinated, 185–86, 322n.11; and Dieudonné, 187, 246, 322n.15; and Hyacinthe, 185–86, 246; and Legion of Equality, 321n.6; and voodoo, 185
Améthyste (princess), 104, 242, 265–66
Amis des Noirs, 77–78, 80–82; *see also* Grégoire, Abbé
André (*commandeur*), 132, 244; *see also* Laborde plantations

Aoua (rebel barge captain), 234; *see also* Bégon; Kerpoisson
Appollon (militia lieutenant at Petit-Goâve), 189–90, 199; *see also* ex-slaves: and mulatto leadership; Faubert; *système portionnaire:* resistance to
Aradas, 26, 41, 281n.59; and voodoo, 58, 285n.133
Arawaks, 51; and Hayti, 236, 288n.28
Artaud, M. (white planter), 161
Assam (slave of Sieur Valette): advised by Pompée, 64, 69, 72; imprisoned, 258–59; interrogation of, 64–65, 251–58, 328n.75, 330nn.10–13; and Makandal, 292n.86, 294n.121; *see also* Jean (slave of Laplaine plantation); poison; Pompée
ateliers, 27–28; *see also commandeurs; marronage;* slaves
Atlas (popular rebel leader), 235; *see also* expeditionary army; Grande-Anse: Abricots—Cap Dame-Marie rebellion
Auberteuil, Hilliard d', 26, 39, 46, 63, 284n.116
August 1791 rebellion: alliances, 112, 245–46, 304nn.108, 110–11; attack on le Cap, 102–4, 266, 301nn.62–63; chronology and geographic movement, 96–101, 111, 260–63, 299n.21; guerrilla tactics, 110; and marronage, 6–7, 49, 75, 94–95, 106–7, 240–41, 263, 295–96n.142; military organization, 109–11; and Morne-Rouge assemblies, 91–95, 240–42, 261–62; negotiations with authorities, 113–17, 245, 305n.125; organization of, 91–96, 243, 260–63, 295–96n.142; and popular violence, 108, 302n.84; premature outbreaks, 95–96, 98–99, 102, 107, 260–63; property losses, 105, 301n.72; rebel numbers,

Rivière, Romaine, 127–29, 138–39, 307–
    8nn.41, 45, 47; *see also* confederate
    army; free blacks; Léogane; voodoo
Robespierre, Maximilien, 85, 163, 297n.18
Rochambeau, General Donatien: assumes
    command of expeditionary army, 221,
    228–29; capitulates to rebel forces, 236;
    commander of West and South, 219; re-
    pression and use of terror, 219–21, 224,
    228–29, 244, 328n.89
Romaine-la-prophétesse. *See* Rivière,
    Romaine
Roume, Philipe: and first civil commis-
    sion, 94, 116, 139–40, 262–63; and
    second civil commission, 195, 197, 201,
    323n.38; and Toussaint's occupation of
    Santo Domingo, 204–6
Rouvray, Marquis de, 74, 102, 300n.46
Rouvray, Mme. de, 102
royalists, 81, 87, 112, 121–22, 127–28,
    130, 139, 157–58, 245–46, 304n.108;
    see also affranchis: armed struggles
    for civil rights; August 1791 rebellion;
    grands blancs; patriots

Saint Domingue: caste system, 17–21, 38,
    192, 239; and colonial representation,
    76–78; constitutional status of, 79–81,
    84, 205–7; early settlement of, 15–16;
    economic and demographic growth, 22–
    25, 280nn.39, 42; on eve of revolution,
    25, 74–76, 87–88; and French Revolu-
    tion, 25, 238–39; population figures, 17,
    19, 25, 278n.14, 280n.42, 304n.109;
    social structure, 17–21; *see also* England;
    expeditionary army; slavery; slaves; slave
    trade
St. Foäche, Stanislas, 36–37; *see also*
    Instructions
Saint-Léger (civil commissioner), 128–29,
    138–9, 140
Saint Marc, 79, 81, 82, 84, 121; *see also*
    Colonial Assembly: at Saint Marc; *Léo-*
    pard
Sannon, Pauléus, 3, 200, 263–64
Sans-Souci (independent band leader), 231;
    see also Dessalines, Jean-Jacques
Santo Domingo: marronage in, 51–56,
    227, 297n.20; Toussaint's occupation

of, 204–6, 211, 323n.38, 324n.57; and
    voodoo, 42, 127–28; *see also* Maniel;
    marronage; Roume, Philipe
Sarrazin, General, 234
Scapin (free black confederate), 126; *see*
    also affranchis: armed struggles for civil
    rights; concordats: of 23 October 1791
Schoelcher, Victor, 2, 264, 323n.43
slavery: absolutism, 33, 36, 39; capitalistic
    orientation of, 34, 36, 281n.65; master-
    slave relationship, 27, 34–39, 44–45,
    65–67, 154–56, 277–78n.7, 283nn.108,
    112; reform measures (1784–85), 33–
    34, 38, 283n.108; and social alienation,
    27, 283n.104; and social structure, 15–
    25, 154–56; violence and terror, 27,
    33–39, 282–83nn.97, 100; and white
    supremacy, 18, 21, 37–38; *see also* slaves
slaves
—and *affranchis*, 53–54, 56, 75, 86–87,
    118, 122–25, 127–29, 131–34, 137–41,
    246
—age distribution of, 27
—in ateliers, 27–30
—conditions of, 28–36
—creolization: and leadership, 30, 74, 86–
    87, 95, 107, 132, 141, 144, 147–48,
    227–29, 231–36, 243–44, 308n.60;
    320n.77; and marronage, 51, 53–55; and
    voodoo, 93–95, 241–42, 264–66
—culture: African influences on, 26, 40–
    41, 57–59, 180–82, 284–86nn.117,
    128–29, 131–33, 140, 145; 290–
    91nn.58, 60–63, 70; 293nn.88, 93;
    297n.5; burials, 44, 286n.145; dances,
    40–42, 284n.120; language, 39–40,
    57–58, 284n.117, 290nn.58, 60–61;
    religion, 36, 41–46, 57–59, 63, 65–66,
    72, 93, 104–5, 127–28, 241–42, 244,
    264–66, 284–86nn.128–29, 133, 140,
    286n.1, 295n.124
—division of labor, 27–31, 282nn.73, 84
—ethnic composition of, 25–26, 59,
    281n.59, 153, 180–81, 287n.24,
    291n.70, 313n.89
—as Executioners of High Justice, 38, 259,
    283n.111, 331n.14
—families, 31, 36, 56, 72, 283n.102
—kitchen gardens, 32–34, 175, 180, 250